Haven't You Heard?

I'M SAKAMOTO

VOLUME

4

ART & STORY

Nami Sano

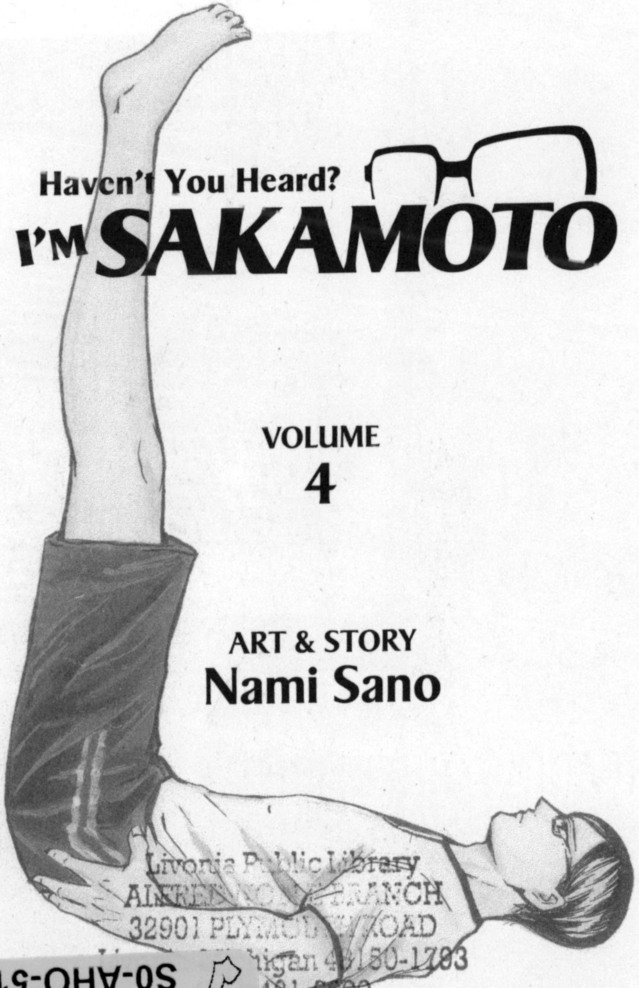

I'm SAKAMOTO

Haven't You Heard? 👓 SEP 12 2016

story and art by NAMI SANO   VOLUME 4

3 9082 13139 2824

TRANSLATION
Adrienne Beck

ADAPTATION
Karis Page

LETTERING AND LAYOUT
Lys Blakeslee

COVER DESIGN
Nicky Lim

PROOFREADER
Shanti Whitesides

PRODUCTION MANAGER
Lissa Pattillo

EDITOR-IN-CHIEF
Adam Arnold

PUBLISHER
Jason DeAngelis

Sakamoto Desuga? Vol.4
©2016 Nami Sano
All Rights reserved.
First published in Japan in 2016 by KADOKAWA CORPORATION ENTERBRAIN.
English translation rights arranged with KADOKAWA CORPORATION
ENTERBRAIN through TOHAN CORPORATION, Tokyo.

Seven Seas books may be purchased in bulk for educational, business, or
promotional use. For information on bulk purchases, please contact Macmillan
Corporate & Premium Sales Department at 1-800-221-7945 (ext 5442)
or write specialmarkets@macmillan.com.

Seven Seas and the Seven Seas logo are trademarks of
Seven Seas Entertainment, LLC.

ISBN: 978-1-626922-88-4

Printed in Canada

First Printing: July 2016

10 9 8 7 6 5 4 3 2 1

FOLLOW US ONLINE: www.gomanga.com

READING DIRECTIONS

This book reads from *right to left*, Japanese style. If
this is your first time reading manga, you start
reading from the top right panel on each page and
take it from there. If you get lost, just follow the
numbered diagram here. It may seem backwards at
first, but you'll get the hang of it! Have fun!!

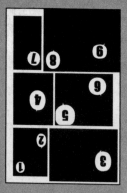

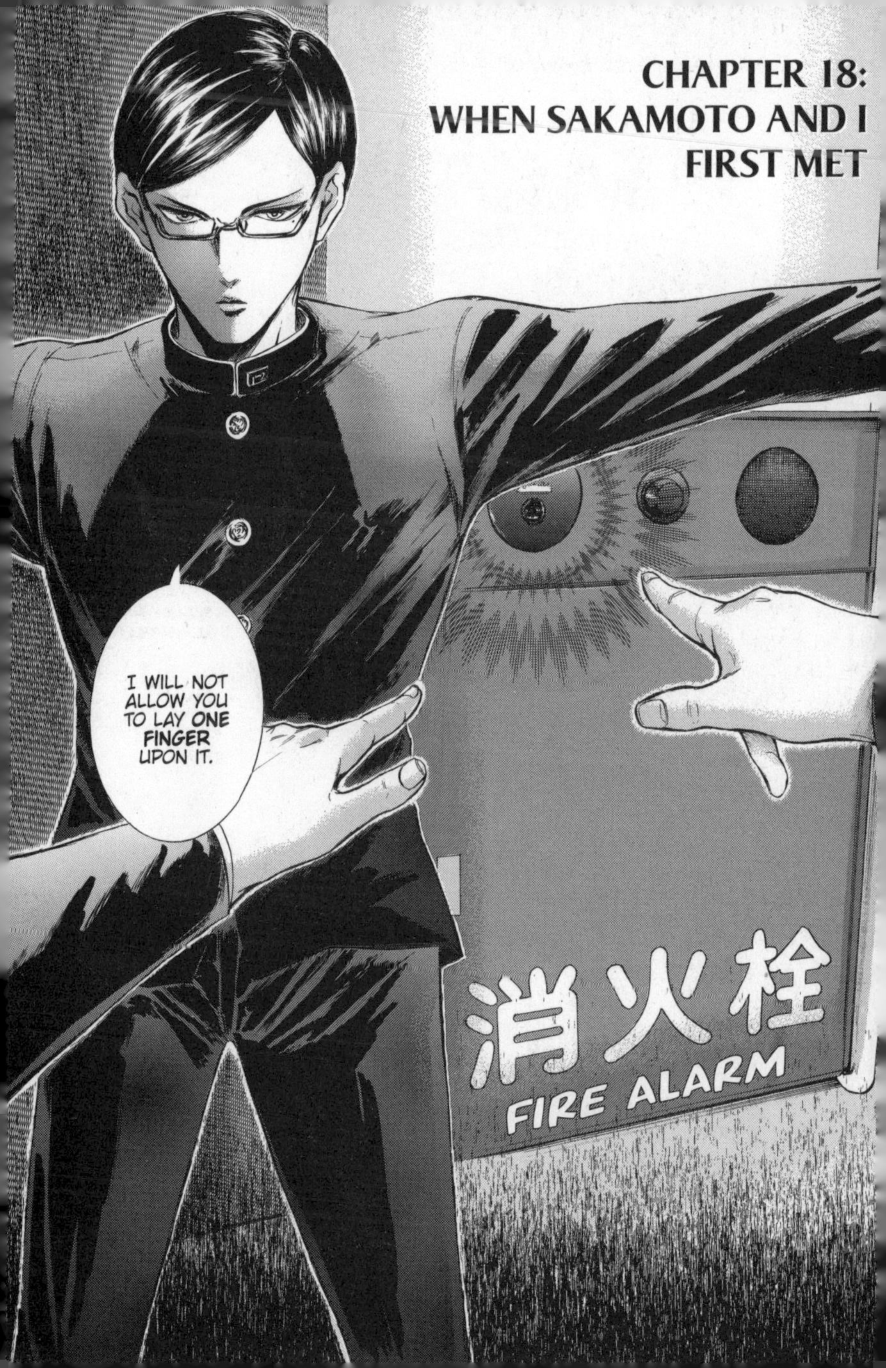
CHAPTER 18: WHEN SAKAMOTO AND I FIRST MET
I WILL NOT ALLOW YOU TO LAY ONE FINGER UPON IT.
消火栓
FIRE ALARM

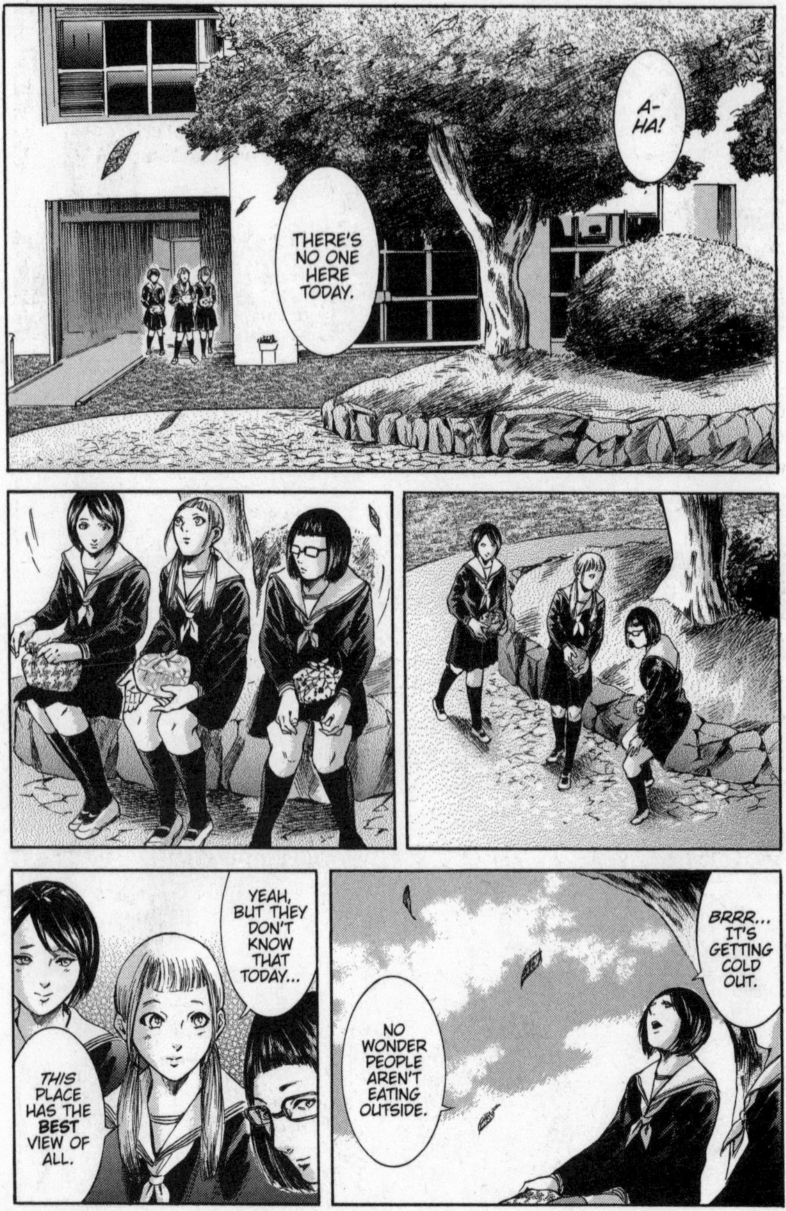
A-HA!
THERE'S NO ONE HERE TODAY.
BRRR... IT'S GETTING COLD OUT.
NO WONDER PEOPLE AREN'T EATING OUTSIDE.
YEAH, BUT THEY DON'T KNOW THAT TODAY...
THIS PLACE HAS THE **BEST** VIEW OF ALL.

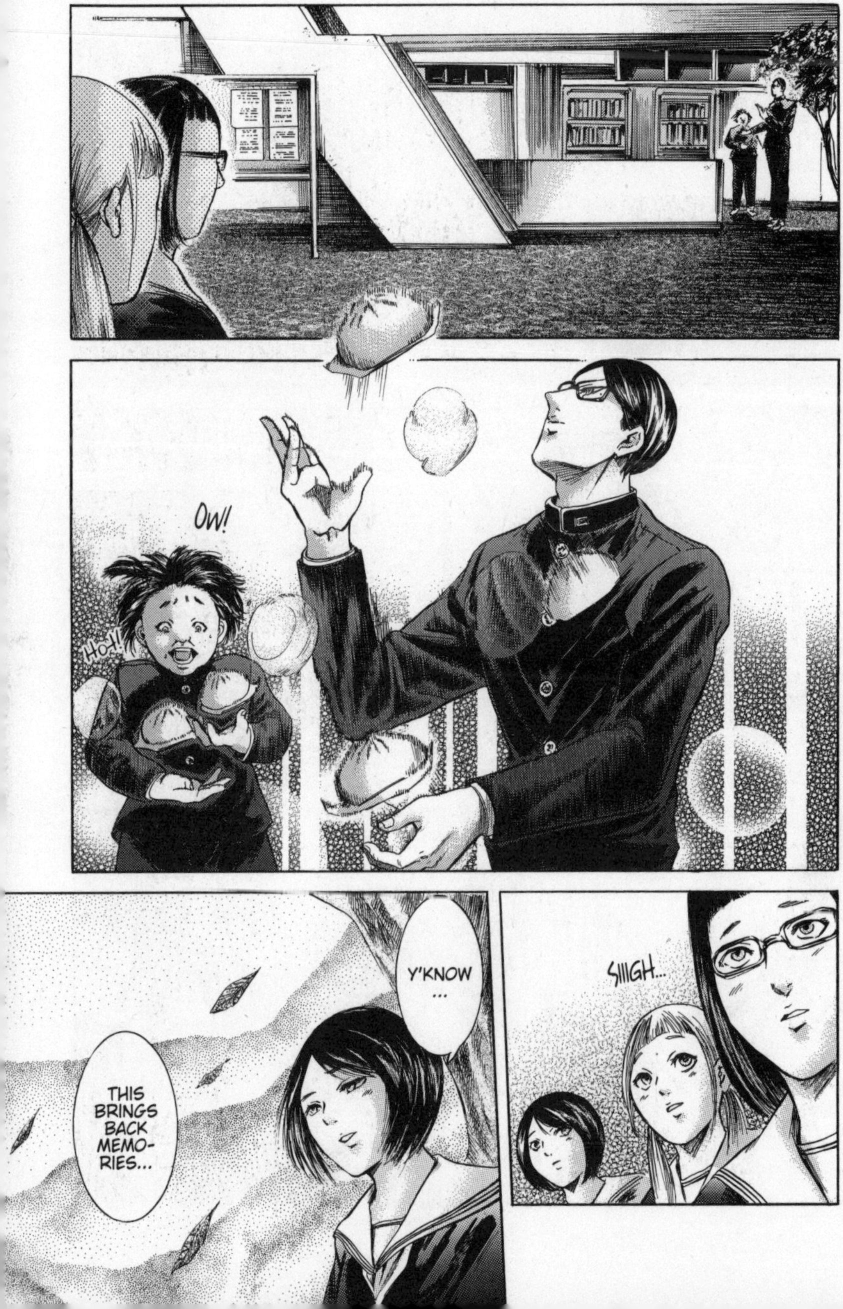
OW!
HO-!!
SIIIGH...
Y'KNOW
...
THIS BRINGS BACK MEMO-RIES...

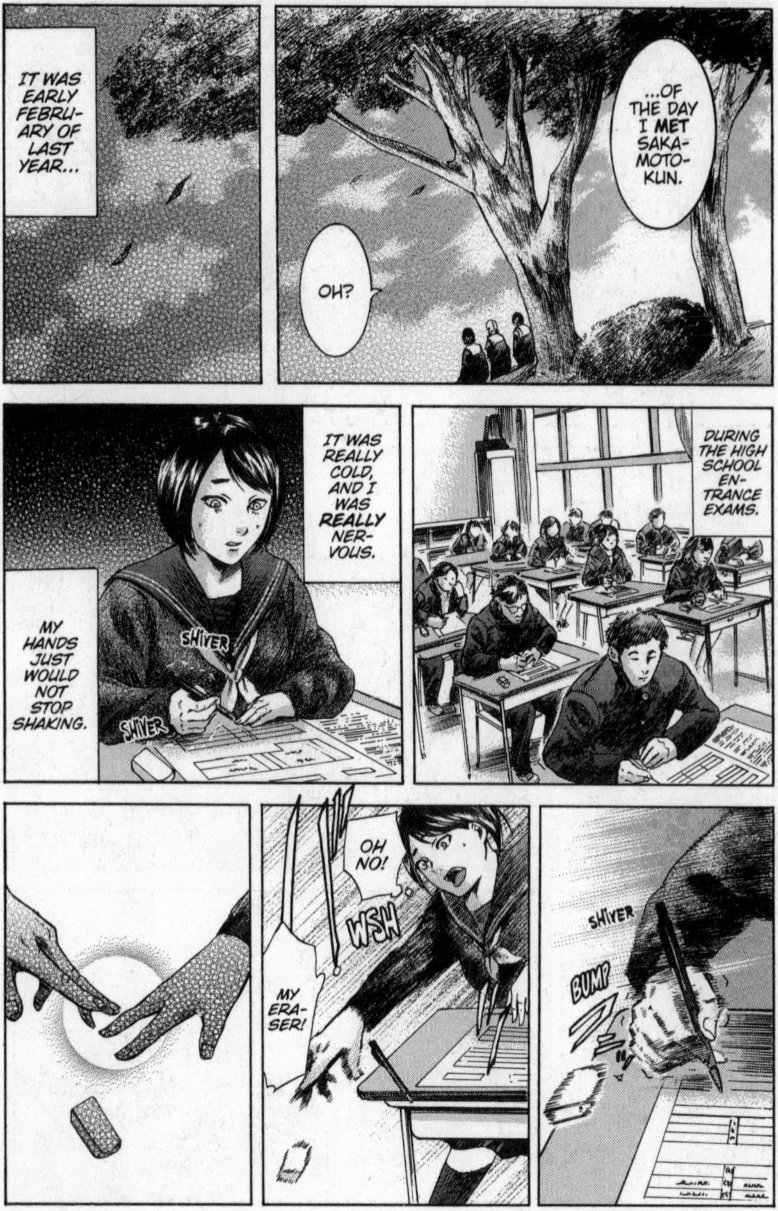
IT WAS EARLY FEBRU-ARY OF LAST YEAR...
...OF THE DAY I MET SAKA-MOTO-KUN.
OH?
DURING THE HIGH SCHOOL EN-TRANCE EXAMS.
IT WAS REALLY COLD, AND I WAS REALLY NER-VOUS.
MY HANDS JUST WOULD NOT STOP SHAKING.
SHIVER
SHIVER
SHIVER
BUMP
OH NO!
WSH
MY ERA-SER!

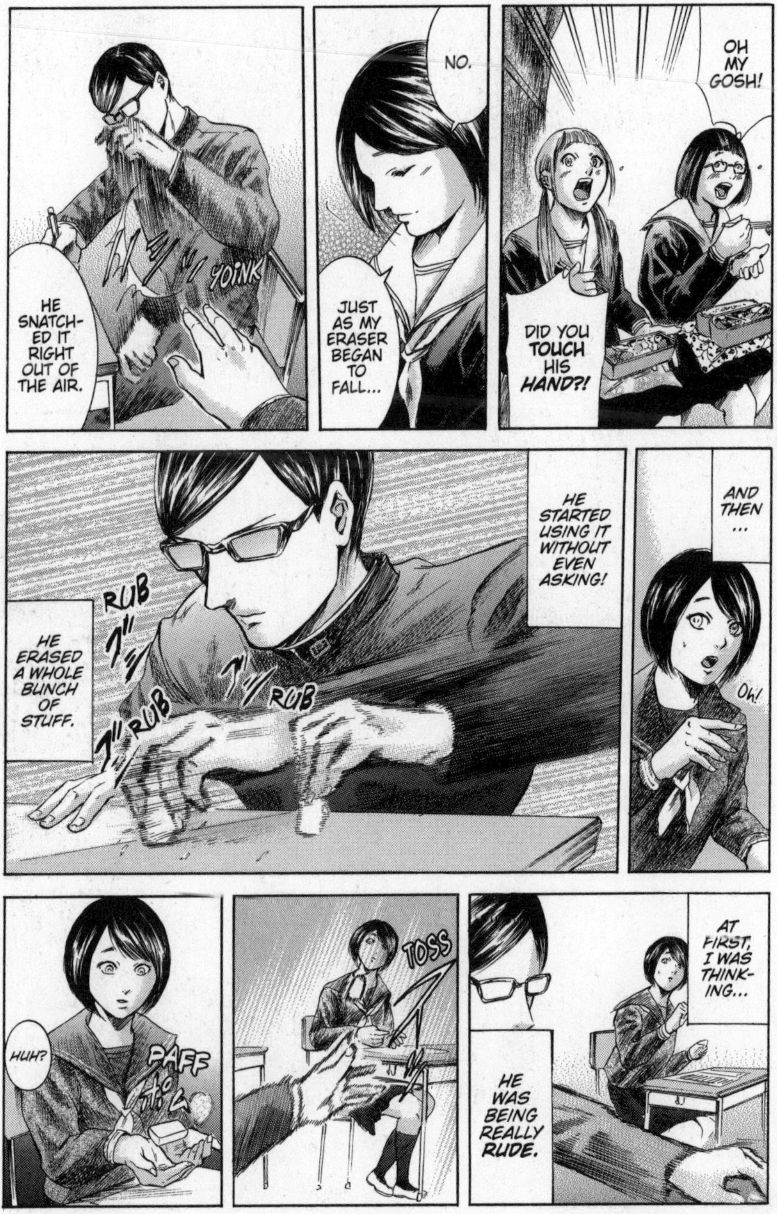
OH MY GOSH!
DID YOU TOUCH HIS HAND?!
NO.
JUST AS MY ERASER BEGAN TO FALL...
YOINK
HE SNATCH-ED IT RIGHT OUT OF THE AIR.
AND THEN ...
Oh!
HE STARTED USING IT WITHOUT EVEN ASKING!
RUB
RUB
RUB
HE ERASED A WHOLE BUNCH OF STUFF.
AT FIRST, I WAS THINK-ING...
HE WAS BEING REALLY RUDE.
TOSS
HUH?
PAFF

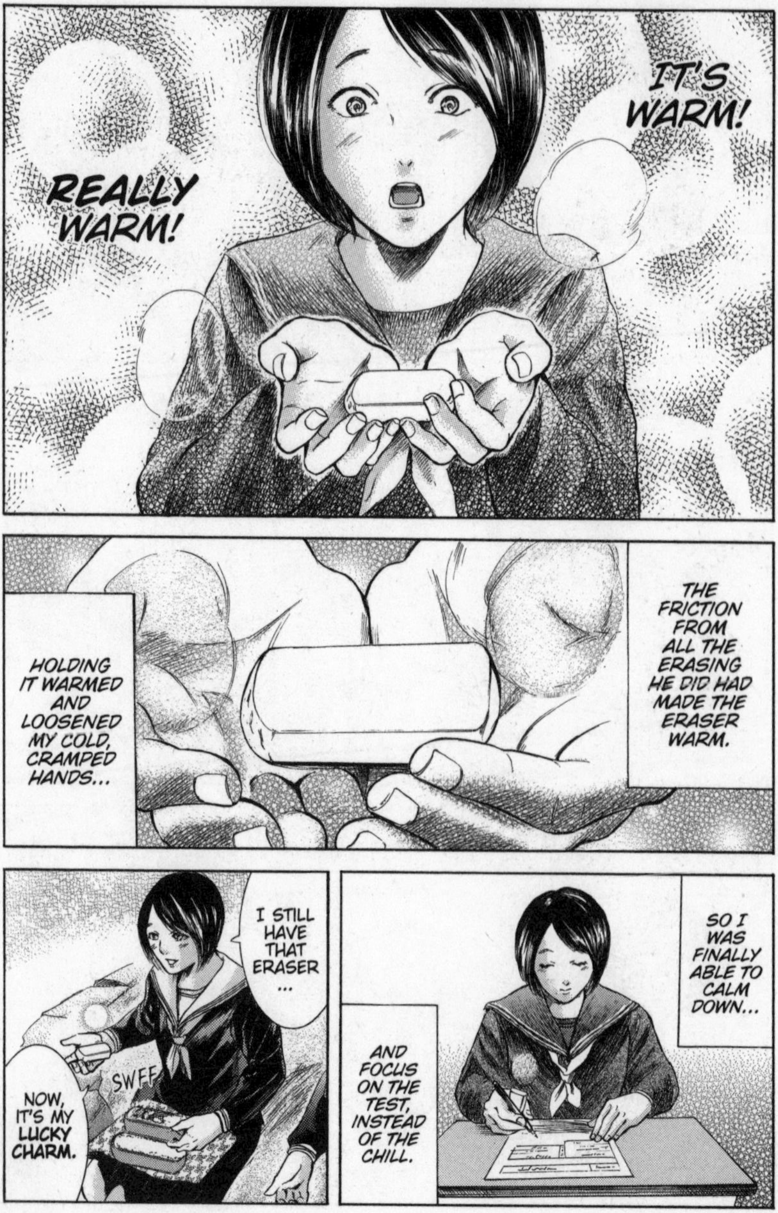
IT'S WARM!
REALLY WARM!
THE FRICTION FROM ALL THE ERASING HE DID HAD MADE THE ERASER WARM.
HOLDING IT WARMED AND LOOSENED MY COLD, CRAMPED HANDS...
SO I WAS FINALLY ABLE TO CALM DOWN...
AND FOCUS ON THE TEST, INSTEAD OF THE CHILL.
I STILL HAVE THAT ERASER...
SWFF
NOW, IT'S MY LUCKY CHARM.

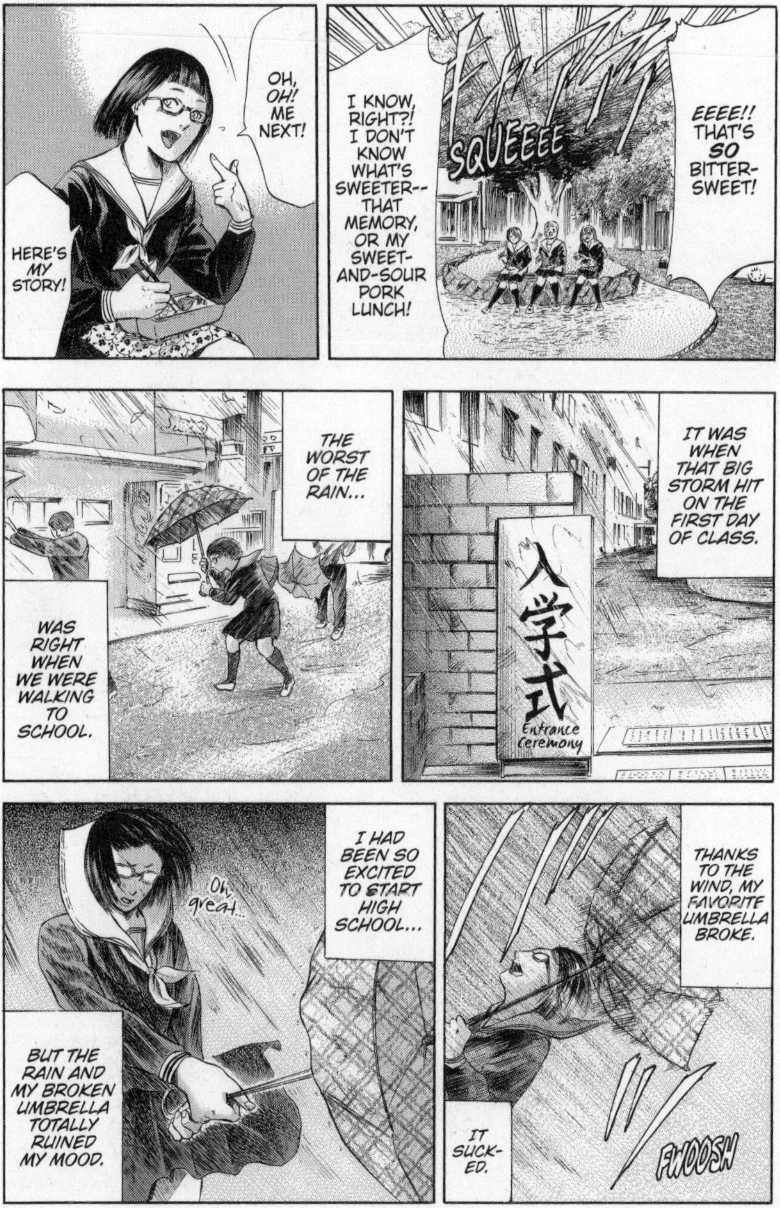
EEEE!! THAT'S SO BITTER-SWEET!
SQUEEEEE
I KNOW, RIGHT?! I DON'T KNOW WHAT'S SWEETER-- THAT MEMORY, OR MY SWEET-AND-SOUR PORK LUNCH!
OH, OH! ME NEXT!
HERE'S MY STORY!
IT WAS WHEN THAT BIG STORM HIT ON THE FIRST DAY OF CLASS.
入学式
Entrance Ceremony
THE WORST OF THE RAIN...
WAS RIGHT WHEN WE WERE WALKING TO SCHOOL.
THANKS TO THE WIND, MY FAVORITE UMBRELLA BROKE.
IT SUCK-ED.
FWOOSH
I HAD BEEN SO EXCITED TO START HIGH SCHOOL...
Oh, great...
BUT THE RAIN AND MY BROKEN UMBRELLA TOTALLY RUINED MY MOOD.

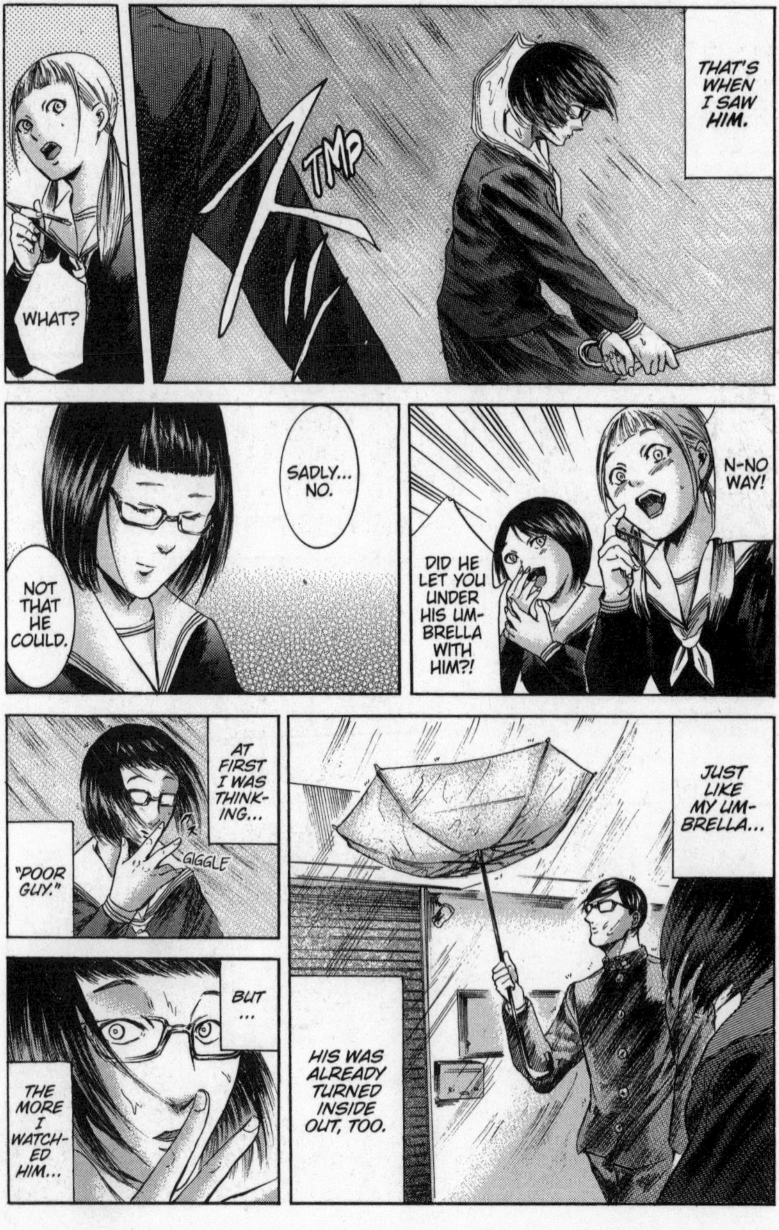
THAT'S WHEN I SAW HIM.
TMP
WHAT?
N-NO WAY!
DID HE LET YOU UNDER HIS UM-BRELLA WITH HIM?!
SADLY... NO.
NOT THAT HE COULD.
JUST LIKE MY UM-BRELLA...
HIS WAS ALREADY TURNED INSIDE OUT, TOO.
AT FIRST I WAS THINK-ING...
GIGGLE
"POOR GUY."
BUT ...
THE MORE I WATCH-ED HIM...

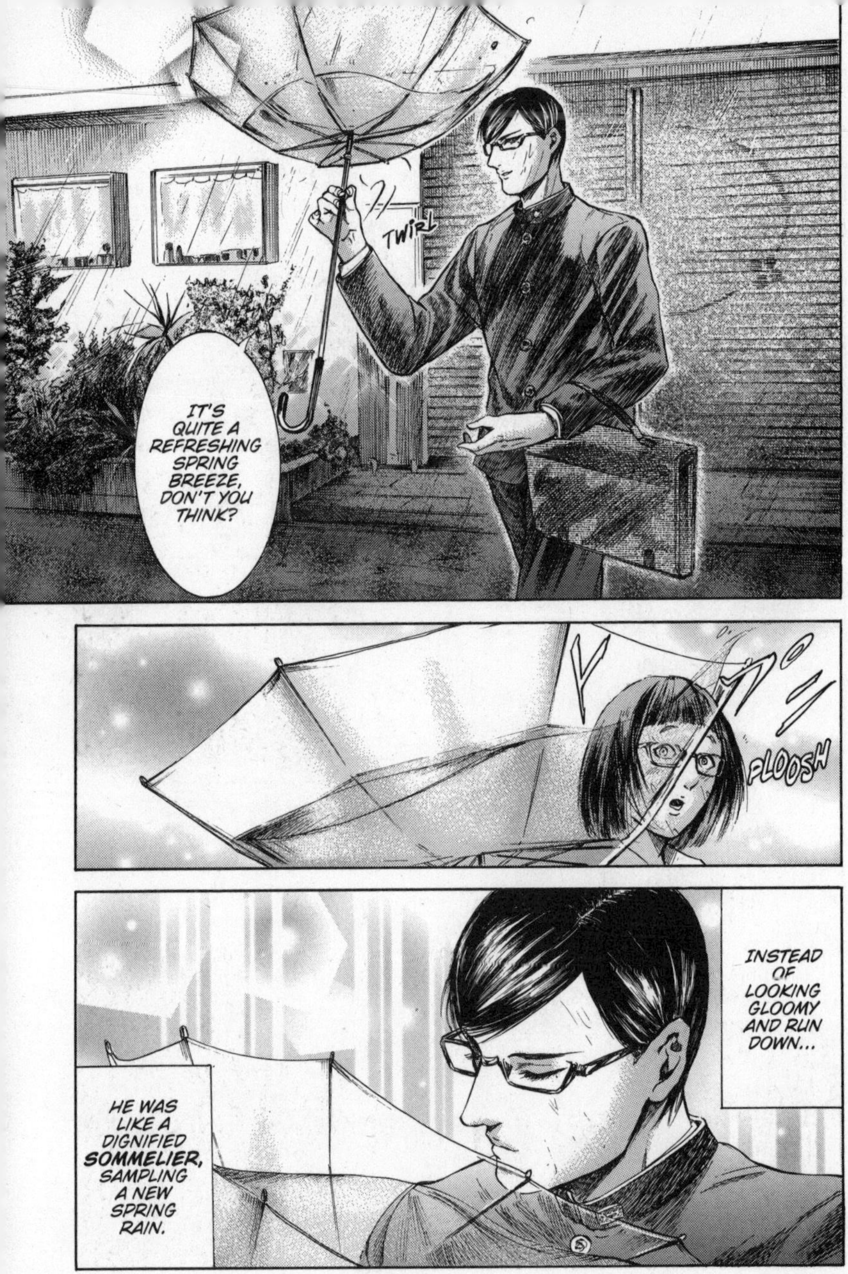
TWIRL
IT'S QUITE A REFRESHING SPRING BREEZE, DON'T YOU THINK?
PLOOSH
INSTEAD OF LOOKING GLOOMY AND RUN DOWN...
HE WAS LIKE A DIGNIFIED **SOMMELIER,** SAMPLING A NEW SPRING RAIN.

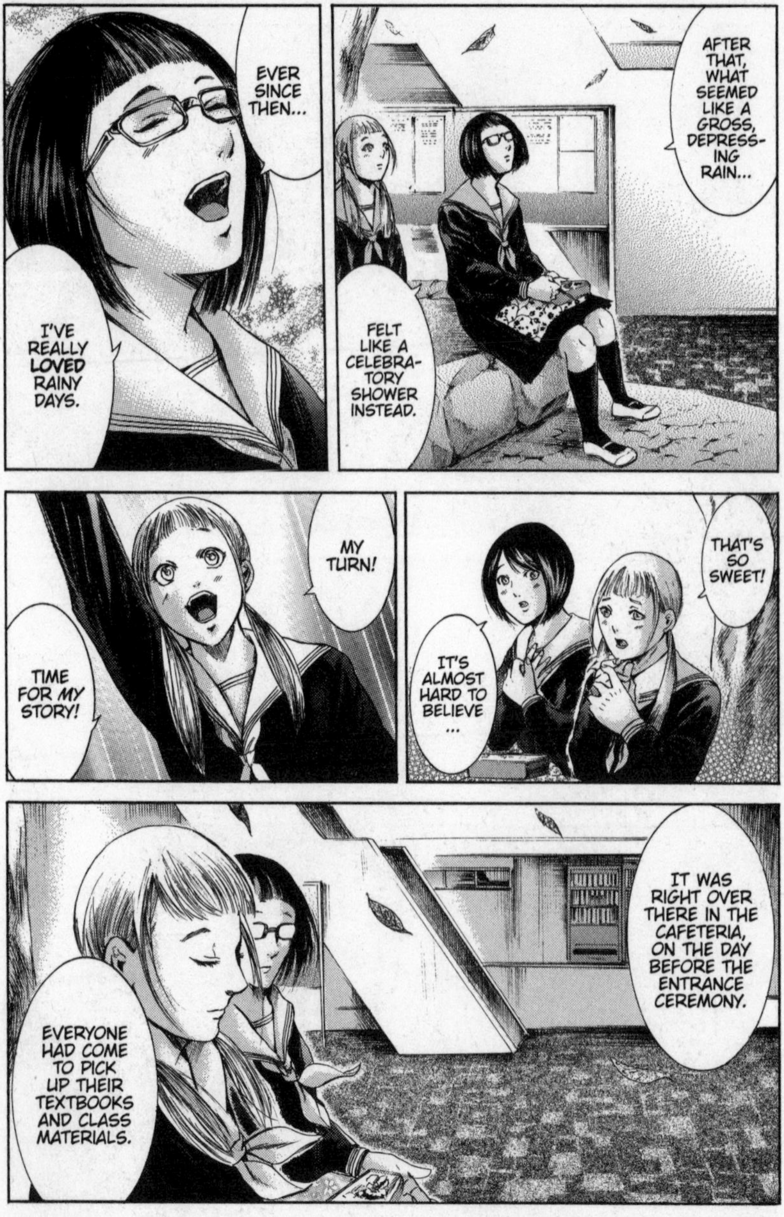
AFTER THAT, WHAT SEEMED LIKE A GROSS, DEPRESSING RAIN...
FELT LIKE A CELEBRATORY SHOWER INSTEAD.
EVER SINCE THEN...
I'VE REALLY LOVED RAINY DAYS.
THAT'S SO SWEET!
IT'S ALMOST HARD TO BELIEVE ...
MY TURN!
TIME FOR MY STORY!
IT WAS RIGHT OVER THERE IN THE CAFETERIA, ON THE DAY BEFORE THE ENTRANCE CEREMONY.
EVERYONE HAD COME TO PICK UP THEIR TEXTBOOKS AND CLASS MATERIALS.

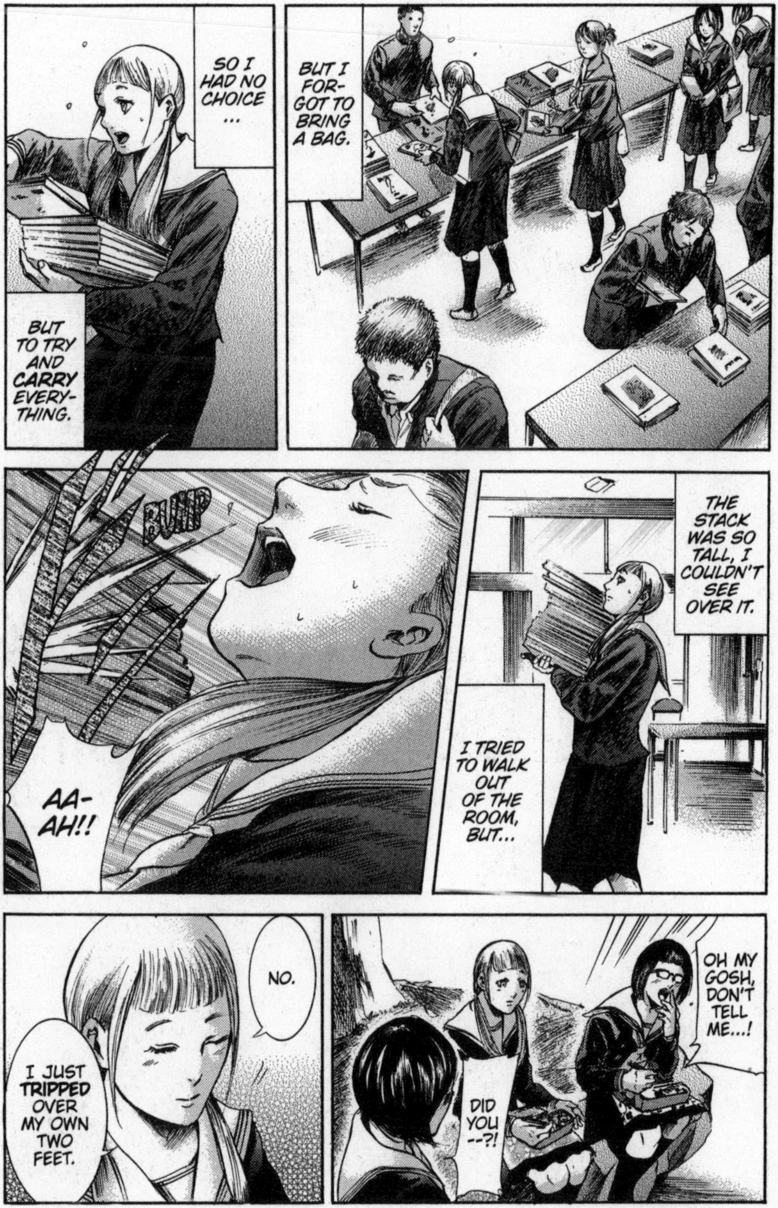
BUT I FOR-GOT TO BRING A BAG.
SO I HAD NO CHOICE ...
BUT TO TRY AND CARRY EVERY-THING.
THE STACK WAS SO TALL, I COULDN'T SEE OVER IT.
I TRIED TO WALK OUT OF THE ROOM, BUT...
BUMP
AA-AH!!
OH MY GOSH, DON'T TELL ME...!
DID YOU --?!
NO.
I JUST TRIPPED OVER MY OWN TWO FEET.

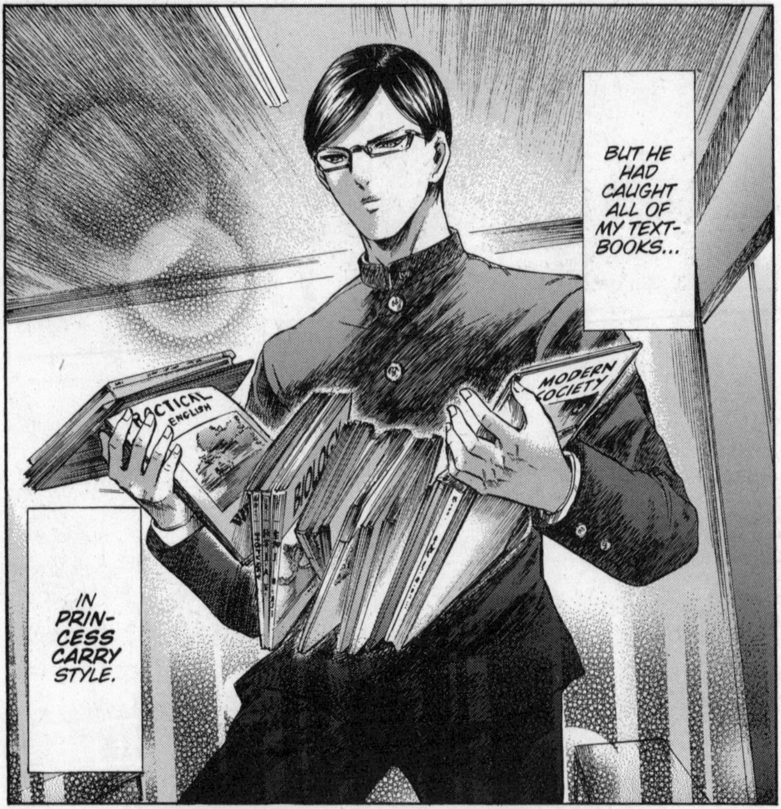
BUT HE HAD CAUGHT ALL OF MY TEXT-BOOKS...
IN PRINCESS CARRY STYLE.
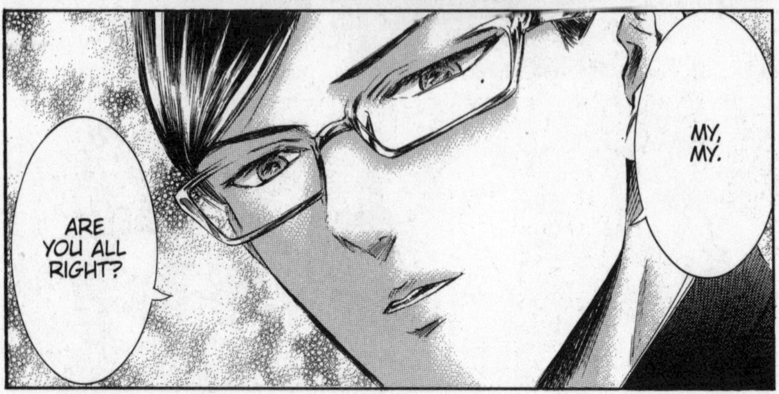
MY, MY.
ARE YOU ALL RIGHT?

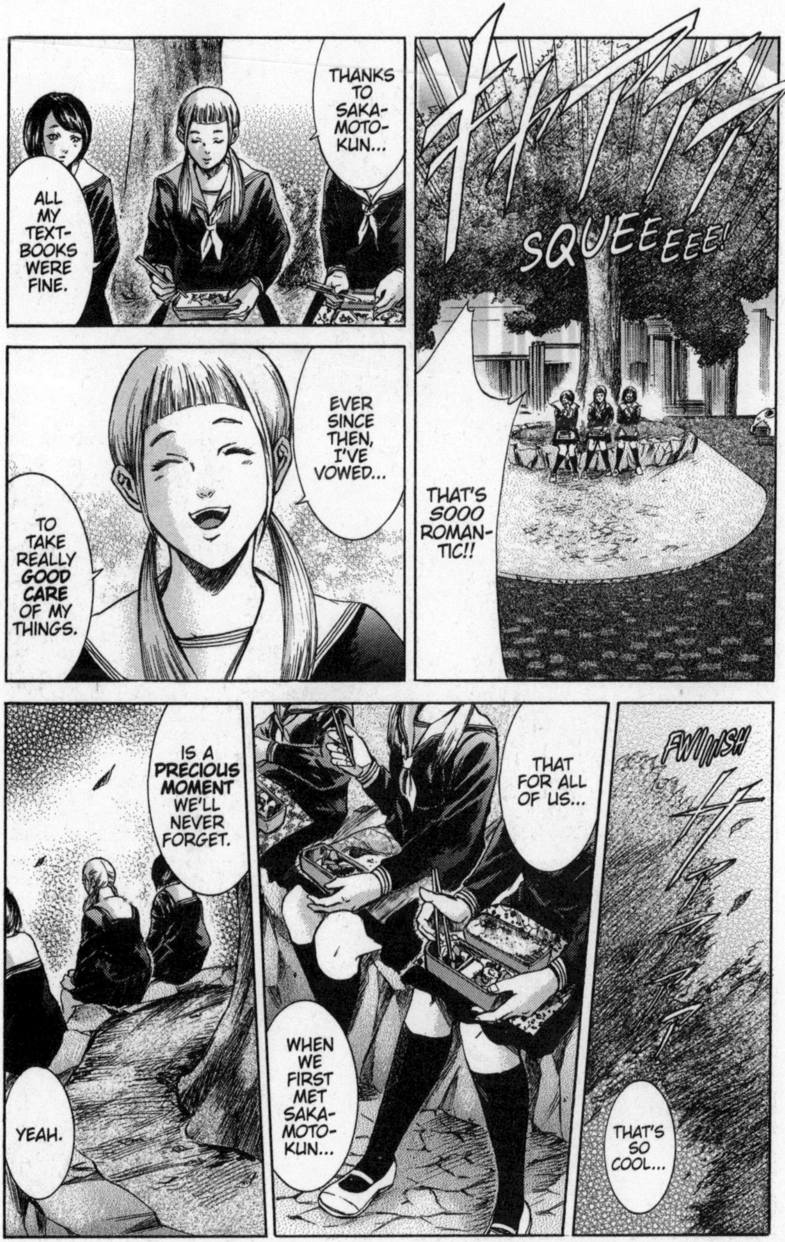
SQUEEEEEE!
THAT'S SOOO ROMANTIC!!
THANKS TO SAKAMOTO-KUN...
ALL MY TEXTBOOKS WERE FINE.
EVER SINCE THEN, I'VE VOWED...
TO TAKE REALLY GOOD CARE OF MY THINGS.
FWIIISH
THAT'S SO COOL...
THAT FOR ALL OF US...
WHEN WE FIRST MET SAKAMOTO-KUN...
IS A PRECIOUS MOMENT WE'LL NEVER FORGET.
YEAH.

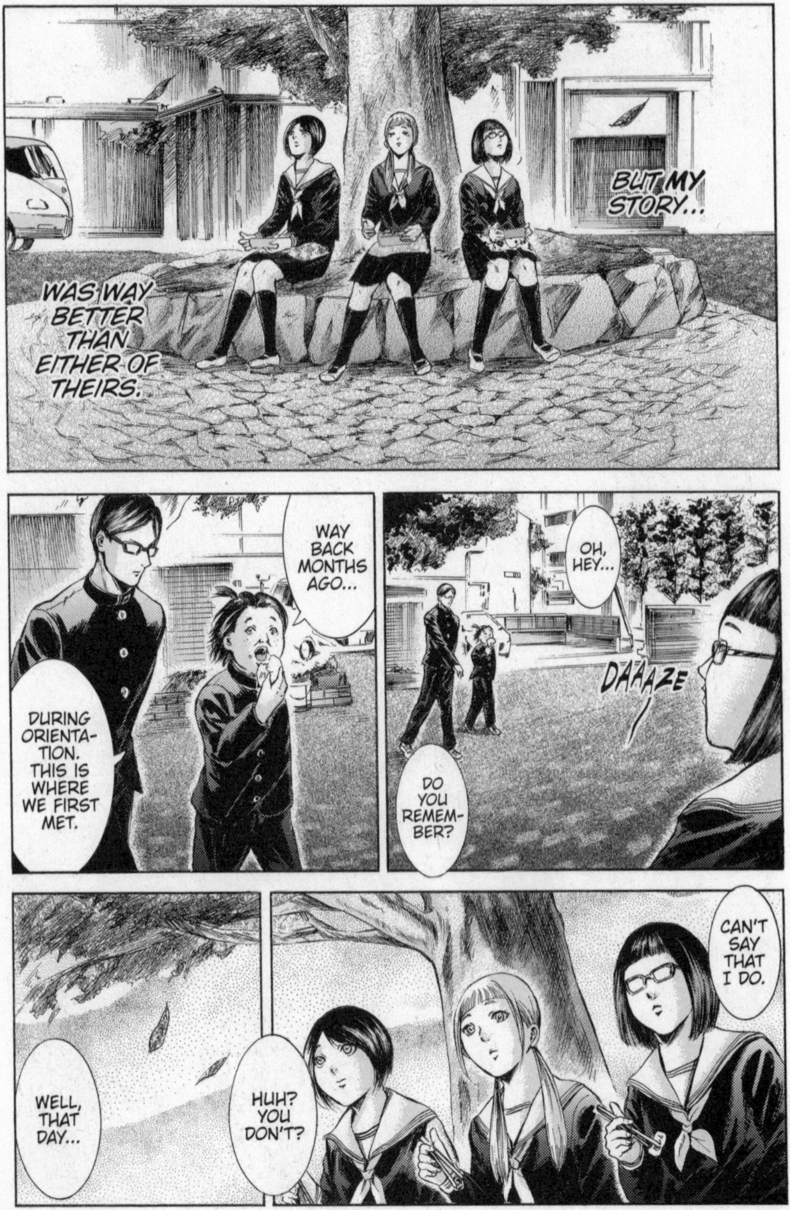
BUT MY STORY...
WAS WAY BETTER THAN EITHER OF THEIRS.
OH, HEY...
DAAAZE
DO YOU REMEMBER?
WAY BACK MONTHS AGO...
DURING ORIENTATION. THIS IS WHERE WE FIRST MET.
CAN'T SAY THAT I DO.
HUH? YOU DON'T?
WELL, THAT DAY...

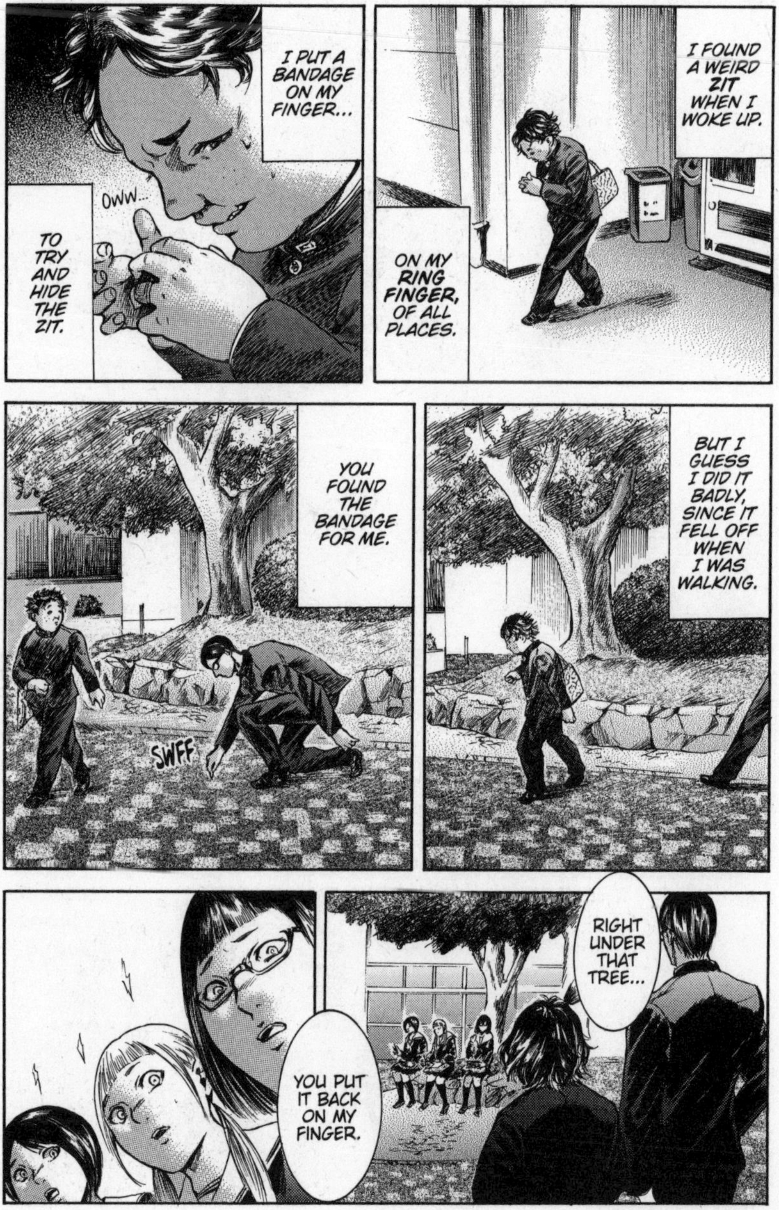
I FOUND A WEIRD ZIT WHEN I WOKE UP.
ON MY RING FINGER, OF ALL PLACES.
I PUT A BANDAGE ON MY FINGER...
OWW...
TO TRY AND HIDE THE ZIT.
BUT I GUESS I DID IT BADLY, SINCE IT FELL OFF WHEN I WAS WALKING.
YOU FOUND THE BANDAGE FOR ME.
SWFF
RIGHT UNDER THAT TREE...
YOU PUT IT BACK ON MY FINGER.

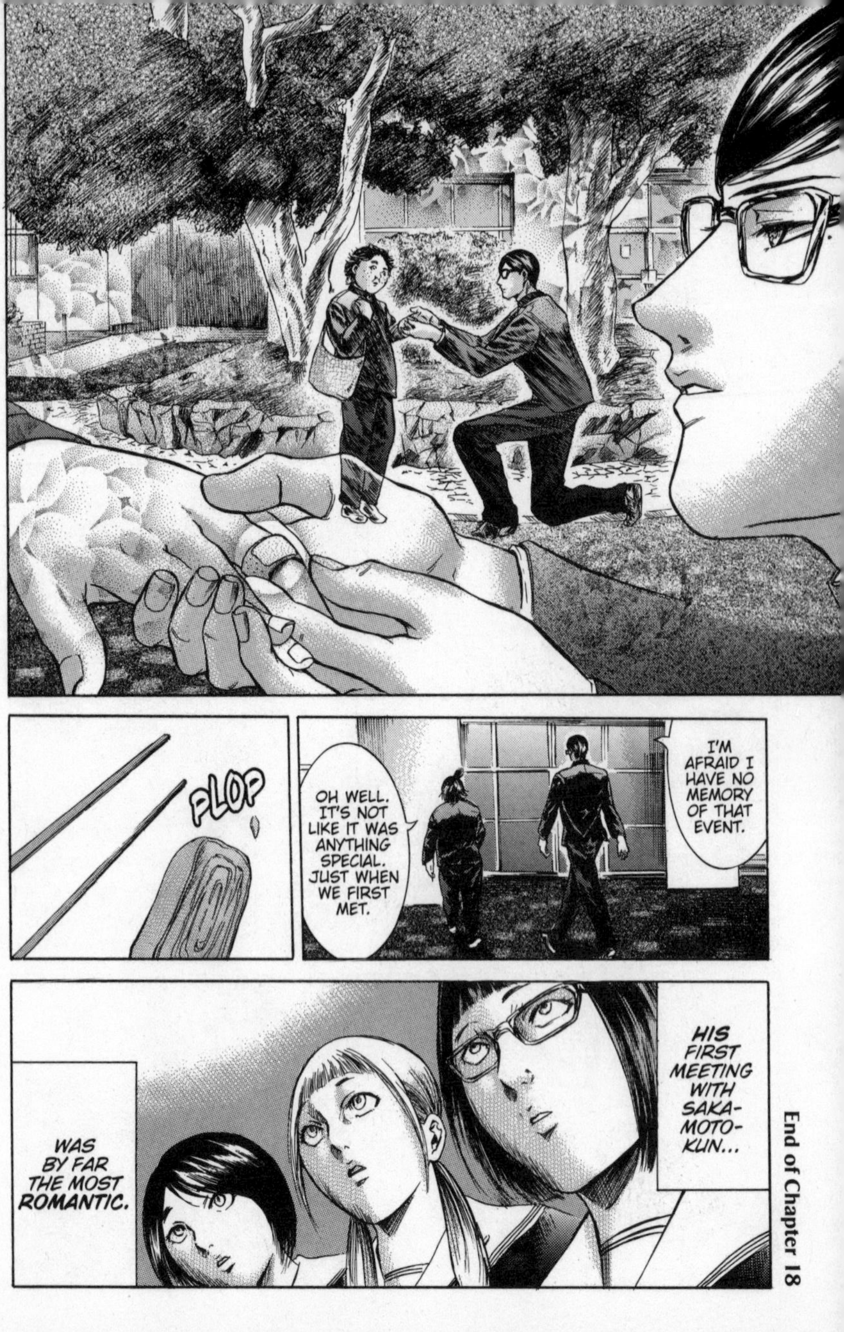
I'M AFRAID I HAVE NO MEMORY OF THAT EVENT.
OH WELL. IT'S NOT LIKE IT WAS ANYTHING SPECIAL. JUST WHEN WE FIRST MET.
PLOP
HIS FIRST MEETING WITH SAKA-MOTO-KUN...
WAS BY FAR THE MOST ROMANTIC.

End of Chapter 18

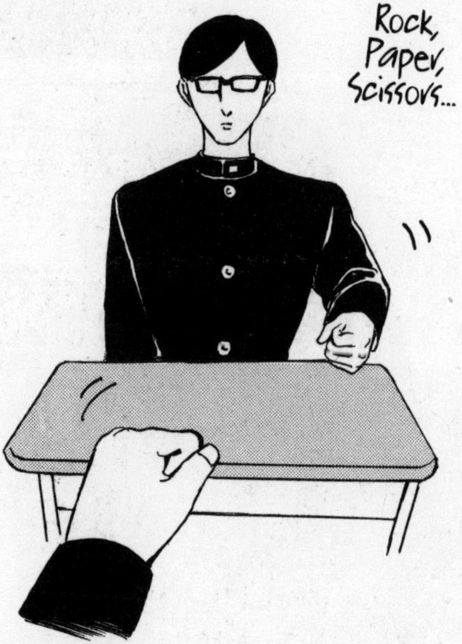
Rock, Paper, Scissors...

Let's Play With
Sakamoto #1

Shoot!
Strength
Magnetic Field
Energy Waves

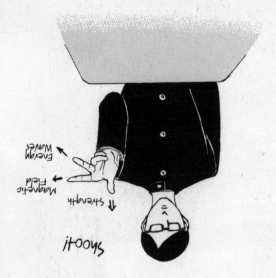

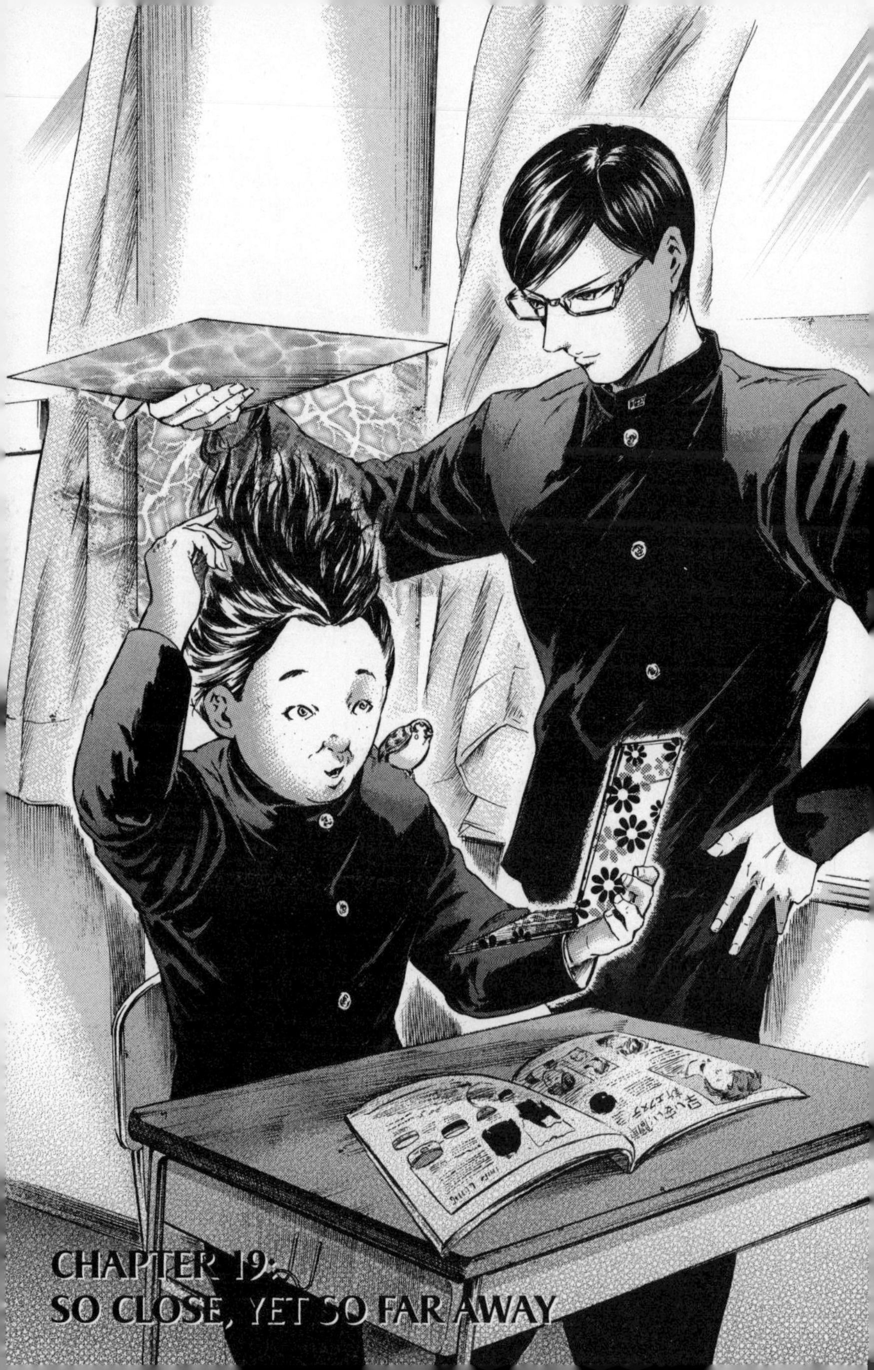
CHAPTER 19:
SO CLOSE, YET SO FAR AWAY

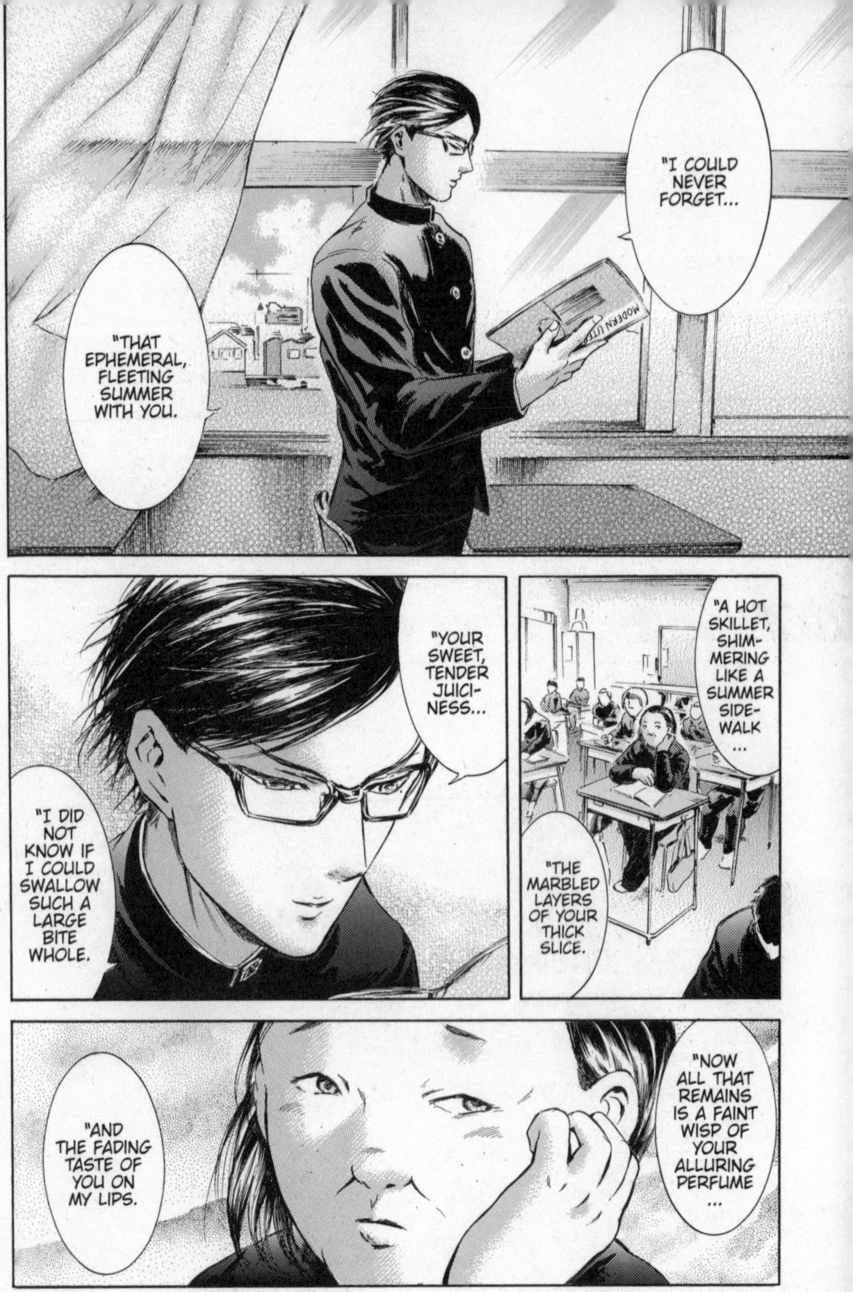
"I COULD NEVER FORGET...
"THAT EPHEMERAL, FLEETING SUMMER WITH YOU.
MODERN LITE
"A HOT SKILLET, SHIMMERING LIKE A SUMMER SIDEWALK ...
"THE MARBLED LAYERS OF YOUR THICK SLICE.
"YOUR SWEET, TENDER JUICINESS...
"I DID NOT KNOW IF I COULD SWALLOW SUCH A LARGE BITE WHOLE.
"NOW ALL THAT REMAINS IS A FAINT WISP OF YOUR ALLURING PERFUME ...
"AND THE FADING TASTE OF YOU ON MY LIPS.

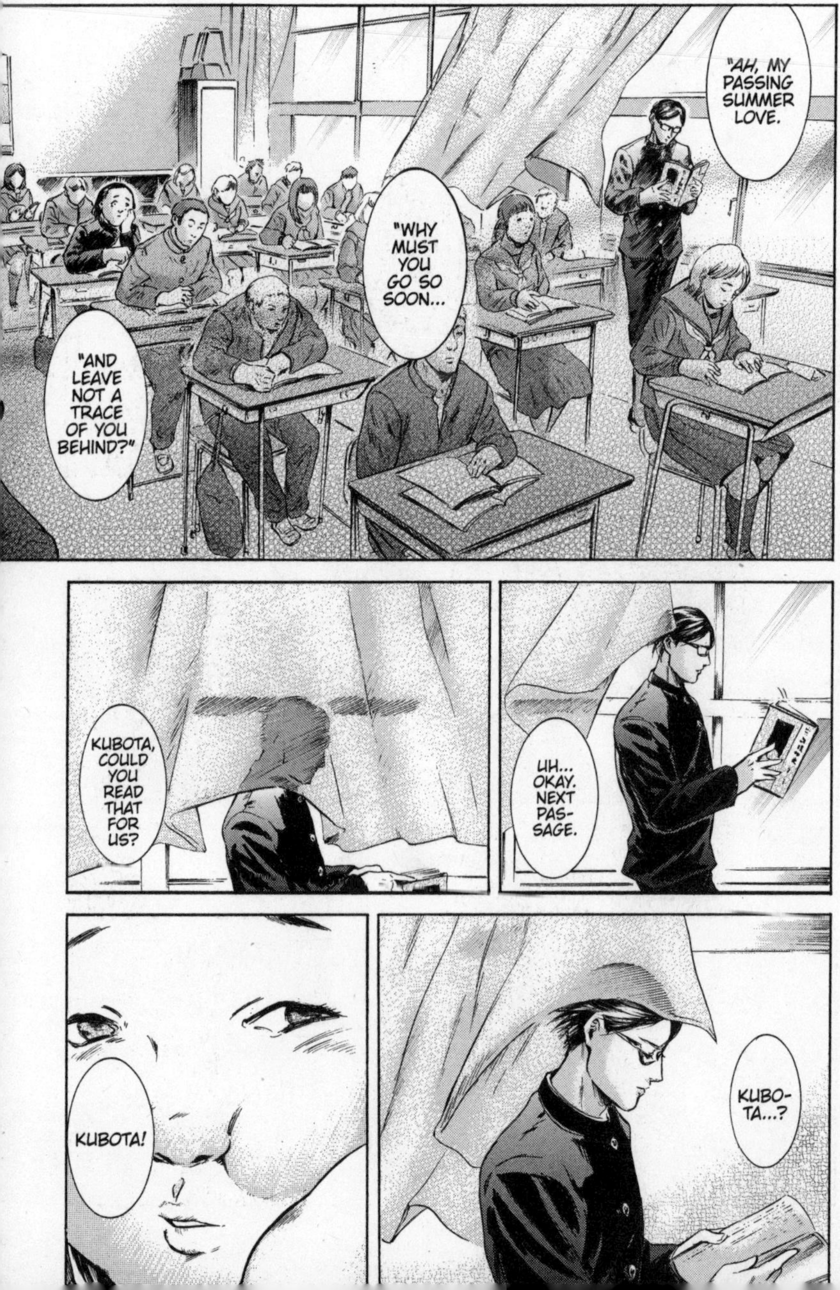
"AH, MY PASSING SUMMER LOVE.
"WHY MUST YOU GO SO SOON...
"AND LEAVE NOT A TRACE OF YOU BEHIND?"
UH... OKAY. NEXT PAS-SAGE.
KUBOTA, COULD YOU READ THAT FOR US?
KUBO-TA...?
KUBOTA!

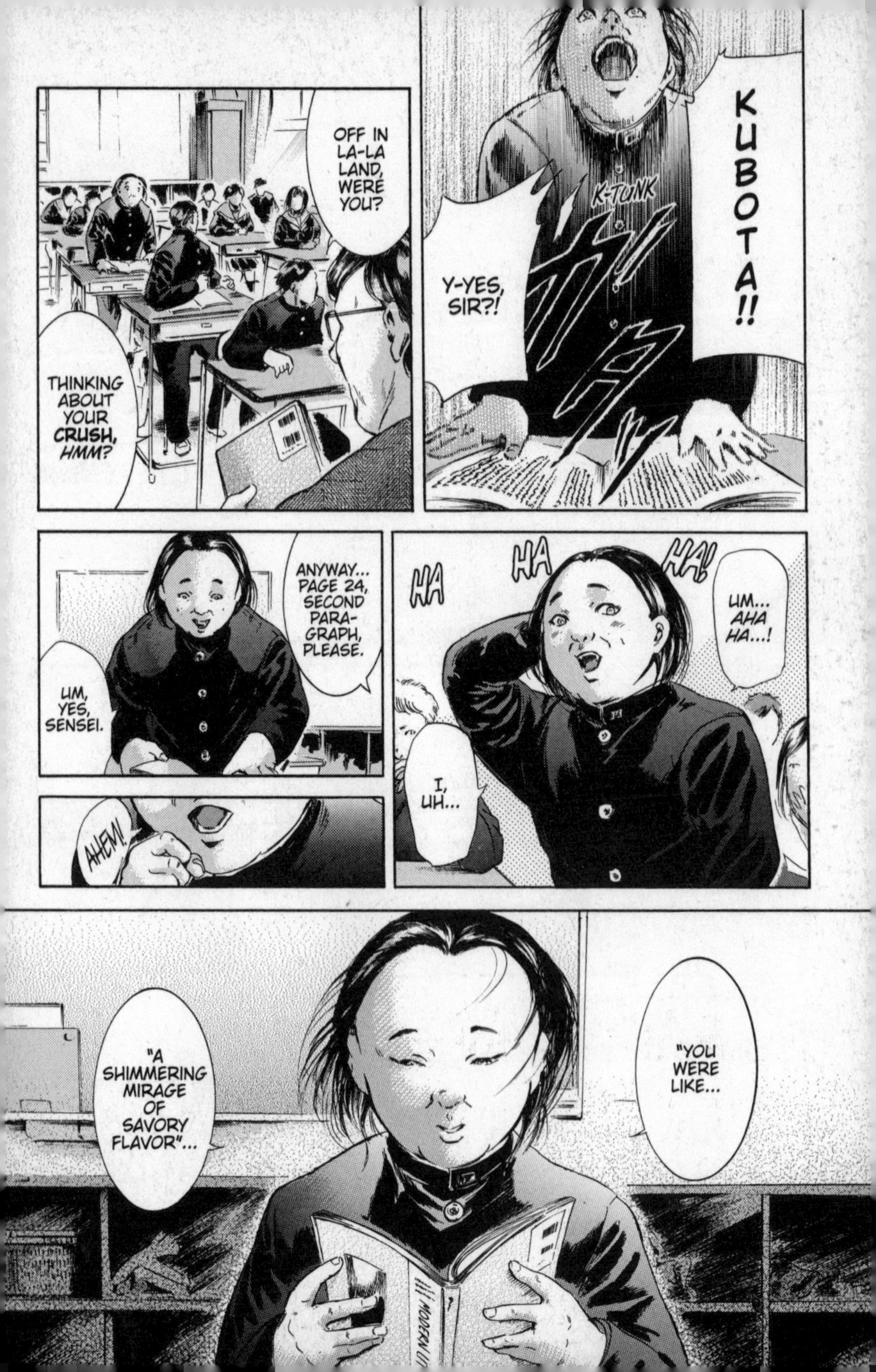
KUBOTA!!
K-TONK
Y-YES, SIR?!
OFF IN LA-LA LAND, WERE YOU?
THINKING ABOUT YOUR CRUSH, HMM?
HA HA HA!
UM... AHA HA...!
I, UH...
ANYWAY... PAGE 24, SECOND PARA-GRAPH, PLEASE.
UM, YES, SENSEI.
AHEM!
"YOU WERE LIKE...
"A SHIMMERING MIRAGE OF SAVORY FLAVOR"...
MODERN LIT

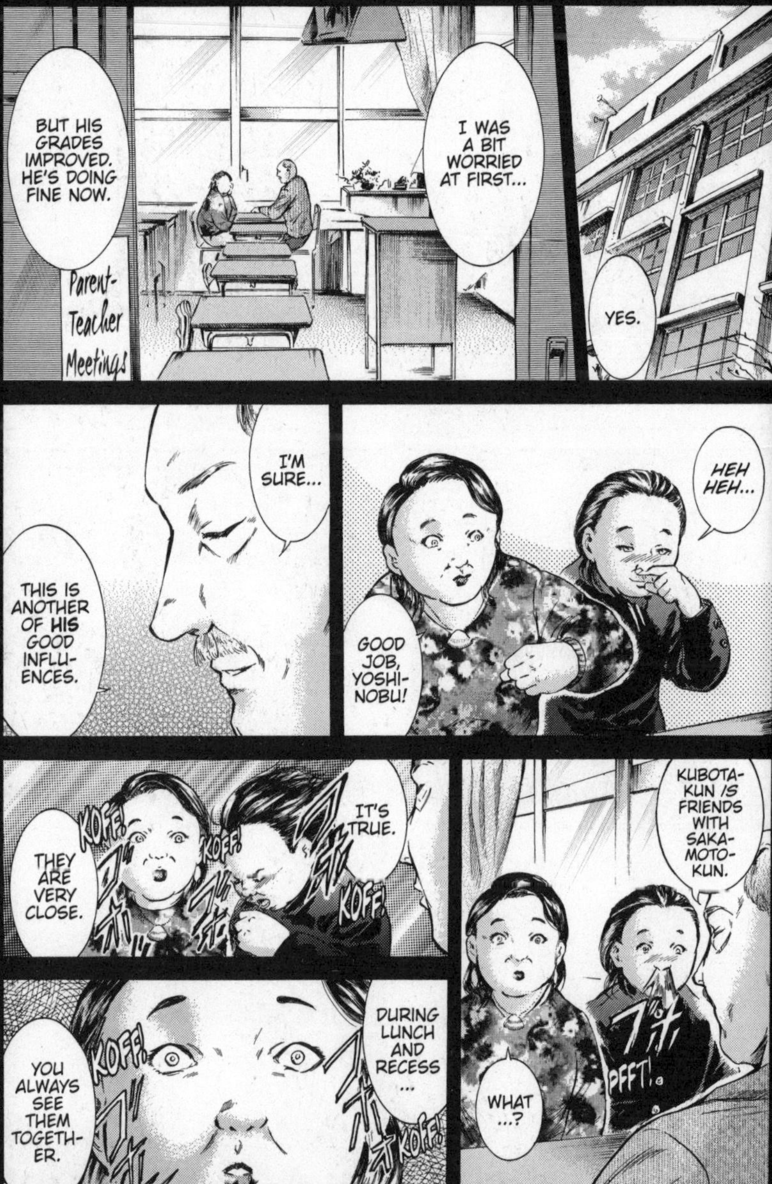
YES.
I WAS A BIT WORRIED AT FIRST...
BUT HIS GRADES IMPROVED. HE'S DOING FINE NOW.
Parent-Teacher Meetings
HEH HEH...
GOOD JOB, YOSHI-NOBU!
I'M SURE...
THIS IS ANOTHER OF **HIS** GOOD INFLU-ENCES.
KUBOTA-KUN *IS* FRIENDS WITH SAKA-MOTO-KUN.
PFFT!
WHAT ...?
IT'S TRUE.
KOFF! KOFF! KOFF!
THEY ARE VERY CLOSE.
DURING LUNCH AND RECESS ...
KOFF! KOFF!
YOU ALWAYS SEE THEM TOGETH-ER.

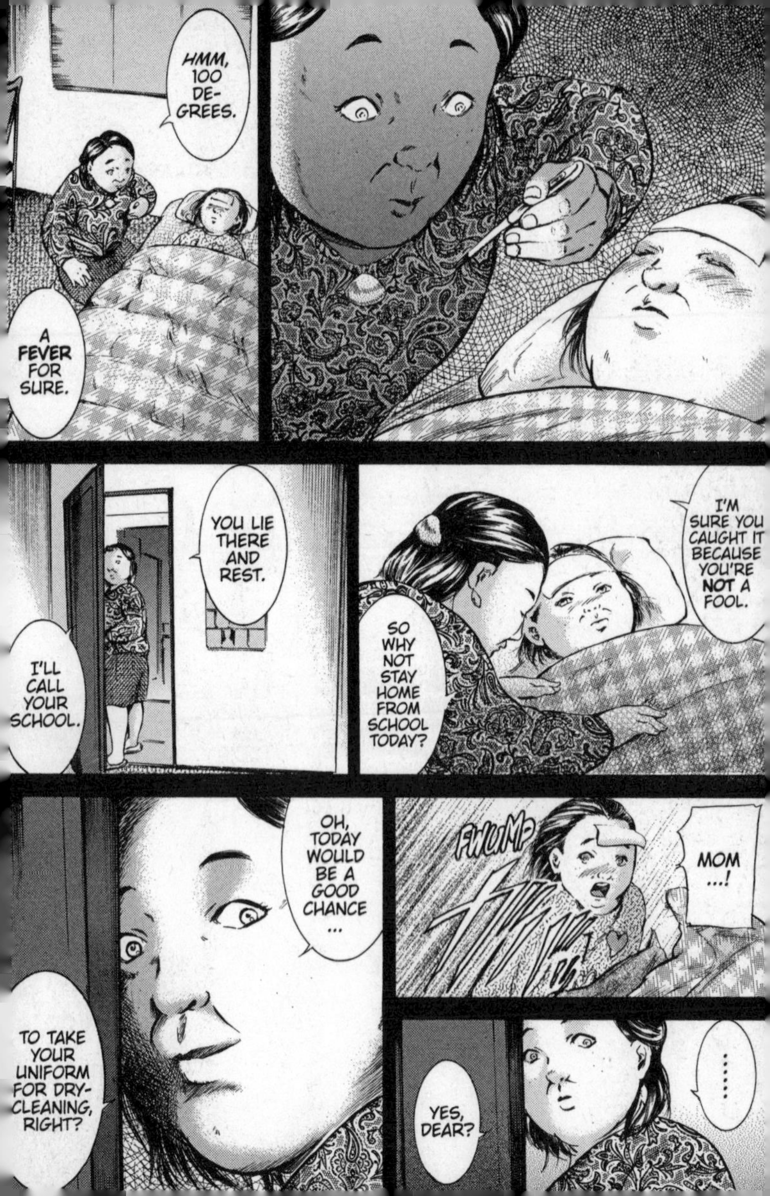
HMM, 100 DE-GREES.
A FEVER FOR SURE.
I'M SURE YOU CAUGHT IT BECAUSE YOU'RE NOT A FOOL.
SO WHY NOT STAY HOME FROM SCHOOL TODAY?
YOU LIE THERE AND REST.
I'LL CALL YOUR SCHOOL.
MOM ...!
FWUMP
......
YES, DEAR?
OH, TODAY WOULD BE A GOOD CHANCE ...
TO TAKE YOUR UNIFORM FOR DRY-CLEANING, RIGHT?

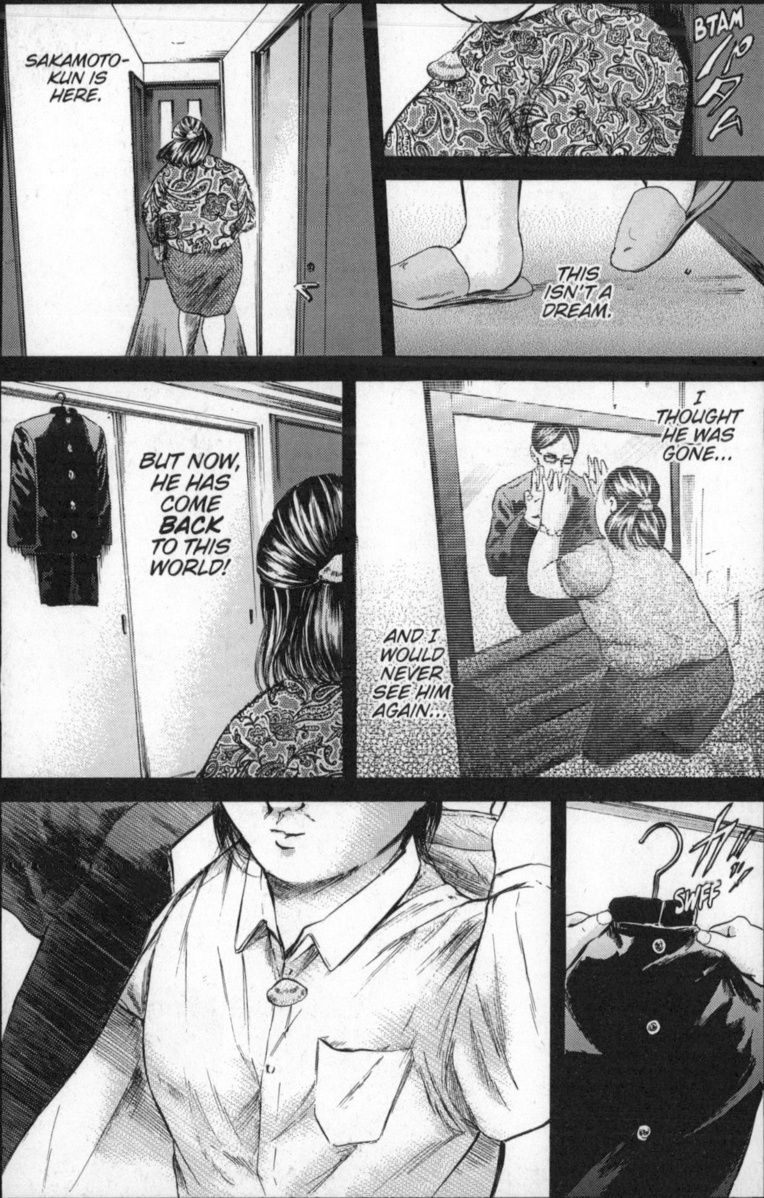
BTAM
THIS ISN'T A DREAM.
SAKAMOTO-KUN IS HERE.
I THOUGHT HE WAS GONE...
AND I WOULD NEVER SEE HIM AGAIN...
BUT NOW, HE HAS COME BACK TO THIS WORLD!
SWFF

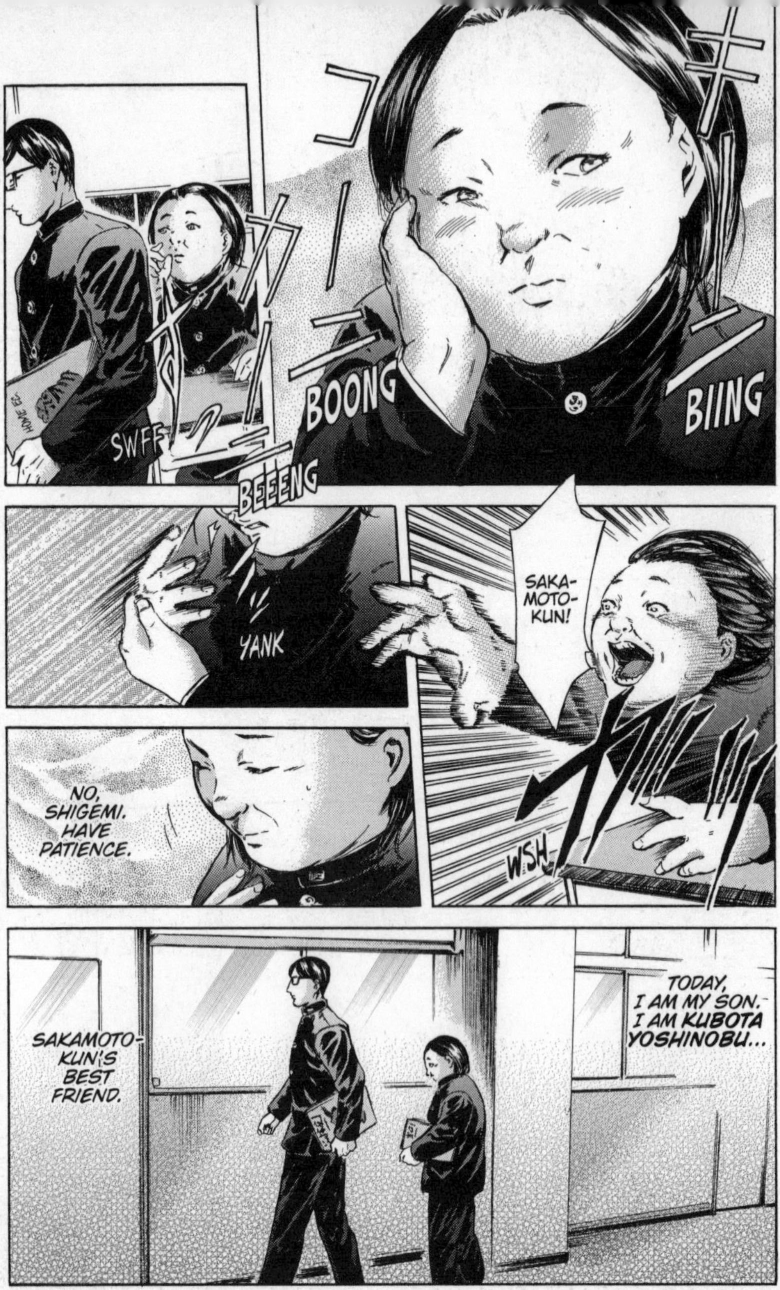
BIING
BOONG
SWFF
HOME EC
BEEENG
SAKA-MOTO-KUN!
WSH
YANK
NO, SHIGEMI. HAVE PATIENCE.
TODAY, I AM MY SON. I AM KUBOTA YOSHINOBU...
SAKAMOTO-KUN'S BEST FRIEND.

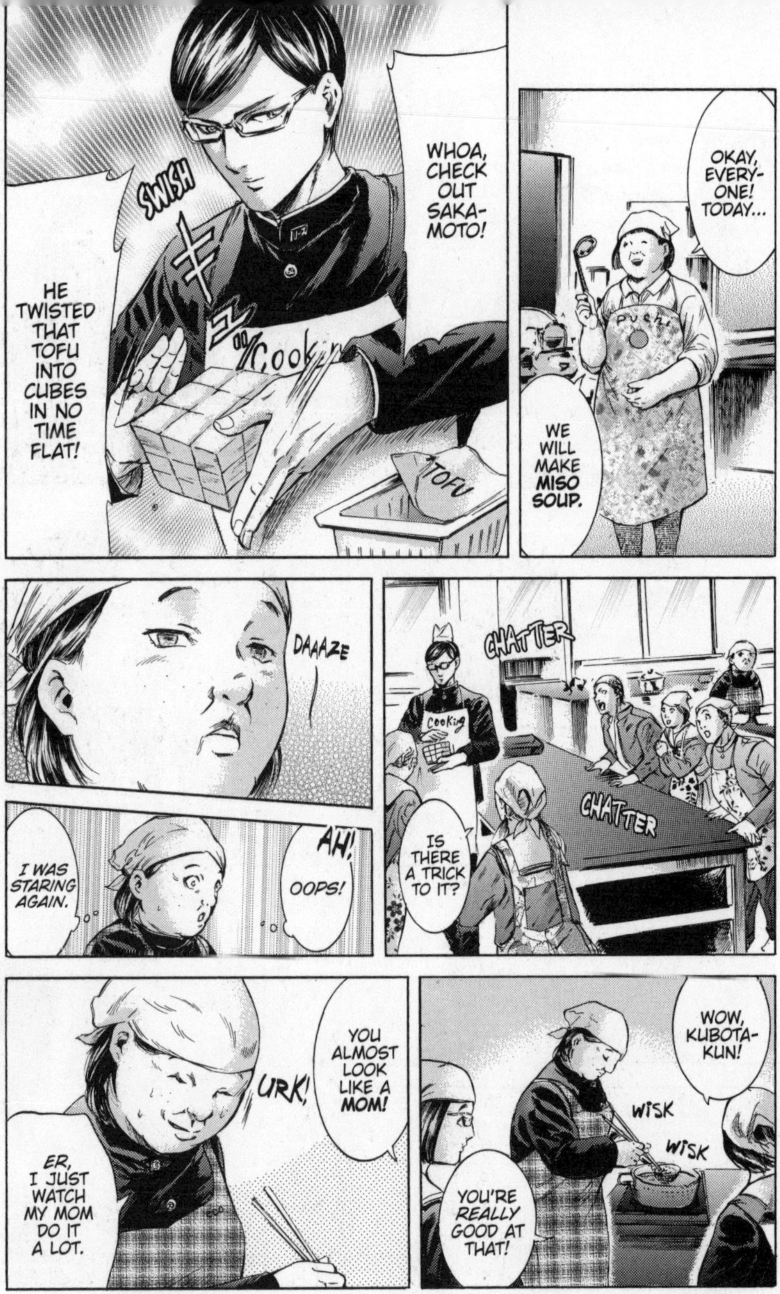
OKAY, EVERY-ONE! TODAY...
WE WILL MAKE MISO SOUP.
WHOA, CHECK OUT SAKA-MOTO!
SWISH
HE TWISTED THAT TOFU INTO CUBES IN NO TIME FLAT!
TOFU
Cooking
CHATTER
CHATTER
IS THERE A TRICK TO IT?
Cooking
DAAAZE
AH!
OOPS!
I WAS STARING AGAIN.
WOW, KUBOTA-KUN!
WISK
WISK
YOU'RE REALLY GOOD AT THAT!
YOU ALMOST LOOK LIKE A MOM!
URK!
ER, I JUST WATCH MY MOM DO IT A LOT.

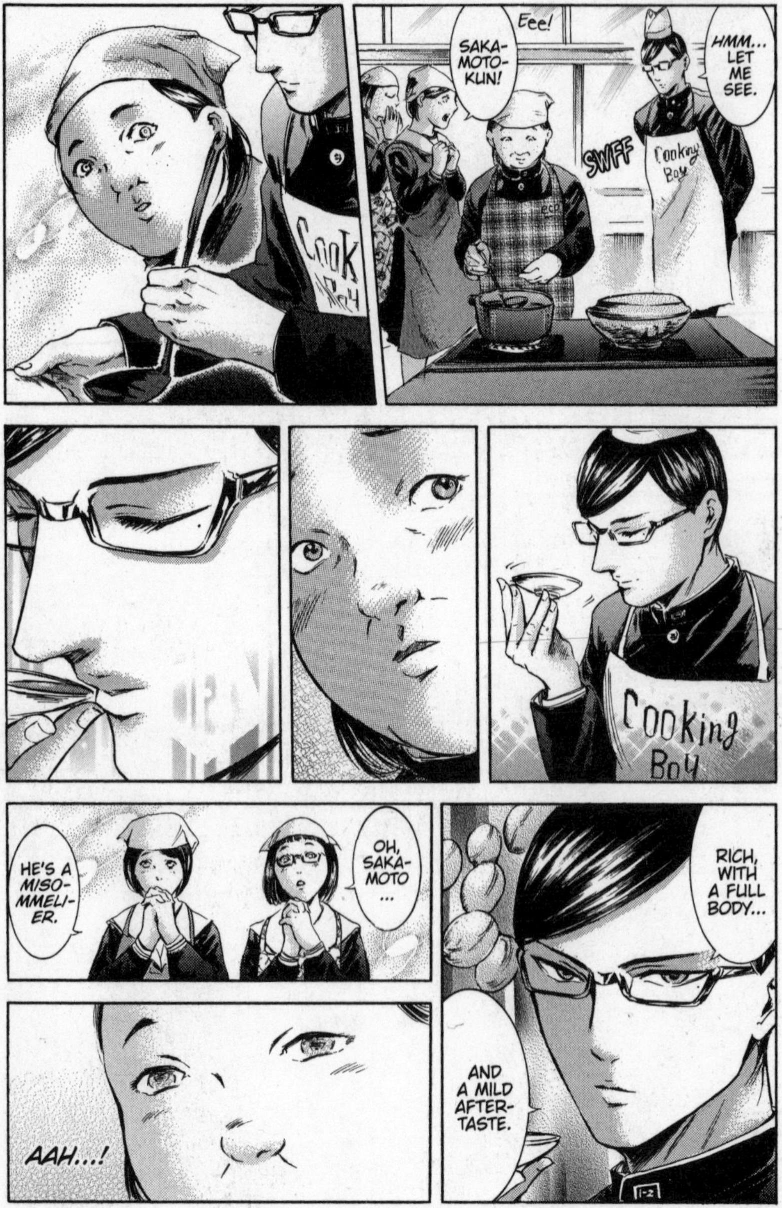
HMM... LET ME SEE.
SWFF
Cooking Boy
SAKA-MOTO-KUN!
Eee!
Cooking Boy
RICH, WITH A FULL BODY...
AND A MILD AFTER-TASTE.
OH, SAKA-MOTO ...
HE'S A MISOM-MMELI-ER.
AAH...!

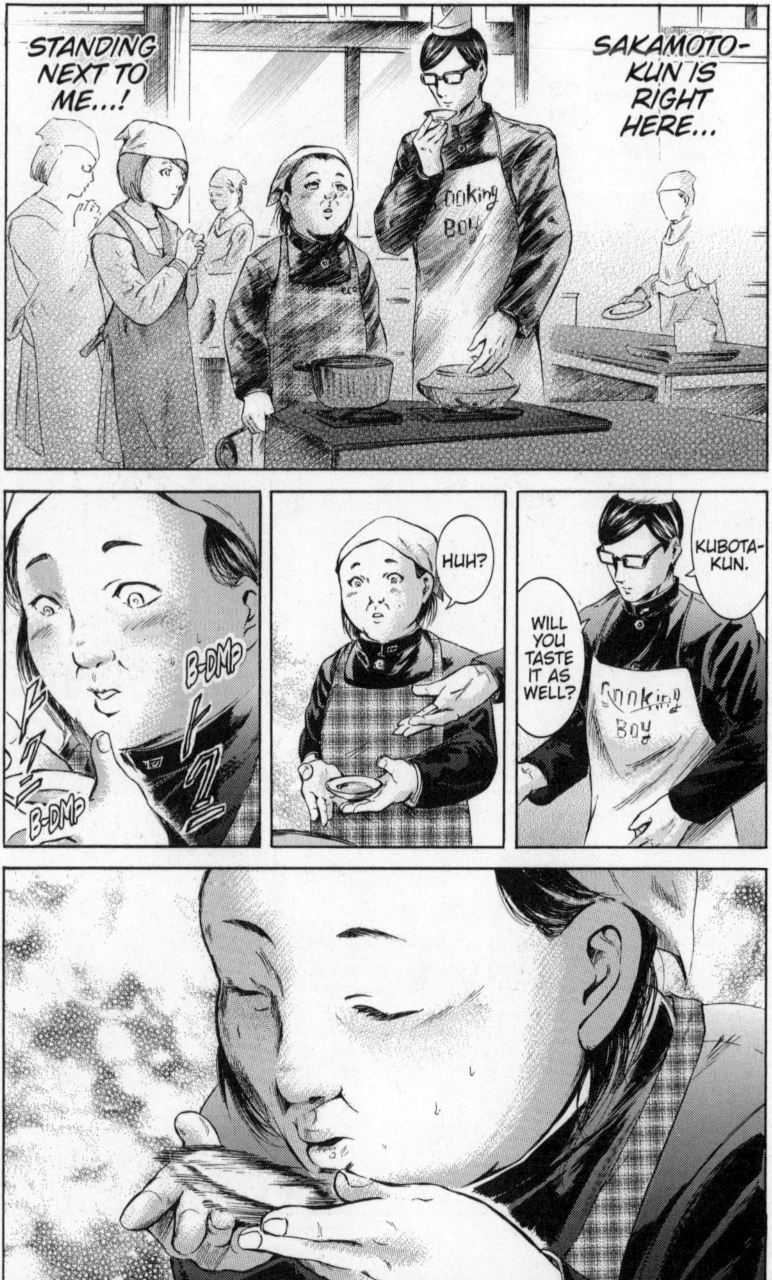
SAKAMOTO-KUN IS RIGHT HERE...
STANDING NEXT TO ME...!
KUBOTA-KUN.
WILL YOU TASTE IT AS WELL?
HUH?
B-DMP
B-DMP

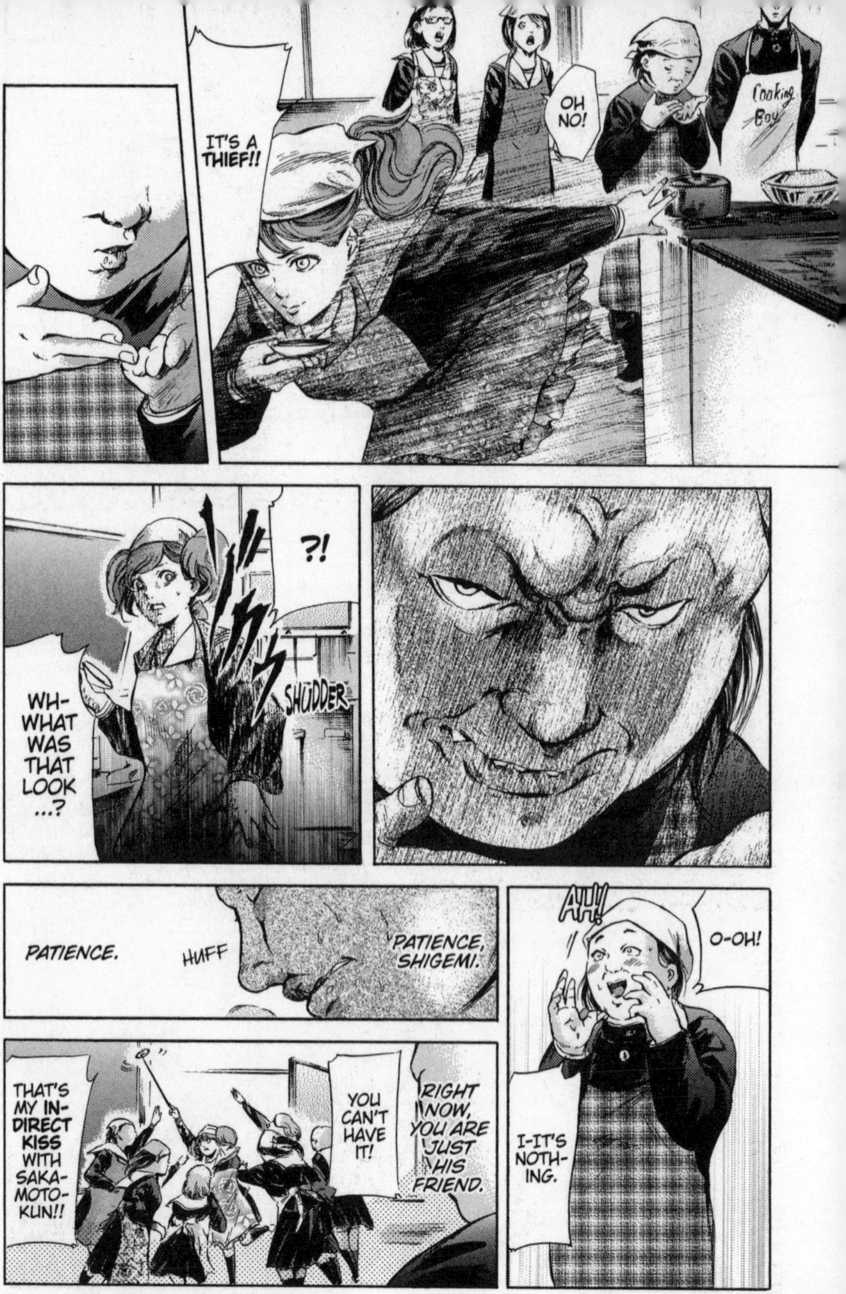
OH NO!
Cooking Boy
IT'S A THIEF!!
?!
WH-WHAT WAS THAT LOOK ...?
SHUDDER
AH!
O-OH!
I-IT'S NOTHING.
PATIENCE, SHIGEMI.
HUFF
PATIENCE.
RIGHT NOW, YOU ARE JUST HIS FRIEND.
YOU CAN'T HAVE IT!
THAT'S MY INDIRECT KISS WITH SAKAMOTO-KUN!!

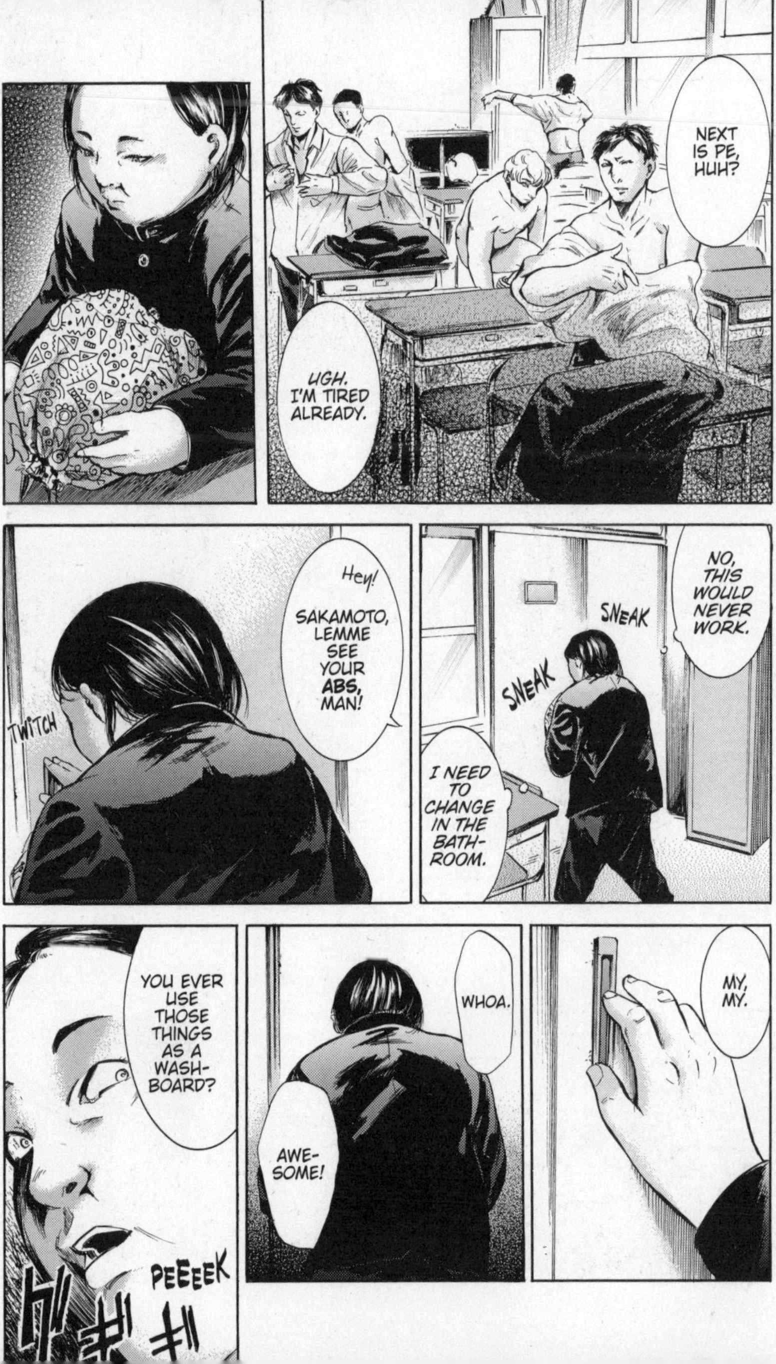
NEXT IS PE, HUH?
UGH. I'M TIRED ALREADY.
NO, THIS WOULD NEVER WORK.
SNEAK
SNEAK
I NEED TO CHANGE IN THE BATHROOM.
Hey!
SAKAMOTO, LEMME SEE YOUR ABS, MAN!
TWITCH
MY, MY.
WHOA.
AWESOME!
YOU EVER USE THOSE THINGS AS A WASHBOARD?
PEEEEK

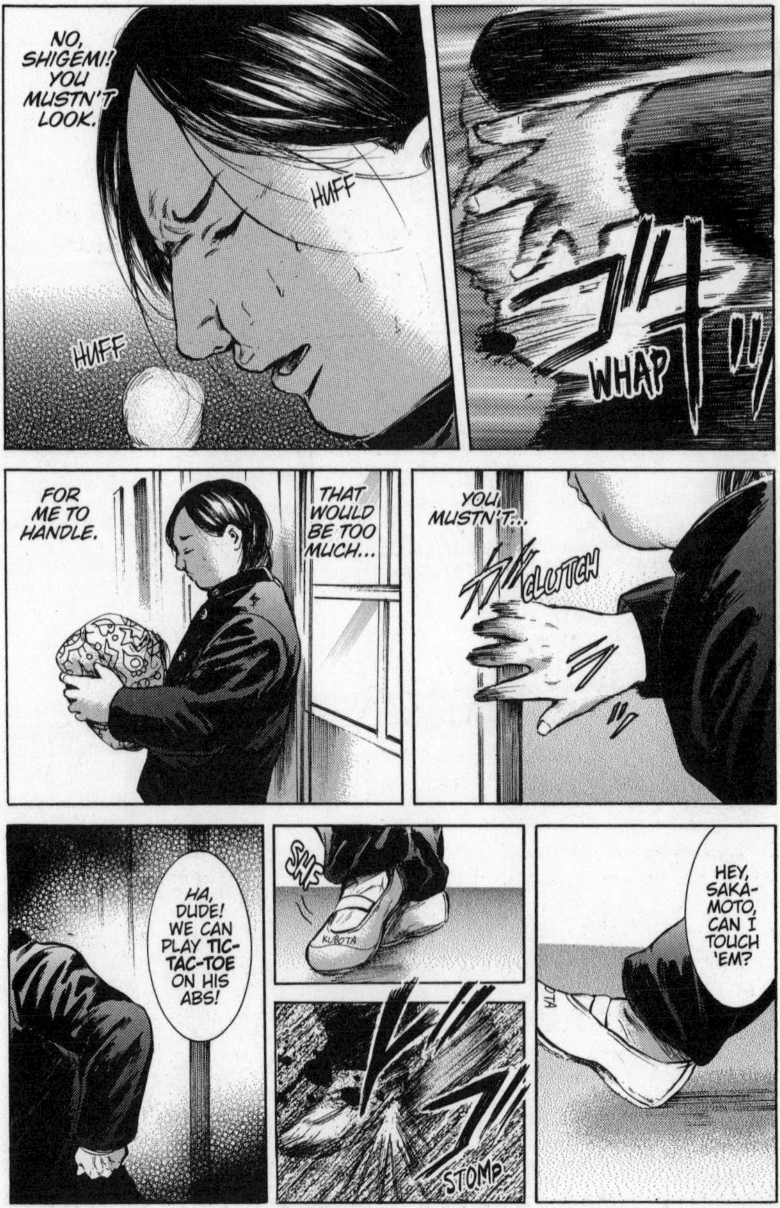
WHAP
NO, SHIGEMI! YOU MUSTN'T LOOK.
HUFF
HUFF
YOU MUSTN'T...
CLUTCH
THAT WOULD BE TOO MUCH...
FOR ME TO HANDLE.
HEY, SAKA-MOTO, CAN I TOUCH 'EM?
SHF
KUBOTA
STOMP
HA, DUDE! WE CAN PLAY TIC-TAC-TOE ON HIS ABS!

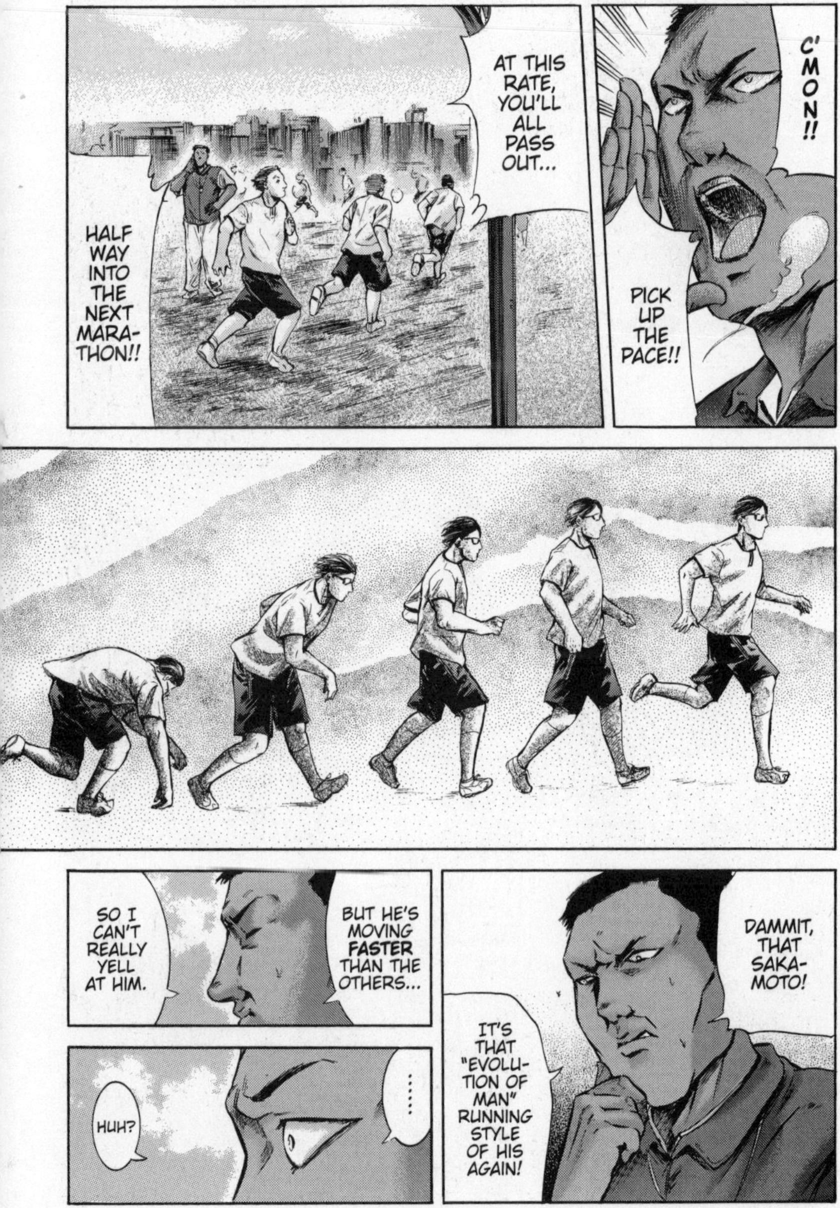
C'MON!!
PICK UP THE PACE!!
AT THIS RATE, YOU'LL ALL PASS OUT...
HALF WAY INTO THE NEXT MARA-THON!!
DAMMIT, THAT SAKA-MOTO!
IT'S THAT "EVOLU-TION OF MAN" RUNNING STYLE OF HIS AGAIN!
BUT HE'S MOVING **FASTER** THAN THE OTHERS...
SO I CAN'T REALLY YELL AT HIM.
......
HUH?

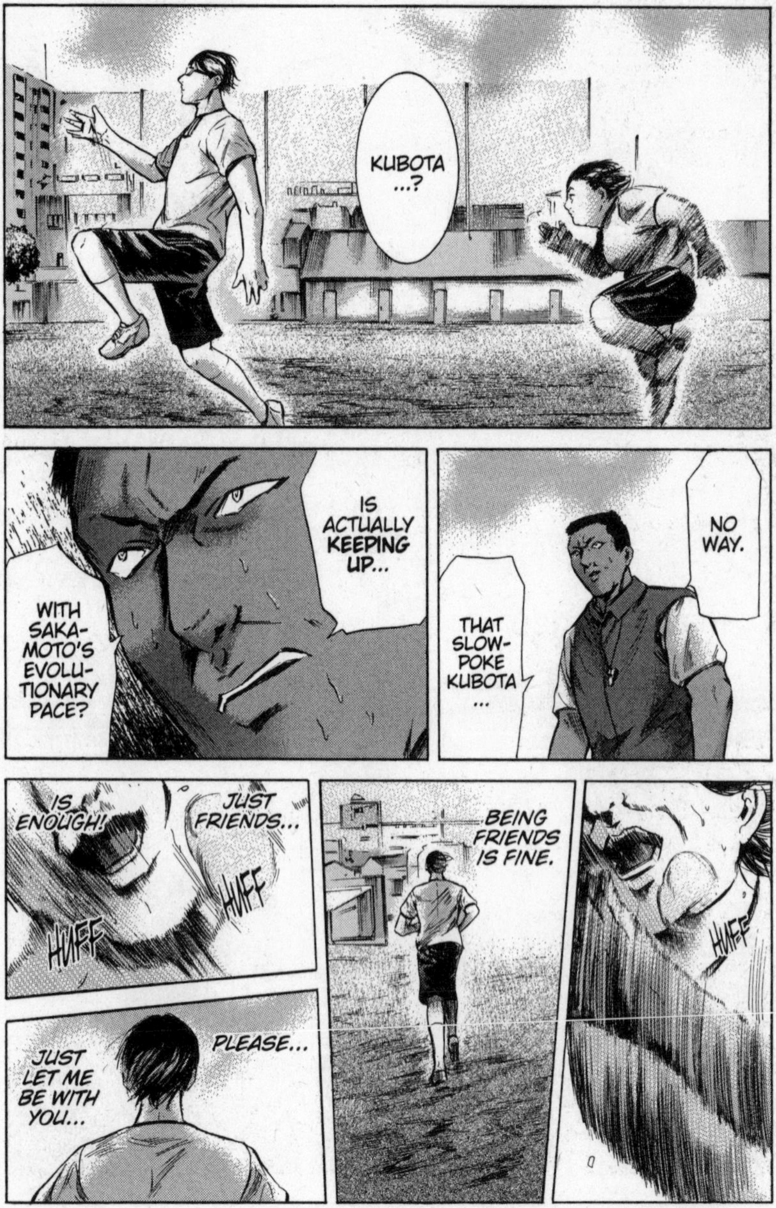
KUBOTA ...?
NO WAY.
THAT SLOW-POKE KUBOTA ...
IS ACTUALLY KEEPING UP...
WITH SAKA-MOTO'S EVOLU-TIONARY PACE?
HUFF
BEING FRIENDS IS FINE.
JUST FRIENDS...
IS ENOUGH!
HUFF
HUFF
PLEASE...
JUST LET ME BE WITH YOU...

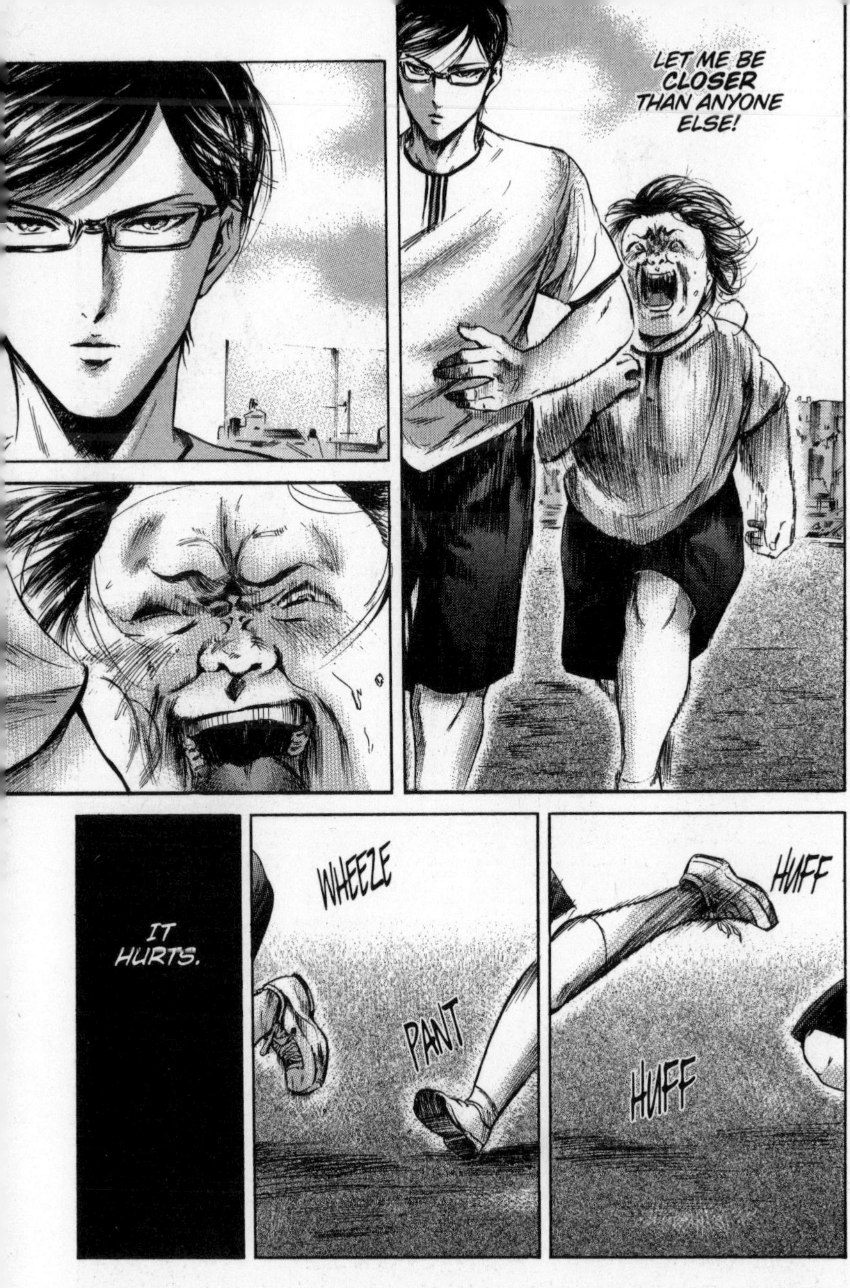
LET ME BE CLOSER THAN ANYONE ELSE!
HUFF
HUFF
WHEEZE
PANT
IT HURTS.

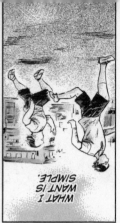

IT HURTS SO MUCH...
WHEEZE
SAKAMOTO-KUN.
EVEN THOUGH I'M THIS CLOSE...
I'LL NEVER...
EVER BE ABLE TO REACH YOU.
SAKA-MOTO-KUN...?
YOU KNOW...
WHAT I WANT IS SIMPLE.

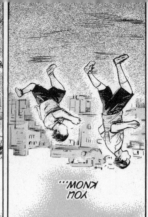

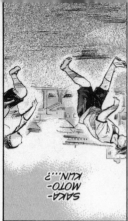

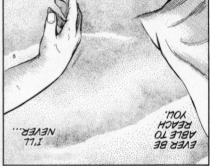

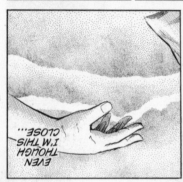

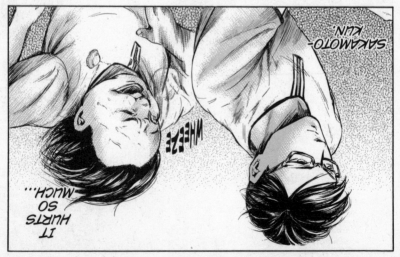

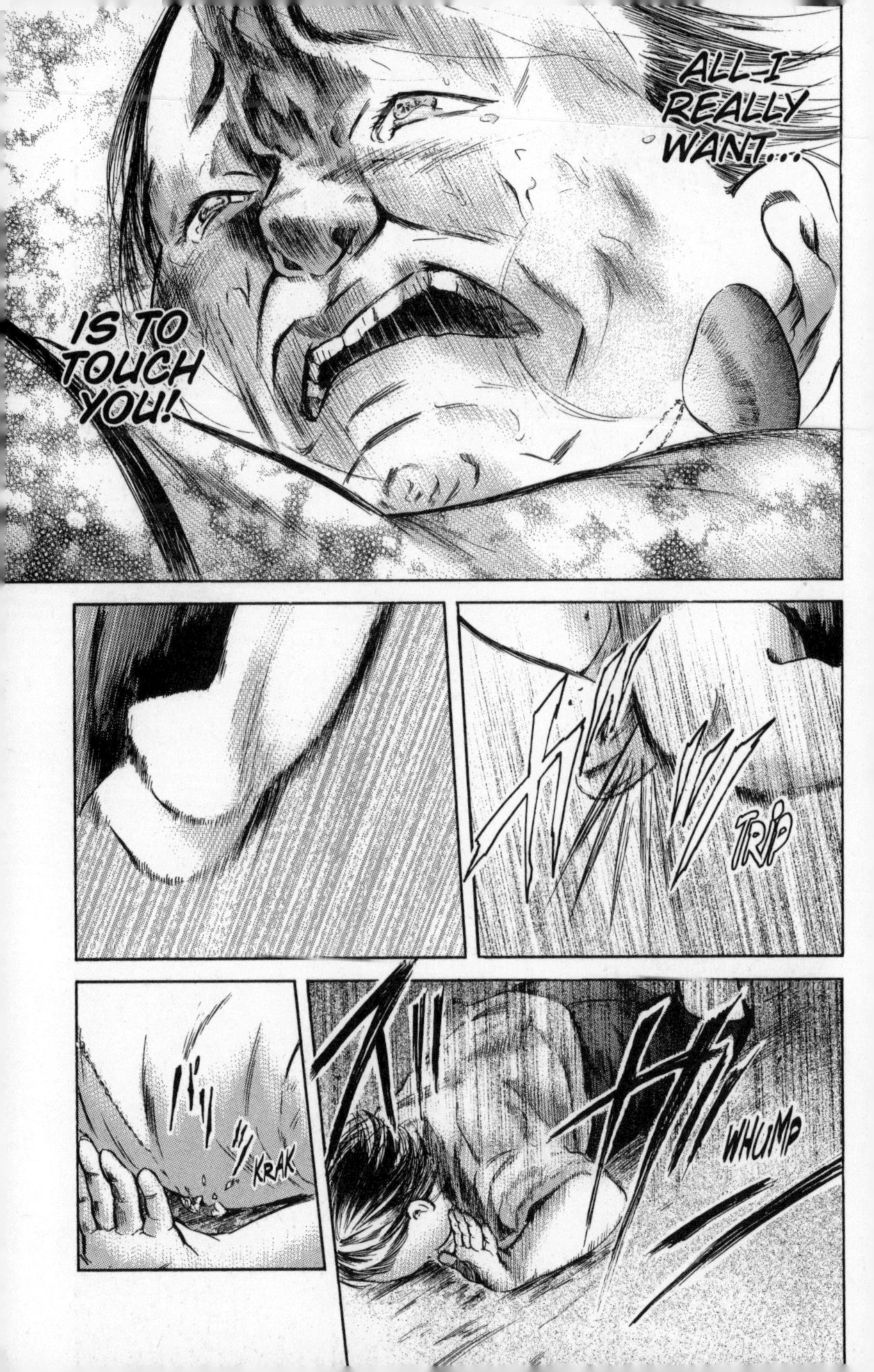
ALL I REALLY WANT...
IS TO TOUCH YOU!
TRIP
WHUMP
KRAK

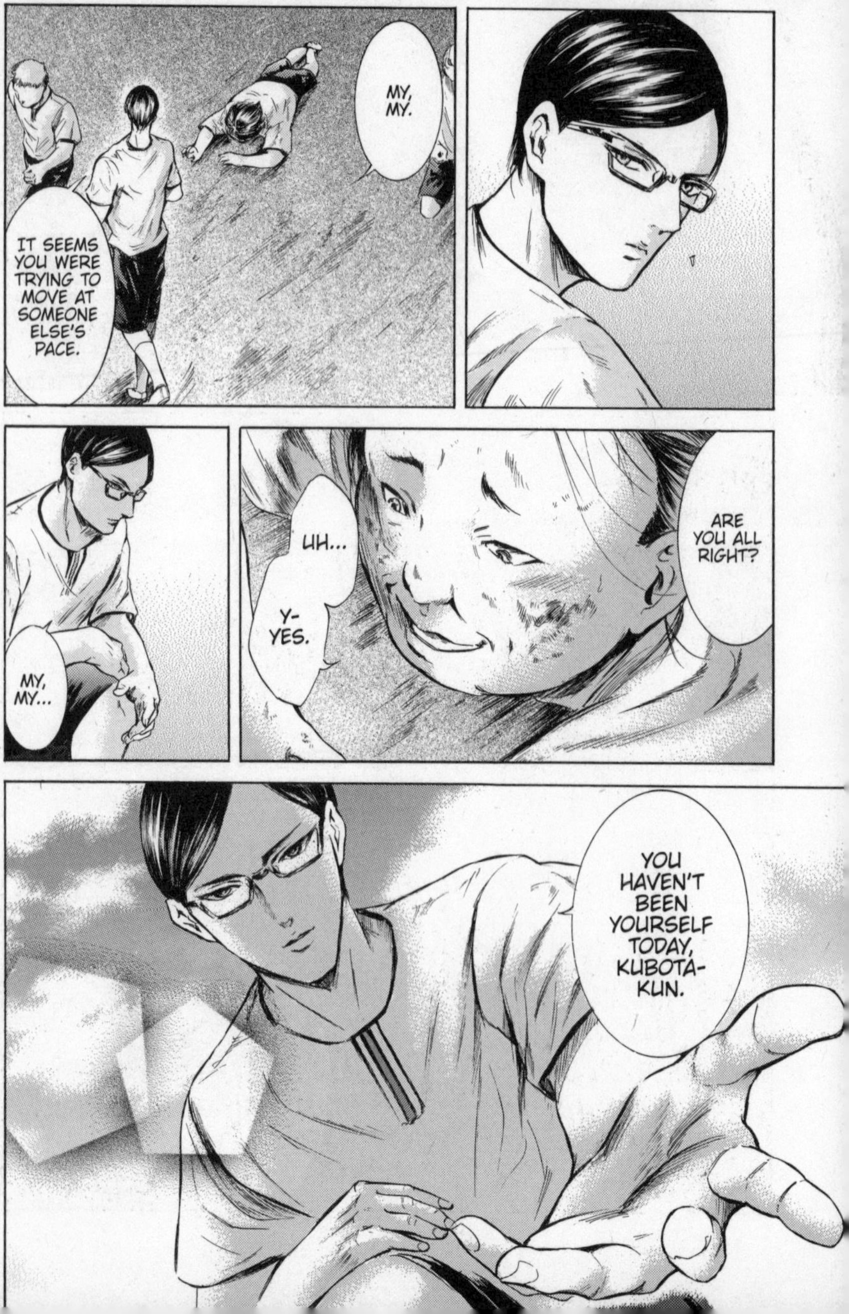
MY, MY.
IT SEEMS YOU WERE TRYING TO MOVE AT SOMEONE ELSE'S PACE.
ARE YOU ALL RIGHT?
UH...
Y-YES.
MY, MY...
YOU HAVEN'T BEEN YOURSELF TODAY, KUBOTA-KUN.

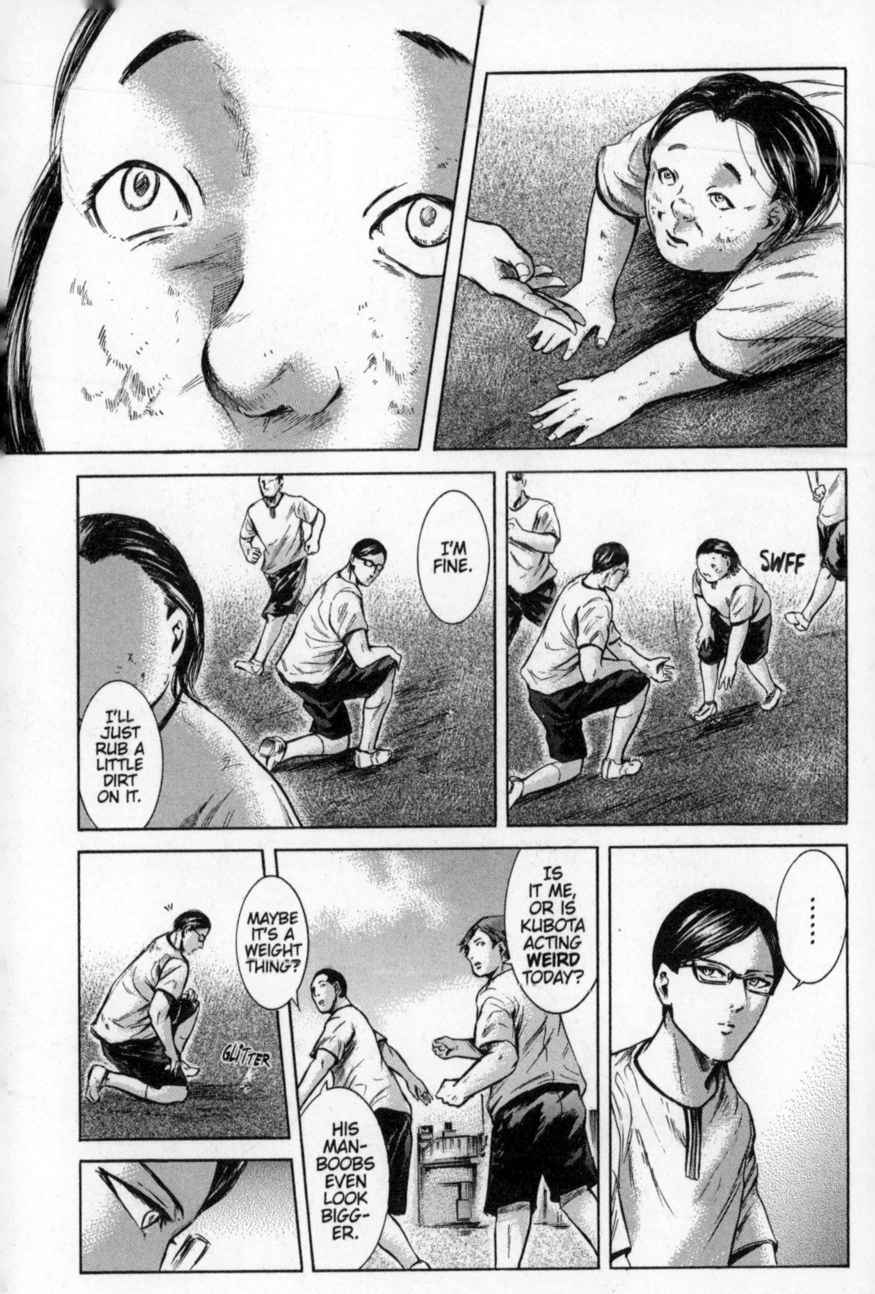
SWFF
I'M FINE.
I'LL JUST RUB A LITTLE DIRT ON IT.
......
IS IT ME, OR IS KUBOTA ACTING WEIRD TODAY?
HIS MAN-BOOBS EVEN LOOK BIGG-ER.
MAYBE IT'S A WEIGHT THING?
GLITTER

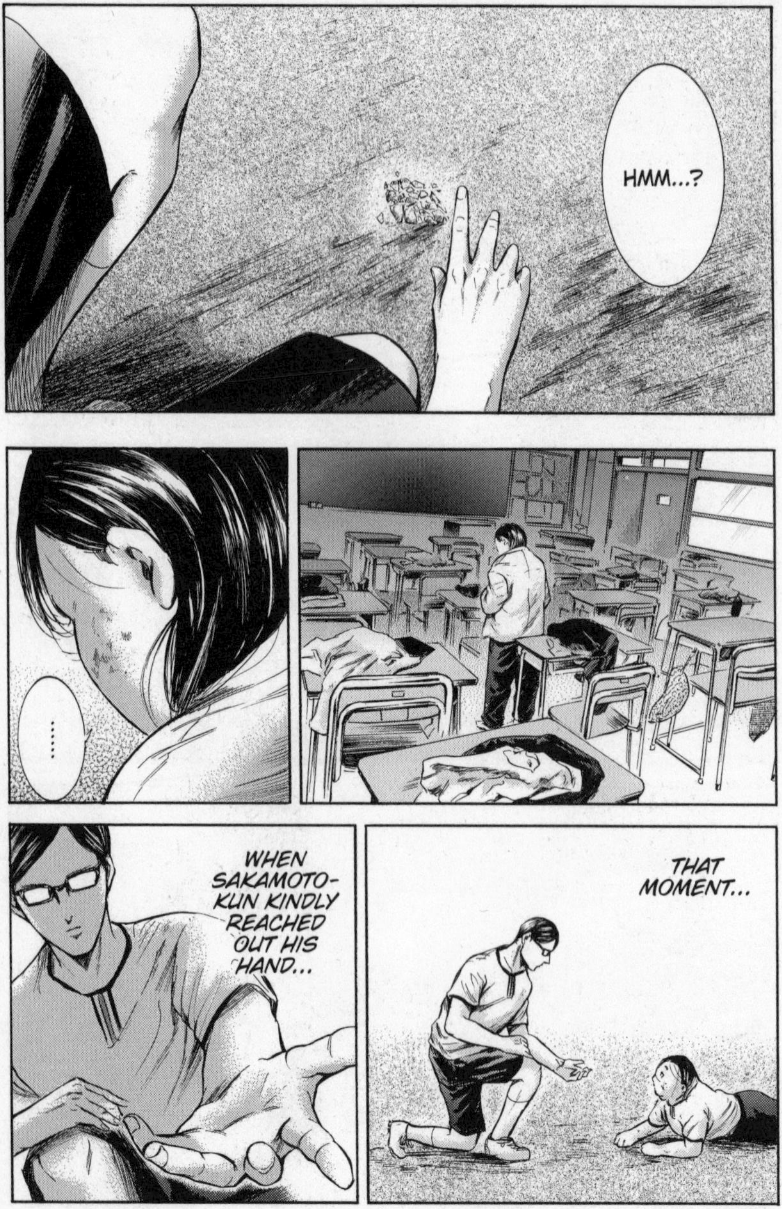
HMM...?
......
THAT MOMENT...
WHEN SAKAMOTO-KUN KINDLY REACHED OUT HIS HAND...

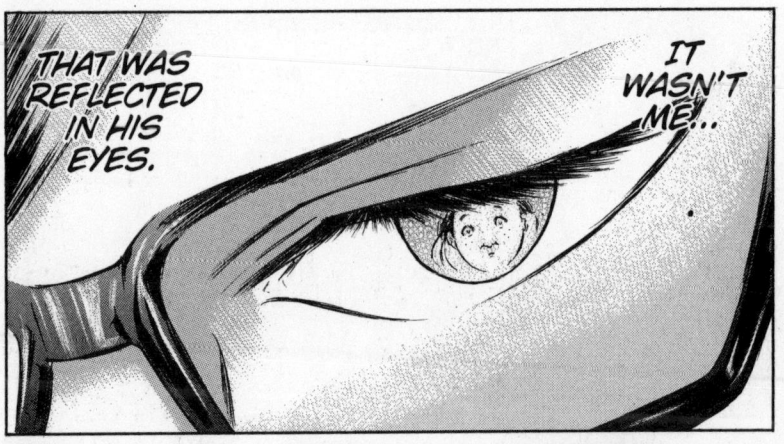

IT WASN'T ME...
THAT WAS REFLECTED IN HIS EYES.
HE WASN'T LOOKING AT ME.
HE WAS SEEING MY SON, YOSHI-NOBU.
I KNEW THAT FROM THE START.
AT LEAST, I THOUGHT I DID...
GOOD-NESS.
I'M SUCH A FOOL.
THAT WAS LIKELY...
MY LAST CHANCE TO TOUCH HIM, TOO.

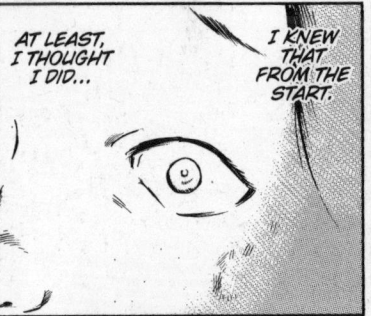

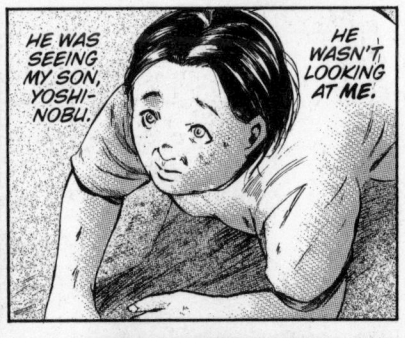

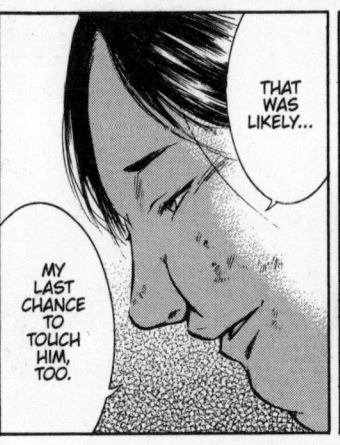

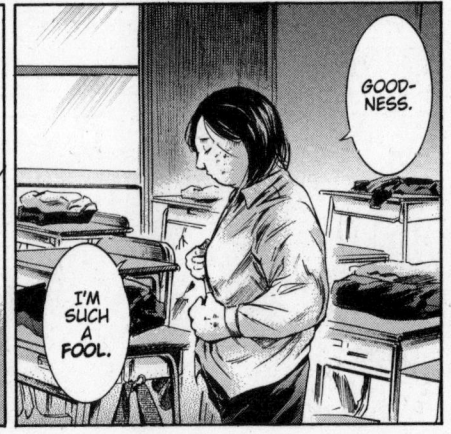

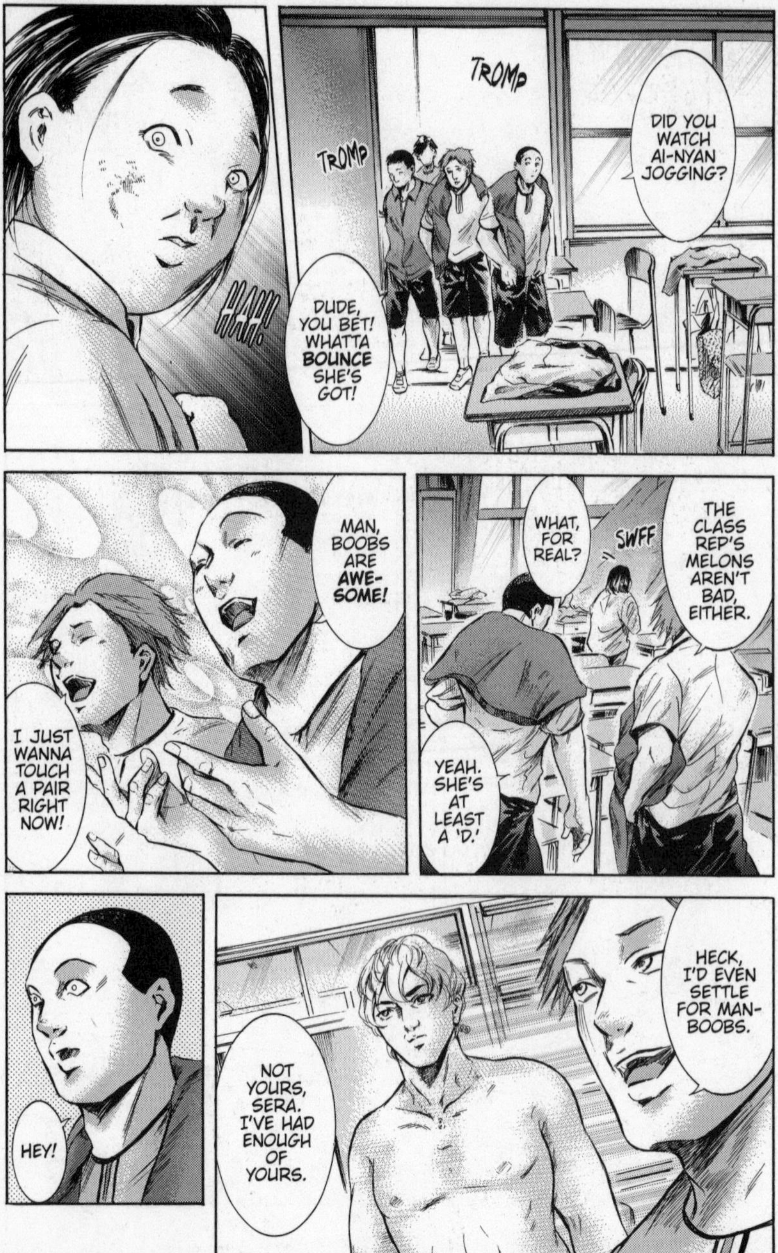
DID YOU WATCH AI-NYAN JOGGING?
TROMP
TROMP
DUDE, YOU BET! WHATTA BOUNCE SHE'S GOT!
HAAH!
THE CLASS REP'S MELONS AREN'T BAD, EITHER.
SWFF
WHAT, FOR REAL?
YEAH. SHE'S AT LEAST A 'D.'
MAN, BOOBS ARE AWE-SOME!
I JUST WANNA TOUCH A PAIR RIGHT NOW!
HECK, I'D EVEN SETTLE FOR MAN-BOOBS.
NOT YOURS, SERA. I'VE HAD ENOUGH OF YOURS.
HEY!

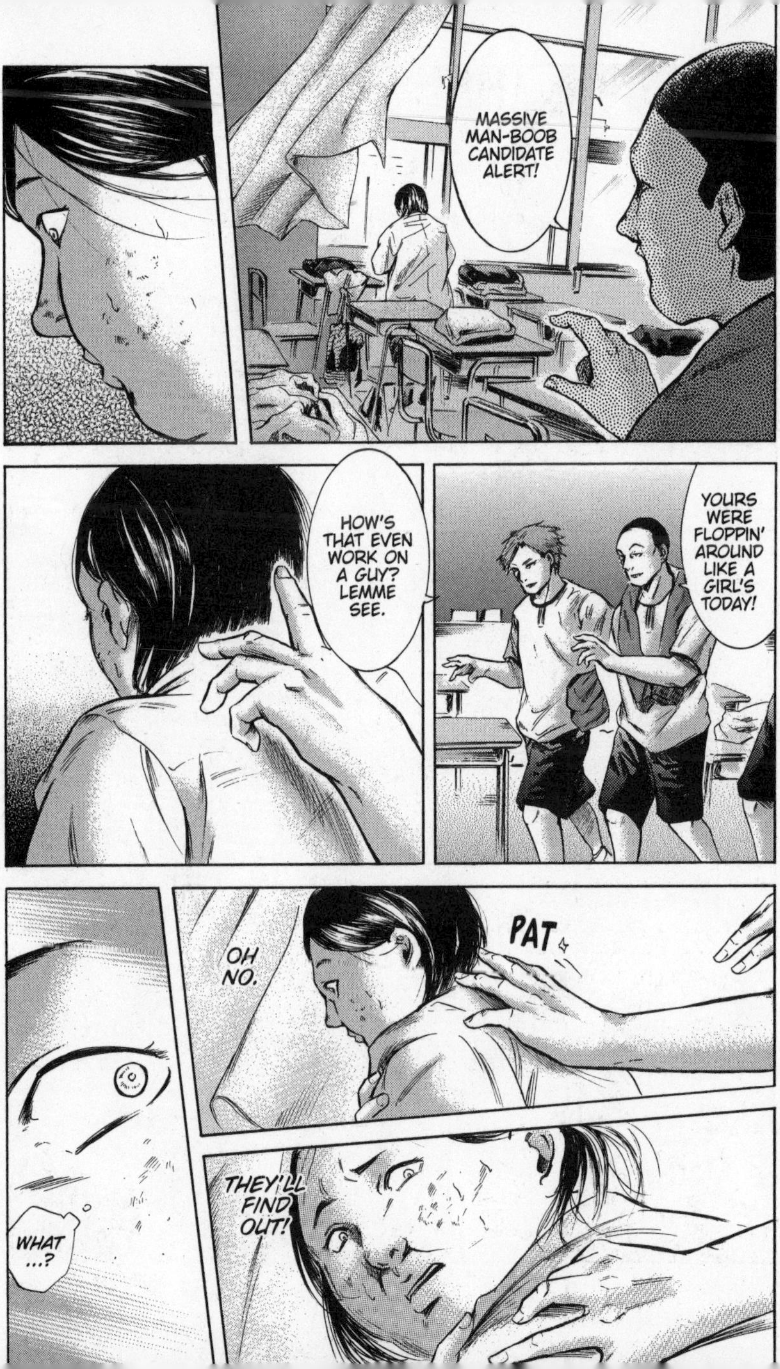
MASSIVE MAN-BOOB CANDIDATE ALERT!
YOURS WERE FLOPPIN' AROUND LIKE A GIRL'S TODAY!
HOW'S THAT EVEN WORK ON A GUY? LEMME SEE.
PAT
OH NO.
THEY'LL FIND OUT!
WHAT ...?

SAKAMOTO-
KUN.

I GIVE
UP.

I...

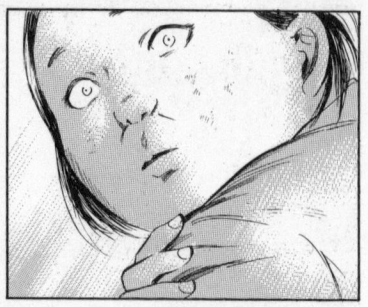

AWW,
YOU'RE
NOT SHY,
ARE YA?

SWFF

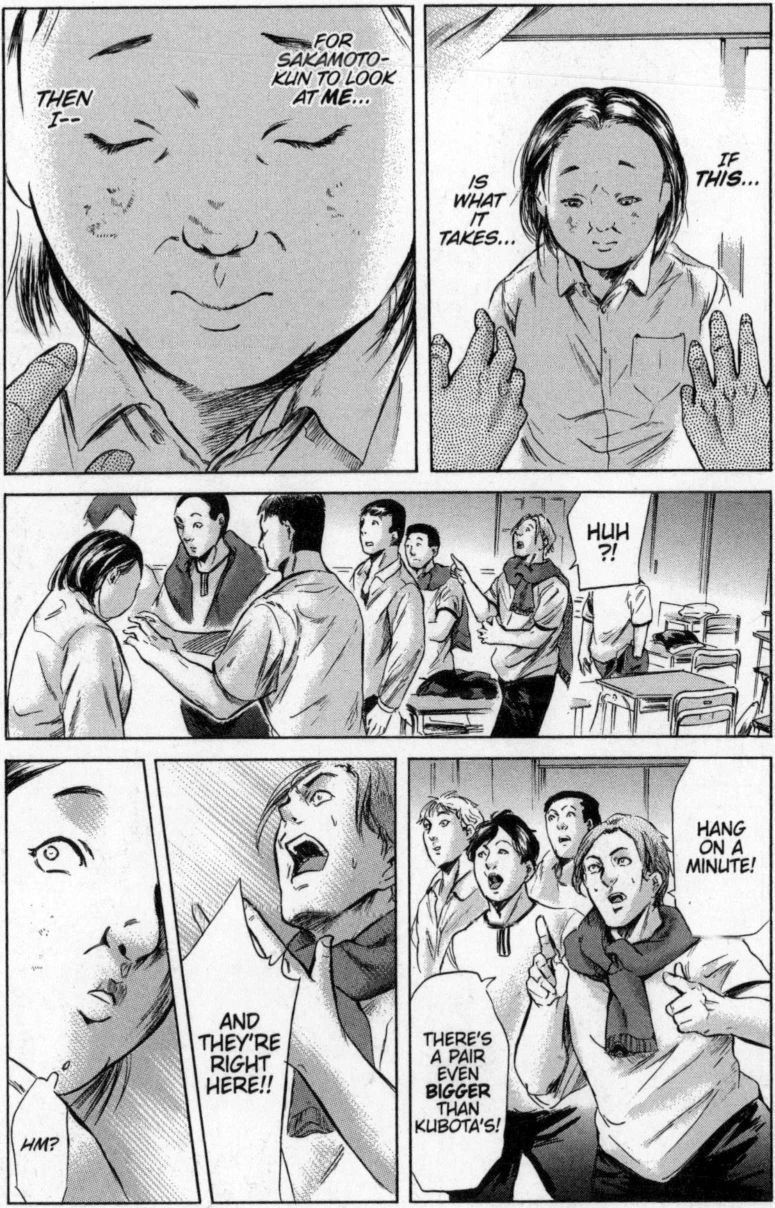
IF THIS...
IS WHAT IT TAKES...
FOR SAKAMOTO-KUN TO LOOK AT ME...
THEN I--
HUH ?!
HANG ON A MINUTE!
THERE'S A PAIR EVEN BIGGER THAN KUBOTA'S!
AND THEY'RE RIGHT HERE!!
HM?

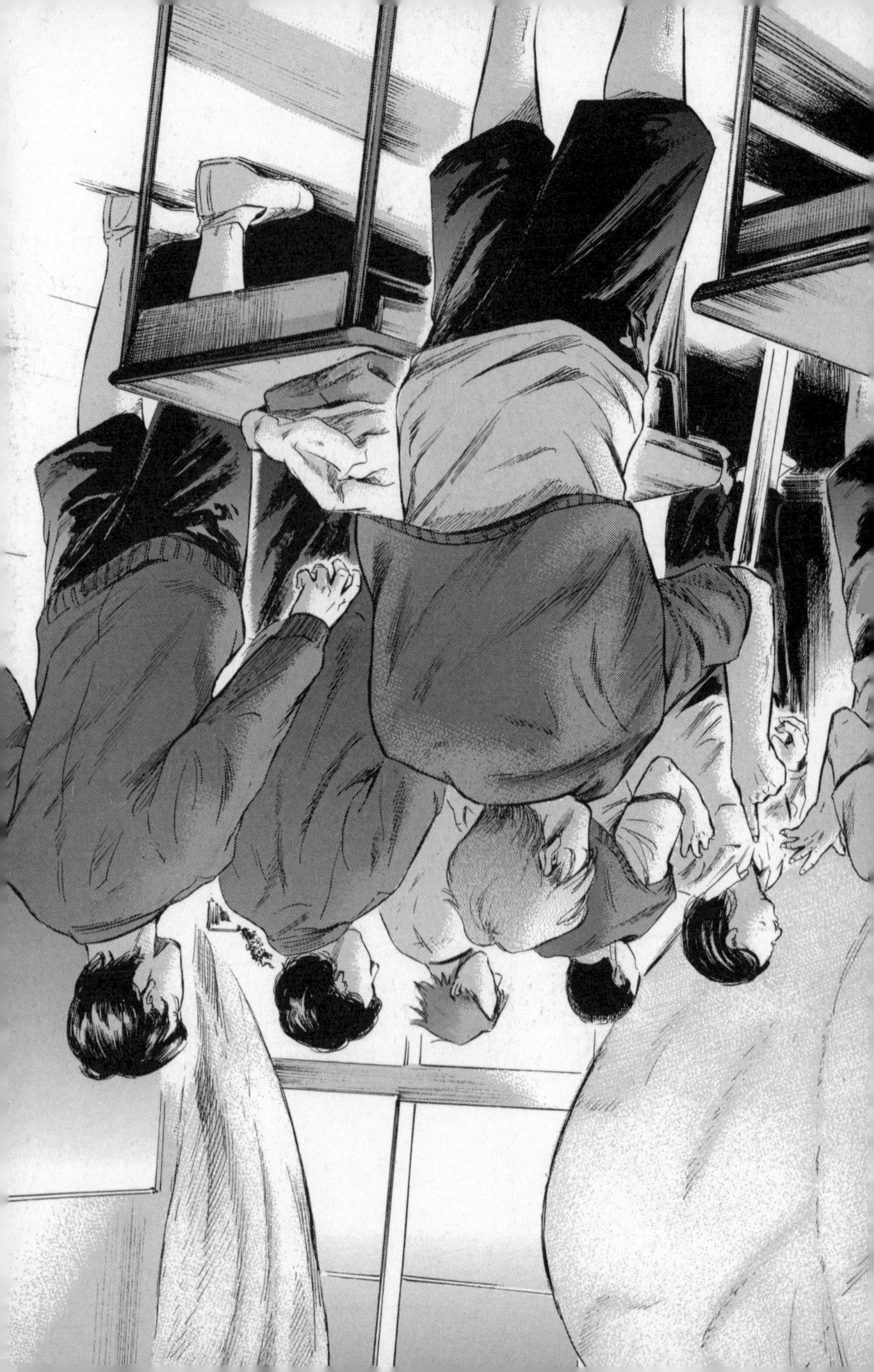

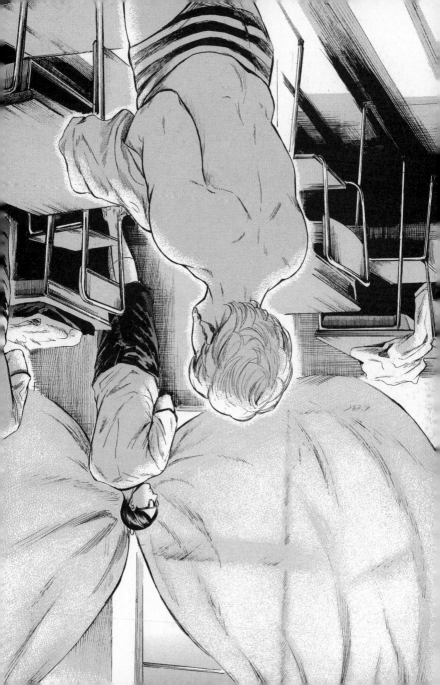

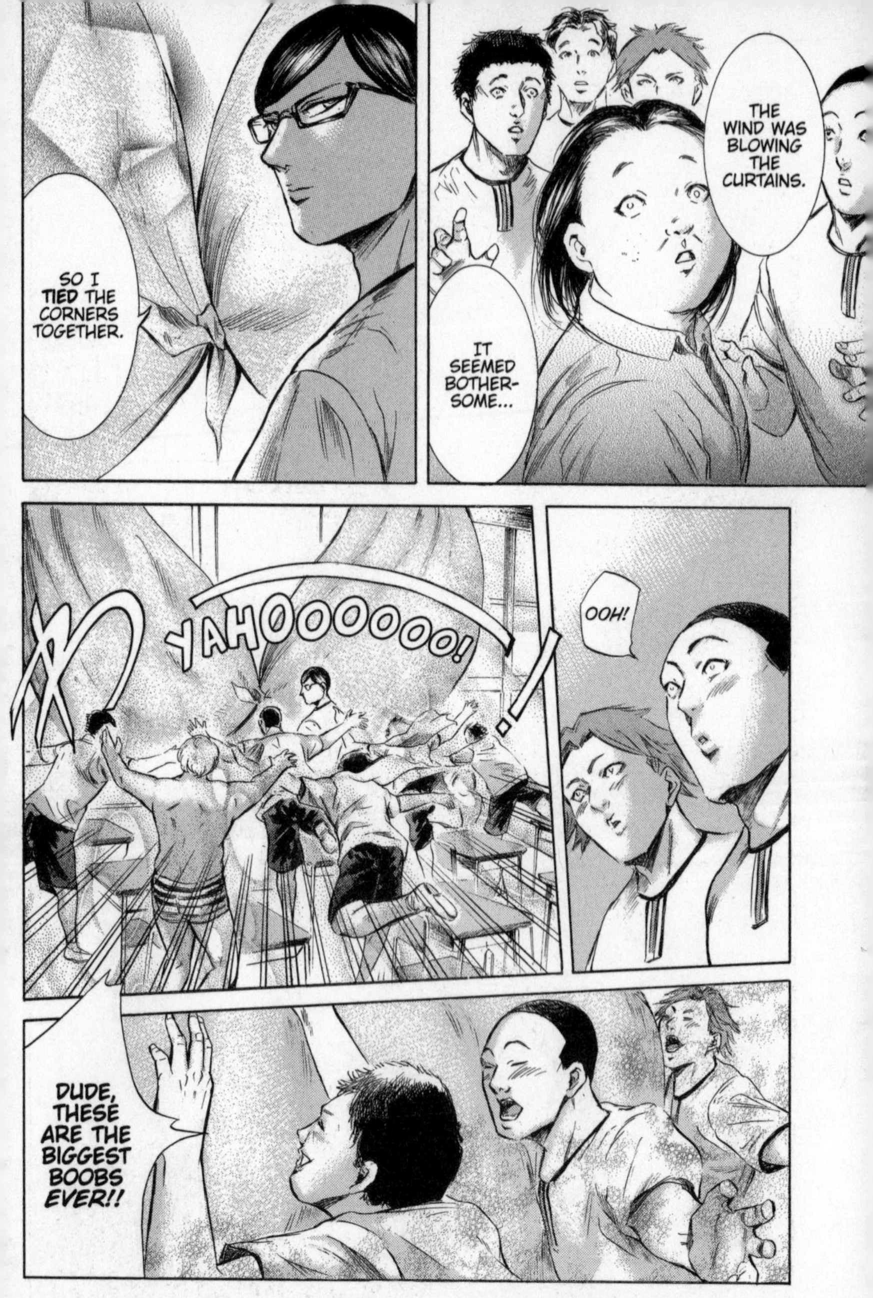
THE WIND WAS BLOWING THE CURTAINS.
IT SEEMED BOTHER-SOME...
SO I TIED THE CORNERS TOGETHER.
OOH!
YAHOOOOOOO!
DUDE, THESE ARE THE BIGGEST BOOBS EVER!!

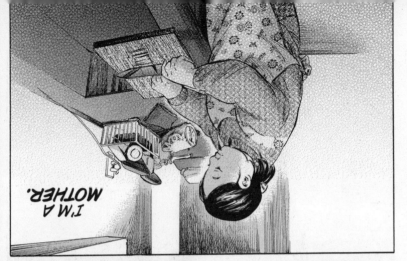

OH.
I'VE SEEN THIS BEFORE...
BUT WHERE...?
AH!
THAT'S RIGHT.
THAT'S THE REAL ME.
I'M A MOTHER.

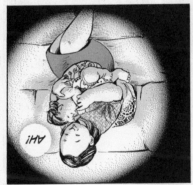

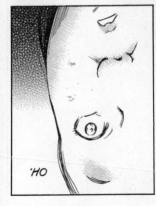

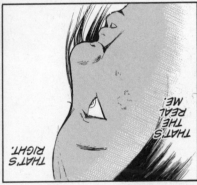

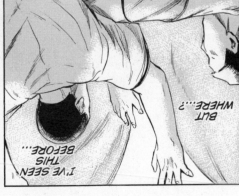

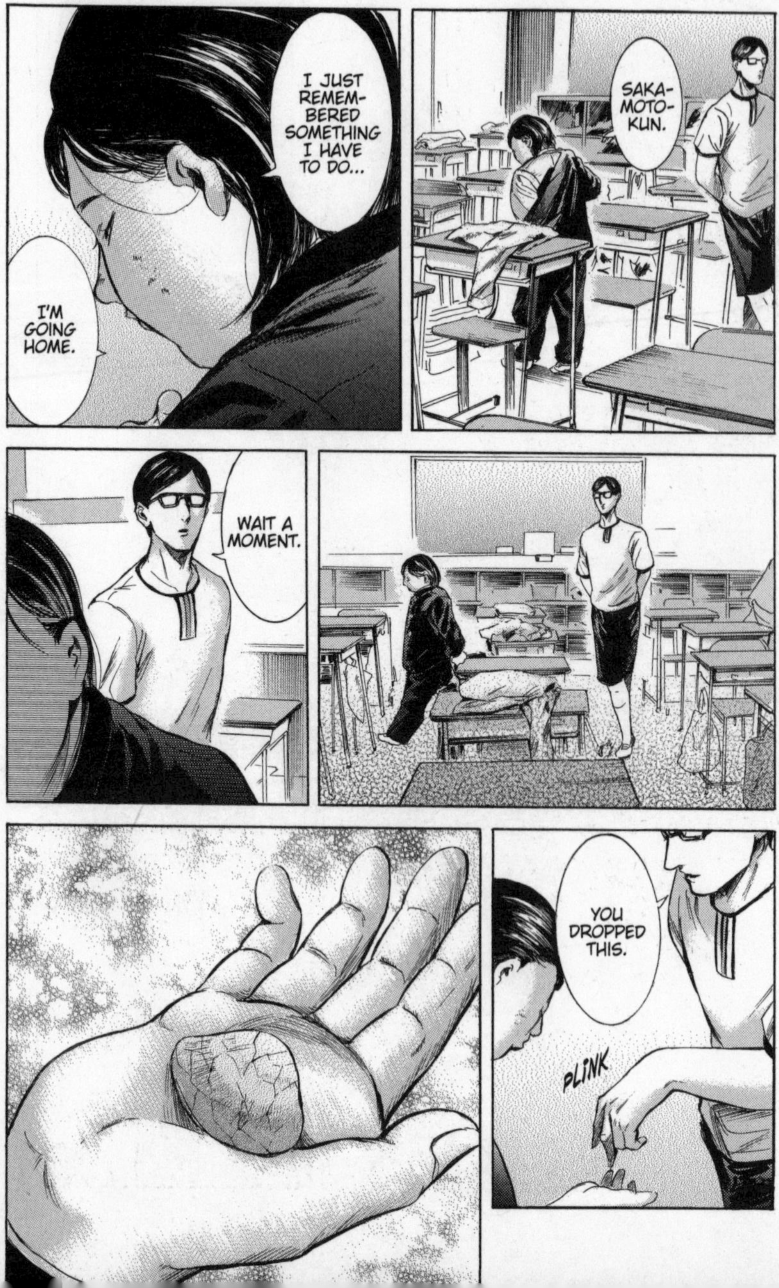
SAKA-MOTO-KUN.
I JUST REMEM-BERED SOMETHING I HAVE TO DO...
I'M GOING HOME.
WAIT A MOMENT.
YOU DROPPED THIS.
PLINK

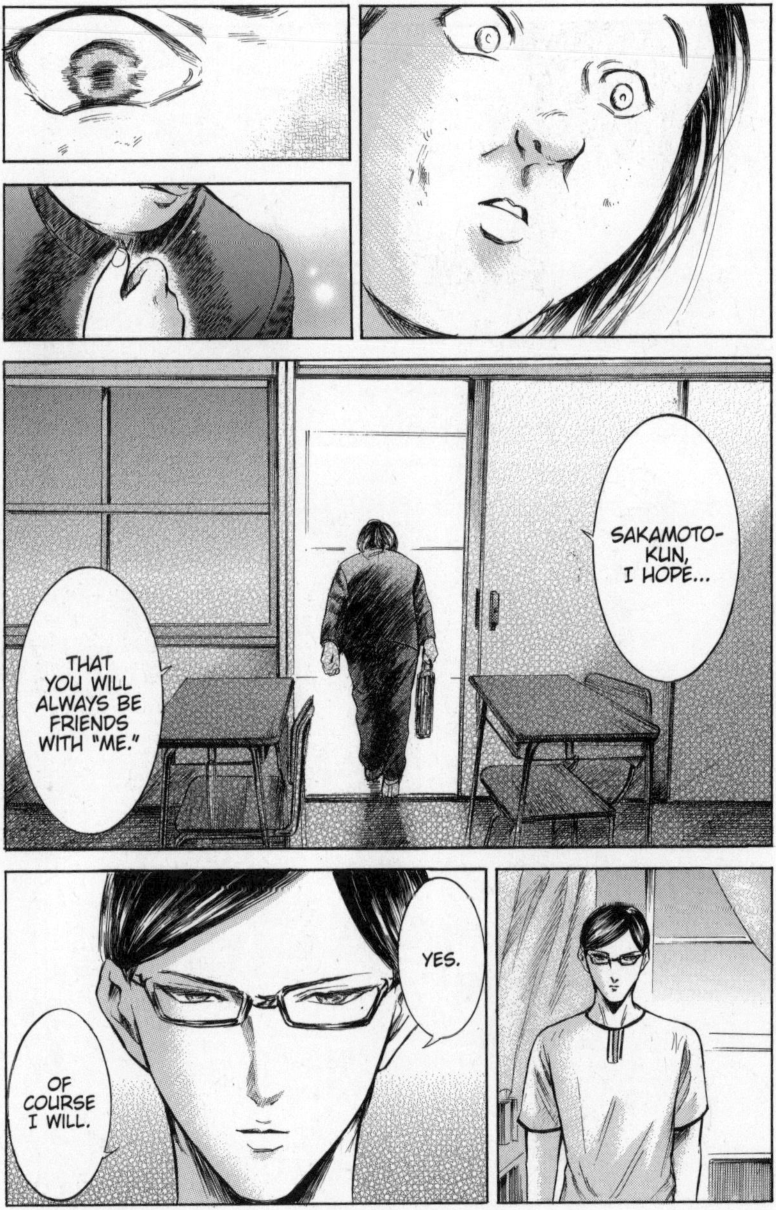
SAKAMOTO-KUN, I HOPE...
THAT YOU WILL ALWAYS BE FRIENDS WITH "ME."
YES.
OF COURSE I WILL.

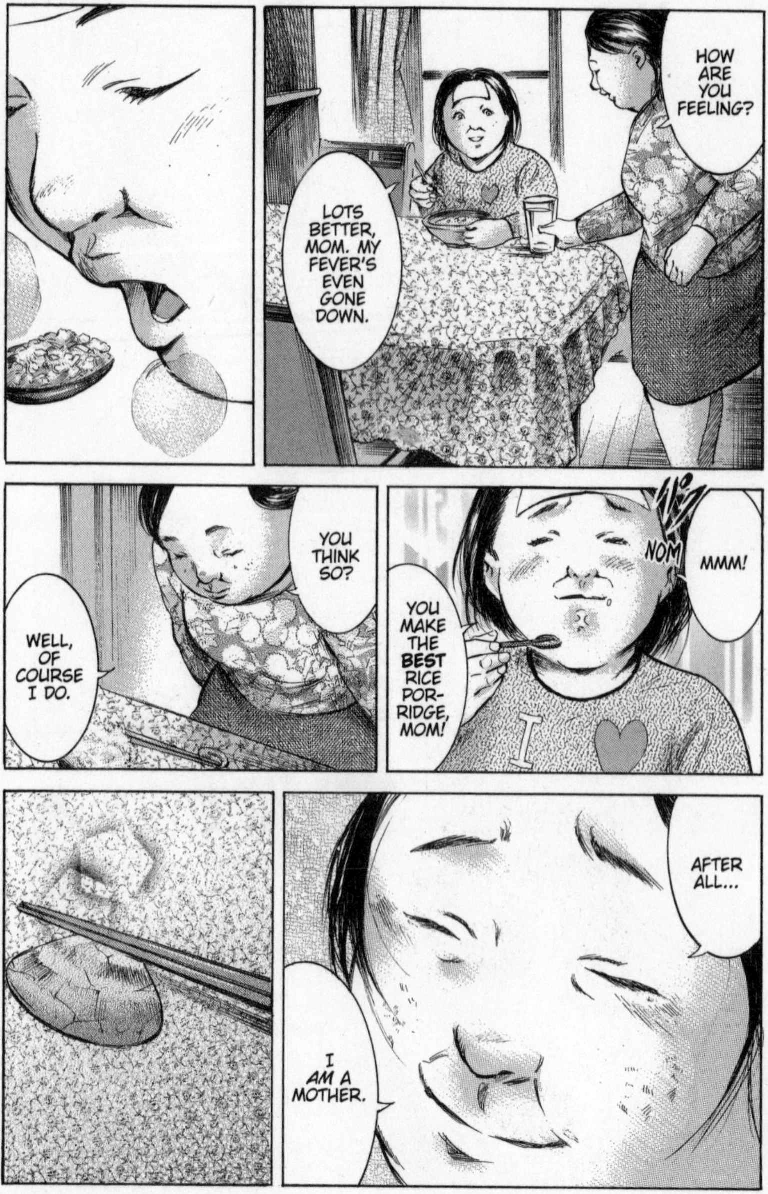
HOW ARE YOU FEELING?
LOTS BETTER, MOM. MY FEVER'S EVEN GONE DOWN.
NOM
MMM!
YOU MAKE THE **BEST** RICE PORRIDGE, MOM!
YOU THINK SO?
WELL, OF COURSE I DO.
AFTER ALL...
I AM A MOTHER.

End of Chapter 19

Look
over...

Let's Play With
Sakamoto #2

Hévé!

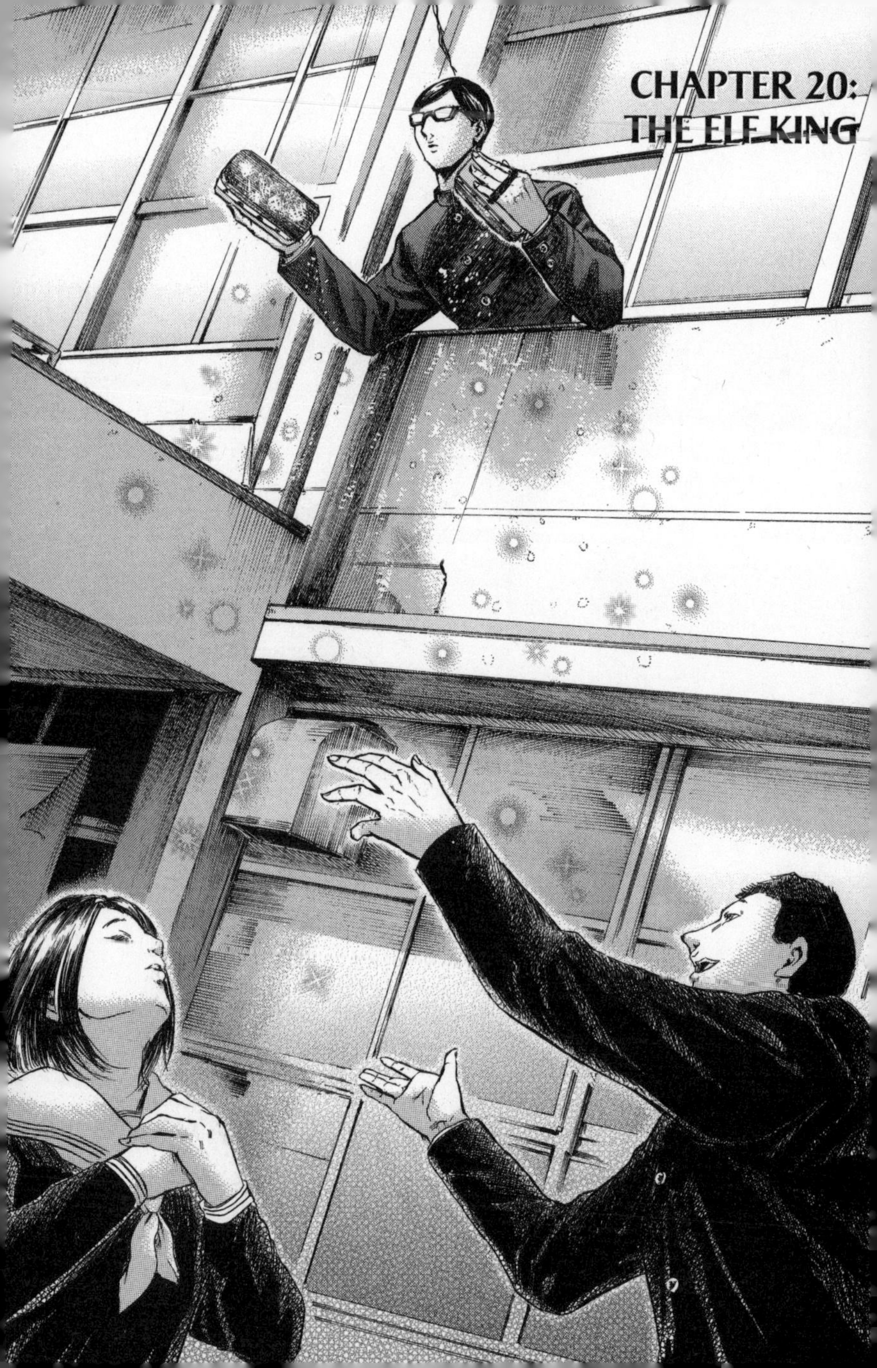
CHAPTER 20:
THE ELF KING

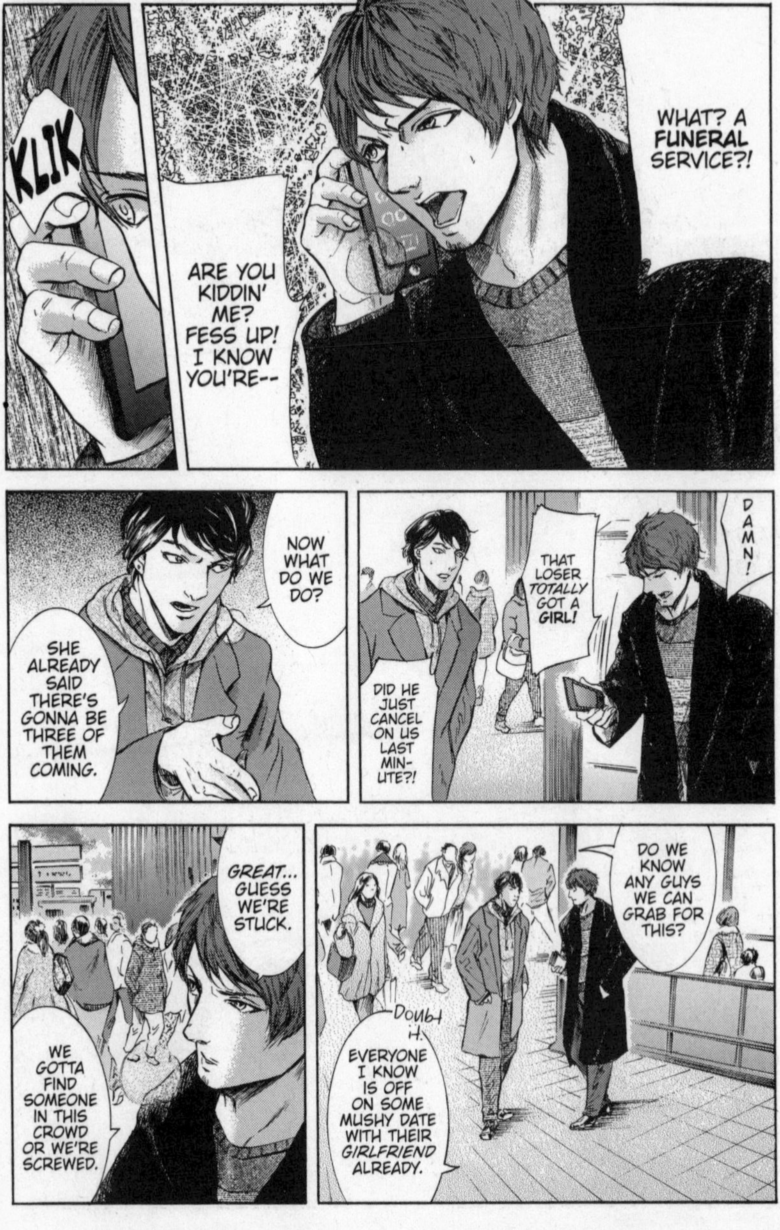
WHAT? A FUNERAL SERVICE?!
ARE YOU KIDDIN' ME? FESS UP! I KNOW YOU'RE--
KLIK
DAMN!
THAT LOSER TOTALLY GOT A GIRL!
DID HE JUST CANCEL ON US LAST MIN-UTE?!
NOW WHAT DO WE DO?
SHE ALREADY SAID THERE'S GONNA BE THREE OF THEM COMING.
DO WE KNOW ANY GUYS WE CAN GRAB FOR THIS?
Doubt it.
EVERYONE I KNOW IS OFF ON SOME MUSHY DATE WITH THEIR GIRLFRIEND ALREADY.
GREAT... GUESS WE'RE STUCK.
WE GOTTA FIND SOMEONE IN THIS CROWD OR WE'RE SCREWED.

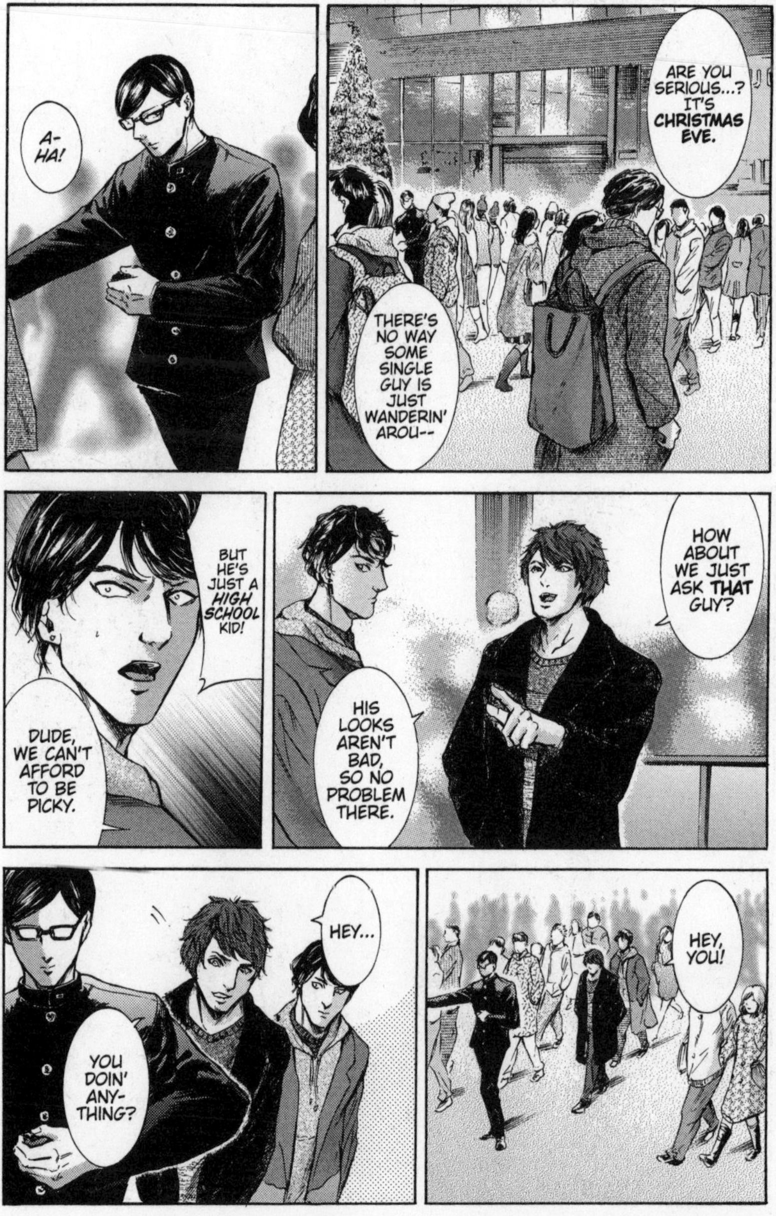
ARE YOU SERIOUS...? IT'S CHRISTMAS EVE.
THERE'S NO WAY SOME SINGLE GUY IS JUST WANDERIN' AROU--
A-HA!
HOW ABOUT WE JUST ASK THAT GUY?
HIS LOOKS AREN'T BAD, SO NO PROBLEM THERE.
BUT HE'S JUST A HIGH SCHOOL KID!
DUDE, WE CAN'T AFFORD TO BE PICKY.
HEY, YOU!
HEY...
YOU DOIN' ANY-THING?

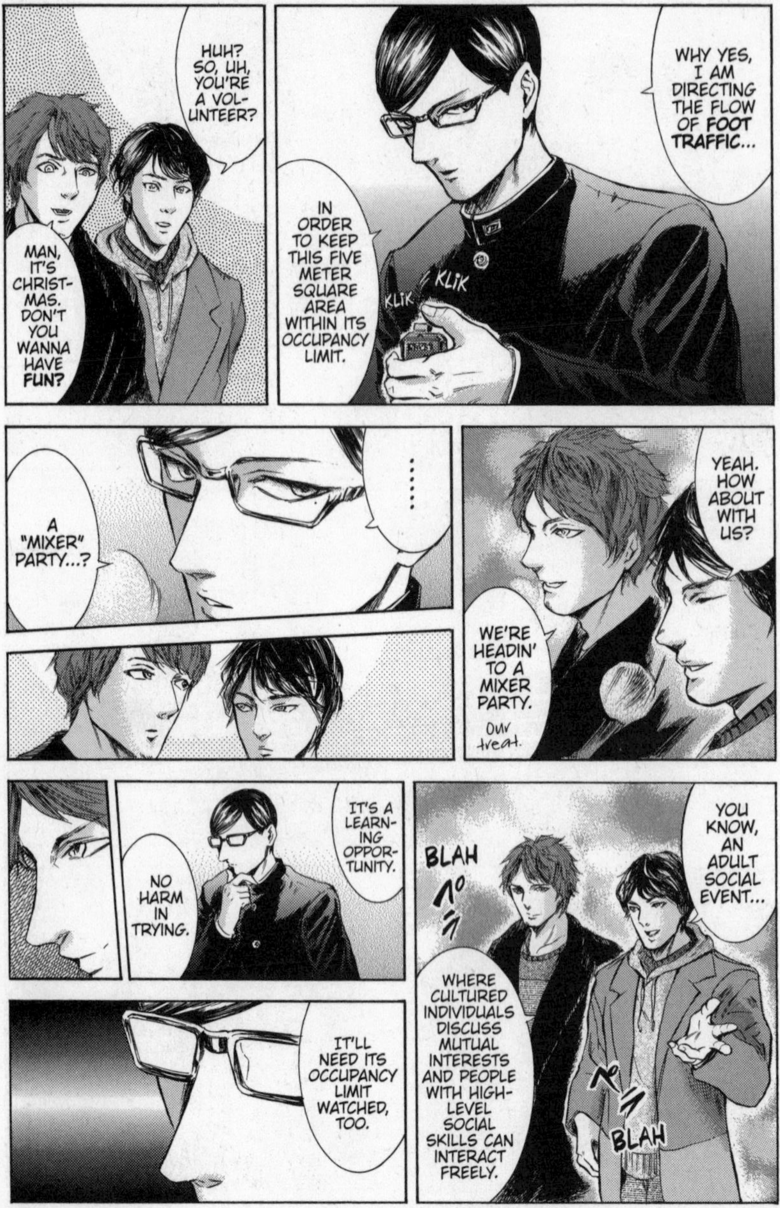
WHY YES, I AM DIRECTING THE FLOW OF FOOT TRAFFIC...
IN ORDER TO KEEP THIS FIVE METER SQUARE AREA WITHIN ITS OCCUPANCY LIMIT.
KLiK
KLiK
HUH? SO, UH, YOU'RE A VOL-UNTEER?
MAN, IT'S CHRIST-MAS. DON'T YOU WANNA HAVE FUN?
YEAH. HOW ABOUT WITH US?
WE'RE HEADIN' TO A MIXER PARTY.
Our treat.
......
A "MIXER" PARTY...?
YOU KNOW, AN ADULT SOCIAL EVENT...
BLAH
WHERE CULTURED INDIVIDUALS DISCUSS MUTUAL INTERESTS AND PEOPLE WITH HIGH-LEVEL SOCIAL SKILLS CAN INTERACT FREELY.
BLAH
IT'S A LEARN-ING OPPOR-TUNITY.
NO HARM IN TRYING.
IT'LL NEED ITS OCCUPANCY LIMIT WATCHED, TOO.

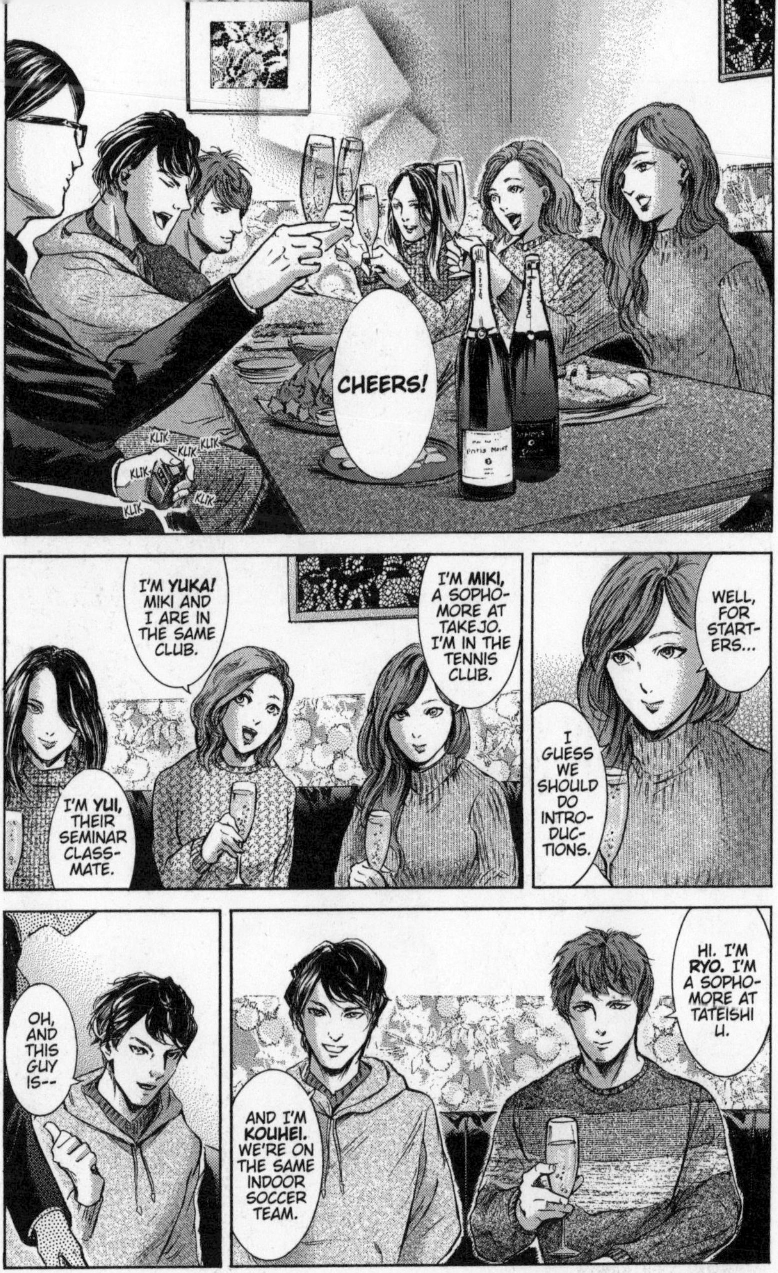
CHEERS!
KLIK KLIK KLIK KLIK KLIK KLIK
WELL, FOR STARTERS...
I GUESS WE SHOULD DO INTRODUCTIONS.
I'M MIKI, A SOPHOMORE AT TAKEJO. I'M IN THE TENNIS CLUB.
I'M YUKA! MIKI AND I ARE IN THE SAME CLUB.
I'M YUI, THEIR SEMINAR CLASSMATE.
HI. I'M RYO. I'M A SOPHOMORE AT TATEISHI U.
AND I'M KOUHEI. WE'RE ON THE SAME INDOOR SOCCER TEAM.
OH, AND THIS GUY IS--

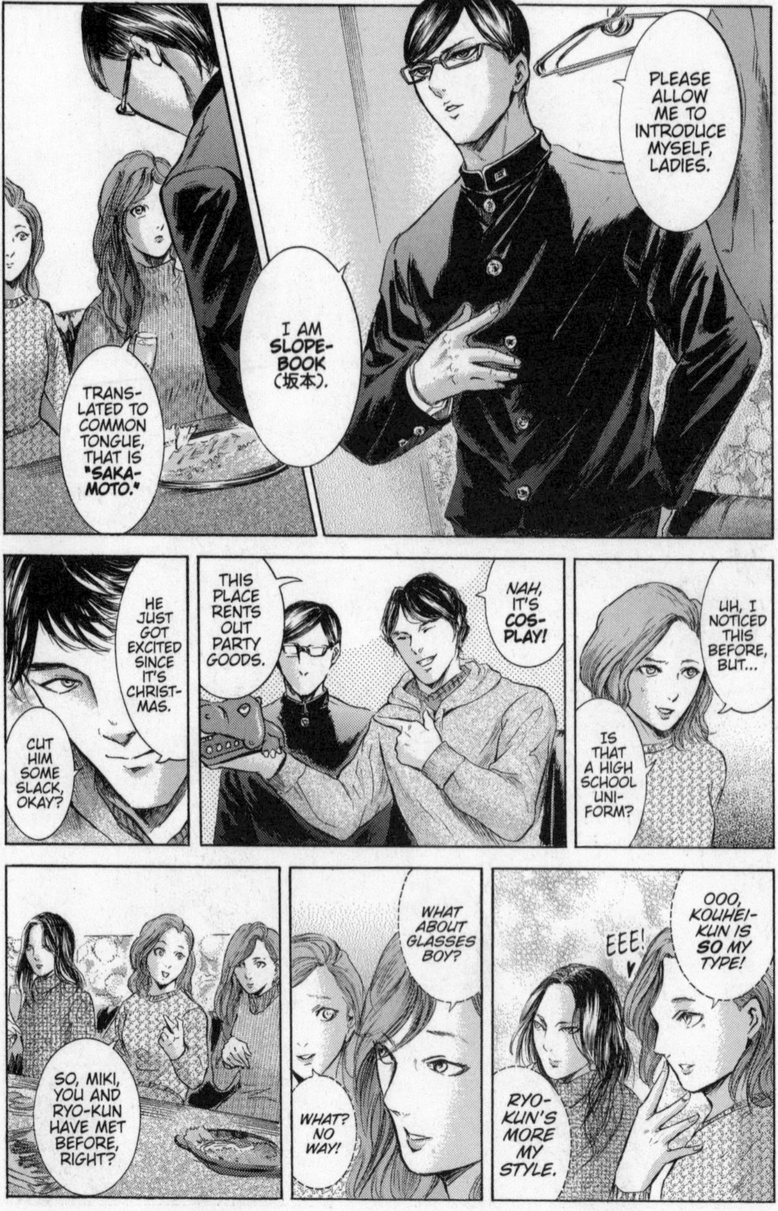
PLEASE ALLOW ME TO INTRODUCE MYSELF, LADIES.
I AM SLOPE-BOOK (坂本).
TRANS-LATED TO COMMON TONGUE, THAT IS "SAKA-MOTO."
UH, I NOTICED THIS BEFORE, BUT...
IS THAT A HIGH SCHOOL UNI-FORM?
NAH, IT'S COS-PLAY!
THIS PLACE RENTS OUT PARTY GOODS.
HE JUST GOT EXCITED SINCE IT'S CHRIST-MAS.
CUT HIM SOME SLACK, OKAY?
OOO, KOUHEI-KUN IS SO MY TYPE!
EEE! ♥
RYO-KUN'S MORE MY STYLE.
WHAT ABOUT GLASSES BOY?
WHAT? NO WAY!
SO, MIKI, YOU AND RYO-KUN HAVE MET BEFORE, RIGHT?

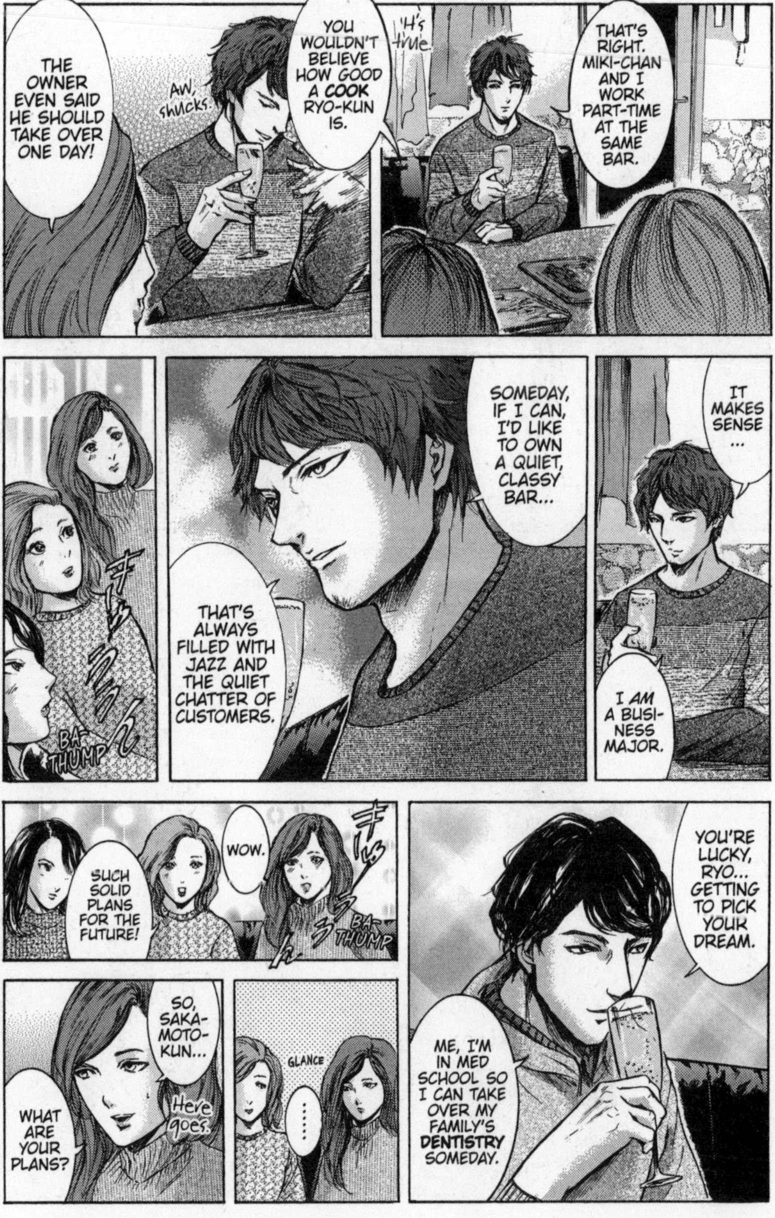
THAT'S RIGHT. MIKI-CHAN AND I WORK PART-TIME AT THE SAME BAR.
It's true.
YOU WOULDN'T BELIEVE HOW GOOD A **COOK** RYO-KUN IS.
AW, shucks.
THE OWNER EVEN SAID HE SHOULD TAKE OVER ONE DAY!
IT MAKES SENSE ...
I *AM* A BUSINESS MAJOR.
SOMEDAY, IF I CAN, I'D LIKE TO OWN A QUIET, CLASSY BAR...
THAT'S ALWAYS FILLED WITH JAZZ AND THE QUIET CHATTER OF CUSTOMERS.
BA-THUMP
YOU'RE LUCKY, RYO... GETTING TO PICK YOUR DREAM.
ME, I'M IN MED SCHOOL SO I CAN TAKE OVER MY FAMILY'S **DENTISTRY** SOMEDAY.
WOW.
BA-THUMP
SUCH SOLID PLANS FOR THE FUTURE!
SO, SAKAMOTO-KUN...
Here goes.
WHAT ARE YOUR PLANS?
GLANCE
......

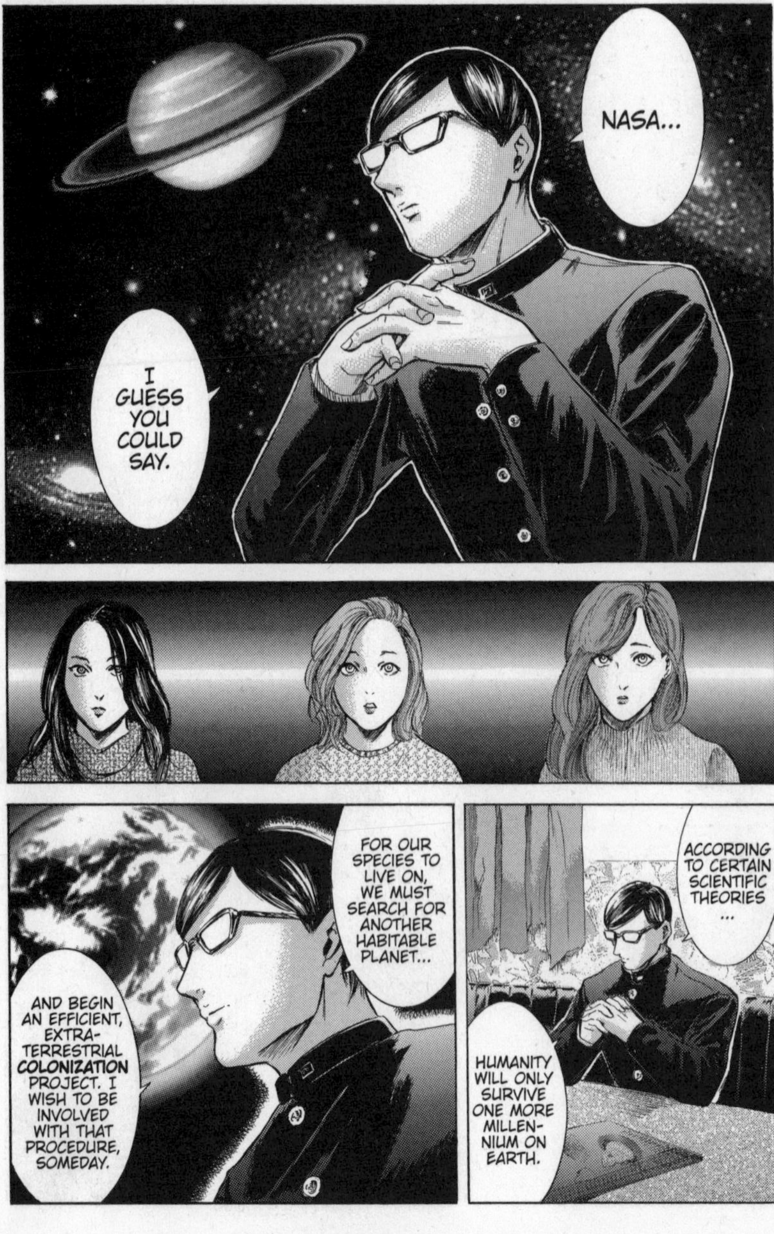
NASA...
I GUESS YOU COULD SAY.
ACCORDING TO CERTAIN SCIENTIFIC THEORIES ...
HUMANITY WILL ONLY SURVIVE ONE MORE MILLEN-NIUM ON EARTH.
FOR OUR SPECIES TO LIVE ON, WE MUST SEARCH FOR ANOTHER HABITABLE PLANET...
AND BEGIN AN EFFICIENT, EXTRA-TERRESTRIAL **COLONIZATION** PROJECT. I WISH TO BE INVOLVED WITH THAT PROCEDURE, SOMEDAY.

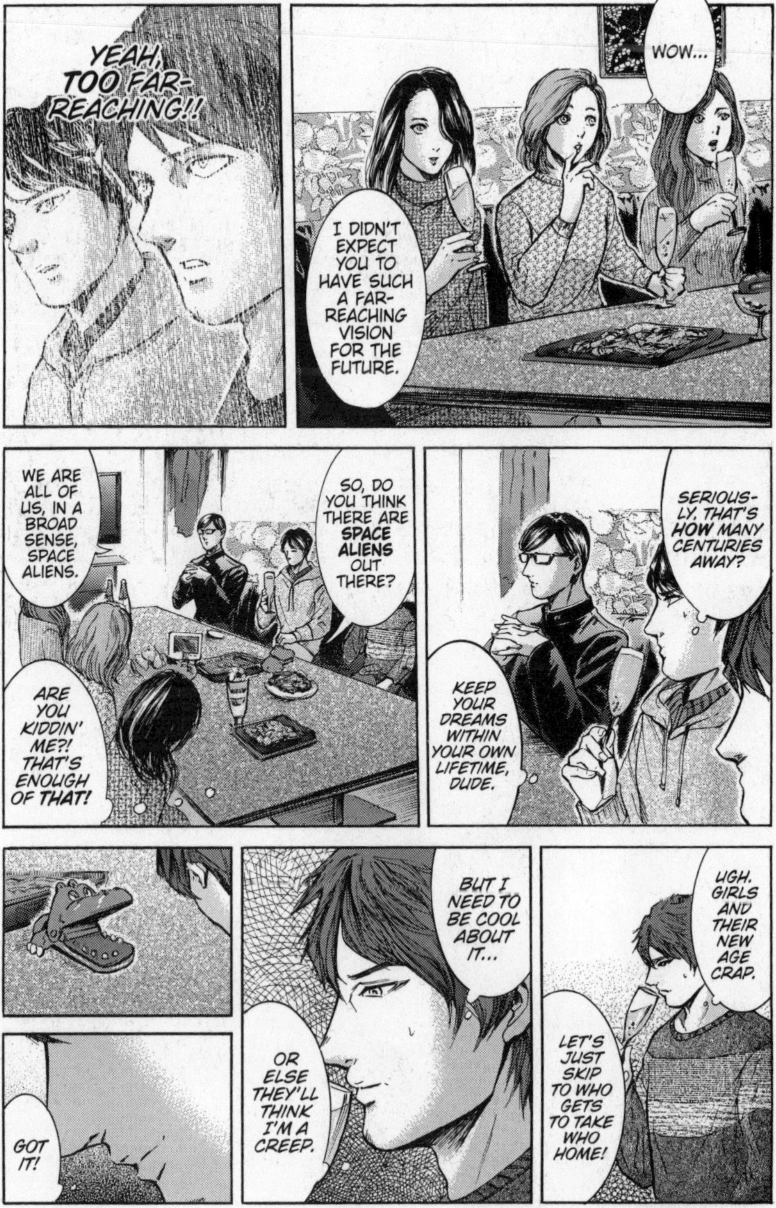
WOW...
I DIDN'T EXPECT YOU TO HAVE SUCH A FAR-REACHING VISION FOR THE FUTURE.
YEAH, TOO FAR-REACHING!!
SERIOUSLY. THAT'S HOW MANY CENTURIES AWAY?
KEEP YOUR DREAMS WITHIN YOUR OWN LIFETIME, DUDE.
SO, DO YOU THINK THERE ARE SPACE ALIENS OUT THERE?
WE ARE ALL OF US, IN A BROAD SENSE, SPACE ALIENS.
ARE YOU KIDDIN' ME?! THAT'S ENOUGH OF THAT!
UGH. GIRLS AND THEIR NEW AGE CRAP.
LET'S JUST SKIP TO WHO GETS TO TAKE WHO HOME!
BUT I NEED TO BE COOL ABOUT IT...
OR ELSE THEY'LL THINK I'M A CREEP.
GOT IT!

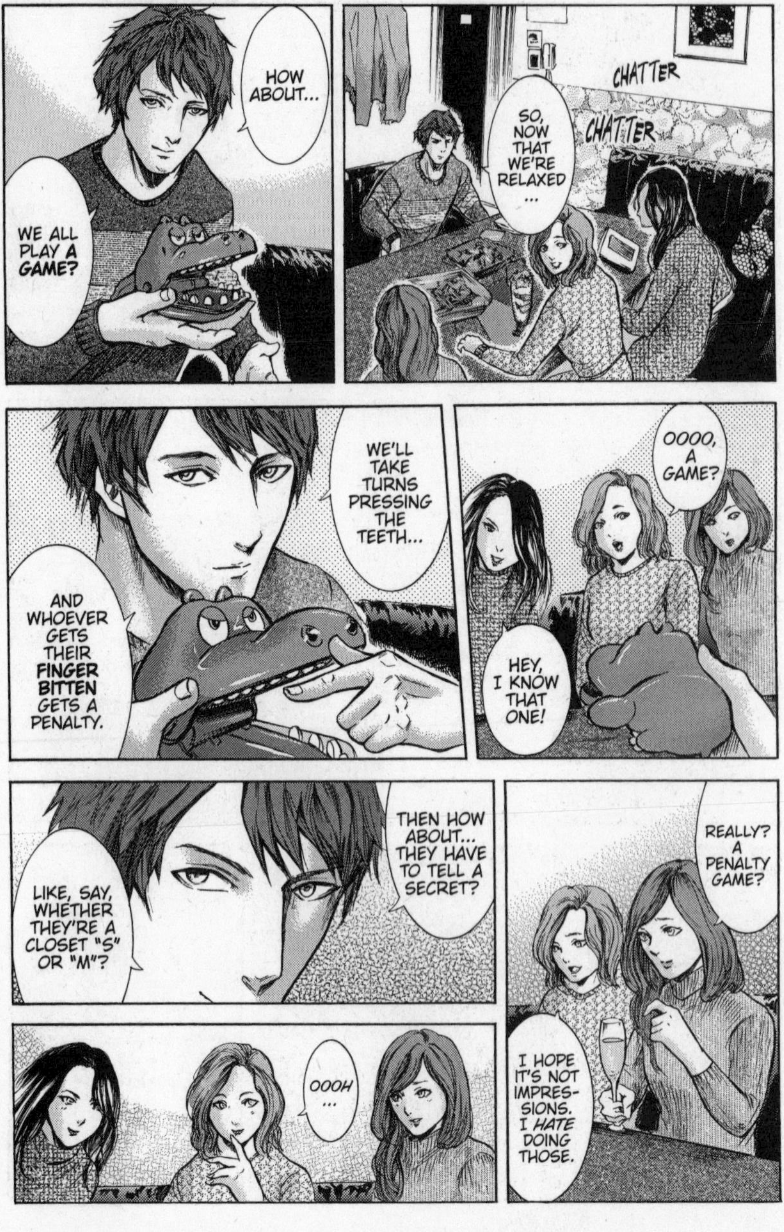
CHATTER
CHATTER
SO, NOW THAT WE'RE RELAXED ...
HOW ABOUT...
WE ALL PLAY A **GAME?**
OOOO, A GAME?
HEY, I KNOW THAT ONE!
WE'LL TAKE TURNS PRESSING THE TEETH...
AND WHOEVER GETS THEIR **FINGER BITTEN** GETS A PENALTY.
REALLY? A PENALTY GAME?
I HOPE IT'S NOT IMPRES-SIONS. I *HATE* DOING THOSE.
THEN HOW ABOUT... THEY HAVE TO TELL A SECRET?
LIKE, SAY, WHETHER THEY'RE A CLOSET "S" OR "M"?
OOOH ...

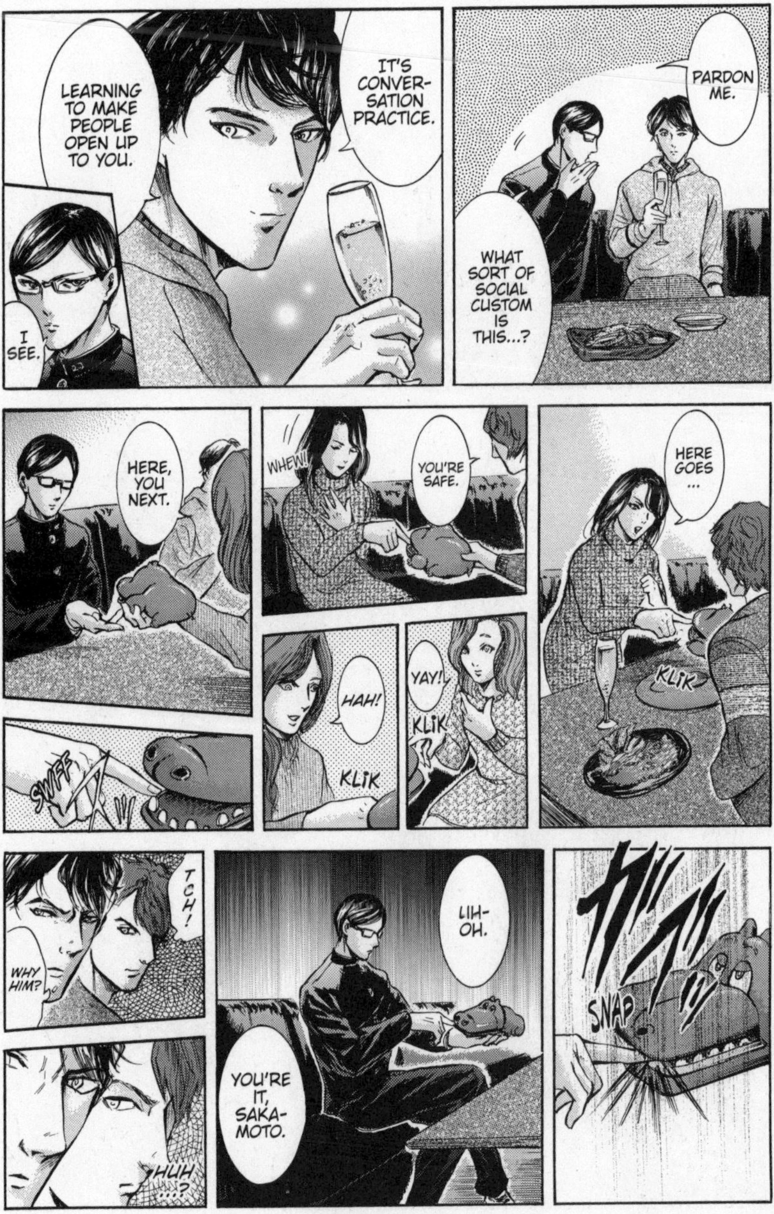
PARDON ME.
WHAT SORT OF SOCIAL CUSTOM IS THIS...?
IT'S CONVERSATION PRACTICE.
LEARNING TO MAKE PEOPLE OPEN UP TO YOU.
I SEE.
HERE GOES...
KLIK
YOU'RE SAFE.
WHEW!
YAY!
KLIK
HAH!
KLIK
HERE, YOU NEXT.
SWIFF
SNAP
UH-OH.
YOU'RE IT, SAKAMOTO.
TCH!
WHY HIM?
HUH...?

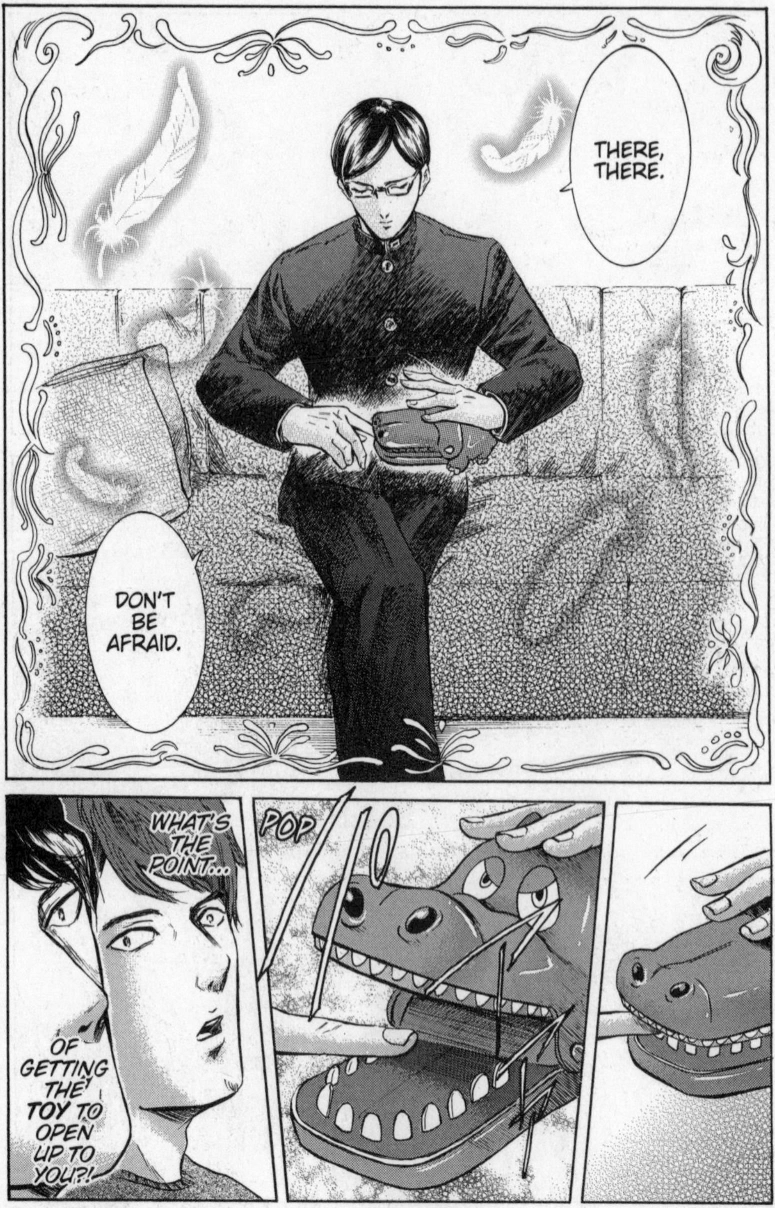
THERE, THERE.
DON'T BE AFRAID.
POP
WHAT'S THE POINT...
OF GETTING THE TOY TO OPEN UP TO YOU?!

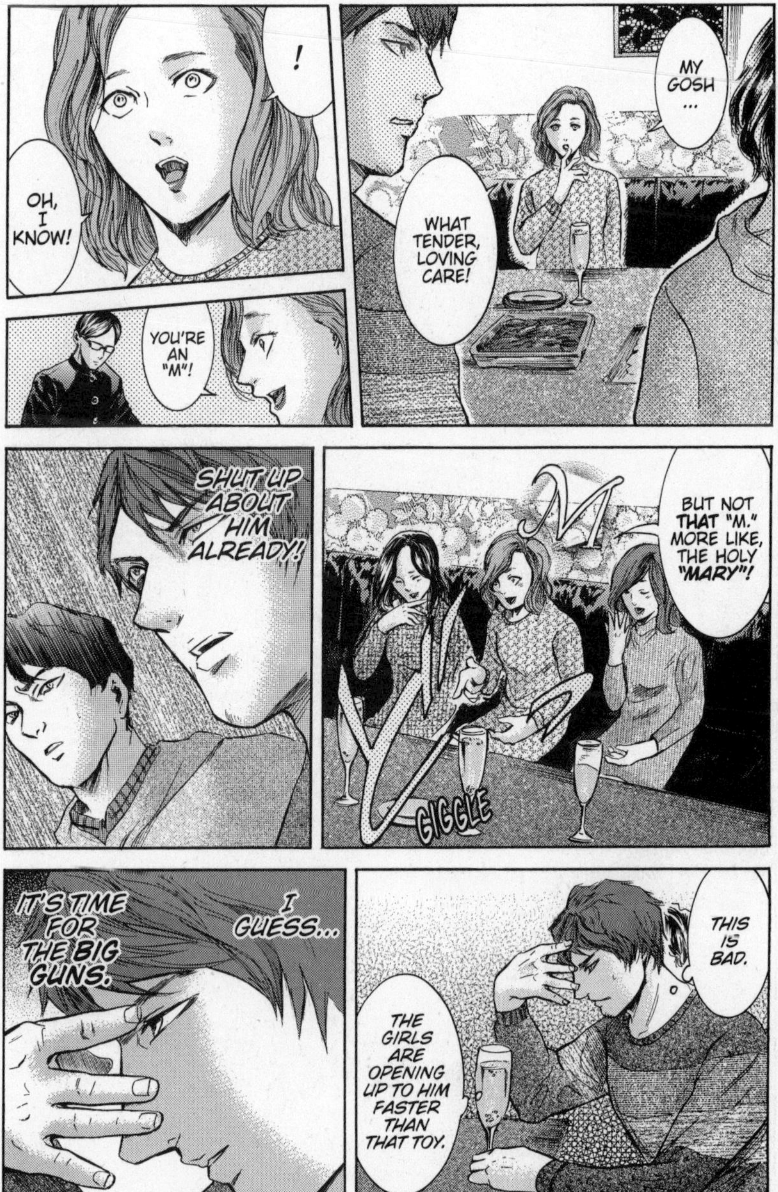
MY GOSH ...
WHAT TENDER, LOVING CARE!
!
OH, I KNOW!
YOU'RE AN "M"!
BUT NOT THAT "M." MORE LIKE, THE HOLY "MARY"!
M
GIGGLE
SHUT UP ABOUT HIM ALREADY!
THIS IS BAD.
THE GIRLS ARE OPENING UP TO HIM FASTER THAN THAT TOY.
I GUESS...
IT'S TIME FOR THE BIG GUNS.

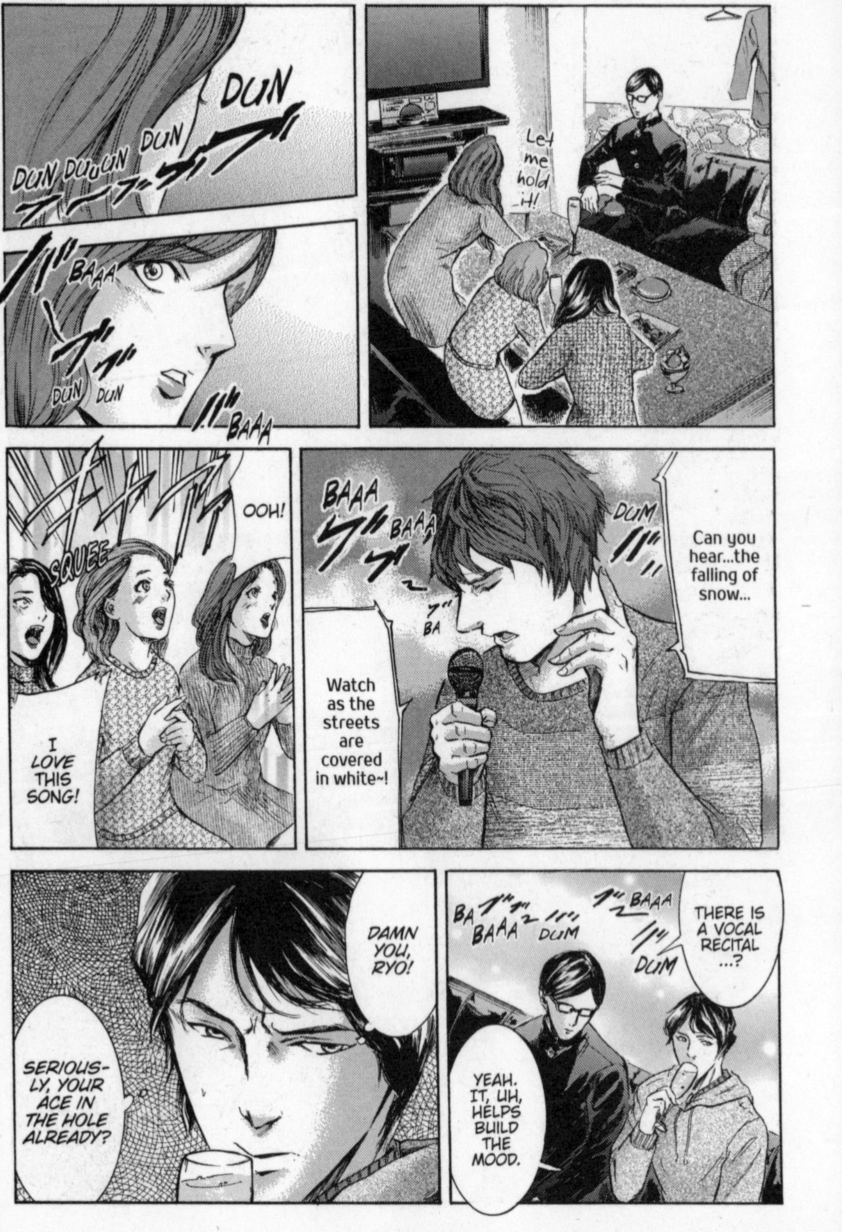
Let me hold it!
DUN DUUUN DUN
DUN
BAAA
DUN DUN
BAAA
DUM
Can you hear...the falling of snow...
BAAA BAAA
BA
Watch as the streets are covered in white~!
OOH!
SQUEE
I LOVE THIS SONG!
THERE IS A VOCAL RECITAL ...?
BAAA
DUM
BA BAAA DUM
YEAH. IT, UH, HELPS BUILD THE MOOD.
DAMN YOU, RYO!
SERIOUSLY, YOUR ACE IN THE HOLE ALREADY?

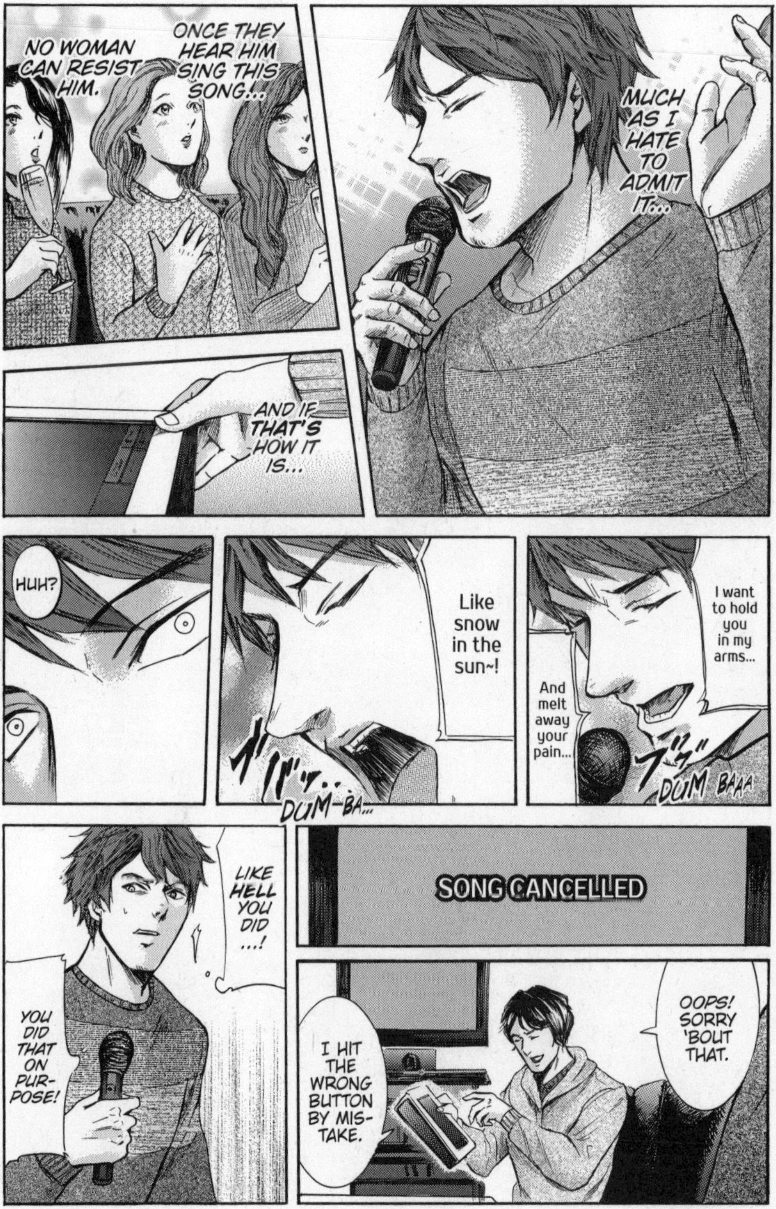
MUCH AS I HATE TO ADMIT IT...
ONCE THEY HEAR HIM SING THIS SONG...
NO WOMAN CAN RESIST HIM.
AND IF THAT'S HOW IT IS...
I want to hold you in my arms...
And melt away your pain...
DUM BAAA
Like snow in the sun~!
DUM-BA...
HUH?
SONG CANCELLED
LIKE HELL YOU DID ...!
YOU DID THAT ON PUR-POSE!
OOPS! SORRY 'BOUT THAT.
I HIT THE WRONG BUTTON BY MIS-TAKE.

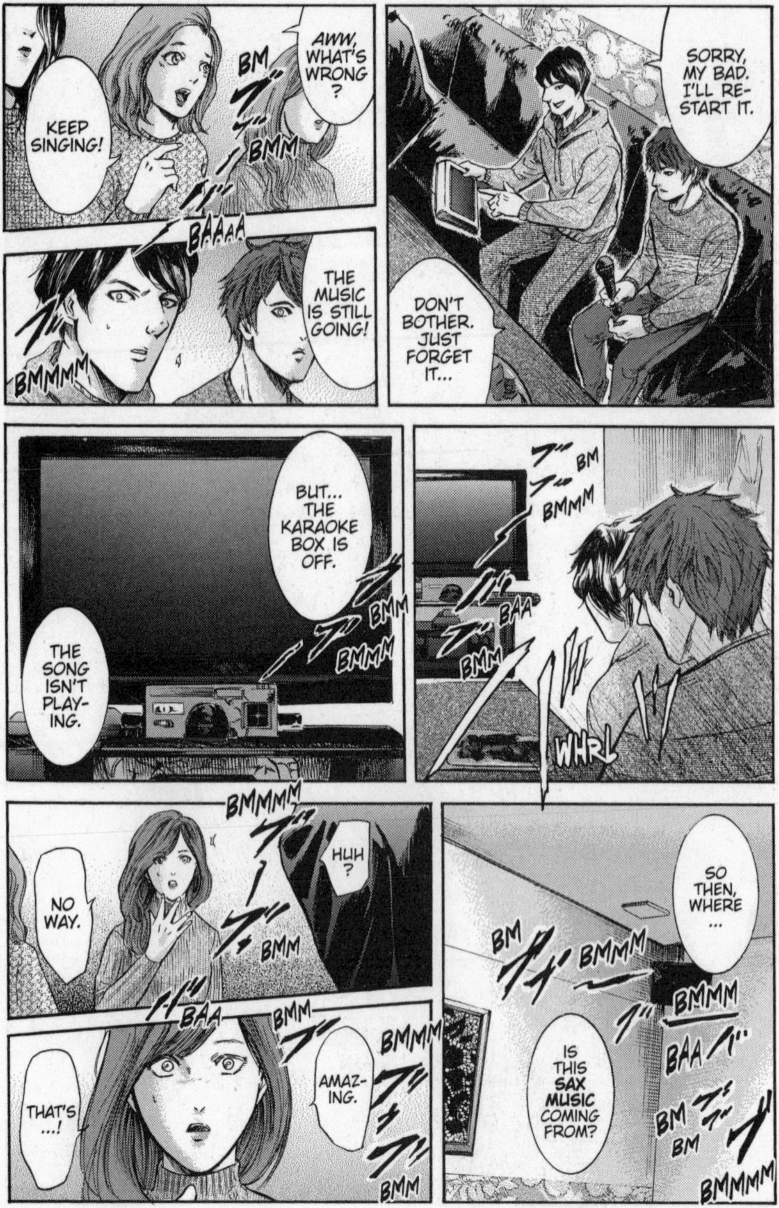
SORRY, MY BAD. I'LL RE-START IT.
DON'T BOTHER. JUST FORGET IT...
AWW, WHAT'S WRONG?
BM
BMM
KEEP SINGING!
BAAAA
THE MUSIC IS STILL GOING!
BMMMM
BM
BMMM
BAA
BMM
WHRL
BUT... THE KARAOKE BOX IS OFF.
BMM
BMMM
THE SONG ISN'T PLAYING.
SO THEN, WHERE...
BM
BMMM
BMMM
BAA
IS THIS SAX MUSIC COMING FROM?
BM
BM
BMMMM
BMMMM
HUH?
BMM
NO WAY.
BAA
BMM
BMMM
AMAZ-ING.
BMM
THAT'S...!

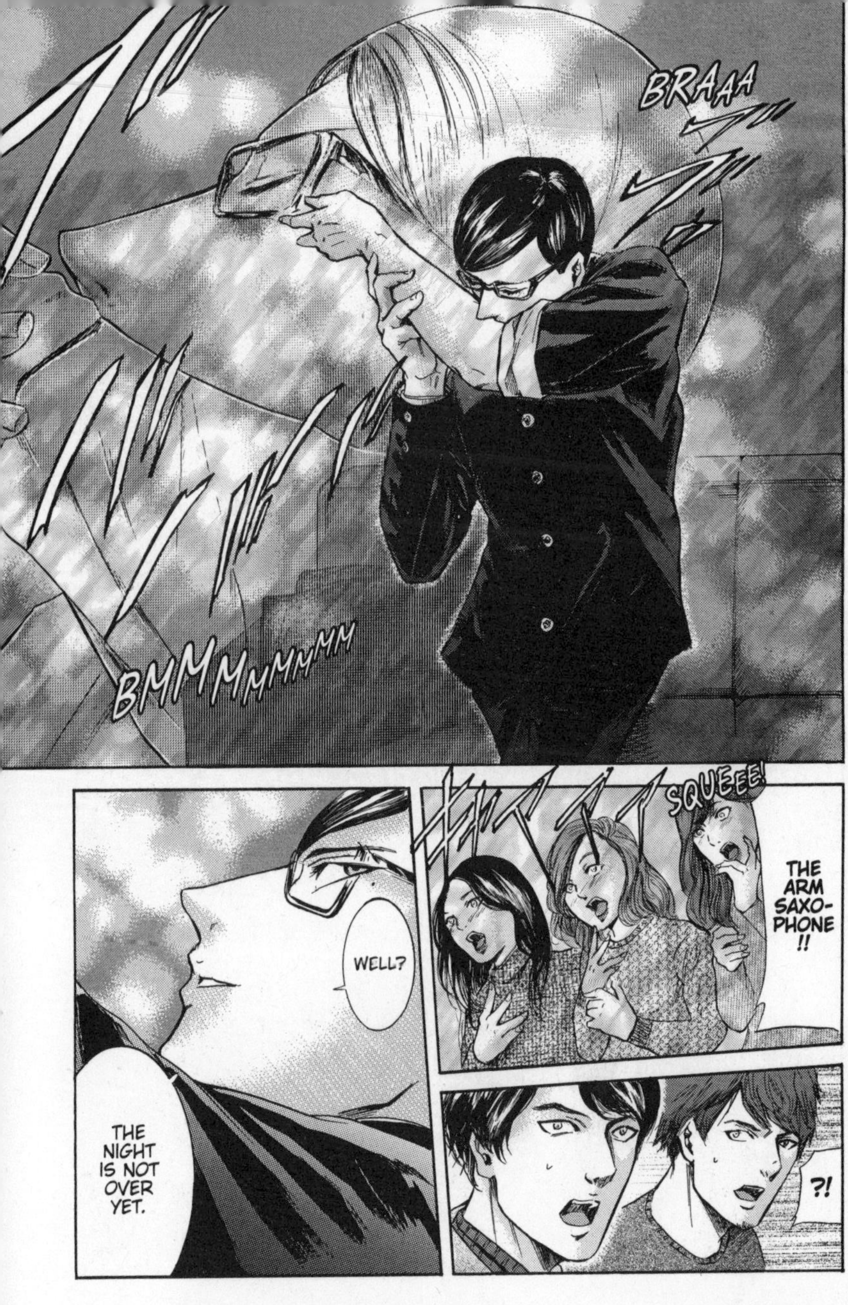
BRAAA
BMMMMMMMM
SQUEEE!
THE ARM SAXO-PHONE !!
?!
WELL?
THE NIGHT IS NOT OVER YET.

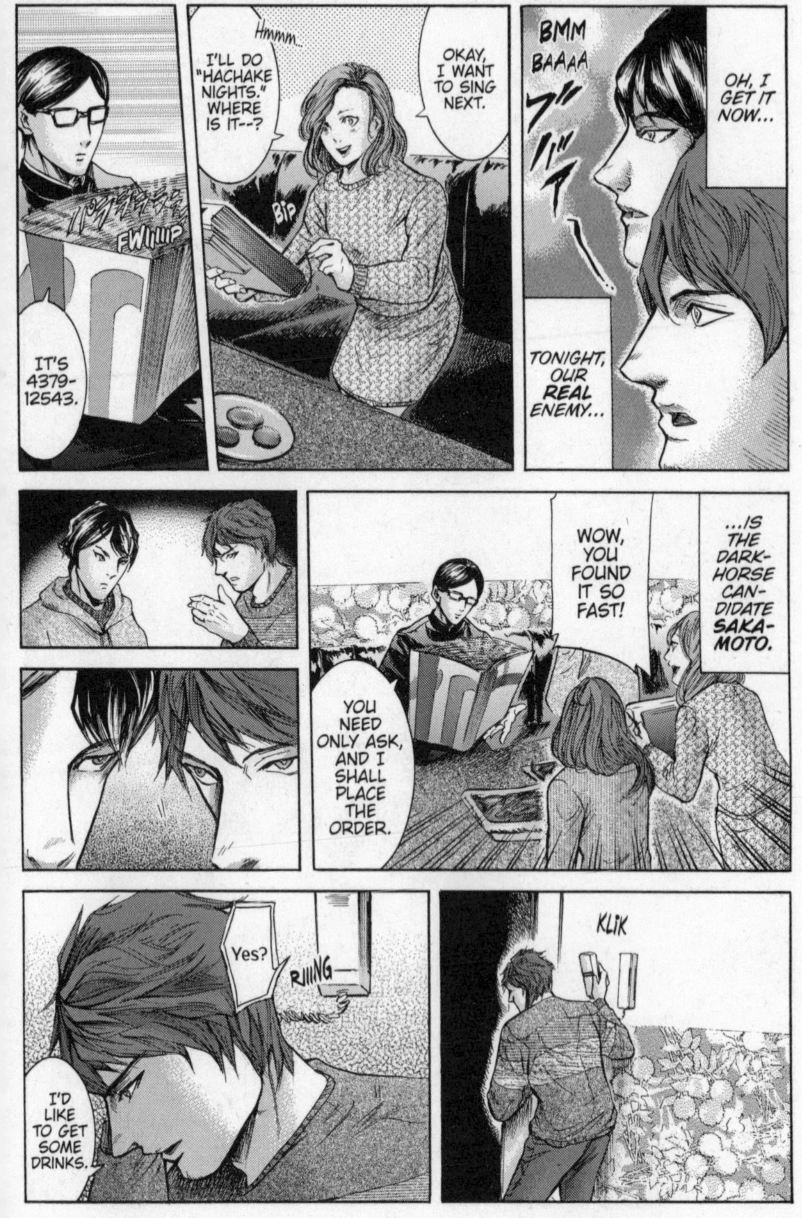
OH, I GET IT NOW...
BMM BAAAA
TONIGHT, OUR REAL ENEMY...
OKAY, I WANT TO SING NEXT.
Hmmm...
I'LL DO "HACHAKE NIGHTS." WHERE IS IT--?
Bip
FWIIIIP
IT'S 4379-12543.
...IS THE DARK-HORSE CAN-DIDATE SAKA-MOTO.
WOW, YOU FOUND IT SO FAST!
YOU NEED ONLY ASK, AND I SHALL PLACE THE ORDER.
KLIK
RIIING—
Yes?
I'D LIKE TO GET SOME DRINKS.

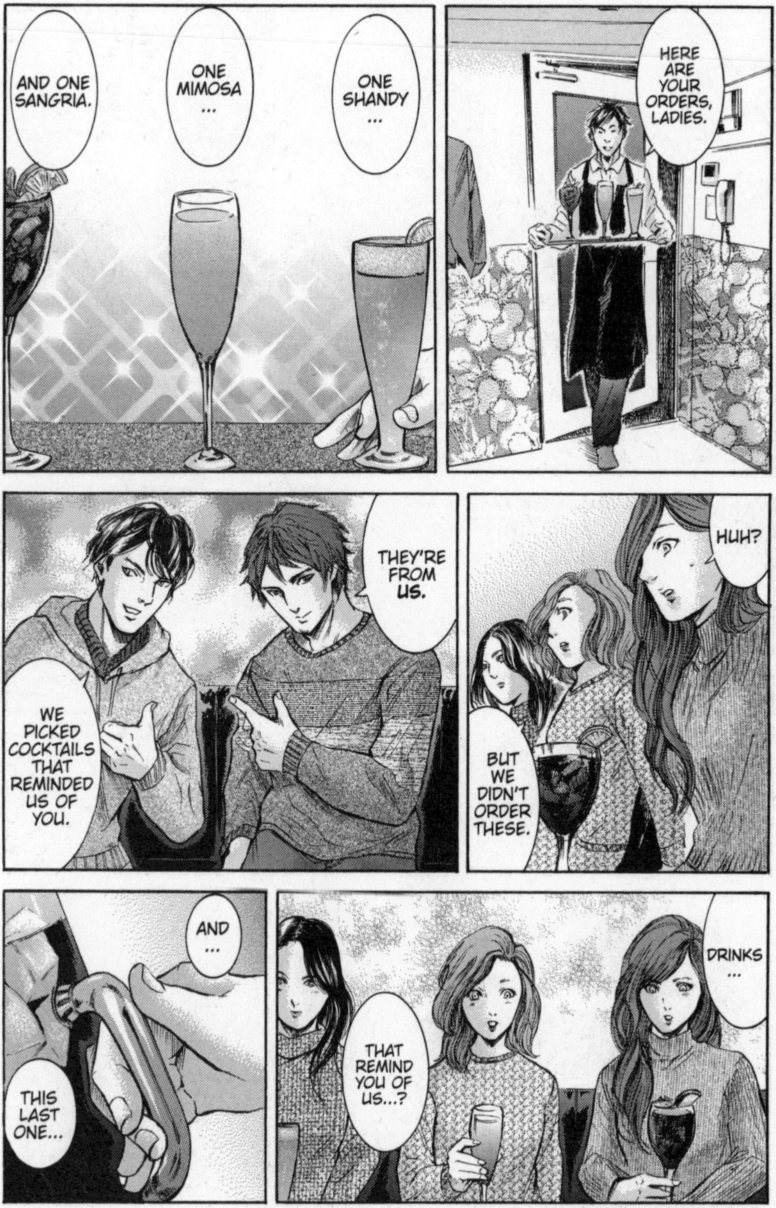
HERE ARE YOUR ORDERS, LADIES.
ONE SHANDY...
ONE MIMOSA...
AND ONE SANGRIA.
HUH?
BUT WE DIDN'T ORDER THESE.
THEY'RE FROM US.
WE PICKED COCKTAILS THAT REMINDED US OF YOU.
DRINKS...
THAT REMIND YOU OF US...?
AND...
THIS LAST ONE...

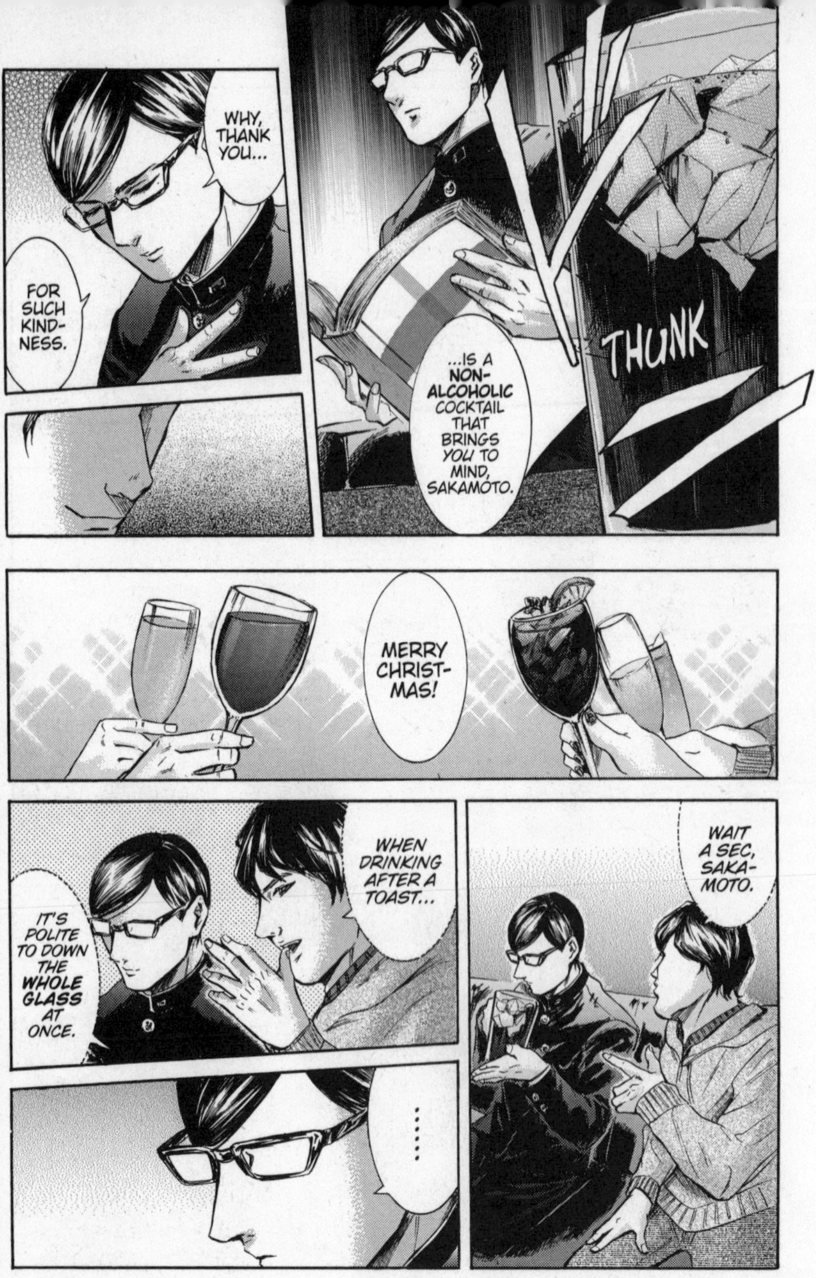
THUNK
...IS A NON-ALCOHOLIC COCKTAIL THAT BRINGS YOU TO MIND, SAKAMOTO.
WHY, THANK YOU...
FOR SUCH KINDNESS.
MERRY CHRISTMAS!
WAIT A SEC, SAKAMOTO.
WHEN DRINKING AFTER A TOAST...
IT'S POLITE TO DOWN THE WHOLE GLASS AT ONCE.
......

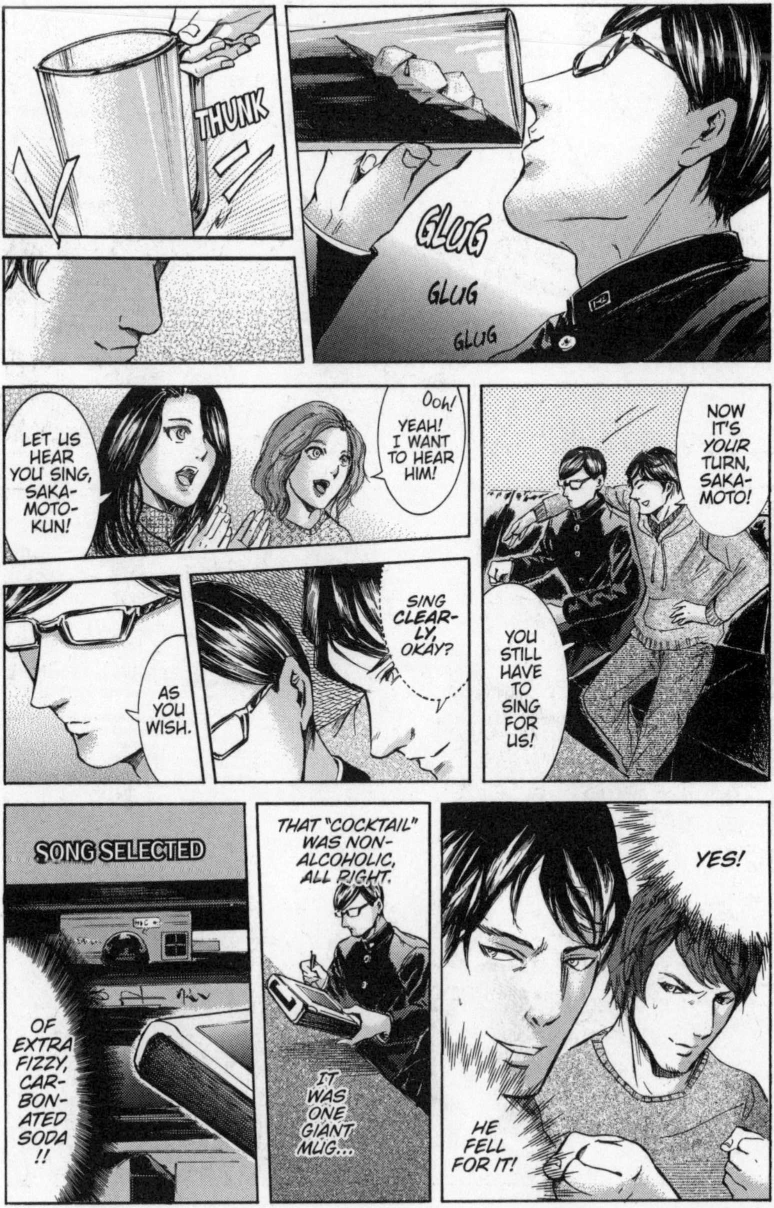
GLUG
GLUG
GLUG
THUNK
NOW IT'S YOUR TURN, SAKAMOTO!
YOU STILL HAVE TO SING FOR US!
Ooh!
YEAH! I WANT TO HEAR HIM!
LET US HEAR YOU SING, SAKAMOTO-KUN!
SING CLEARLY, OKAY?
AS YOU WISH.
YES!
HE FELL FOR IT!
THAT "COCKTAIL" WAS NON-ALCOHOLIC, ALL RIGHT.
IT WAS ONE GIANT MUG...
SONG SELECTED
OF EXTRA FIZZY, CARBONATED SODA!!

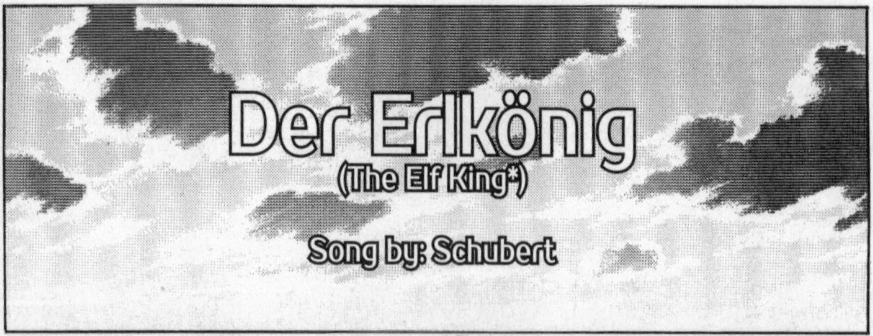
Der Erlkönig
(The Elf King*)
Song by: Schubert

※The Japanese name for this song is 魔王, meaning "The Devil."

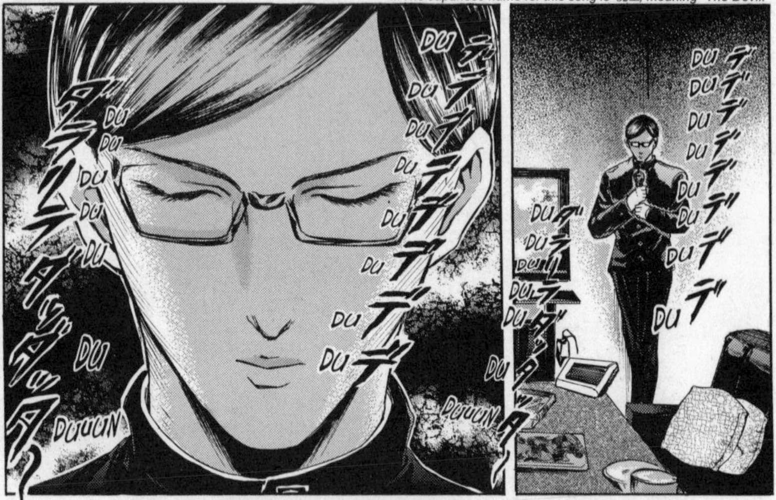
DU DU DU DU DU DU DU DU DU
DU DU DU DU DU DUUUN
DU DU DU DU DU DU DU DU DU DU DU DUUUN

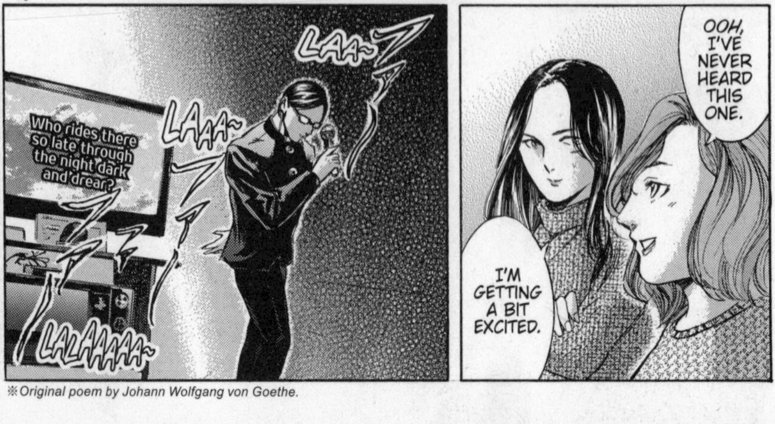
OOH, I'VE NEVER HEARD THIS ONE.
I'M GETTING A BIT EXCITED.
LAA~
LAAA~
Who rides there so late through the night dark and drear?
LALAAAAA~

※Original poem by Johann Wolfgang von Goethe.

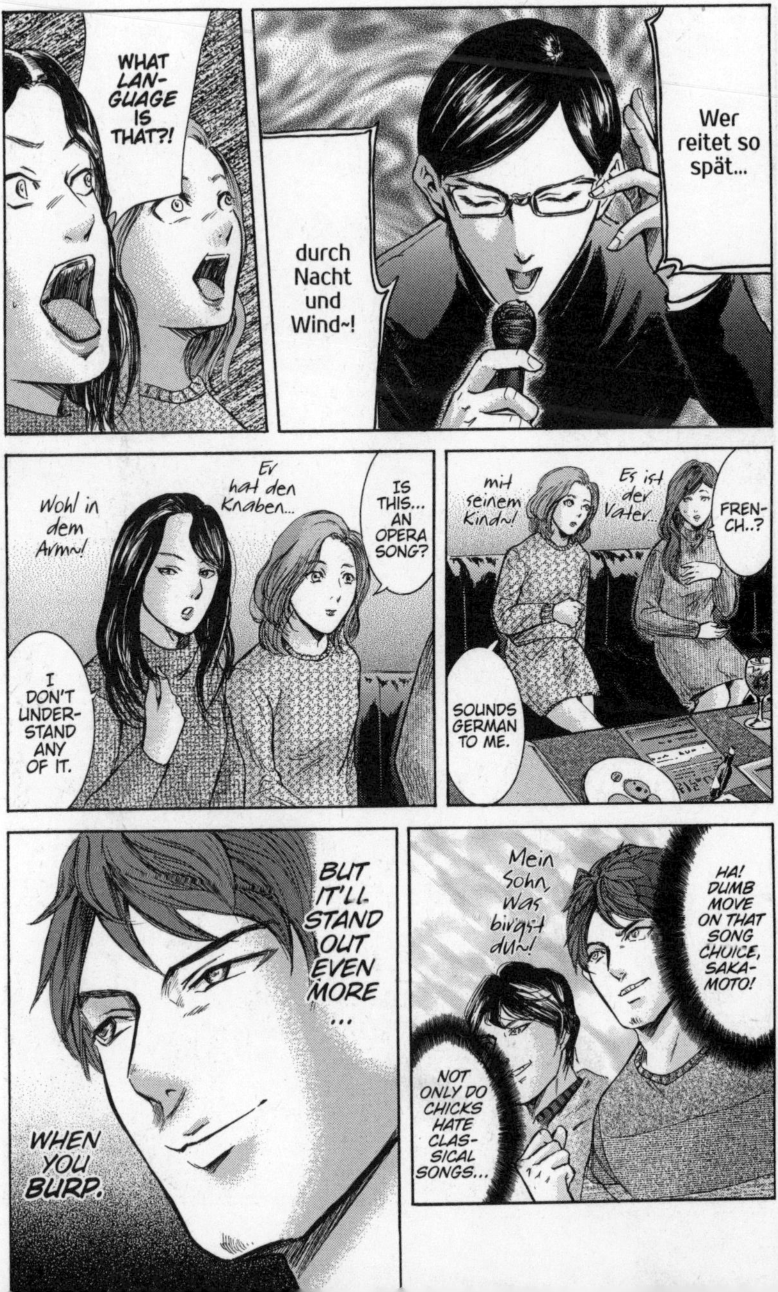
Wer reitet so spät...
durch Nacht und Wind~!
WHAT LANGUAGE IS THAT?!
Es ist der Vater...
FRENCH..?
mit seinem Kind~!
SOUNDS GERMAN TO ME.
Er hat den Knaben...
IS THIS... AN OPERA SONG?
Wohl in dem Arm~!
I DON'T UNDERSTAND ANY OF IT.
HA! DUMB MOVE ON THAT SONG CHUICE, SAKAMOTO!
Mein Sohn, was birgst du~!
NOT ONLY DO CHICKS HATE CLASSICAL SONGS...
BUT IT'LL STAND OUT EVEN MORE...
WHEN YOU BURP.

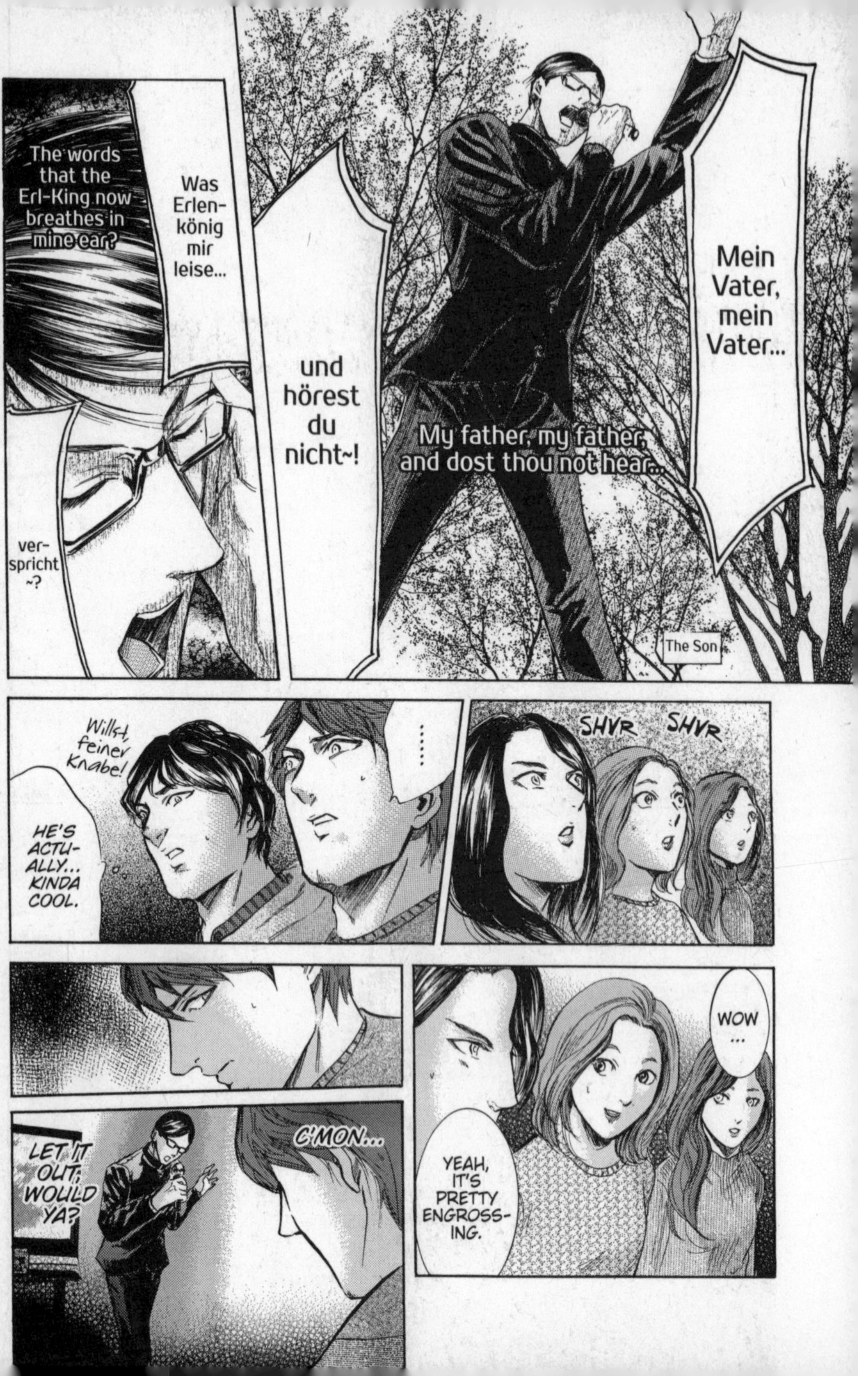
Mein Vater, mein Vater...
My father, my father, and dost thou not hear...
The Son
und hörest du nicht~!
Was Erlenkönig mir leise...
The words that the Erl-King now breathes in mine ear?
ver-spricht ~?
SHVR SHVR
......
Willst, feiner Knabe!
HE'S ACTU-ALLY... KINDA COOL.
WOW ...
YEAH, IT'S PRETTY ENGROSS-ING.
C'MON...
LET IT OUT, WOULD YA?

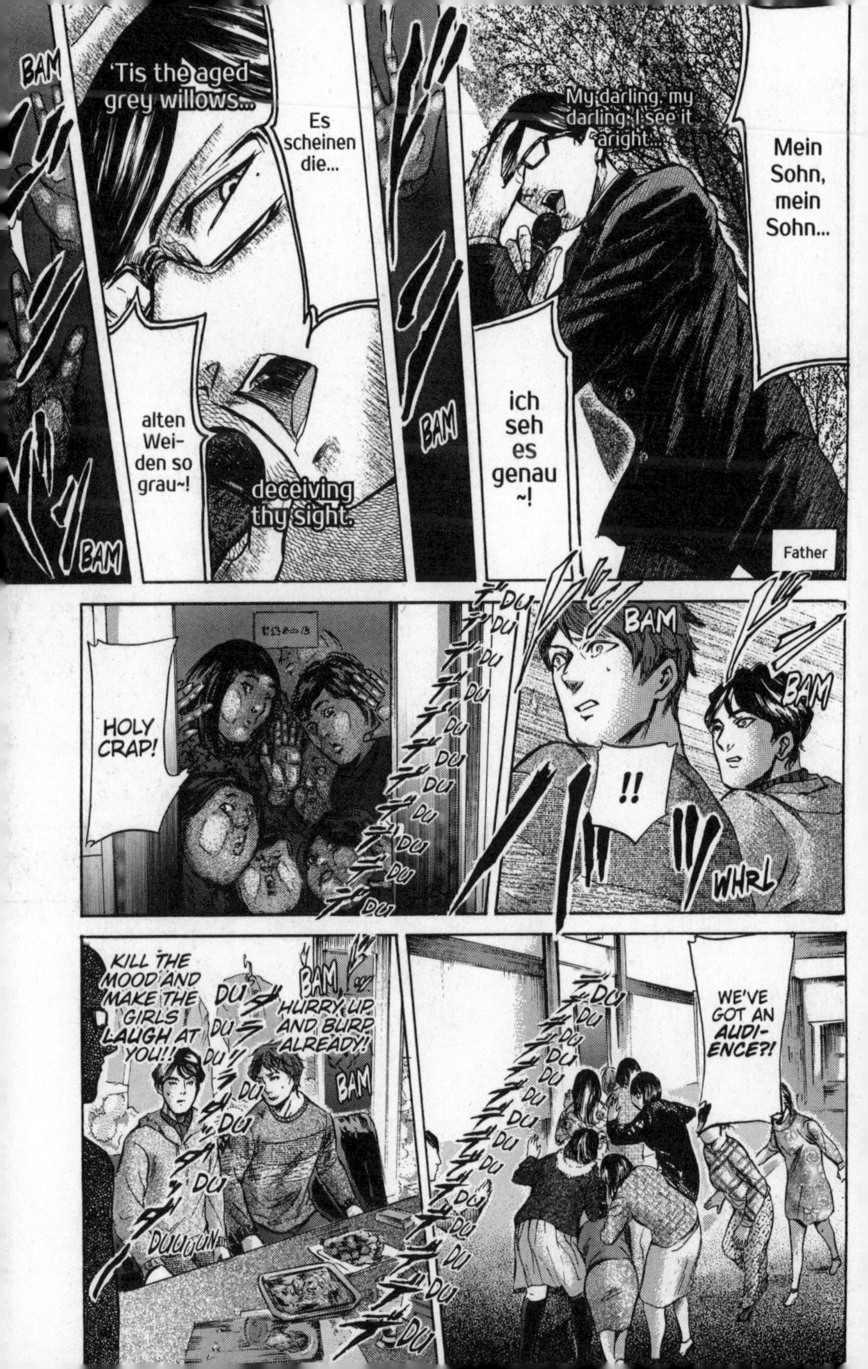
Father
Mein Sohn, mein Sohn...
My darling, my darling, I see it aright...
ich seh es genau ~!
BAM
Es scheinen die...
'Tis the aged grey willows...
alten Wei-den so grau~!
deceiving thy sight.
BAM
BAM
BAM
BAM
!!
WHRL
DU DU DU DU DU DU DU DU DU DU DU
HOLY CRAP!
WE'VE GOT AN AUDI-ENCE?!
DU DU DU DU DU DU DU DU DU DU DU DU DU
BAM,
HURRY UP AND BURP ALREADY!
BAM
KILL THE MOOD AND MAKE THE GIRLS LAUGH AT YOU!!
DU DU DU DU DU DU
DUUUUN

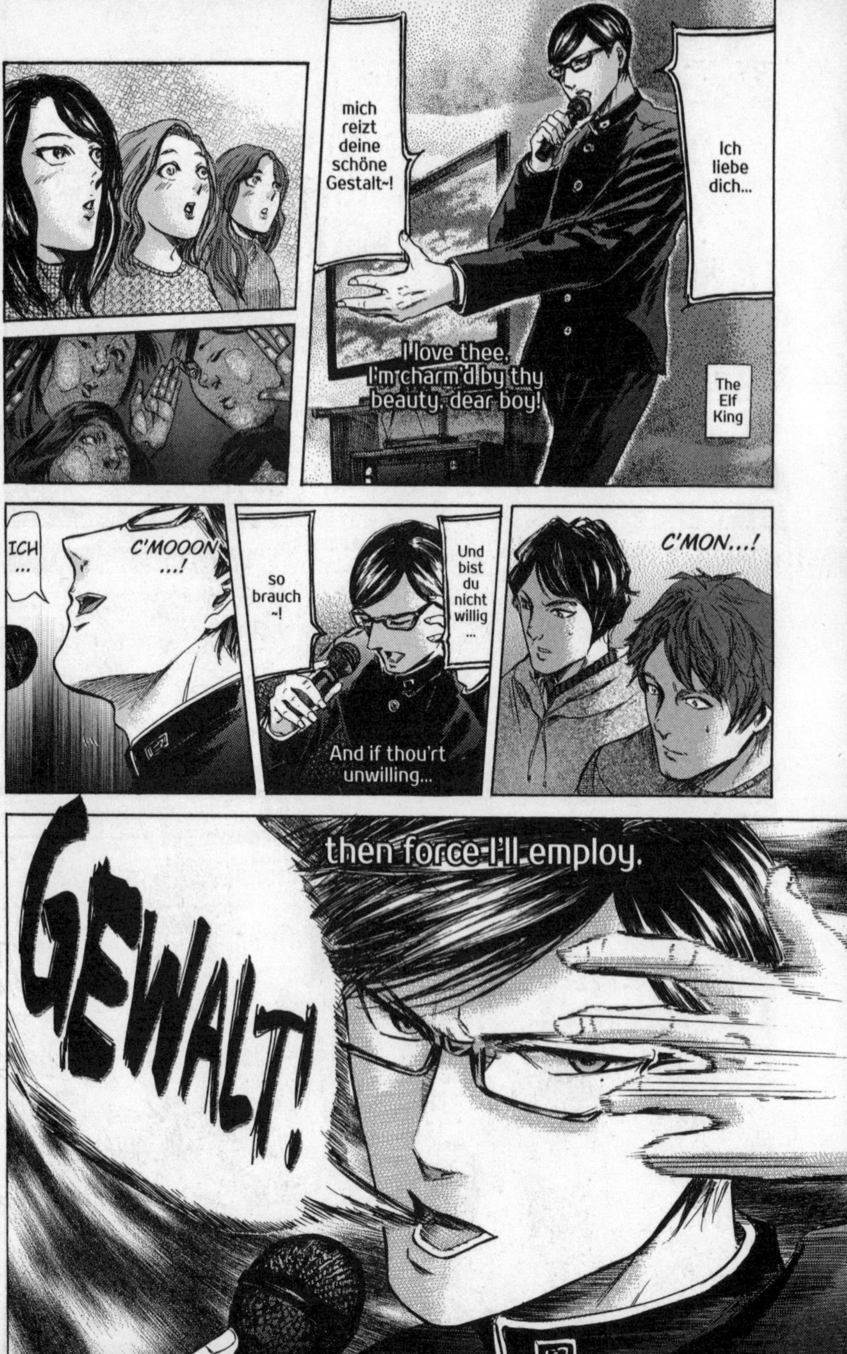
The Elf King
Ich liebe dich...
mich reizt deine schöne Gestalt~!
I love thee, I'm charm'd by thy beauty, dear boy!
C'MON...!
Und bist du nicht willig ...
so brauch ~!
And if thou'rt unwilling...
C'MOOON ...!
ICH ...
then force I'll employ.
GEWALT!

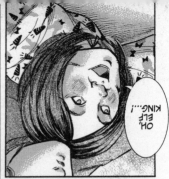

UH...
WAS THAT ...?
HE SOUNDS LIKE A NATIVE SPEAK-ER!!
HE EVEN MADE THE BURP WORK FOR HIM!!
WHUM
OH, ELF KING...!

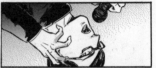

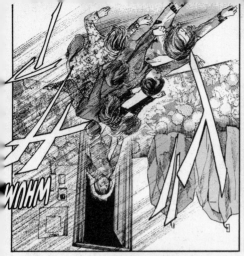

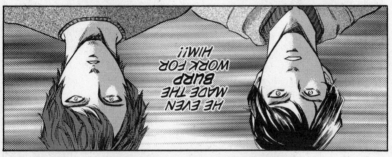

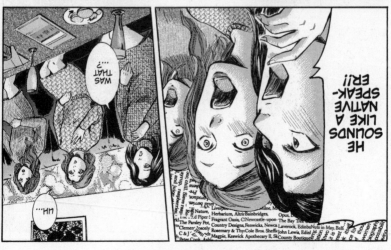

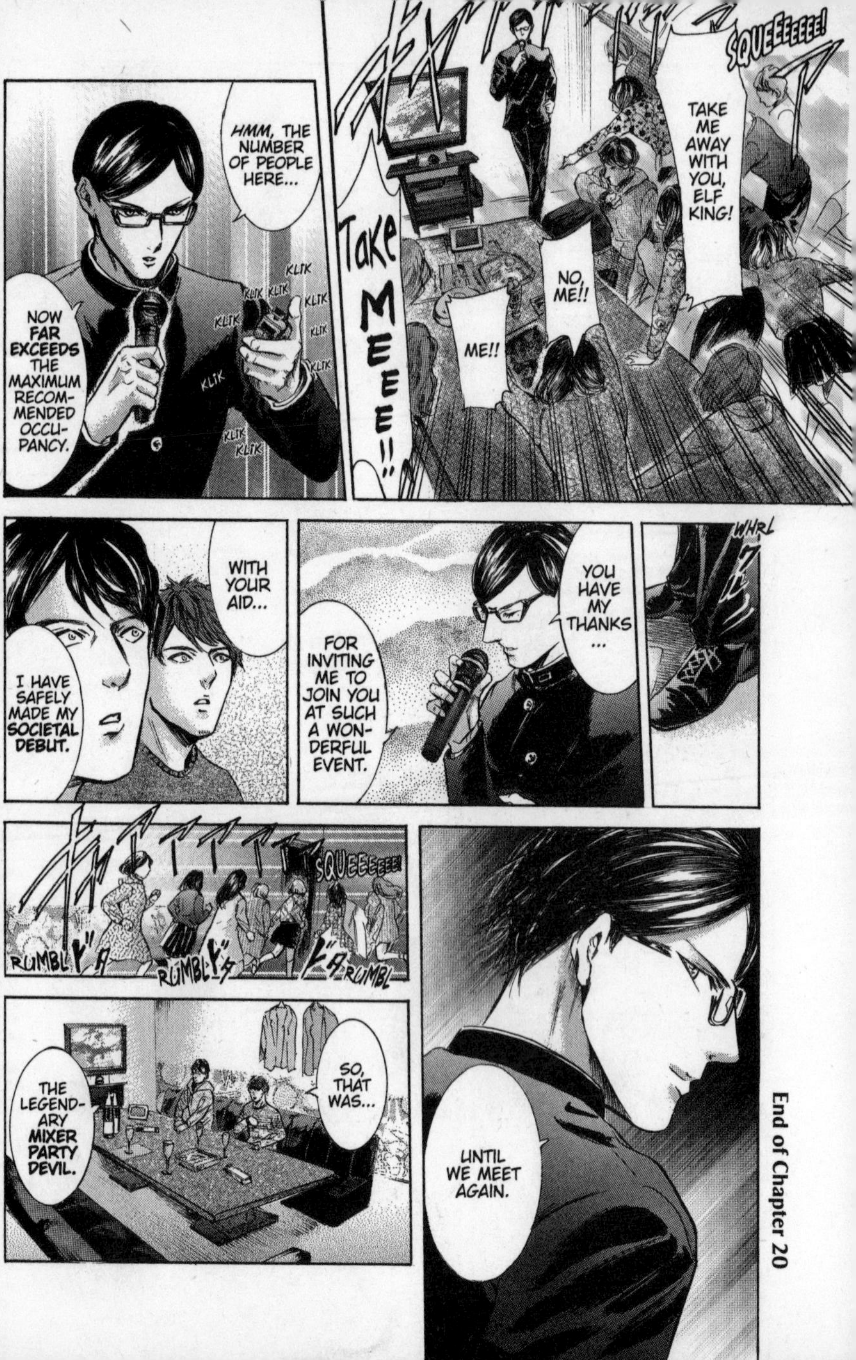
SQUEEEEEEE!
TAKE ME AWAY WITH YOU, ELF KING!
NO, ME!!
ME!!
Take MEEE!!
HMM, THE NUMBER OF PEOPLE HERE...
NOW FAR EXCEEDS THE MAXIMUM RECOMMENDED OCCUPANCY.
KLIK KLIK KLIK KLIK KLIK KLIK KLIK KLIK KLIK
WHRL
YOU HAVE MY THANKS...
FOR INVITING ME TO JOIN YOU AT SUCH A WONDERFUL EVENT.
WITH YOUR AID...
I HAVE SAFELY MADE MY SOCIETAL DEBUT.
UNTIL WE MEET AGAIN.
SQUEEEEEEE!
RUMBL RUMBL RUMBL
SO, THAT WAS...
THE LEGENDARY MIXER PARTY DEVIL.

End of Chapter 20

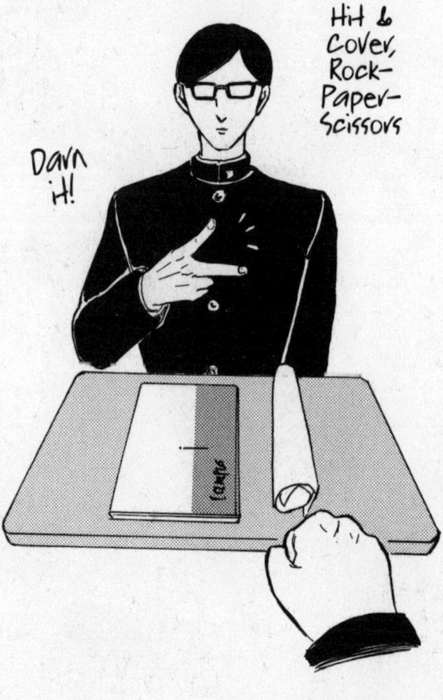
Hit & Cover, Rock-Paper-Scissors
Darn it!

Let's Play With Sakamoto #3

VWEEEM

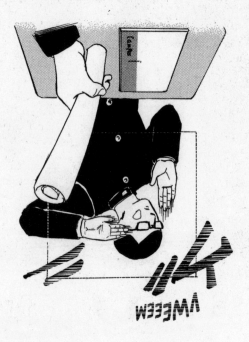

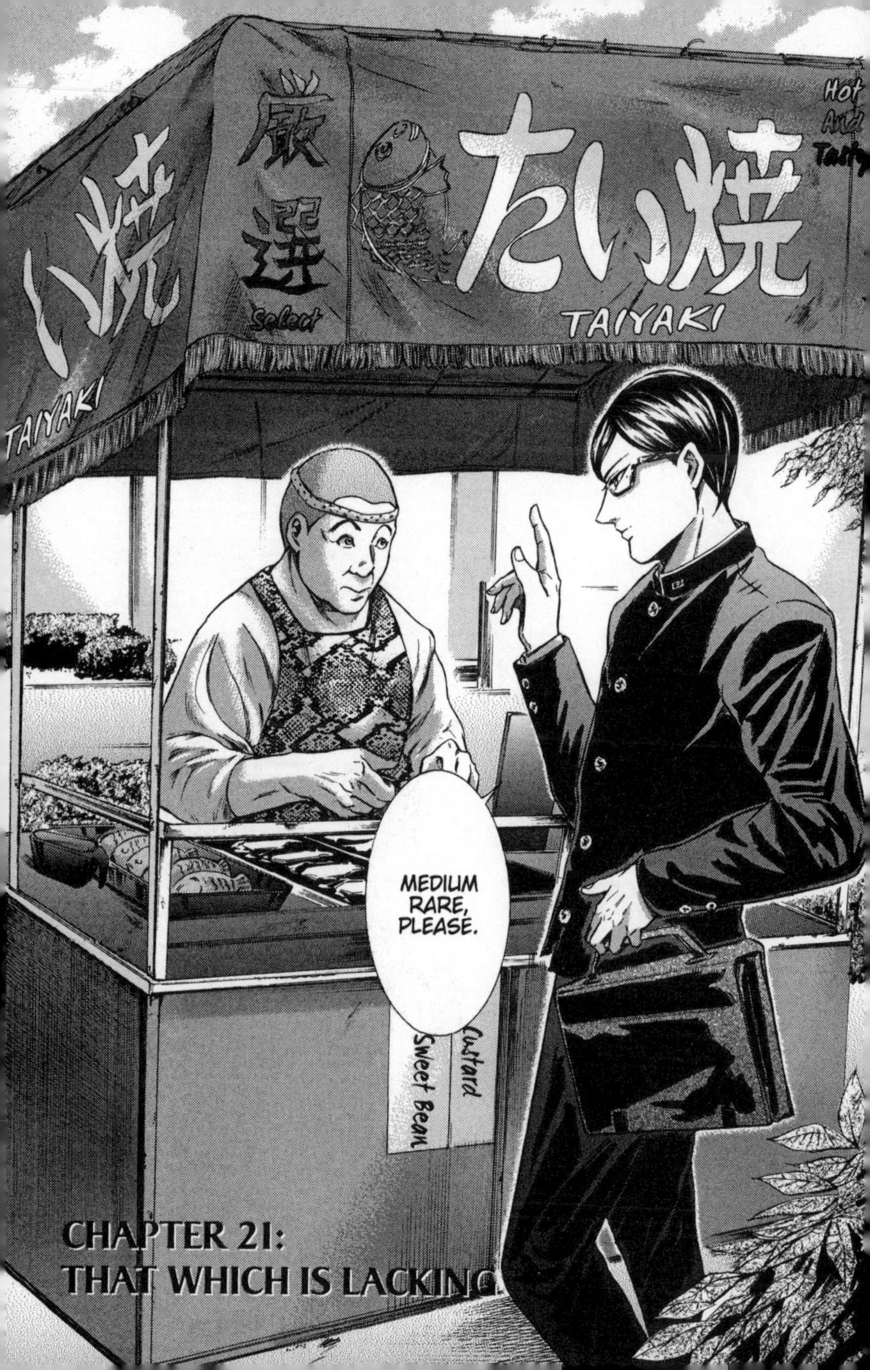
たい焼
TAIYAKI
厳選
Select
TAIYAKI
MEDIUM RARE, PLEASE.
Custard
Sweet Bean
CHAPTER 21:
THAT WHICH IS LACKING

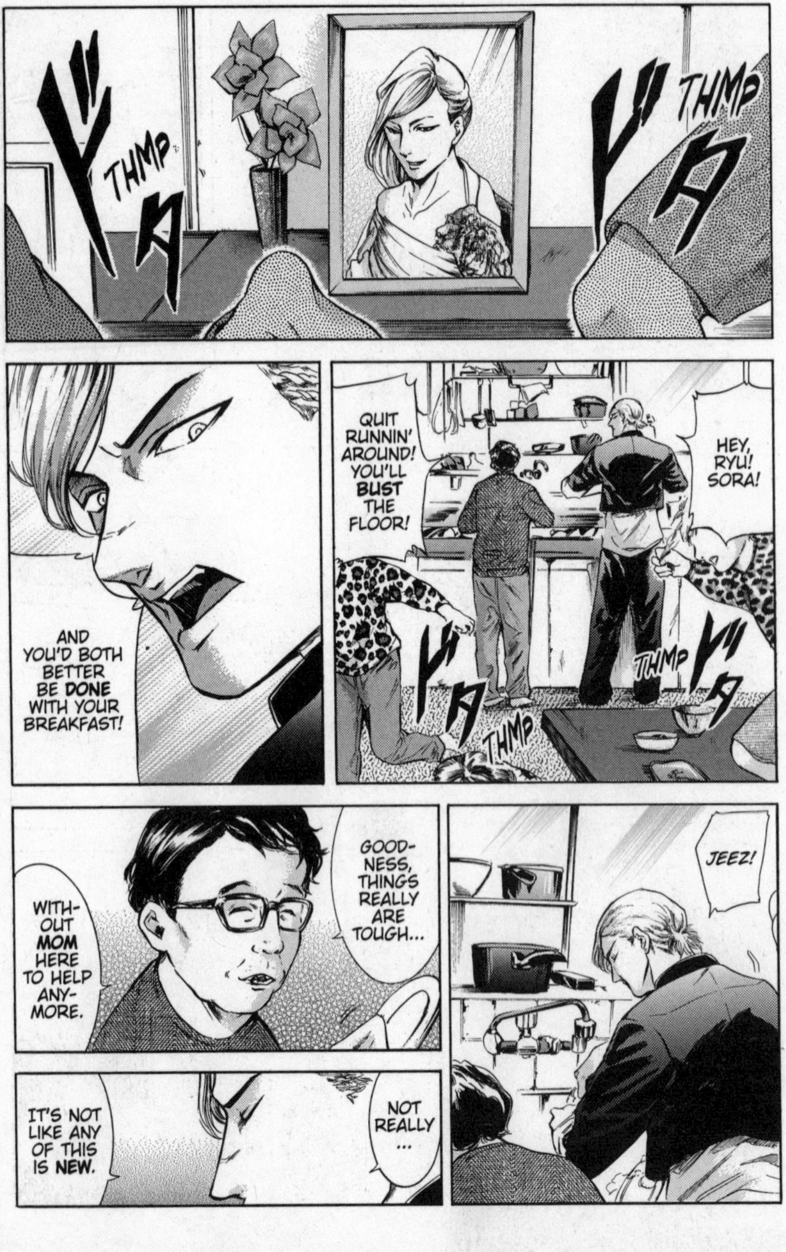
THMP
THMP
HEY, RYU! SORA!
QUIT RUNNIN' AROUND! YOU'LL BUST THE FLOOR!
THMP
THMP
AND YOU'D BOTH BETTER BE DONE WITH YOUR BREAKFAST!
JEEZ!
GOODNESS, THINGS REALLY ARE TOUGH...
WITHOUT MOM HERE TO HELP ANYMORE.
NOT REALLY ...
IT'S NOT LIKE ANY OF THIS IS NEW.

......
SHO.
HOW ABOUT YOU COME WITH ME TO A FRENCH RESTAURANT TONIGHT?
HUH ...?
I, UH... WANT TO...
INTRO-DUCE YOU TO SOME-ONE... A LADY.
?!
WHRL
THERE'S A CHANCE SHE MAY BE YOUR NEW MOTHER SOMEDAY.
WHAT THE HELL, DAD?!
HAVE YOU LOST YOUR MIND?!
SHO ...
YOUR LITTLE BROTH-ERS...
THEY DESERVE TO GROW UP WITH A MOM.

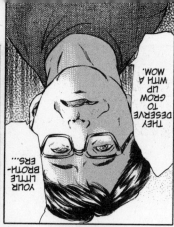

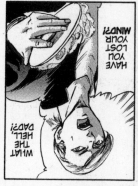

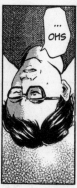

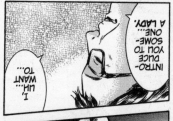

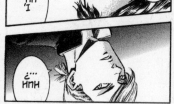

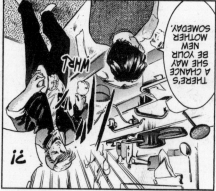

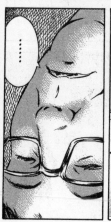

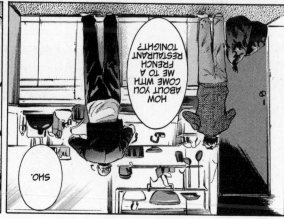

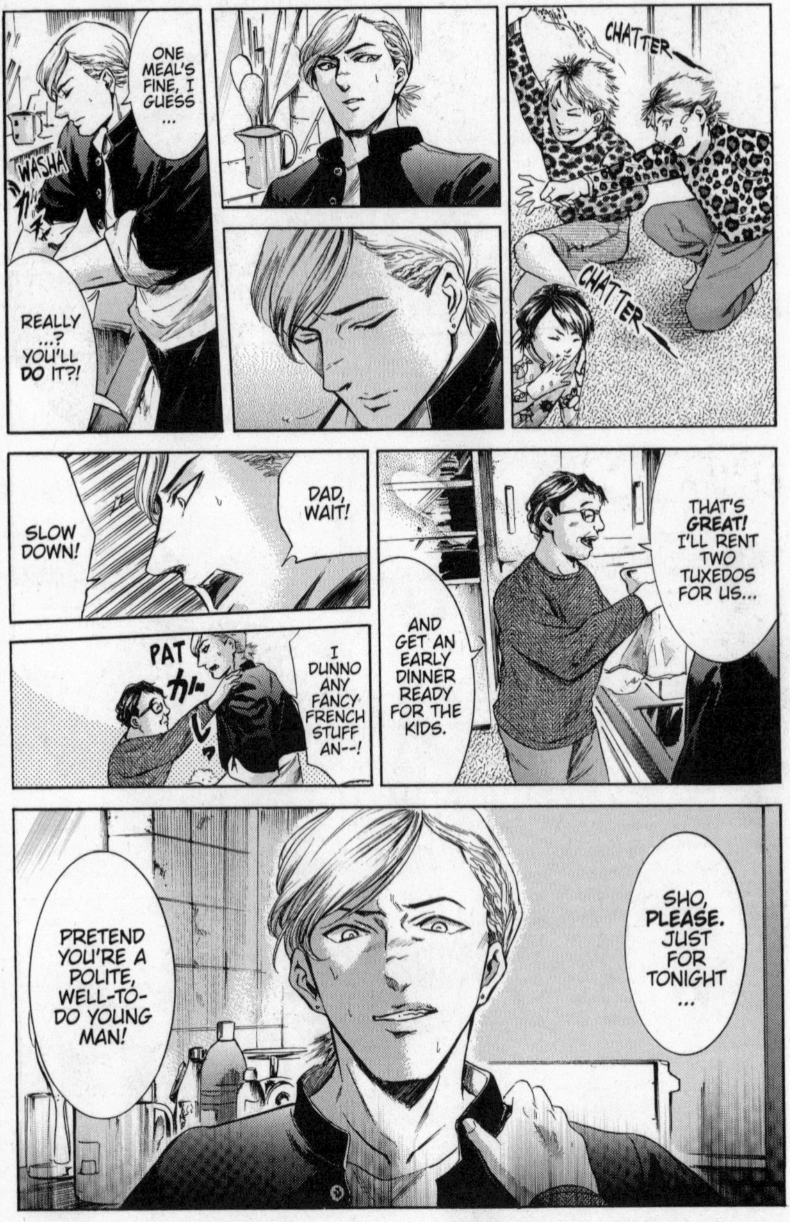
CHATTER
CHATTER
ONE MEAL'S FINE, I GUESS...
WASHA
REALLY...? YOU'LL DO IT?!
THAT'S GREAT! I'LL RENT TWO TUXEDOS FOR US...
AND GET AN EARLY DINNER READY FOR THE KIDS.
DAD, WAIT!
SLOW DOWN!
I DUNNO ANY FANCY FRENCH STUFF AN--!
PAT
SHO, PLEASE. JUST FOR TONIGHT...
PRETEND YOU'RE A POLITE, WELL-TO-DO YOUNG MAN!

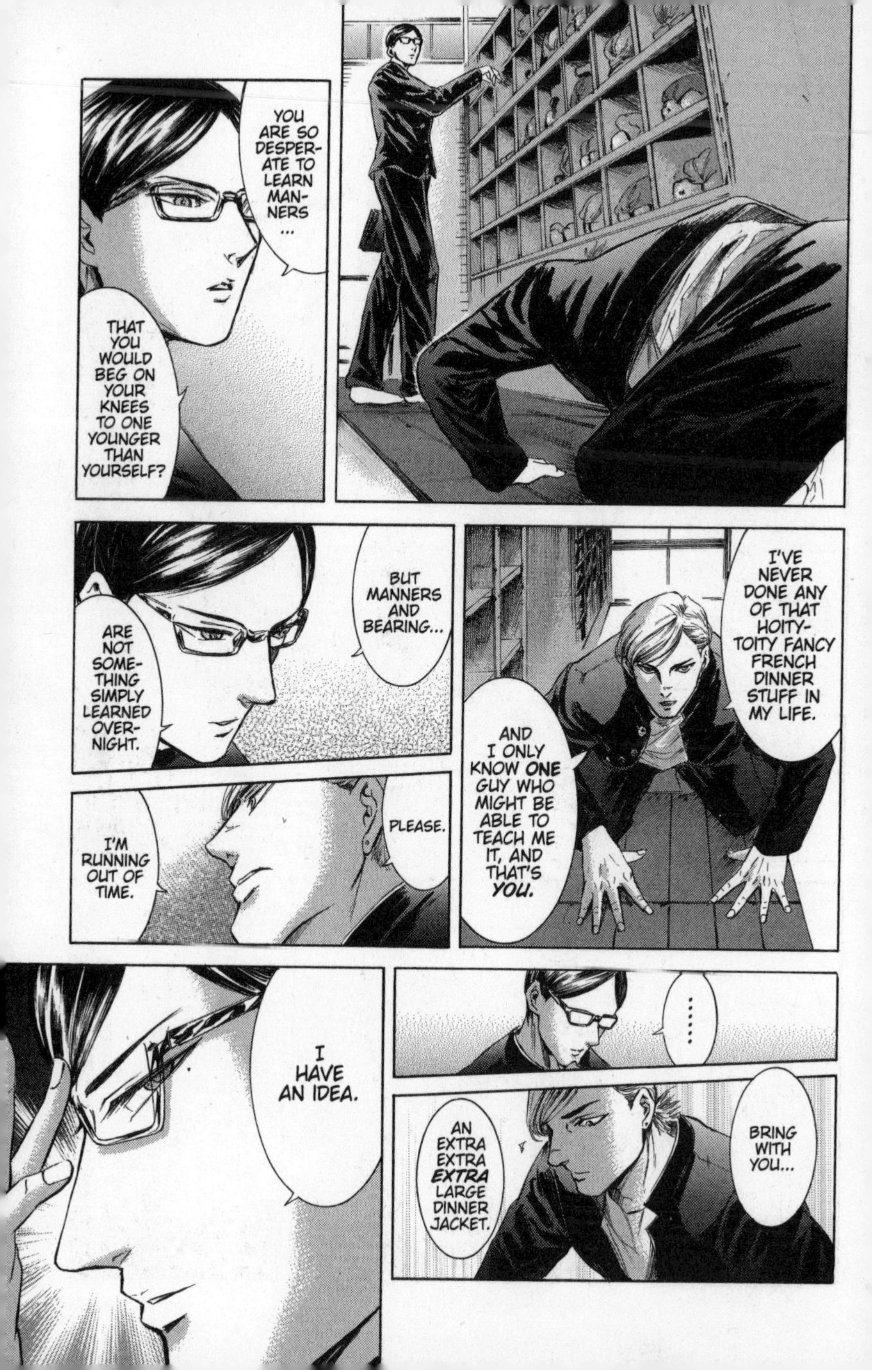
YOU ARE SO DESPER-ATE TO LEARN MAN-NERS ...
THAT YOU WOULD BEG ON YOUR KNEES TO ONE YOUNGER THAN YOURSELF?
I'VE NEVER DONE ANY OF THAT HOITY-TOITY FANCY FRENCH DINNER STUFF IN MY LIFE.
AND I ONLY KNOW **ONE** GUY WHO MIGHT BE ABLE TO TEACH ME IT, AND THAT'S ***YOU.***
BUT MANNERS AND BEARING...
ARE NOT SOME-THING SIMPLY LEARNED OVER-NIGHT.
PLEASE.
I'M RUNNING OUT OF TIME.
.....
BRING WITH YOU...
AN EXTRA EXTRA ***EXTRA*** LARGE DINNER JACKET.
I HAVE AN IDEA.

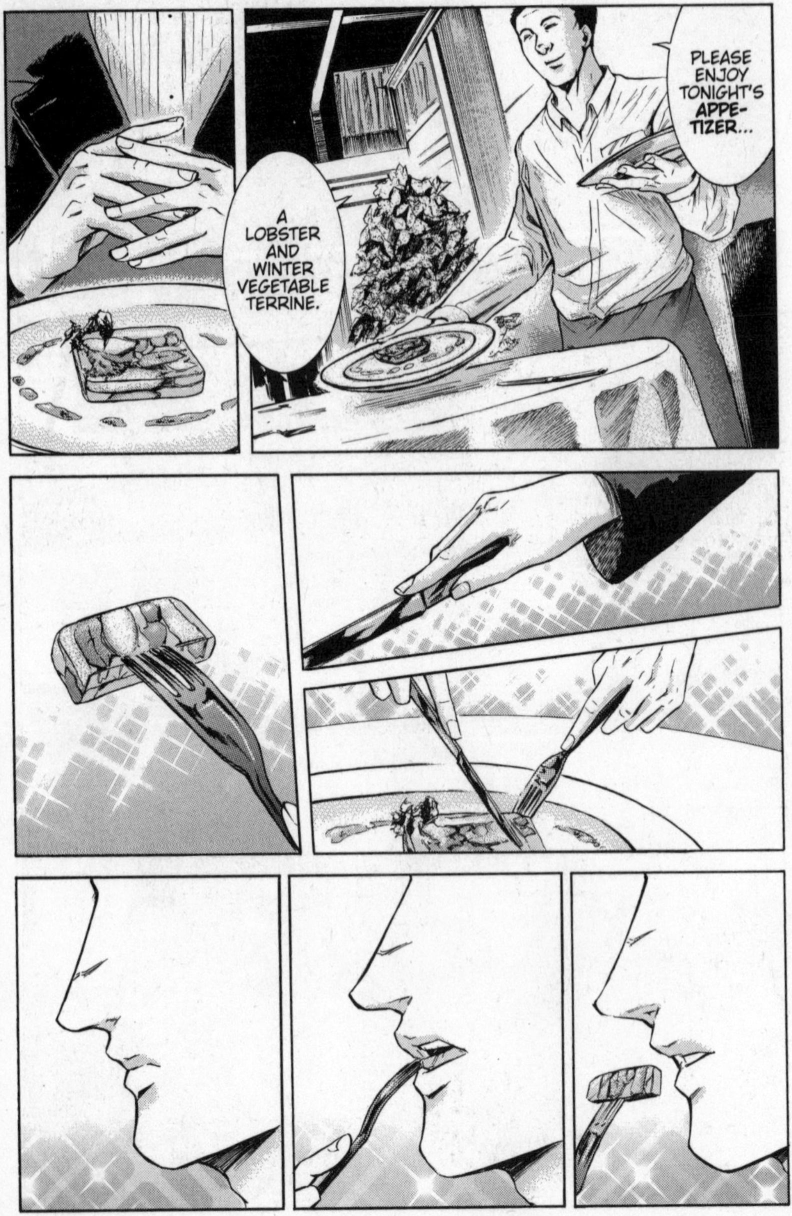
PLEASE ENJOY TONIGHT'S APPE-TIZER...
A LOBSTER AND WINTER VEGETABLE TERRINE.

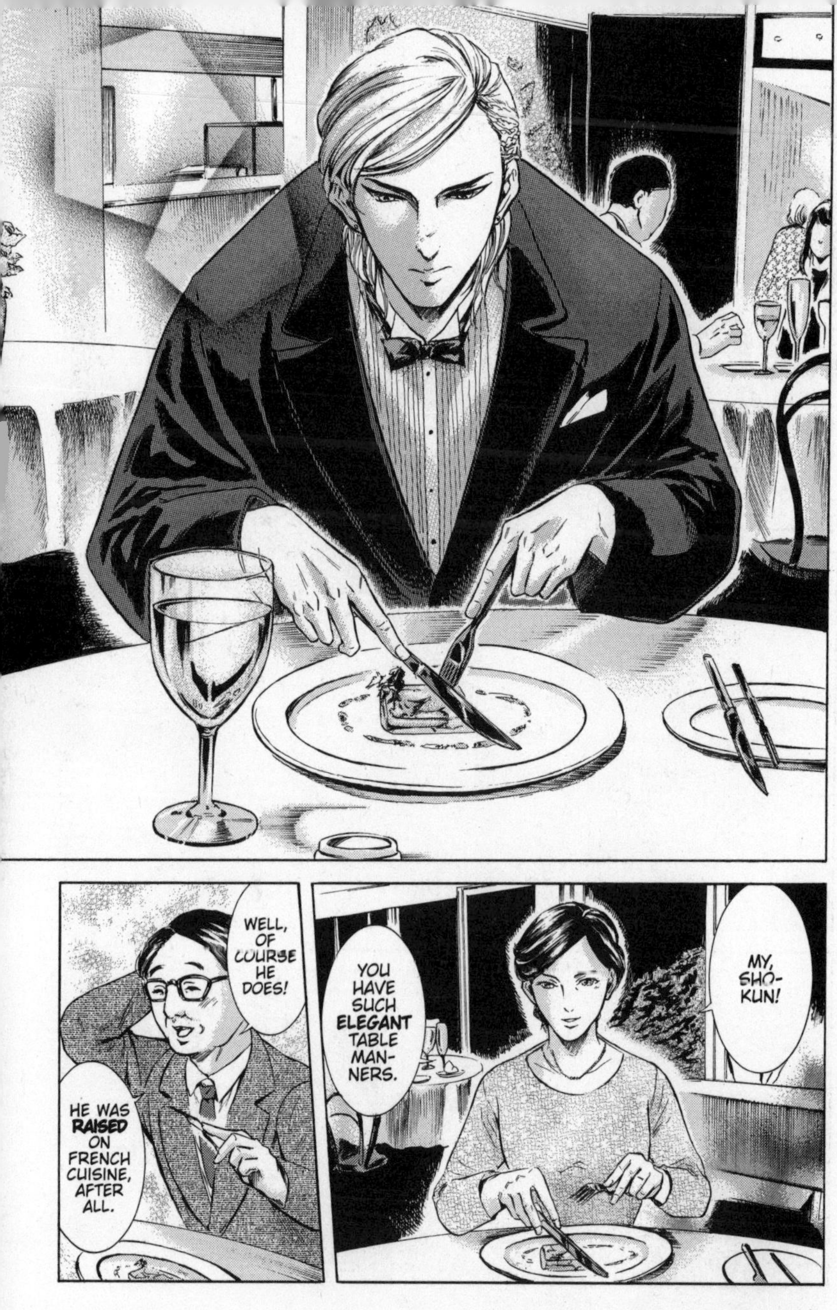
MY, SHO-KUN!
YOU HAVE SUCH **ELEGANT** TABLE MAN-NERS.
WELL, OF COURSE HE DOES!
HE WAS **RAISED** ON FRENCH CUISINE, AFTER ALL.

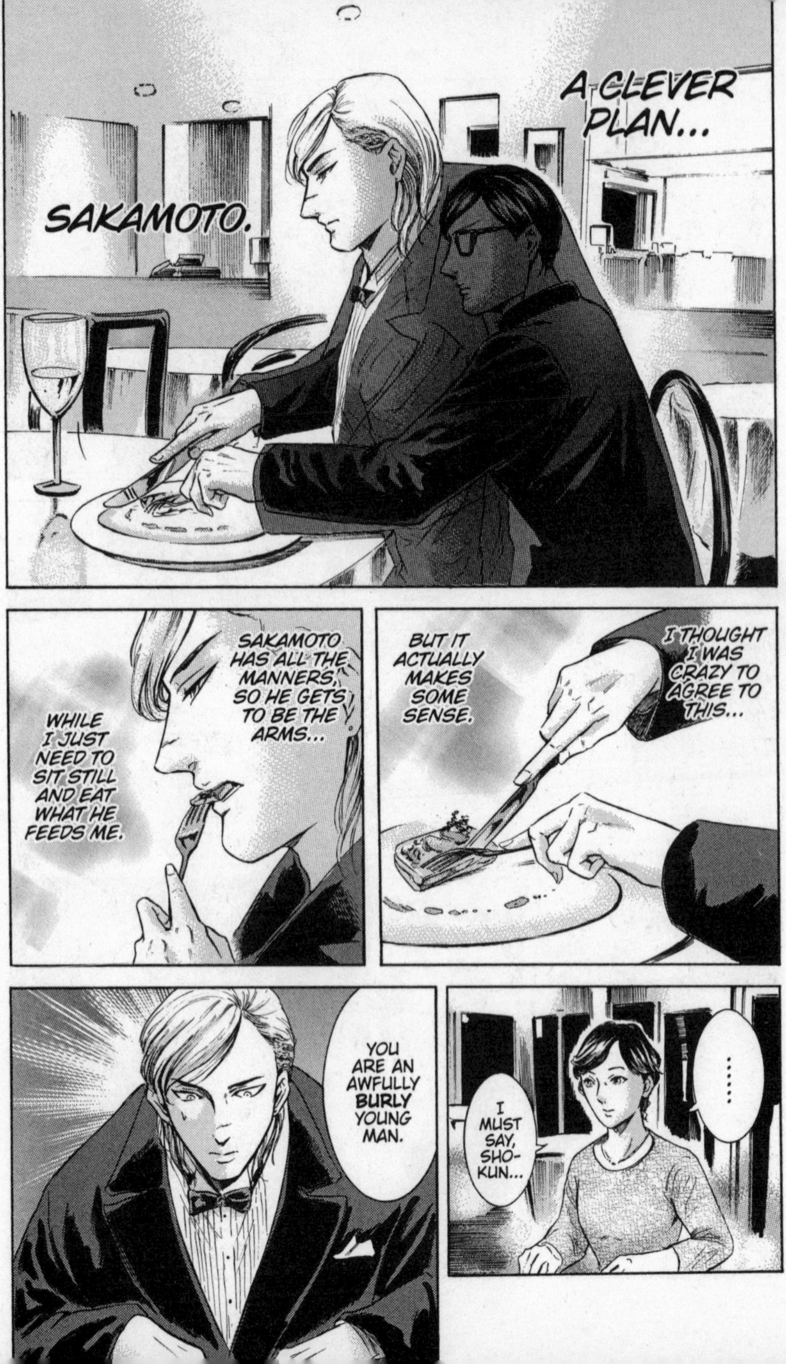
A CLEVER PLAN...
SAKAMOTO.
I THOUGHT I WAS CRAZY TO AGREE TO THIS...
BUT IT ACTUALLY MAKES SOME SENSE.
SAKAMOTO HAS ALL THE MANNERS, SO HE GETS TO BE THE ARMS...
WHILE I JUST NEED TO SIT STILL AND EAT WHAT HE FEEDS ME.
......
I MUST SAY, SHO-KUN...
YOU ARE AN AWFULLY **BURLY** YOUNG MAN.

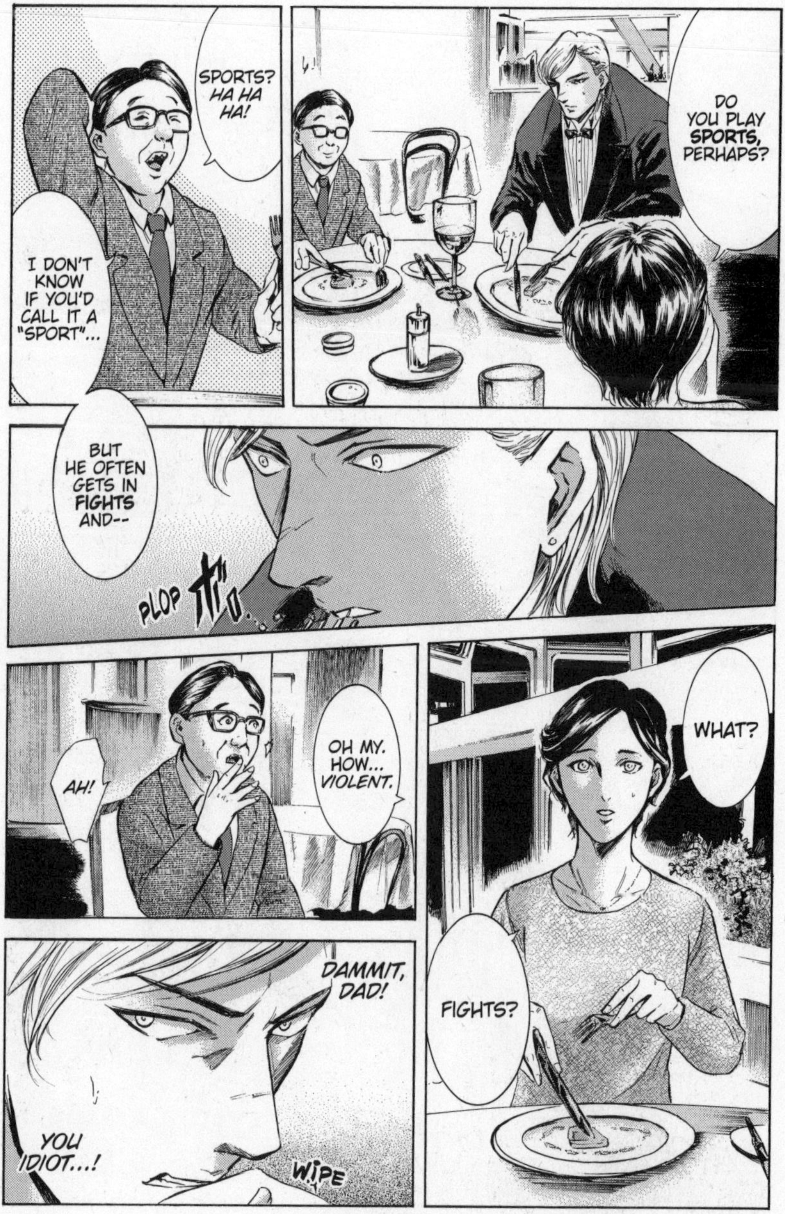
DO YOU PLAY SPORTS, PERHAPS?
SPORTS? HA HA HA!
I DON'T KNOW IF YOU'D CALL IT A "SPORT"...
BUT HE OFTEN GETS IN FIGHTS AND--
PLOP
WHAT?
FIGHTS?
OH MY. HOW... VIOLENT.
AH!
DAMMIT, DAD!
YOU IDIOT...!
WIPE

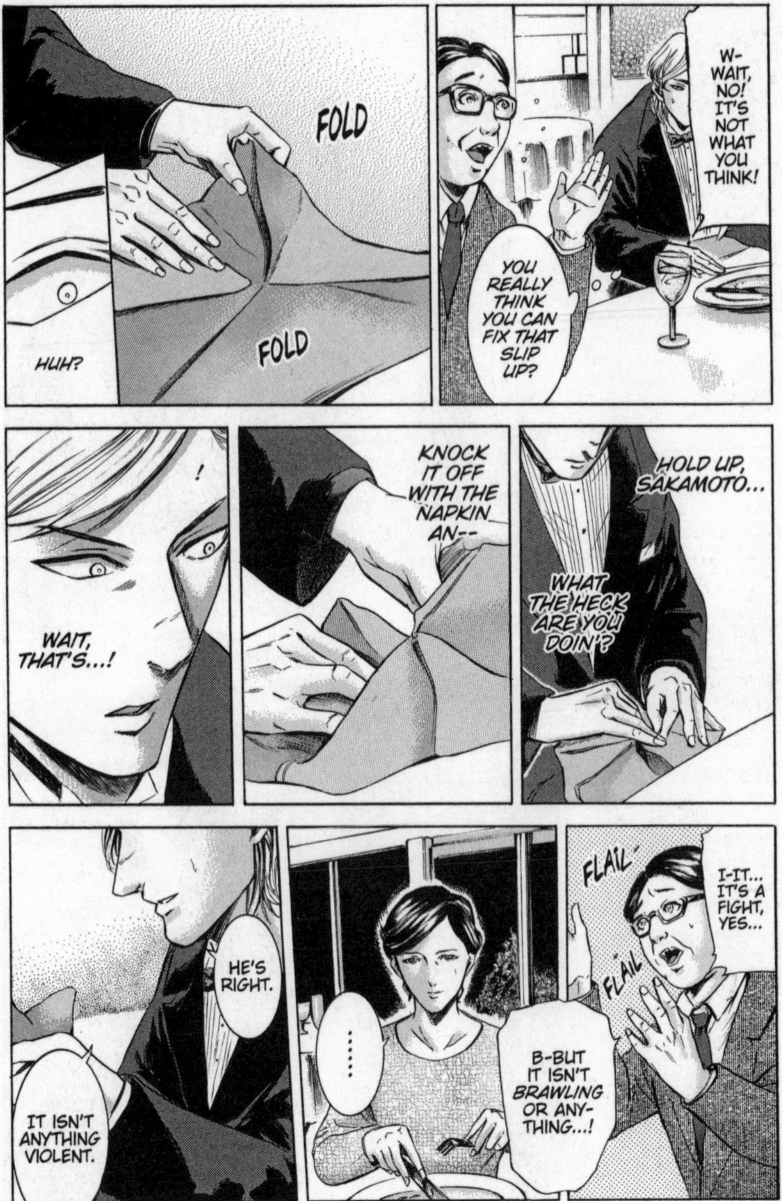
W-WAIT, NO! IT'S NOT WHAT YOU THINK!
YOU REALLY THINK YOU CAN FIX THAT SLIP UP?
FOLD
FOLD
HUH?
HOLD UP, SAKAMOTO...
WHAT THE HECK ARE YOU DOIN'?
KNOCK IT OFF WITH THE NAPKIN AN--
!
WAIT, THAT'S...!
I-IT... IT'S A FIGHT, YES...
FLAIL
FLAIL
B-BUT IT ISN'T BRAWLING OR ANY-THING...!
......
HE'S RIGHT.
IT ISN'T ANYTHING VIOLENT.

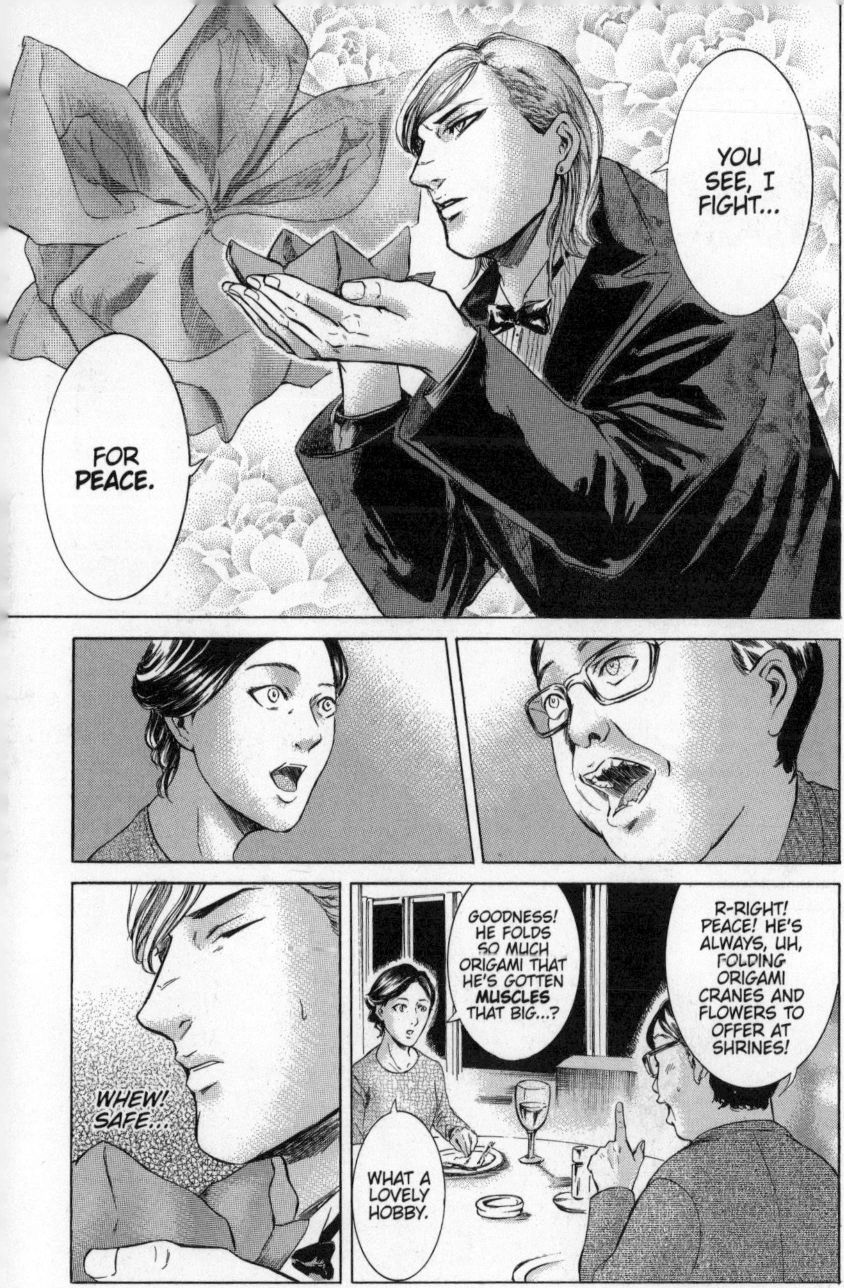
YOU SEE, I FIGHT...
FOR PEACE.
R-RIGHT! PEACE! HE'S ALWAYS, UH, FOLDING ORIGAMI CRANES AND FLOWERS TO OFFER AT SHRINES!
GOODNESS! HE FOLDS SO MUCH ORIGAMI THAT HE'S GOTTEN **MUSCLES** THAT BIG...?
WHAT A LOVELY HOBBY.
WHEW! SAFE...

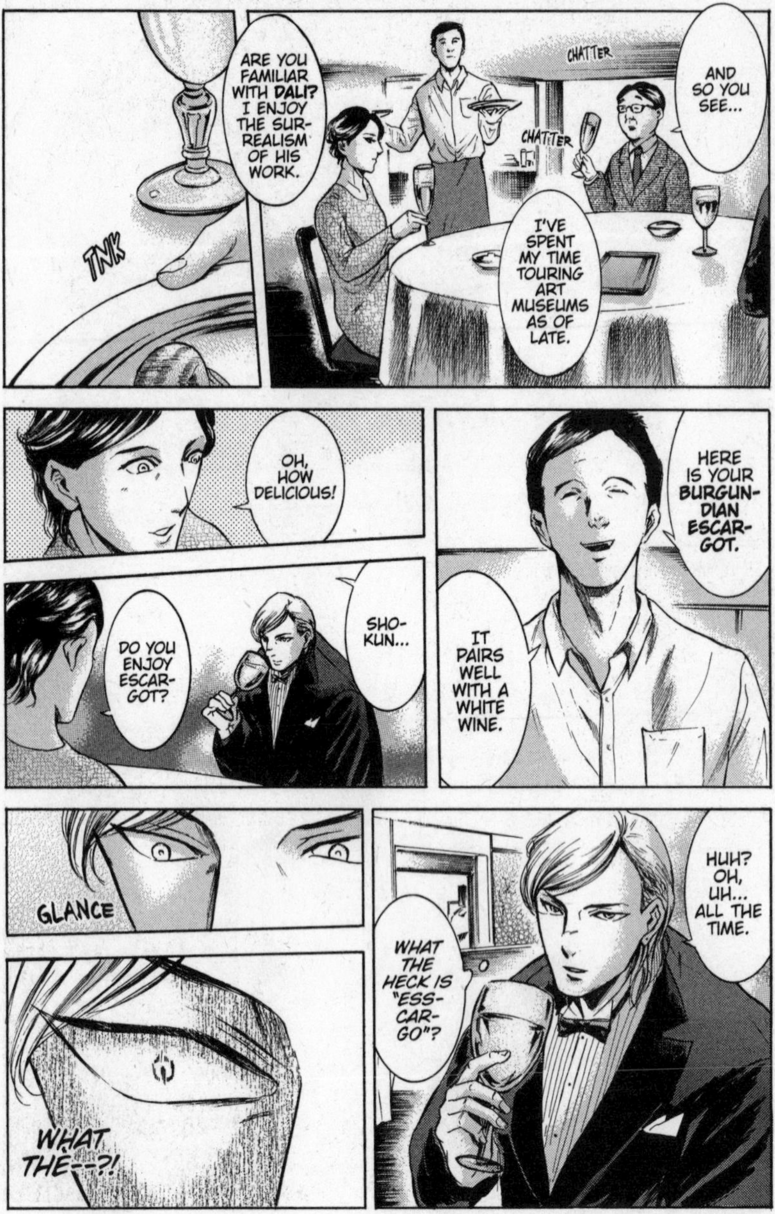
AND SO YOU SEE...
CHATTER
CHATTER
I'VE SPENT MY TIME TOURING ART MUSEUMS AS OF LATE.
ARE YOU FAMILIAR WITH DALI? I ENJOY THE SURREALISM OF HIS WORK.
TNK
HERE IS YOUR BURGUNDIAN ESCARGOT.
IT PAIRS WELL WITH A WHITE WINE.
OH, HOW DELICIOUS!
SHO-KUN...
DO YOU ENJOY ESCARGOT?
HUH? OH, UH... ALL THE TIME.
WHAT THE HECK IS "ESS-CAR-GO"?
GLANCE
WHAT THE--?!

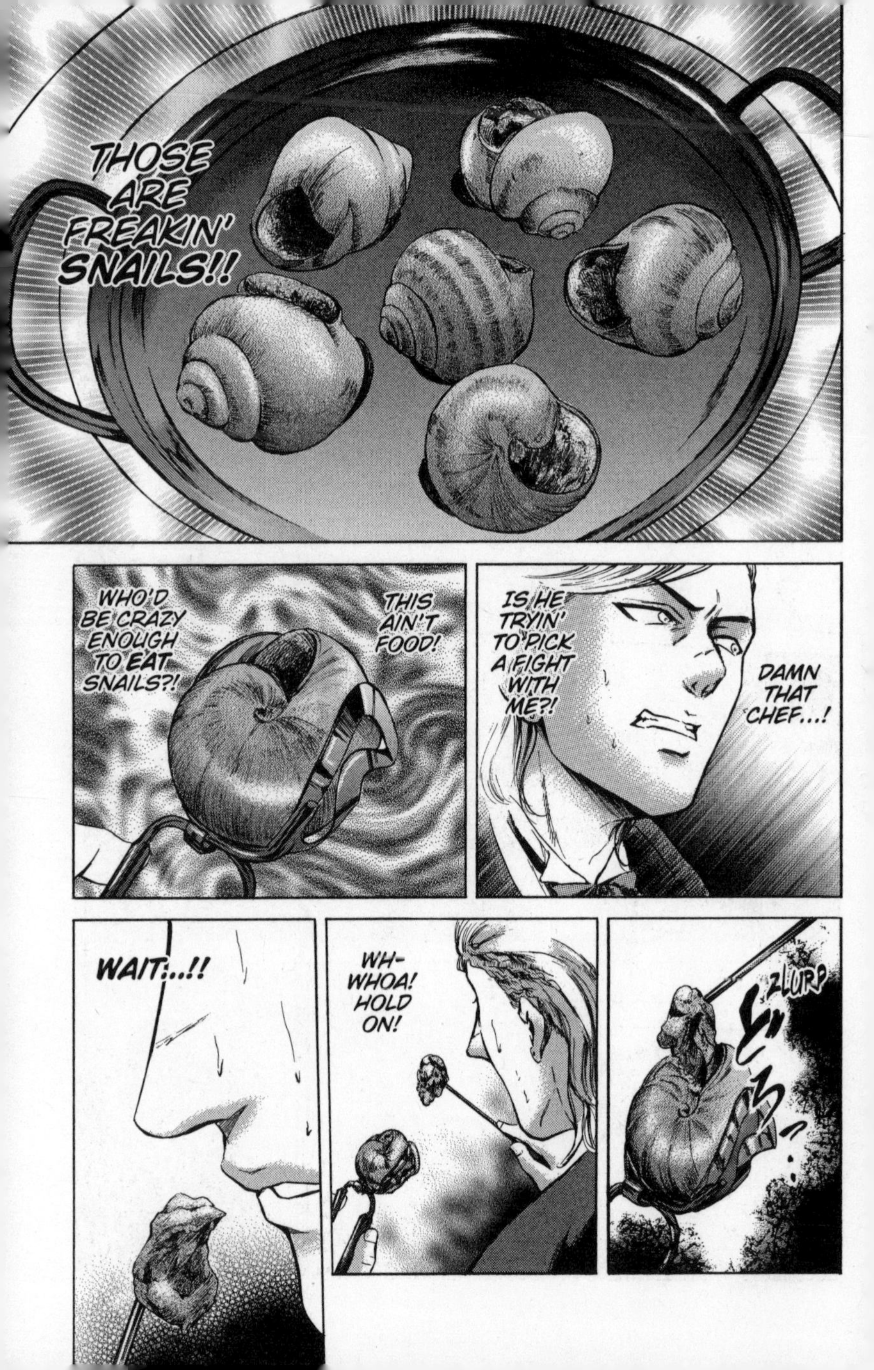
THOSE ARE FREAKIN' SNAILS!!
DAMN THAT CHEF...!
IS HE TRYIN' TO PICK A FIGHT WITH ME?!
THIS AIN'T FOOD!
WHO'D BE CRAZY ENOUGH TO EAT SNAILS?!
ZLURP
WH- WHOA! HOLD ON!
WAIT...!!

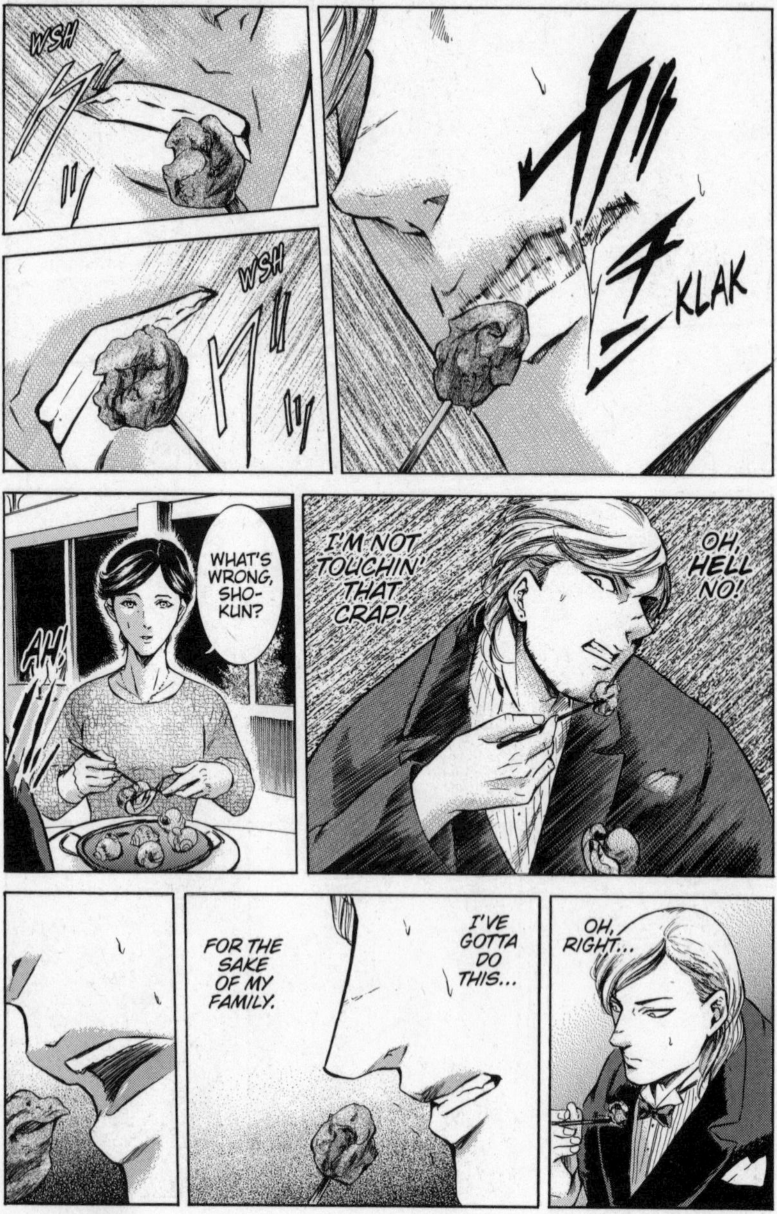
KLAK
WSH
WSH
OH, HELL NO!
I'M NOT TOUCHIN' THAT CRAP!
WHAT'S WRONG, SHO-KUN?
AH!
OH, RIGHT...
I'VE GOTTA DO THIS...
FOR THE SAKE OF MY FAMILY.

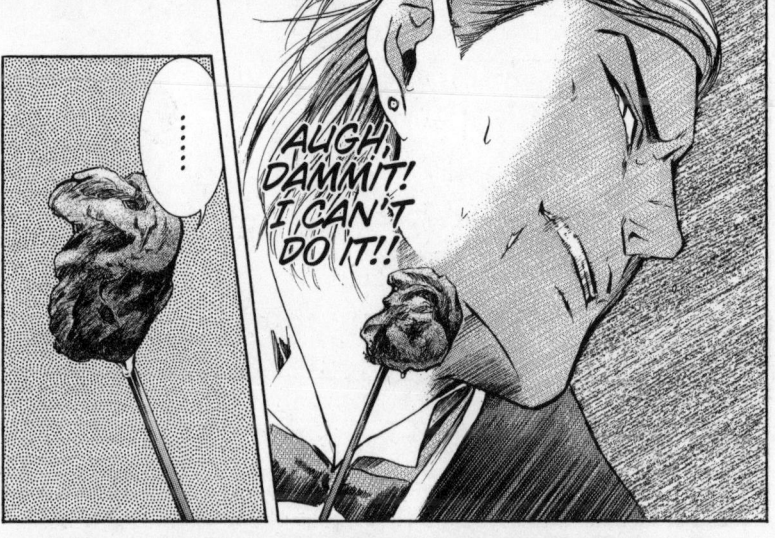

AUGH, DAMMIT! I CAN'T DO IT!!
......
TINK
JEEZ, ANYONE WHO EATS THESE THINGS...
TINK
TINK
MUST BE A TOTAL NUT-CASE.
SKFF
SKFF
HUH?
TWRL
WHAT?
TWITCH

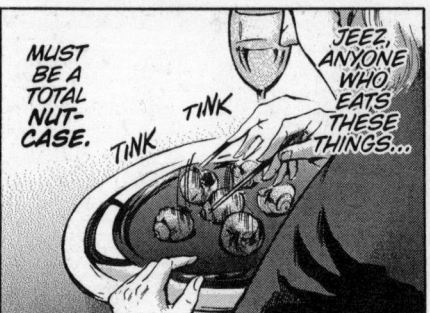

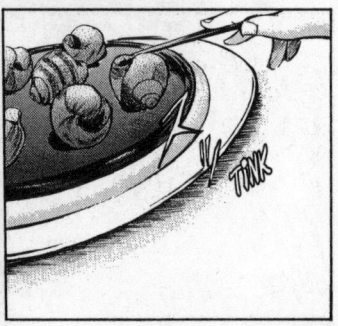

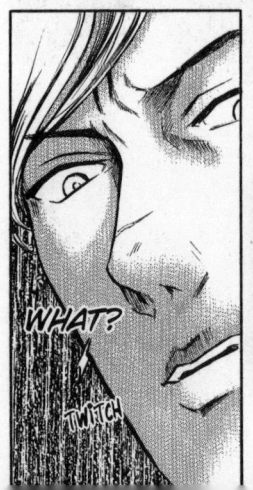

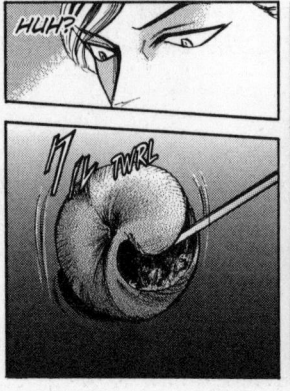

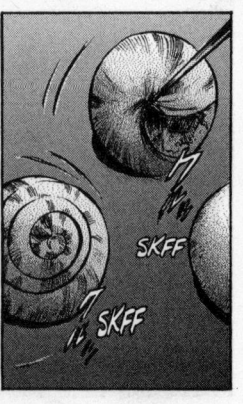

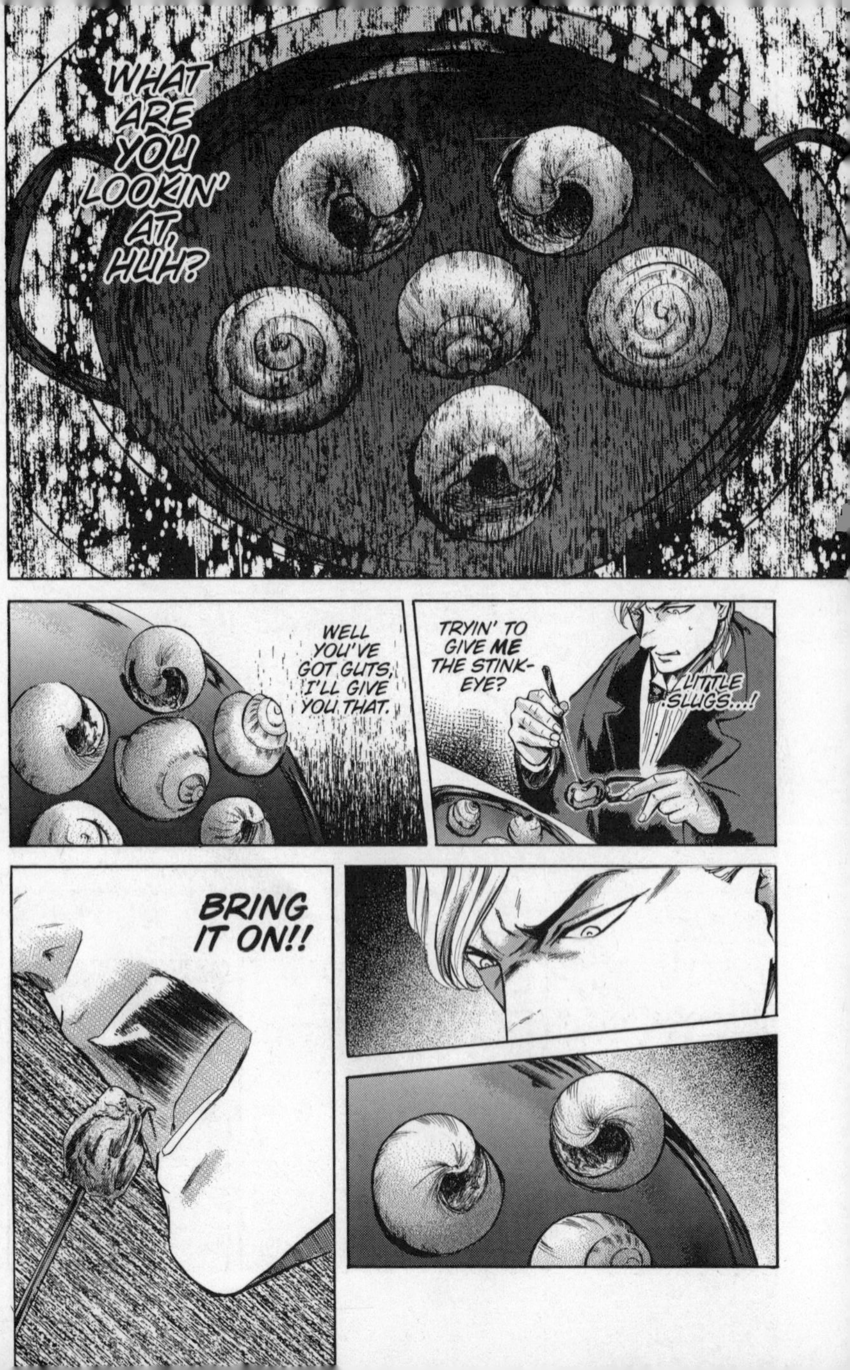
WHAT ARE YOU LOOKIN' AT, HUH?
TRYIN' TO GIVE ME THE STINK-EYE?
LITTLE SLUGS...!
WELL YOU'VE GOT GUTS, I'LL GIVE YOU THAT.
BRING IT ON!!

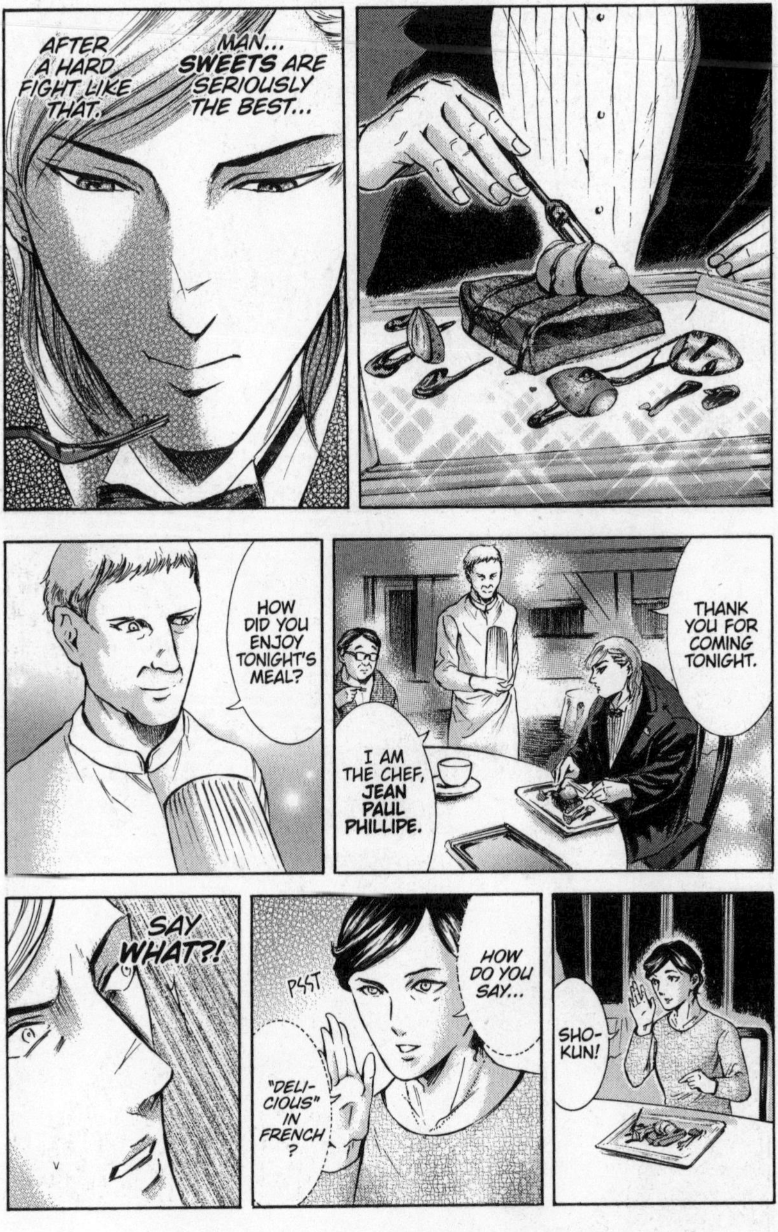
MAN... SWEETS ARE SERIOUSLY THE BEST...
AFTER A HARD FIGHT LIKE THAT.
THANK YOU FOR COMING TONIGHT.
I AM THE CHEF, JEAN PAUL PHILLIPE.
HOW DID YOU ENJOY TONIGHT'S MEAL?
SHO-KUN!
HOW DO YOU SAY...
PSST
"DELICIOUS" IN FRENCH?
SAY WHAT?!

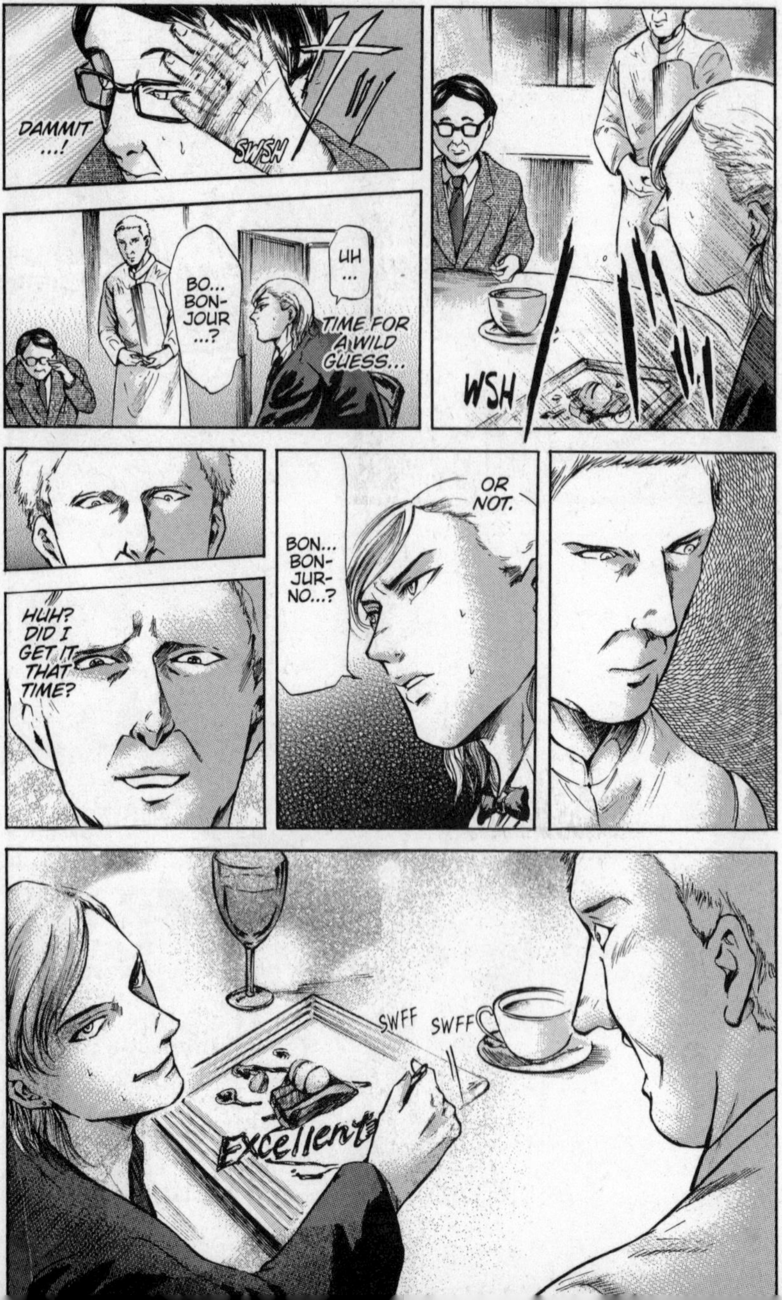
WSH
DAMMIT ...!
SWSH
BO... BONJOUR ...?
UH ...
TIME FOR A WILD GUESS...
BON... BONJURNO...?
OR NOT.
HUH? DID I GET IT THAT TIME?
SWFF
SWFF
Excellent

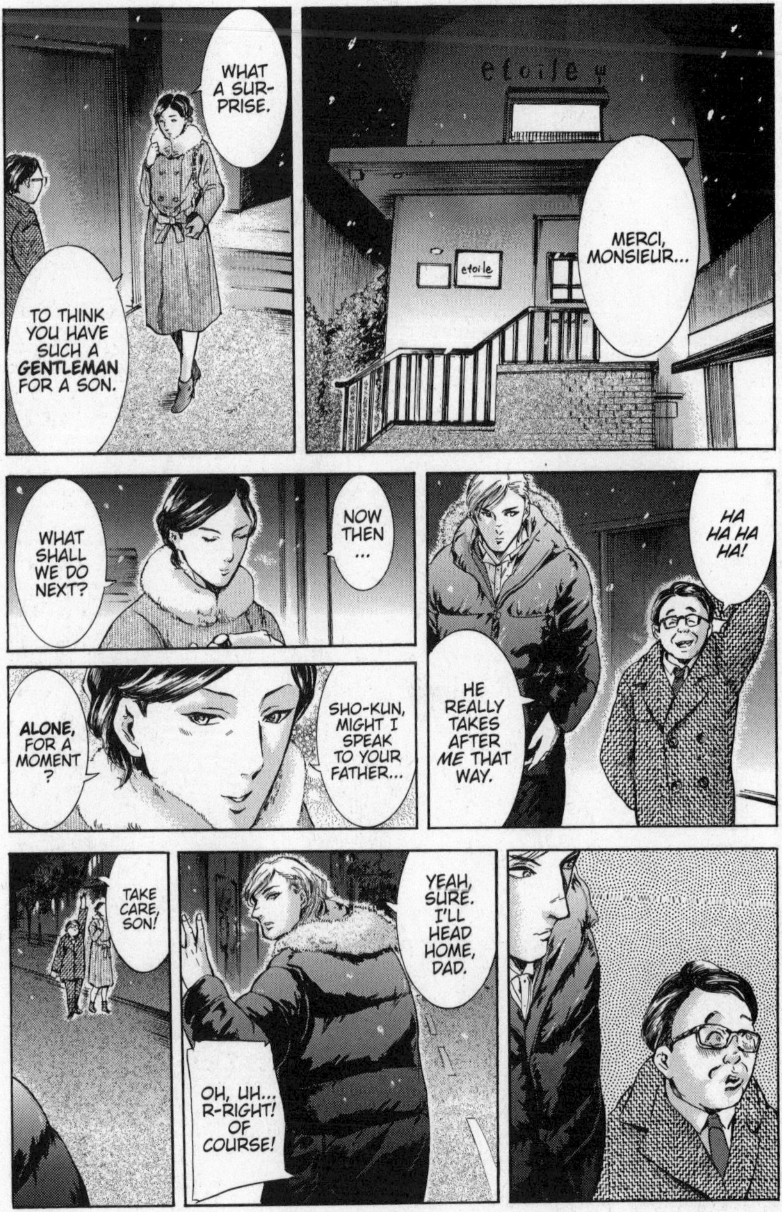
etoile
MERCI, MONSIEUR...
etoile
WHAT A SUR-PRISE.
TO THINK YOU HAVE SUCH A **GENTLEMAN** FOR A SON.
HA HA HA HA!
HE REALLY TAKES AFTER *ME* THAT WAY.
NOW THEN ...
WHAT SHALL WE DO NEXT?
SHO-KUN, MIGHT I SPEAK TO YOUR FATHER...
ALONE, FOR A MOMENT ?
YEAH, SURE. I'LL HEAD HOME, DAD.
OH, UH... R-RIGHT! OF COURSE!
TAKE CARE, SON!

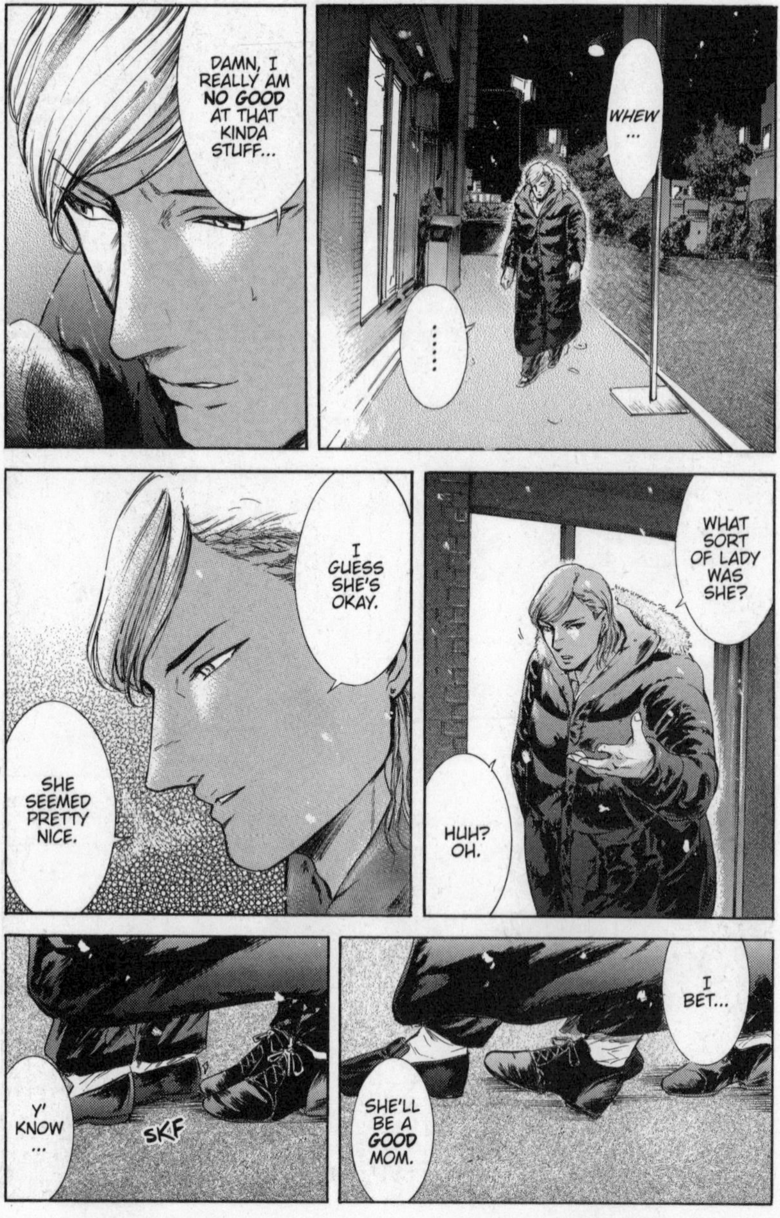
WHEW ...
......
DAMN, I REALLY AM NO GOOD AT THAT KINDA STUFF...
WHAT SORT OF LADY WAS SHE?
HUH? OH.
I GUESS SHE'S OKAY.
SHE SEEMED PRETTY NICE.
I BET...
SHE'LL BE A GOOD MOM.
SKF
Y' KNOW ...

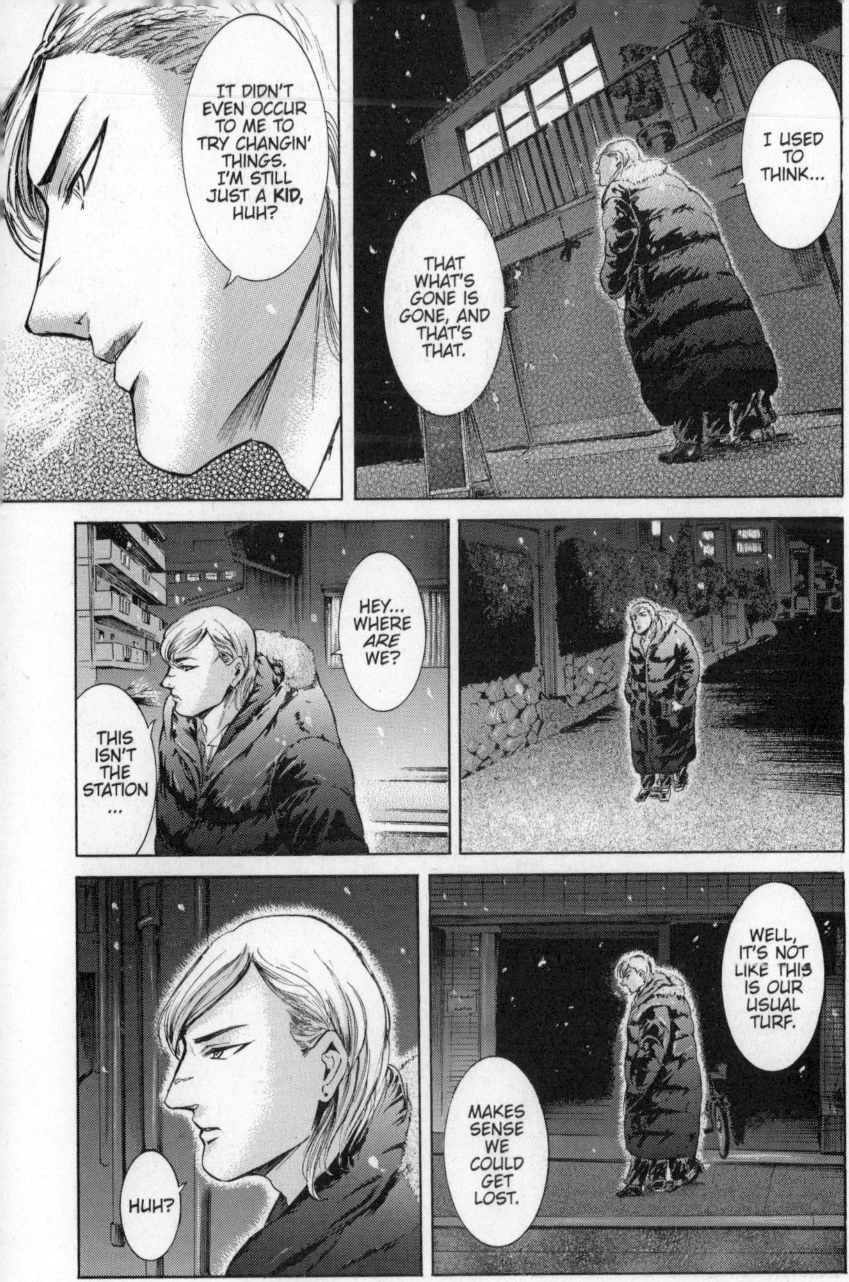
I USED TO THINK...
THAT WHAT'S GONE IS GONE, AND THAT'S THAT.
IT DIDN'T EVEN OCCUR TO ME TO TRY CHANGIN' THINGS. I'M STILL JUST A KID, HUH?
HEY... WHERE ARE WE?
THIS ISN'T THE STATION ...
WELL, IT'S NOT LIKE THIS IS OUR USUAL TURF.
MAKES SENSE WE COULD GET LOST.
HUH?

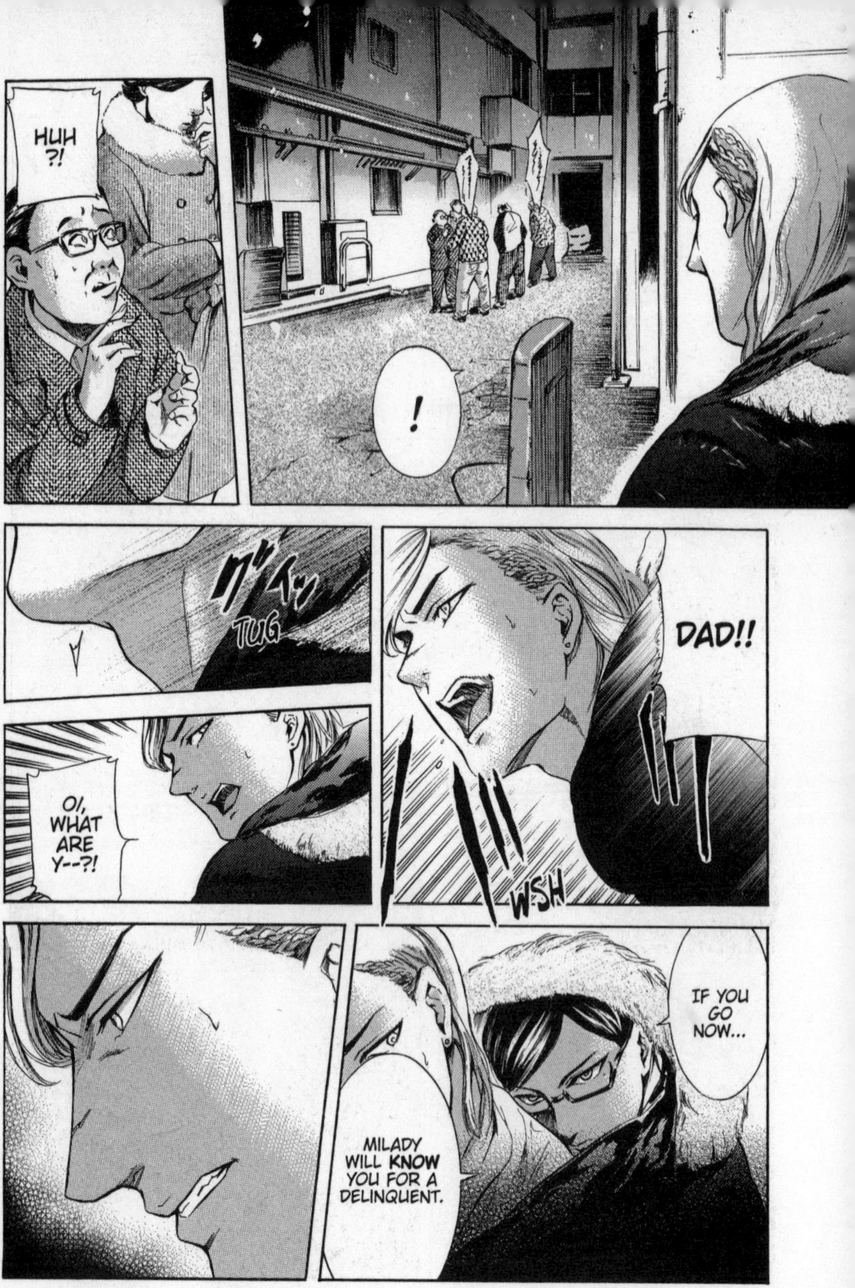
!
HUH ?!
DAD!!
WSH
TUG
OI, WHAT ARE Y--?!
IF YOU GO NOW...
MILADY WILL **KNOW** YOU FOR A DELINQUENT.

YO, SAKA- MOTO...

EEEK!

I'M SORRY! I'M SORRY! I'M SORRRRY!!

NO.

YOU KNOW HOW TO FIGHT?

THEN IT'S TIME WE SWITCH THINGS UP.

SIR, IF YOU WOULD PLEASE ABSTAIN.

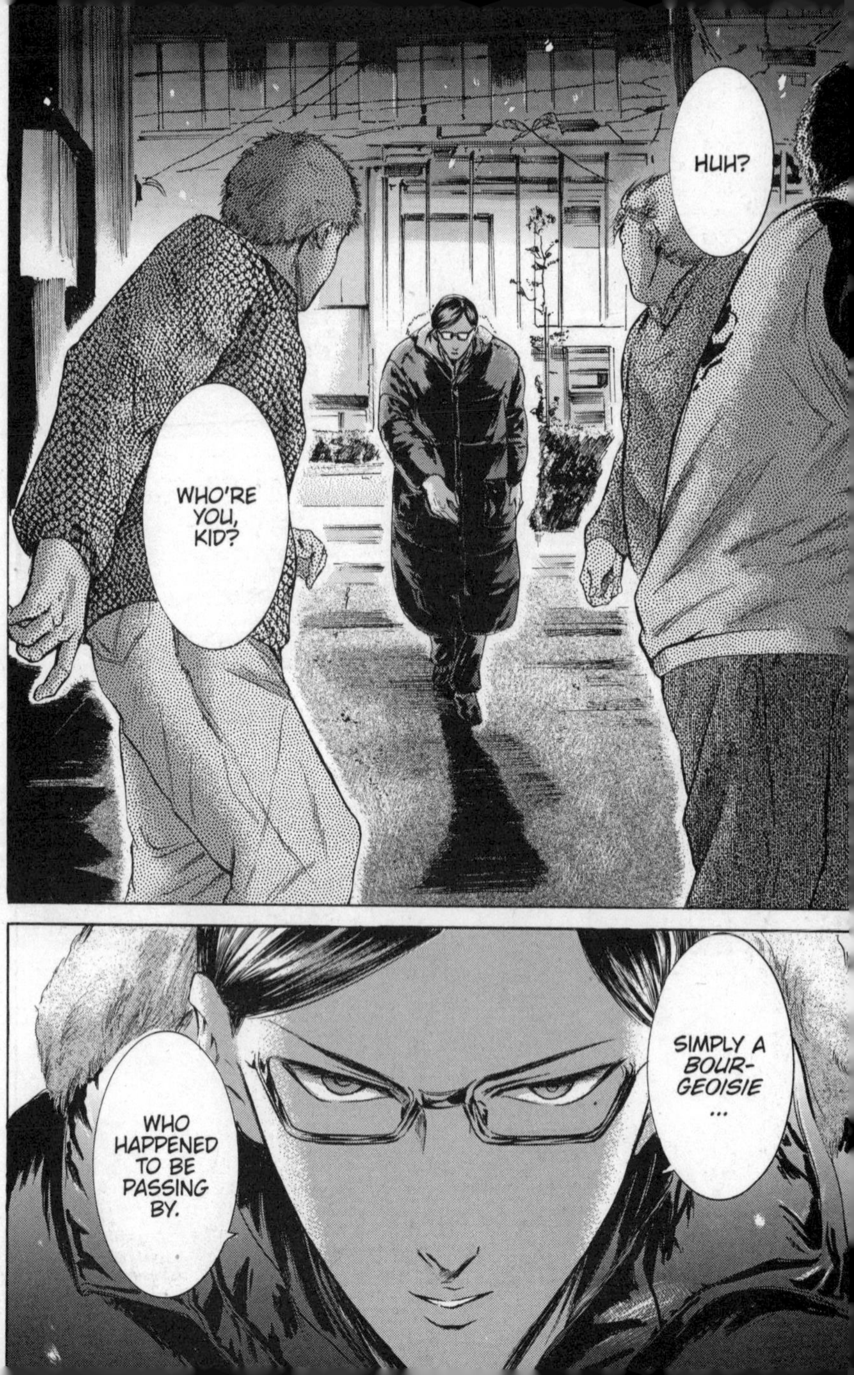
HUH?
WHO'RE YOU, KID?
SIMPLY A BOURGEOISIE ...
WHO HAPPENED TO BE PASSING BY.

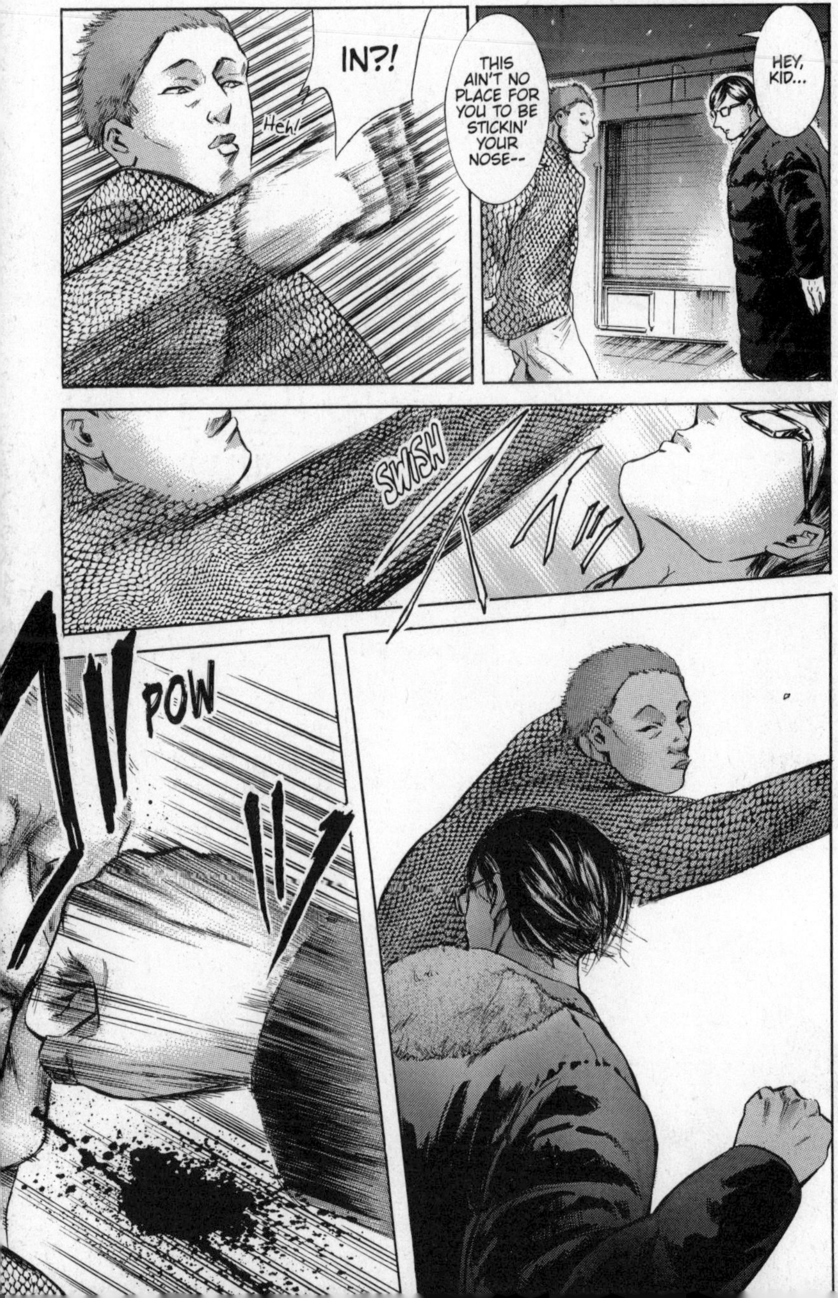
HEY, KID...
THIS AIN'T NO PLACE FOR YOU TO BE STICKIN' YOUR NOSE--
IN?!
Heh!
SWISH
POW

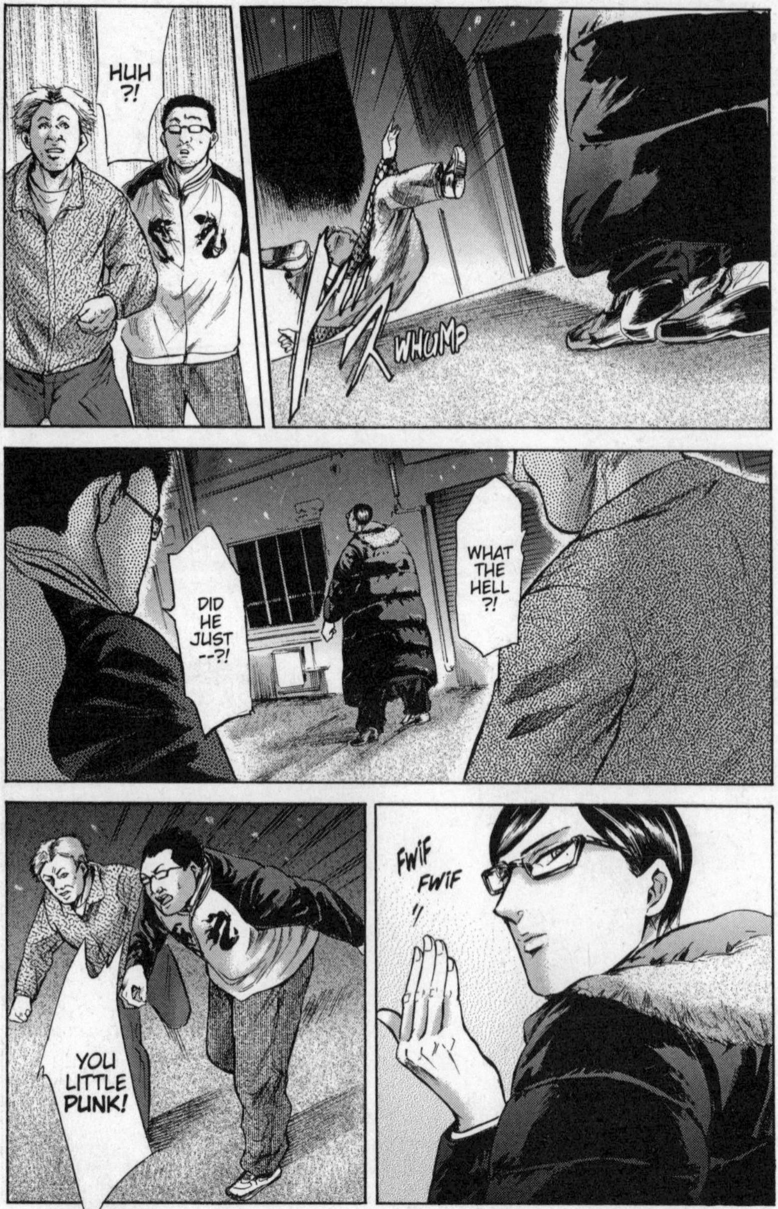
WHUMP
HUH ?!
WHAT THE HELL ?!
DID HE JUST --?!
FWIF FWIF
YOU LITTLE PUNK!

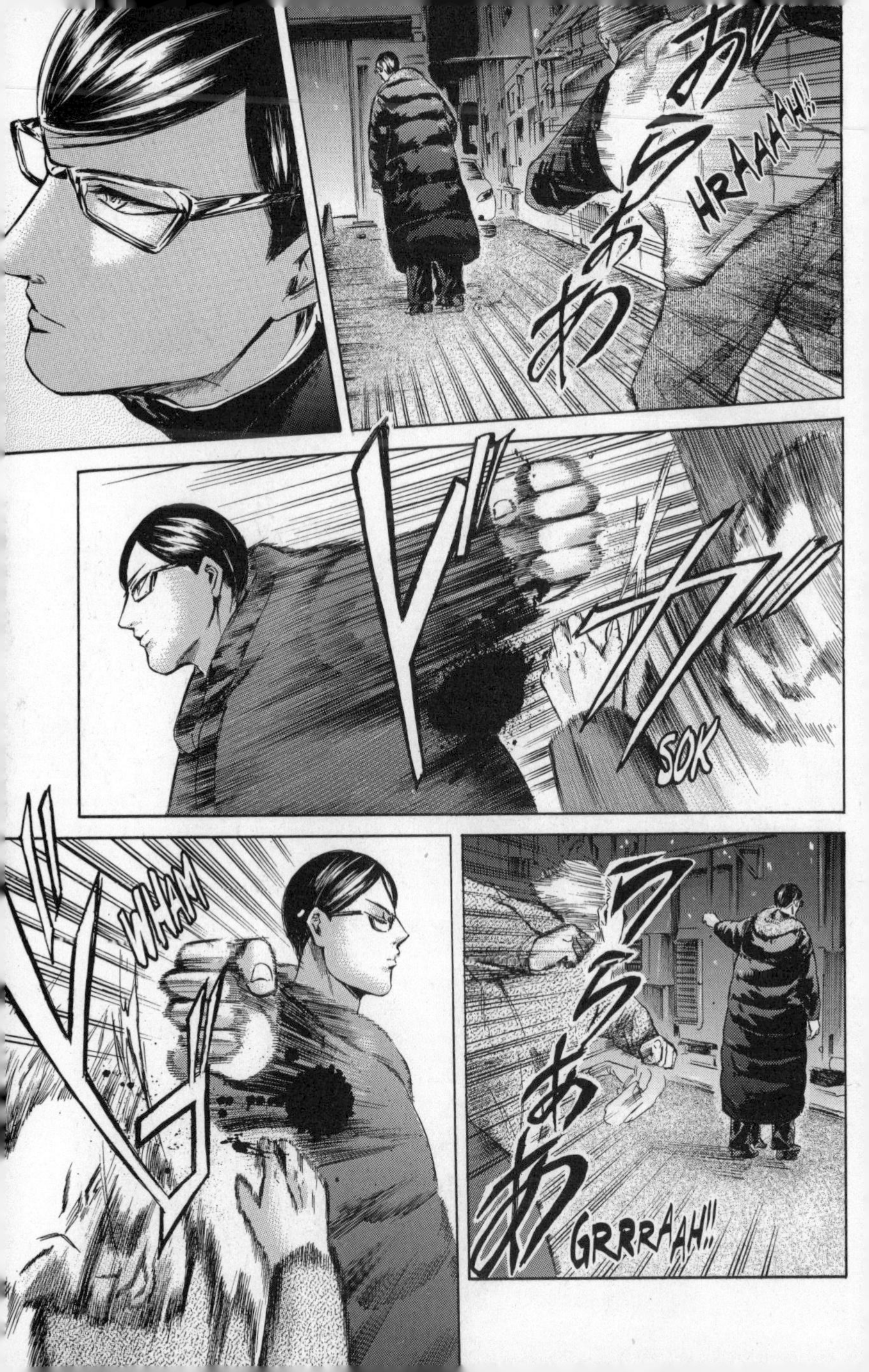
うらああ
HRAAAAH!!
SOK
うらああ
GRRRAAH!!
WHAM

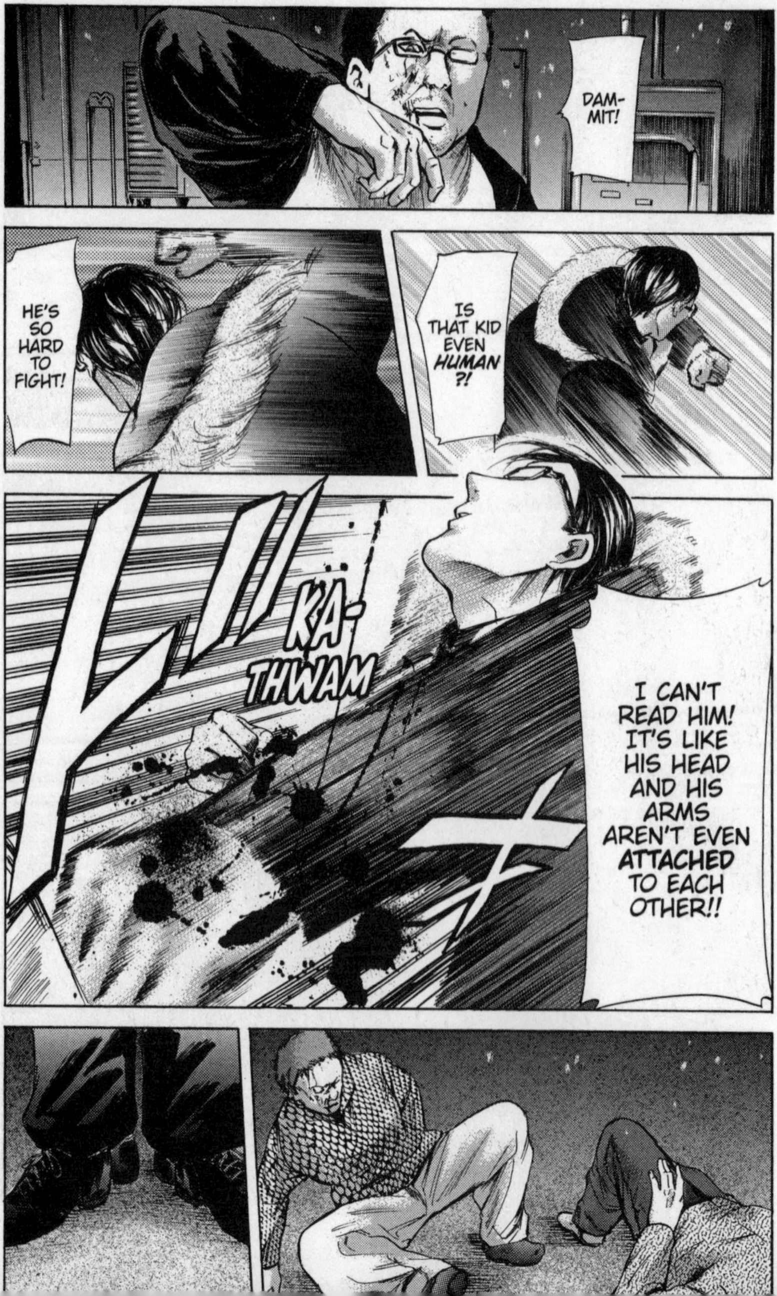
DAM-MIT!
IS THAT KID EVEN HUMAN?!
HE'S SO HARD TO FIGHT!
KA-THWAM
I CAN'T READ HIM! IT'S LIKE HIS HEAD AND HIS ARMS AREN'T EVEN ATTACHED TO EACH OTHER!!

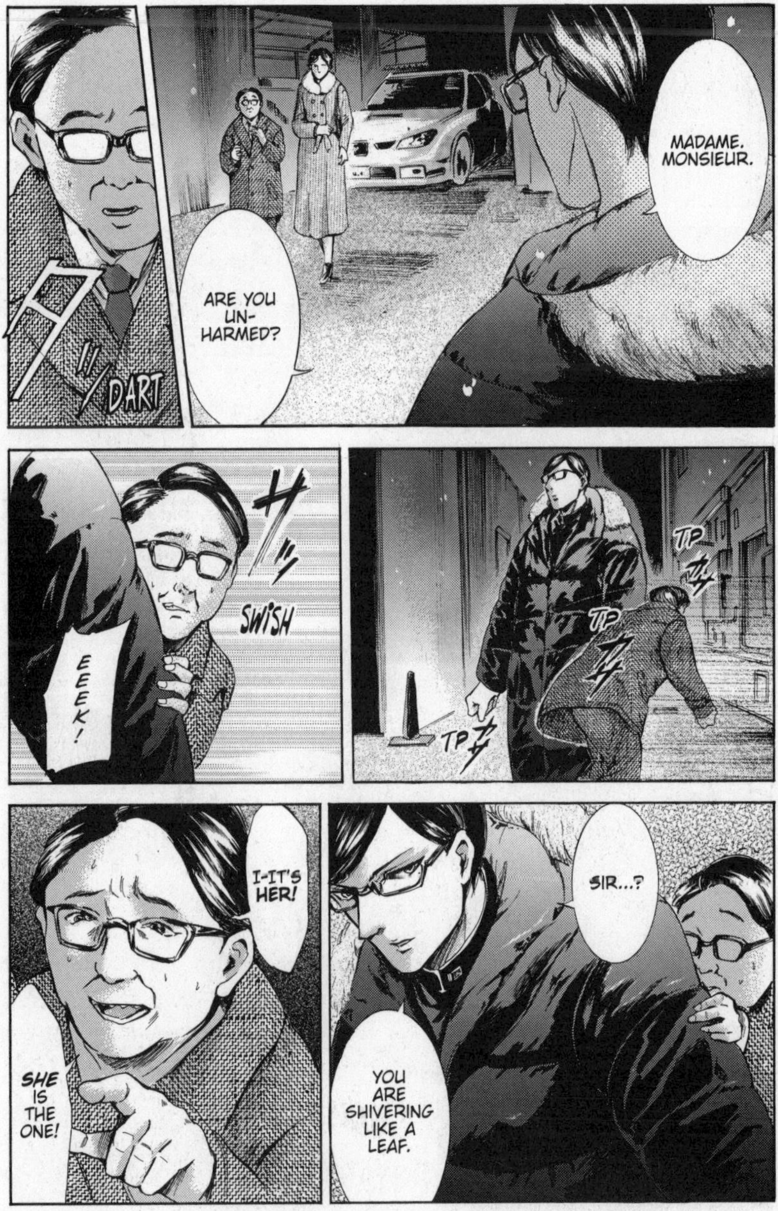
MADAME. MONSIEUR.
ARE YOU UN-HARMED?
DART
TP
TP
TP
SWISH
EEEK!
SIR...?
YOU ARE SHIVERING LIKE A LEAF.
I-IT'S HER!
SHE IS THE ONE!

THIS WAS ALL PART OF HER *SCAM!*
UM, I-I MEANT IT!
I R-REALLY *DON'T* HAVE ANY MONEY!
DON'T LIE TO ME.
HOW ELSE COULD YOU RAISE SUCH A **PRINCELY** SON?

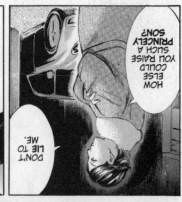

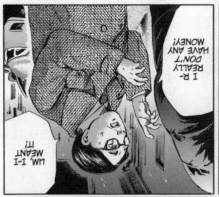

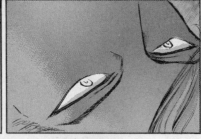

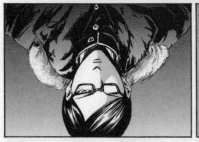

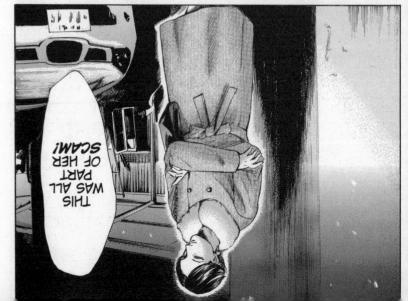

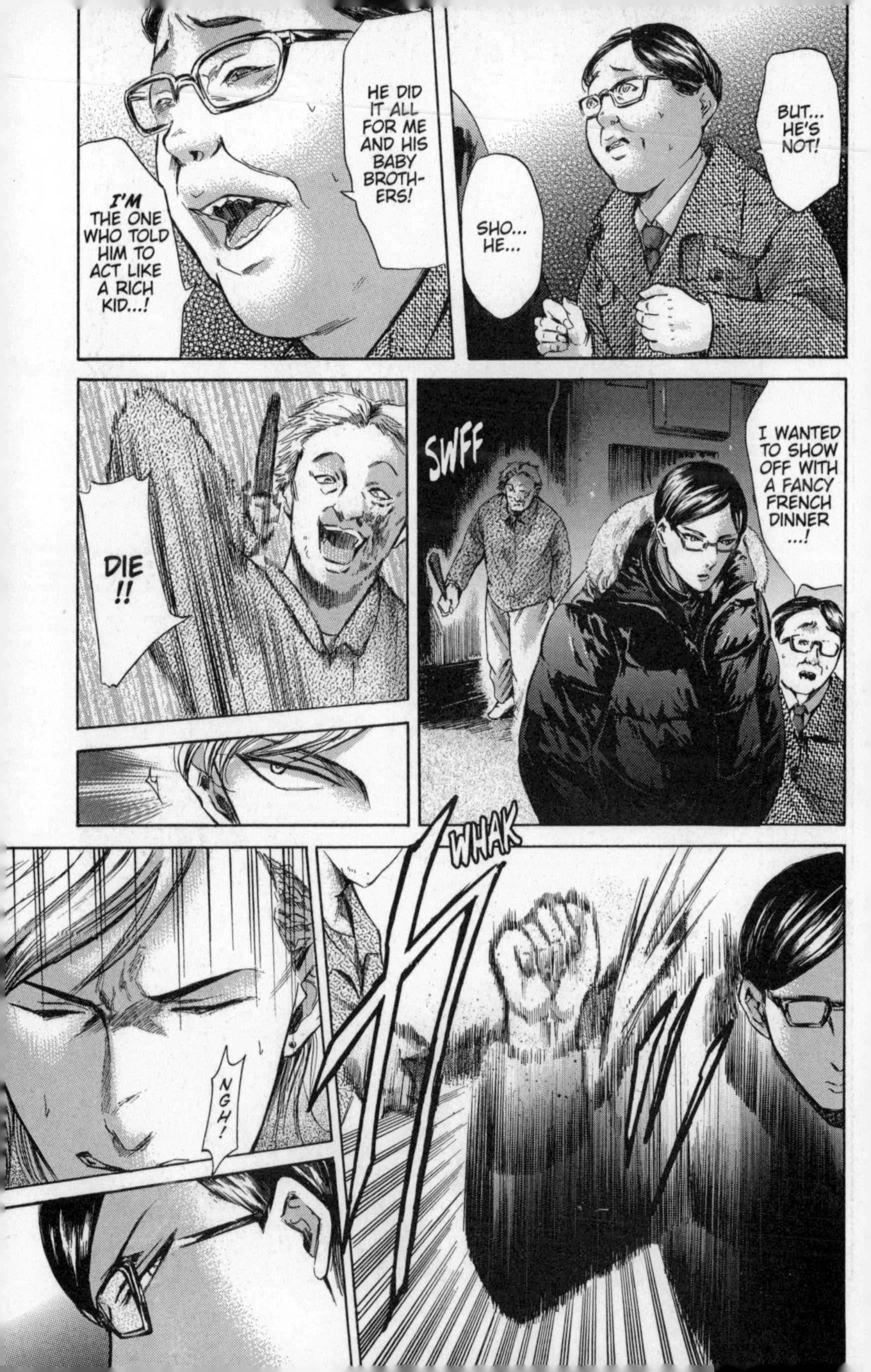
BUT... HE'S NOT!
SHO... HE...
HE DID IT ALL FOR ME AND HIS BABY BROTH-ERS!
I'M THE ONE WHO TOLD HIM TO ACT LIKE A RICH KID...!
I WANTED TO SHOW OFF WITH A FANCY FRENCH DINNER ...!
SWFF
DIE !!
WHAK
NGH!

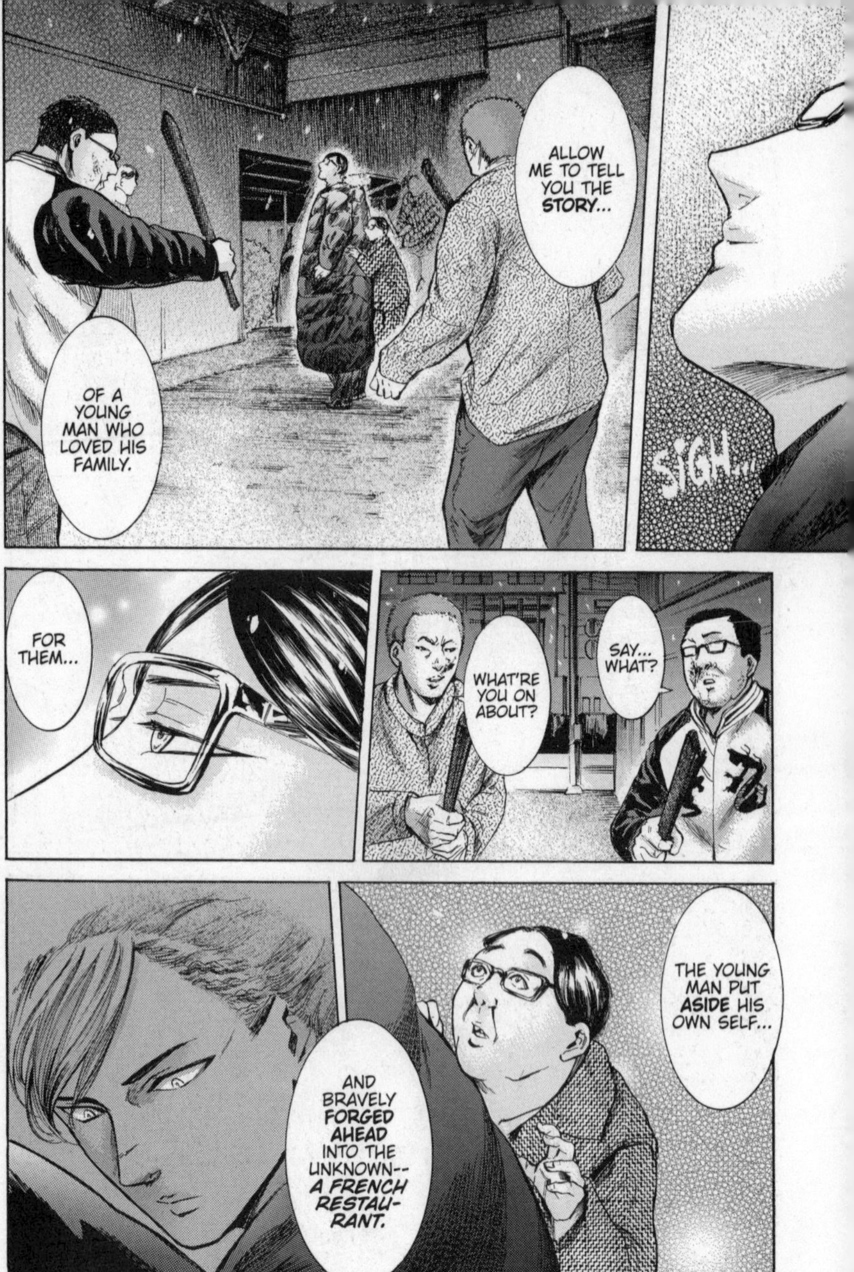
SIGH...
ALLOW ME TO TELL YOU THE STORY...
OF A YOUNG MAN WHO LOVED HIS FAMILY.
SAY... WHAT?
WHAT'RE YOU ON ABOUT?
FOR THEM...
THE YOUNG MAN PUT ASIDE HIS OWN SELF...
AND BRAVELY FORGED AHEAD INTO THE UNKNOWN-- A FRENCH RESTAU-RANT.

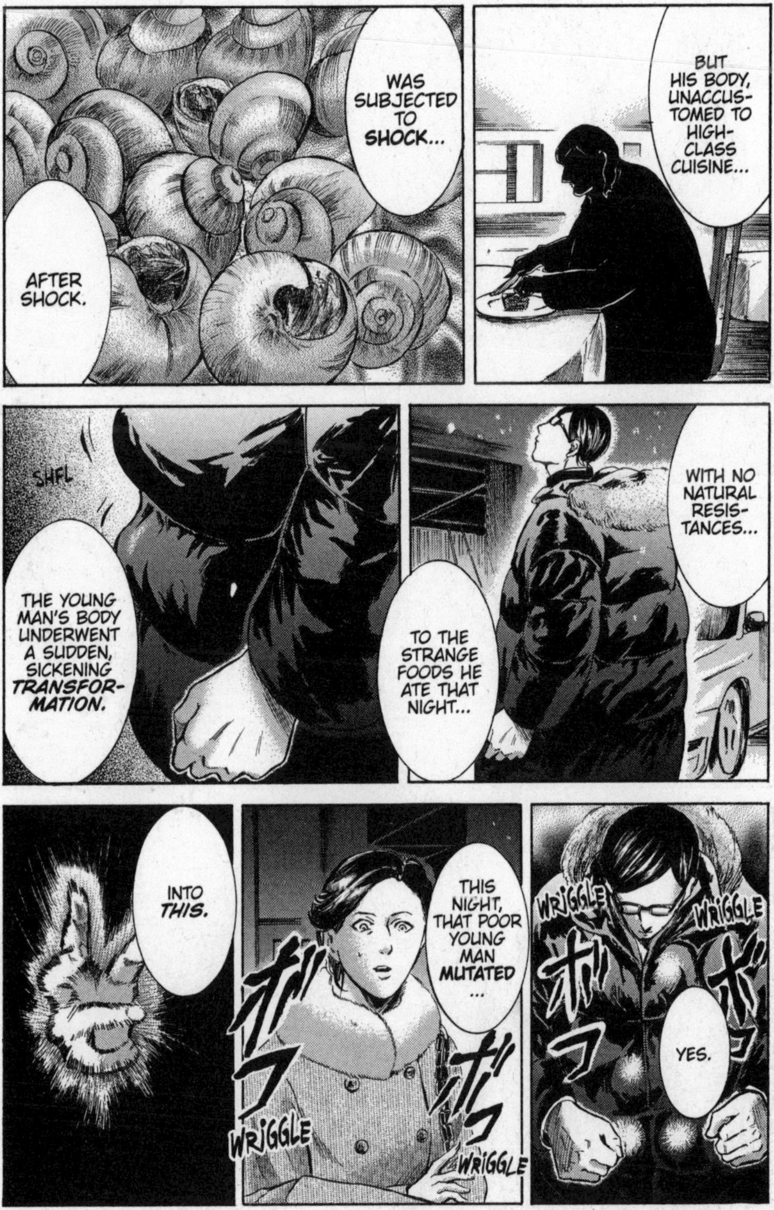
BUT HIS BODY, UNACCUSTOMED TO HIGH-CLASS CUISINE...
WAS SUBJECTED TO SHOCK...
AFTER SHOCK.
WITH NO NATURAL RESISTANCES...
TO THE STRANGE FOODS HE ATE THAT NIGHT...
SHFL
THE YOUNG MAN'S BODY UNDERWENT A SUDDEN, SICKENING TRANSFORMATION.
WRIGGLE
WRIGGLE
YES.
THIS NIGHT, THAT POOR YOUNG MAN MUTATED...
WRIGGLE
WRIGGLE
INTO THIS.

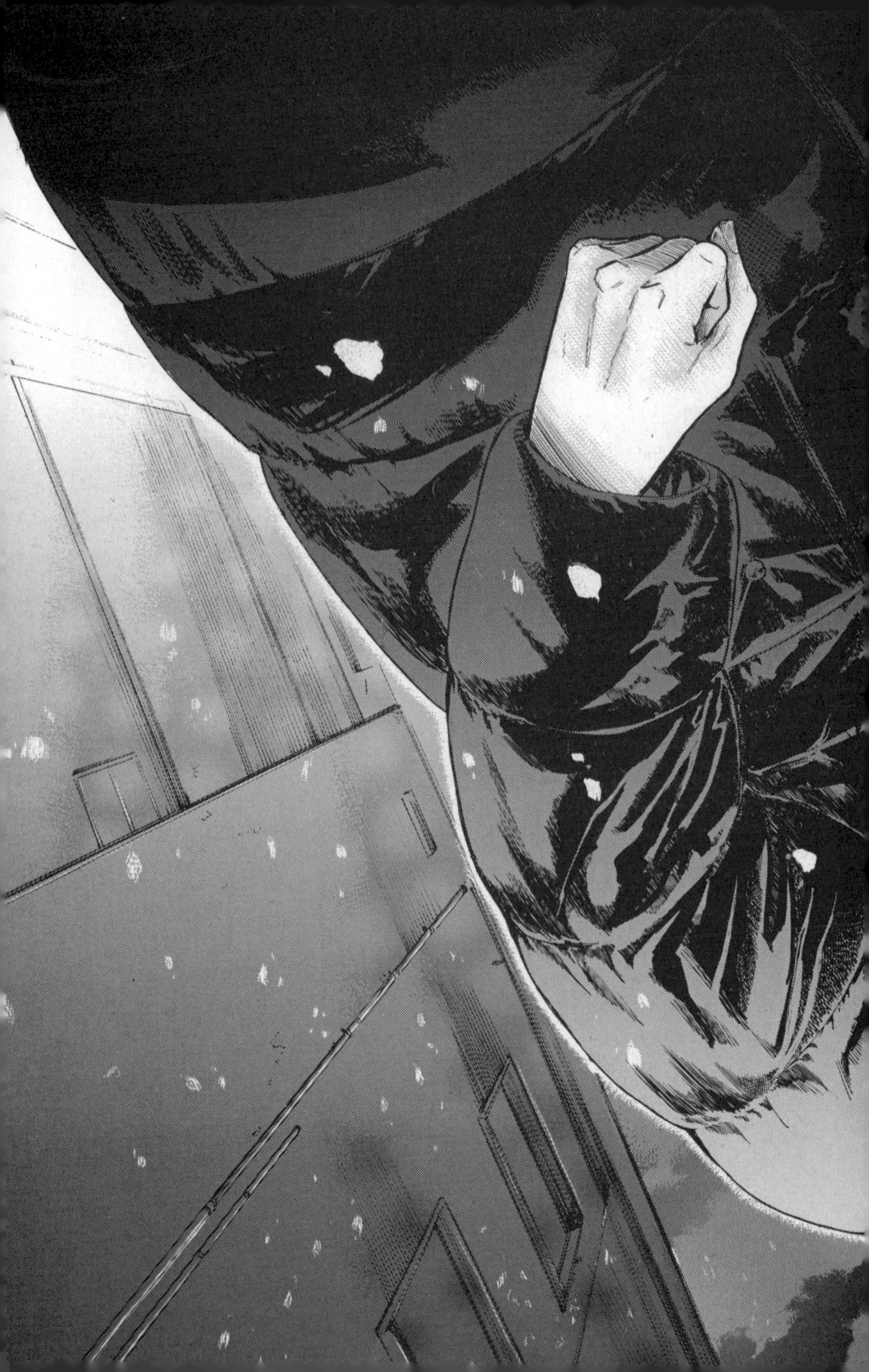

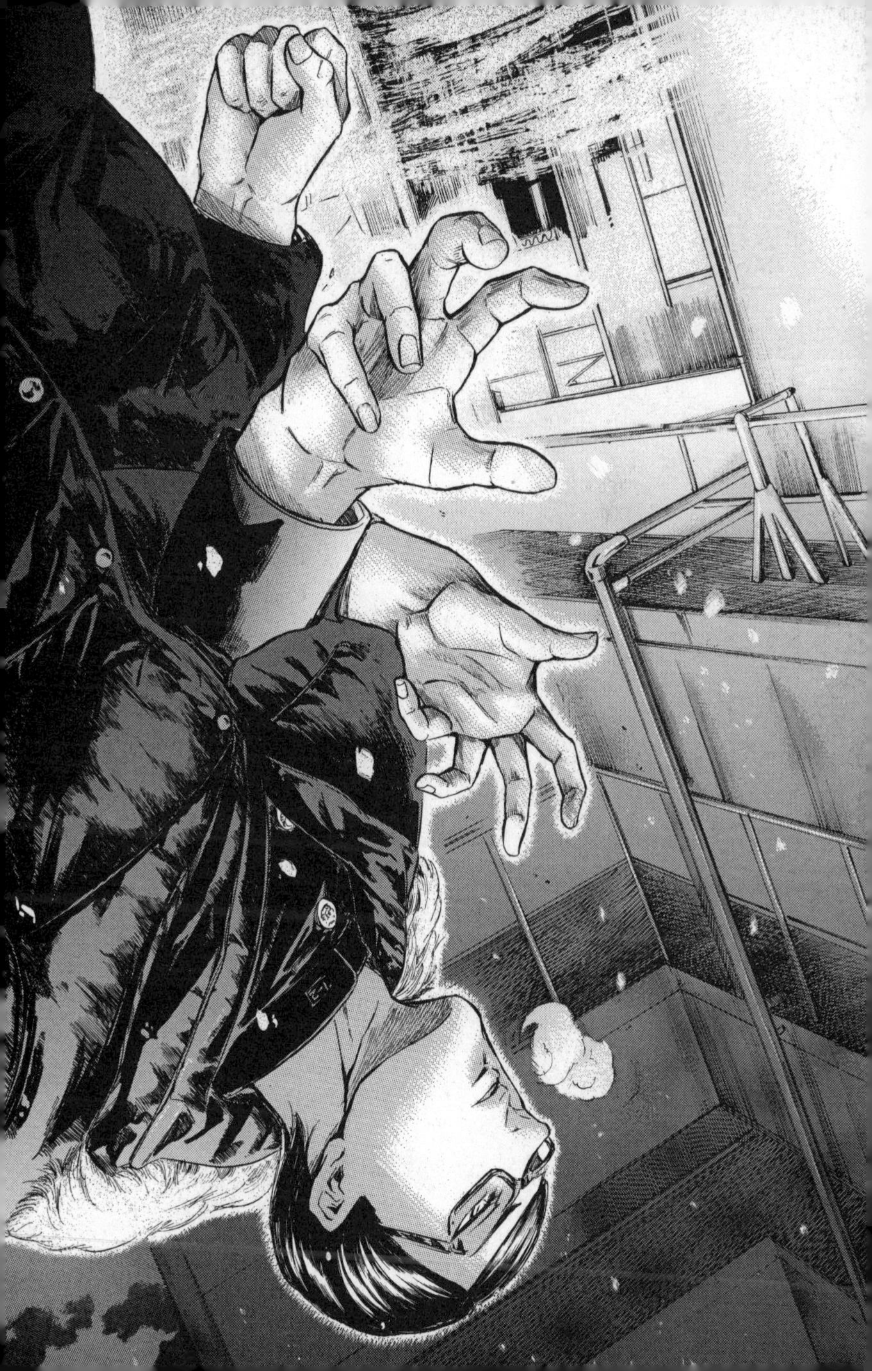

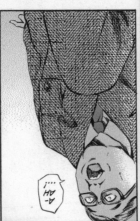

AH…!

AAAAAAAAAH!

THUMP

I-IT'S A MON-STER!!

AAAAH!!

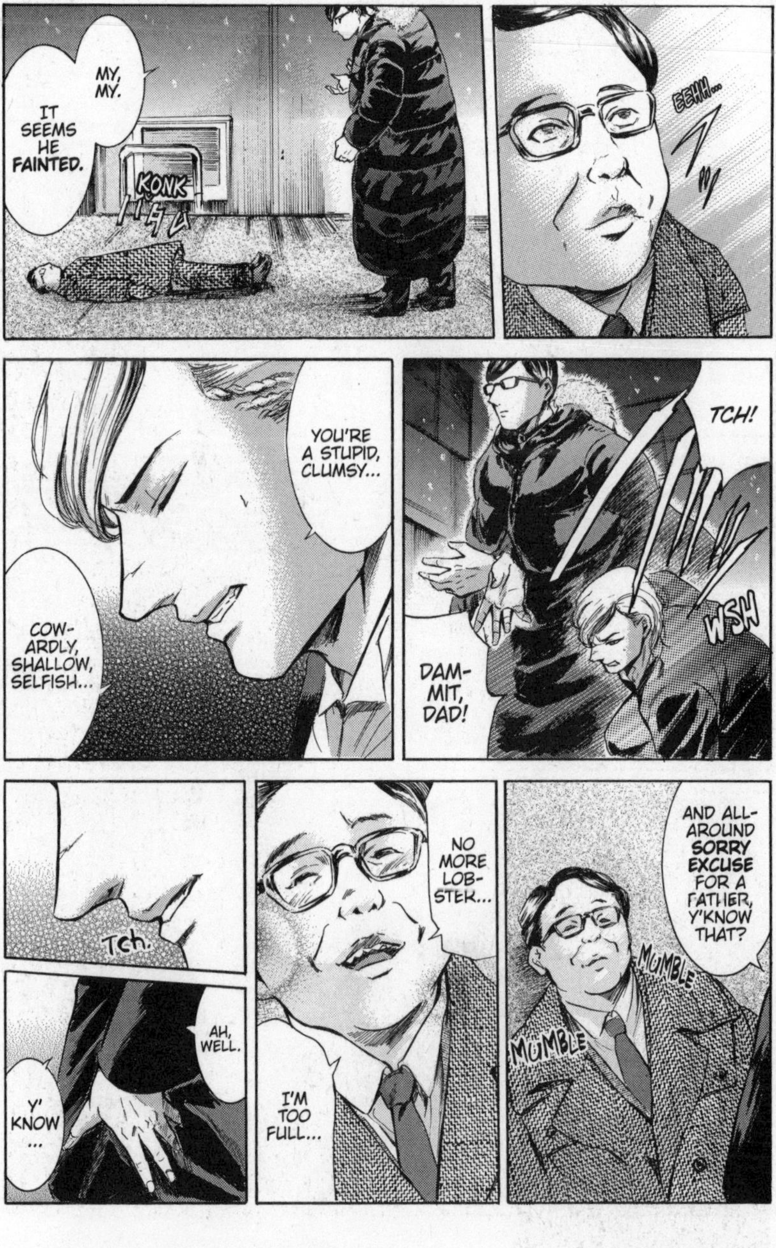
EEHH...
MY, MY.
IT SEEMS HE FAINTED.
KONK
TCH!
WSH
DAMMIT, DAD!
YOU'RE A STUPID, CLUMSY...
COWARDLY, SHALLOW, SELFISH...
AND ALL-AROUND SORRY EXCUSE FOR A FATHER, Y'KNOW THAT?
MUMBLE
MUMBLE
NO MORE LOBSTER...
I'M TOO FULL...
Tch.
AH, WELL.
Y' KNOW ...

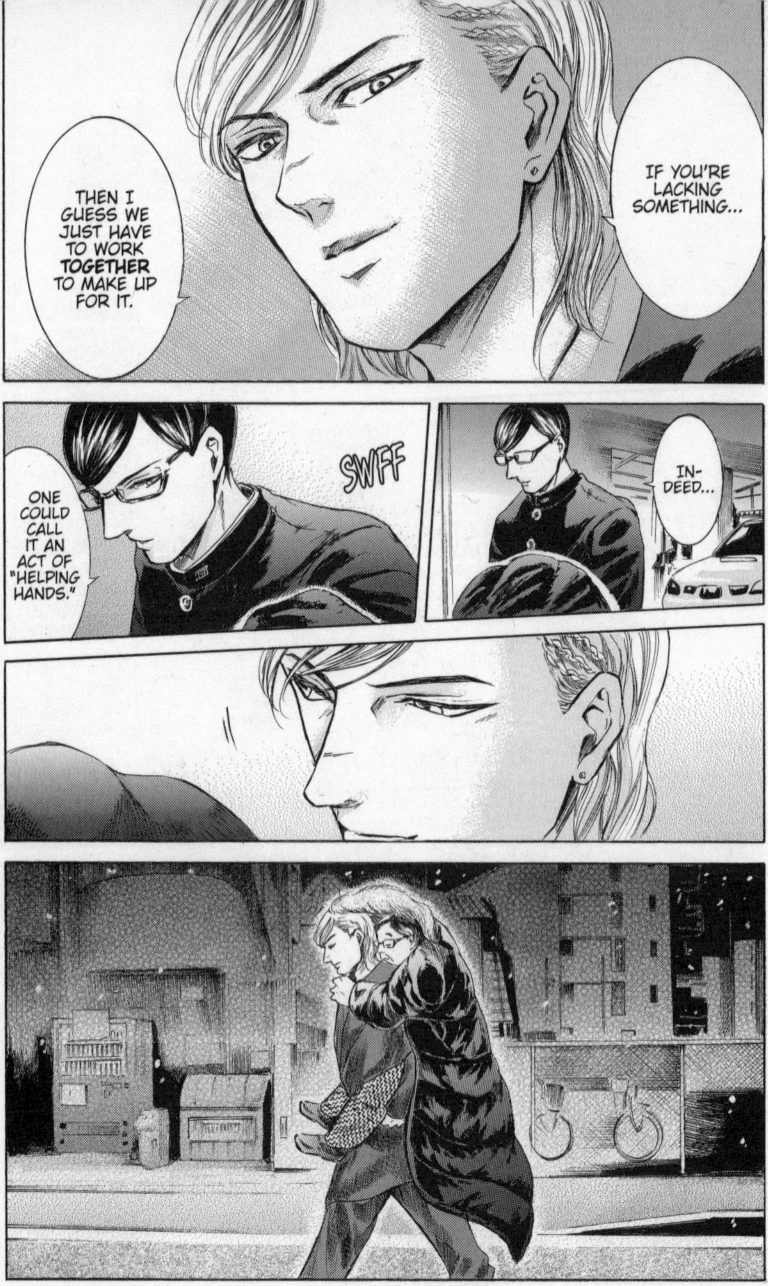
IF YOU'RE LACKING SOMETHING...
THEN I GUESS WE JUST HAVE TO WORK **TOGETHER** TO MAKE UP FOR IT.
IN-DEED...
SWFF
ONE COULD CALL IT AN ACT OF "HELPING HANDS."

End of Chapter 21

Let's Play with
Sakamoto #4

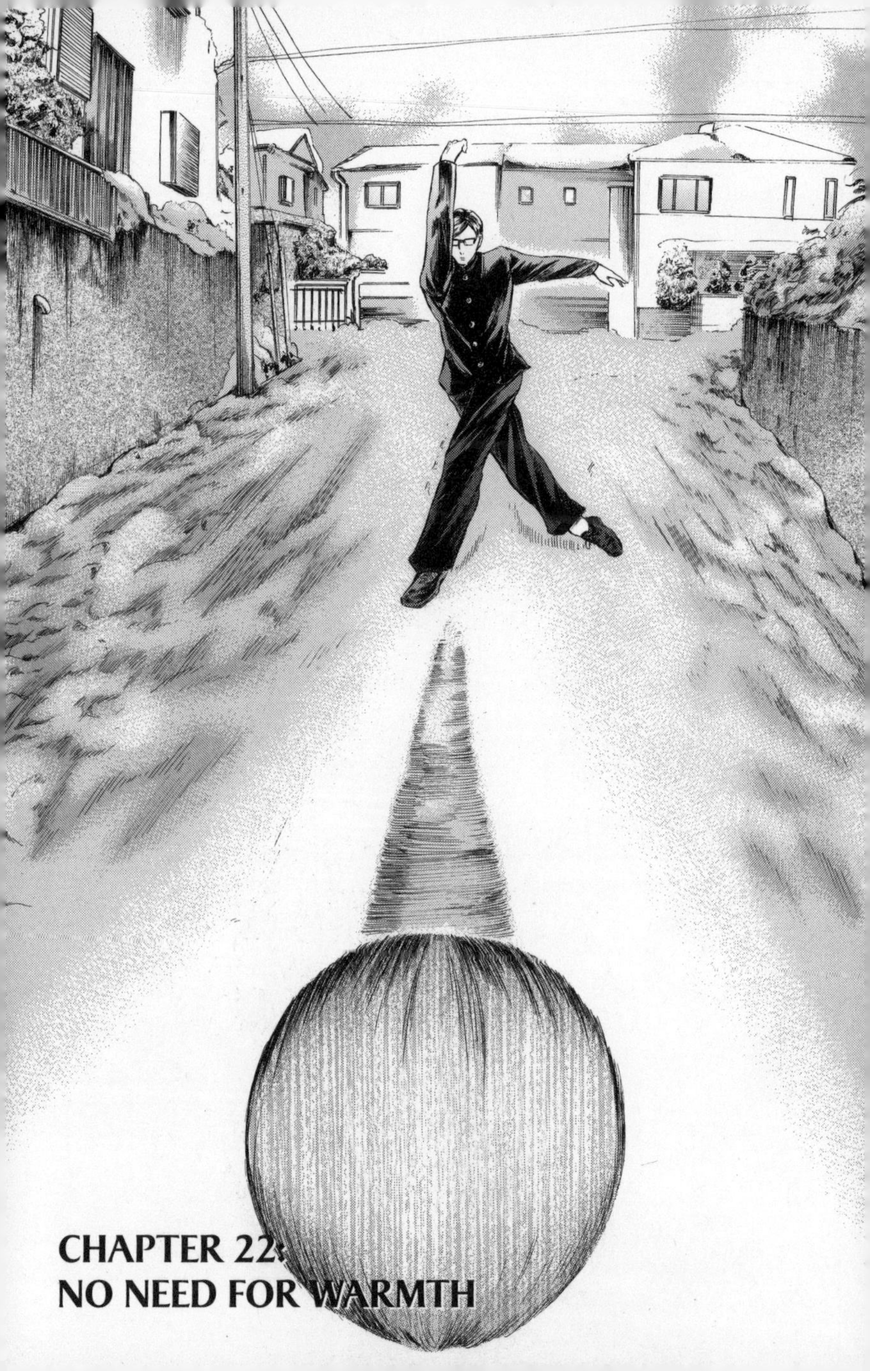

CHAPTER 22: NO NEED FOR WARMTH

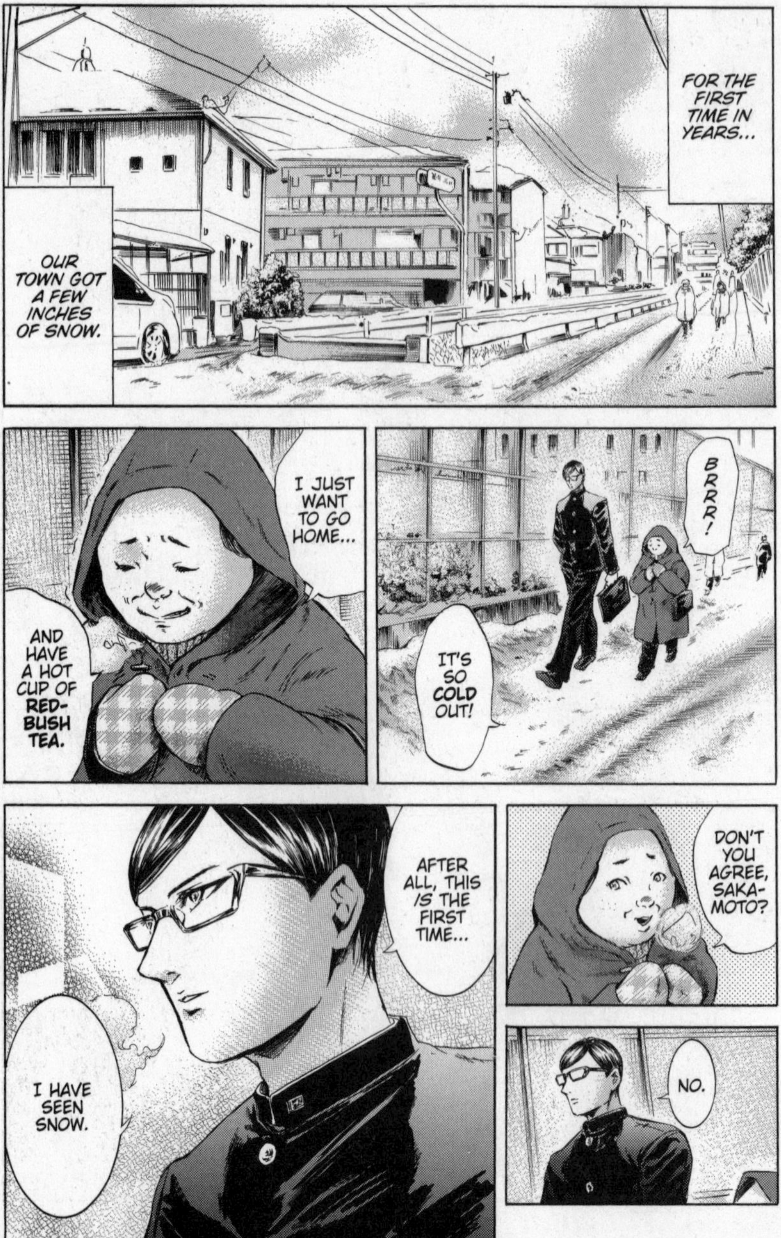
FOR THE FIRST TIME IN YEARS...
OUR TOWN GOT A FEW INCHES OF SNOW.
BRRR!
IT'S SO COLD OUT!
I JUST WANT TO GO HOME...
AND HAVE A HOT CUP OF RED-BUSH TEA.
DON'T YOU AGREE, SAKA-MOTO?
NO.
AFTER ALL, THIS IS THE FIRST TIME...
I HAVE SEEN SNOW.

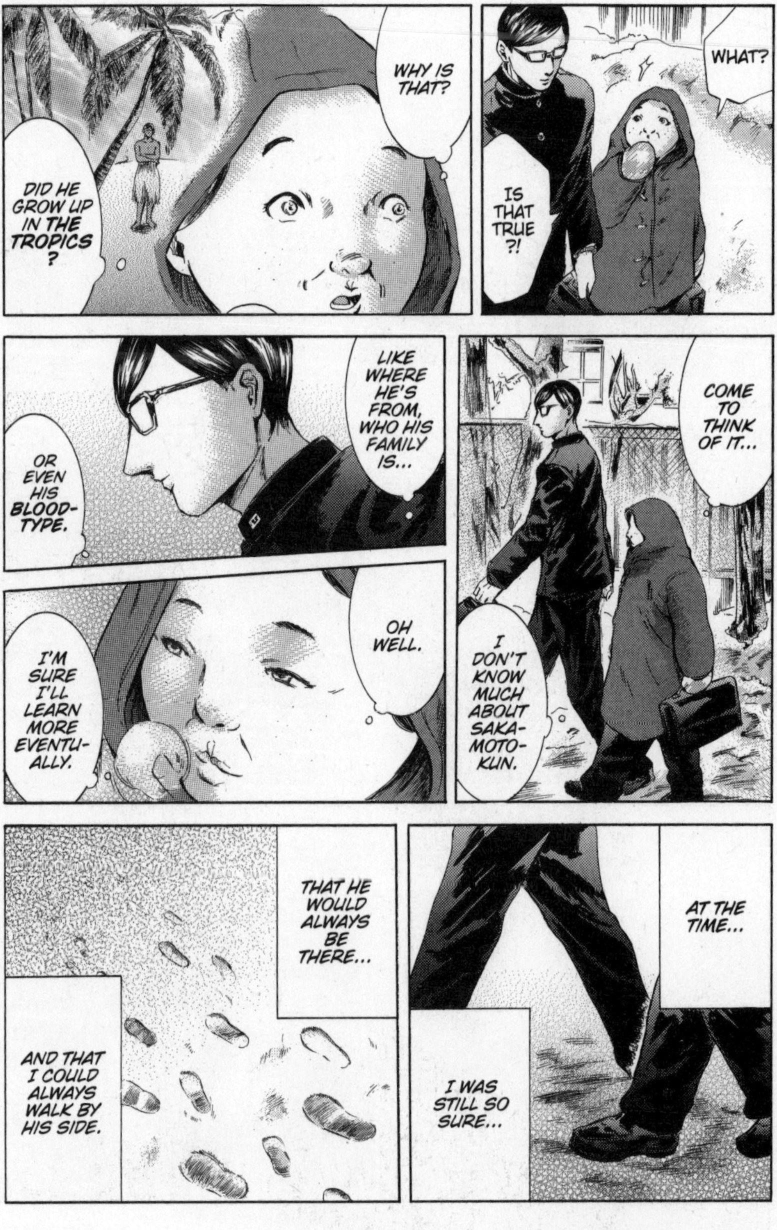
WHAT?
IS THAT TRUE ?!
WHY IS THAT?
DID HE GROW UP IN THE TROPICS ?
COME TO THINK OF IT...
I DON'T KNOW MUCH ABOUT SAKA-MOTO-KUN.
LIKE WHERE HE'S FROM, WHO HIS FAMILY IS...
OR EVEN HIS BLOOD-TYPE.
OH WELL.
I'M SURE I'LL LEARN MORE EVENTU-ALLY.
AT THE TIME...
I WAS STILL SO SURE...
THAT HE WOULD ALWAYS BE THERE...
AND THAT I COULD ALWAYS WALK BY HIS SIDE.

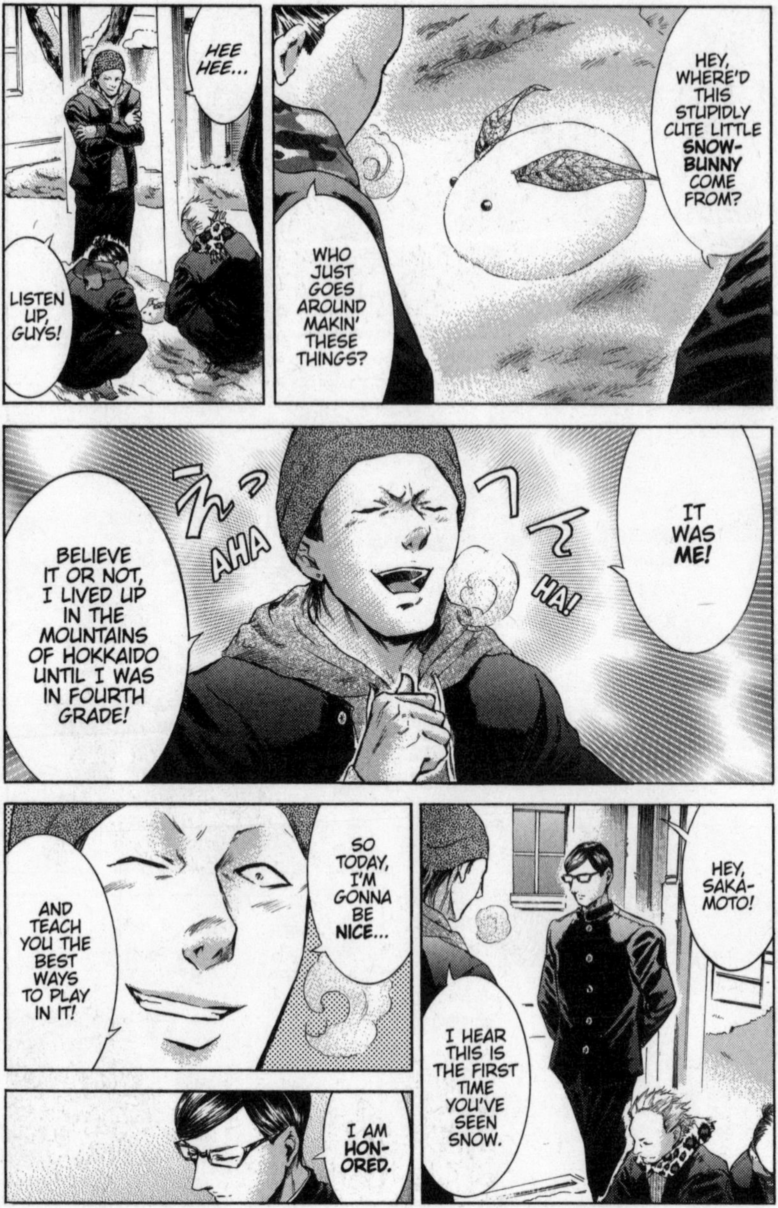
HEY, WHERE'D THIS STUPIDLY CUTE LITTLE **SNOW-BUNNY** COME FROM?
WHO JUST GOES AROUND MAKIN' THESE THINGS?
HEE HEE...
LISTEN UP, GUYS!
IT WAS **ME!**
HA!
AHA
BELIEVE IT OR NOT, I LIVED UP IN THE MOUNTAINS OF HOKKAIDO UNTIL I WAS IN FOURTH GRADE!
HEY, SAKA-MOTO!
I HEAR THIS IS THE FIRST TIME YOU'VE SEEN SNOW.
SO TODAY, I'M GONNA BE **NICE...**
AND TEACH YOU THE BEST WAYS TO PLAY IN IT!
I AM HON-ORED.

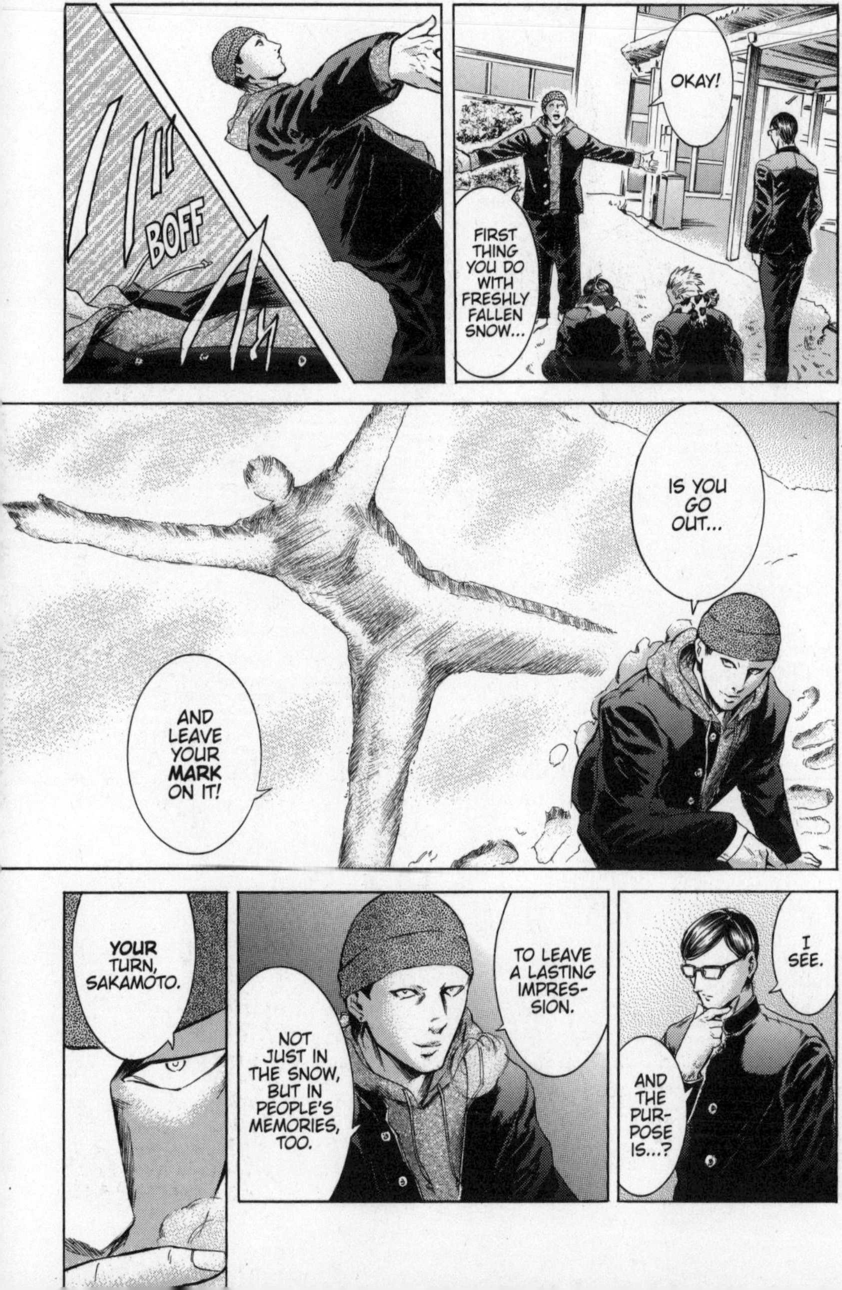
OKAY!
FIRST THING YOU DO WITH FRESHLY FALLEN SNOW...
BOFF
IS YOU GO OUT...
AND LEAVE YOUR **MARK** ON IT!
I SEE.
AND THE PUR-POSE IS...?
TO LEAVE A LASTING IMPRES-SION.
NOT JUST IN THE SNOW, BUT IN PEOPLE'S MEMORIES, TOO.
YOUR TURN, SAKAMOTO.

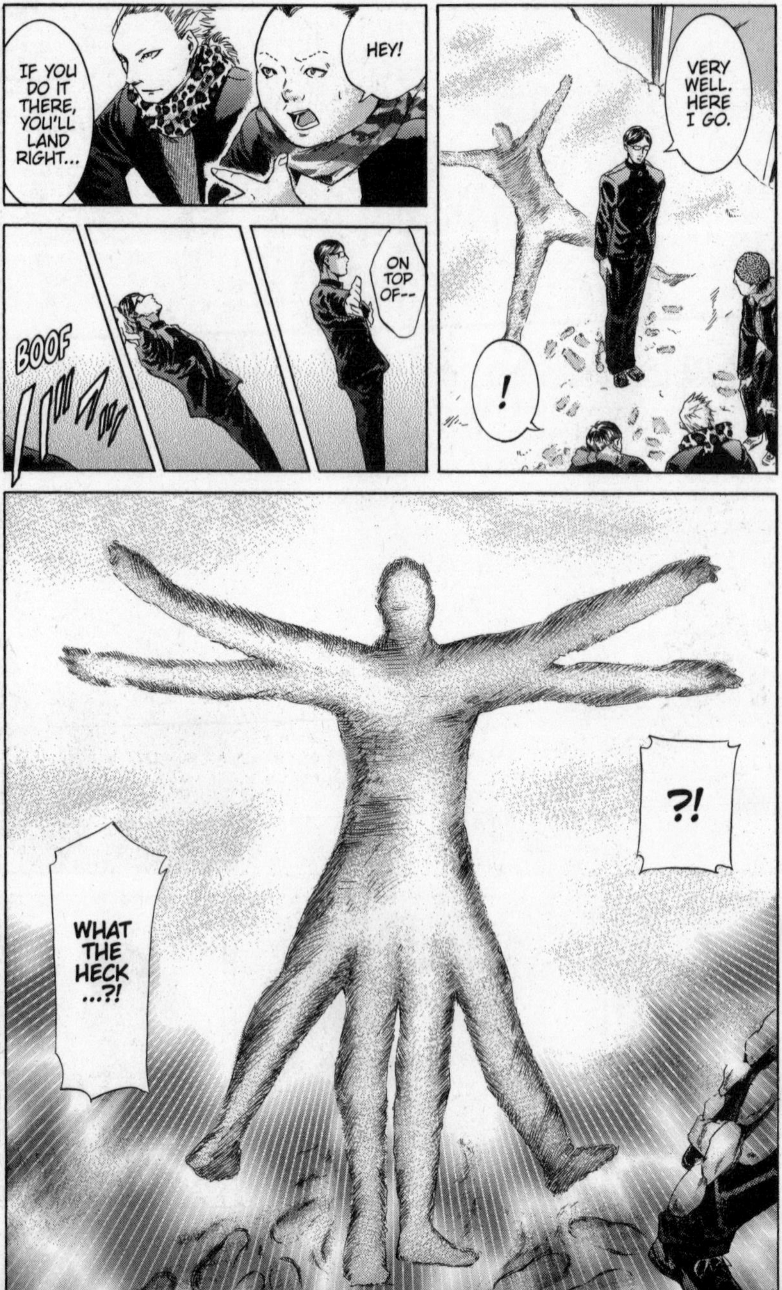
VERY WELL. HERE I GO.
!
HEY!
IF YOU DO IT THERE, YOU'LL LAND RIGHT...
ON TOP OF--
BOOF
?!
WHAT THE HECK ...?!

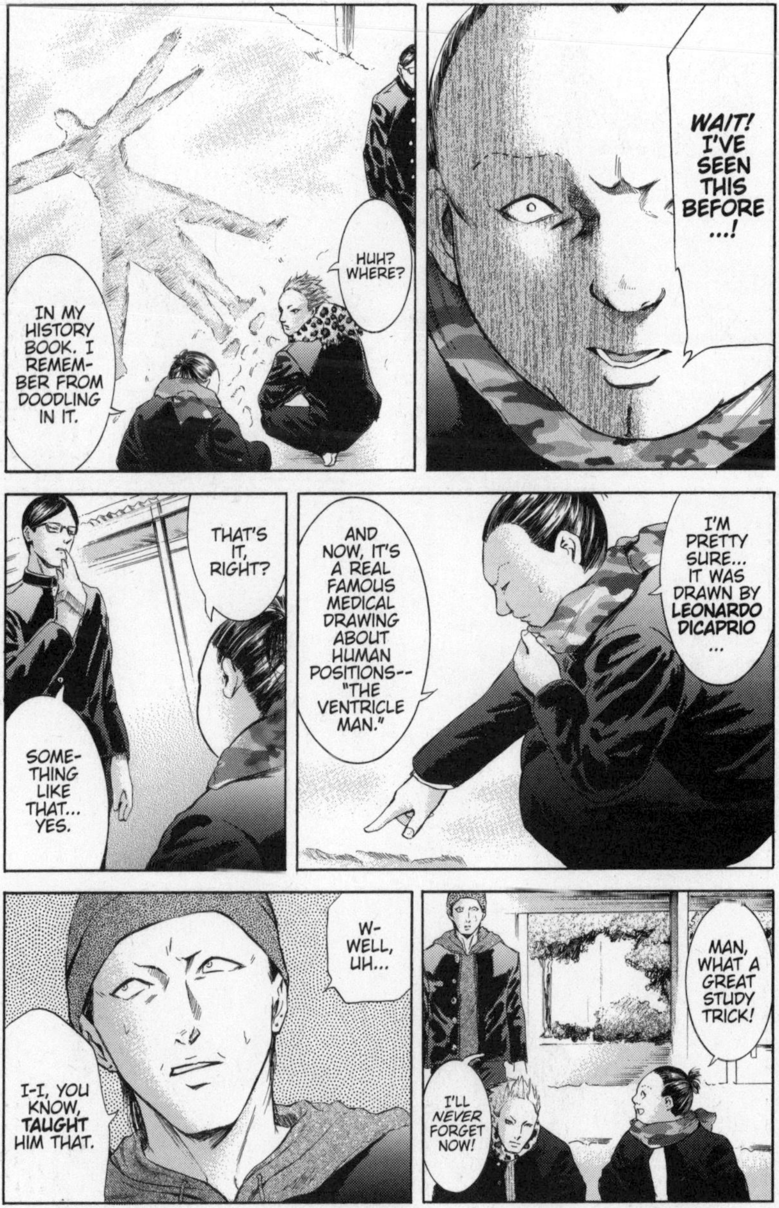
WAIT! I'VE SEEN THIS BEFORE ...!
HUH? WHERE?
IN MY HISTORY BOOK. I REMEMBER FROM DOODLING IN IT.
I'M PRETTY SURE... IT WAS DRAWN BY LEONARDO DICAPRIO ...
AND NOW, IT'S A REAL FAMOUS MEDICAL DRAWING ABOUT HUMAN POSITIONS-- "THE VENTRICLE MAN."
THAT'S IT, RIGHT?
SOME-THING LIKE THAT... YES.
MAN, WHAT A GREAT STUDY TRICK!
I'LL NEVER FORGET NOW!
W-WELL, UH...
I-I, YOU KNOW, TAUGHT HIM THAT.

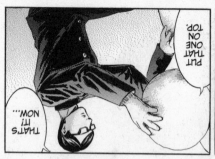

BING BONG
BEENG BOONG
YO, SAKA-MOTO!
TIME FOR YOUR NEXT LESSON-- MAKIN' A SNOWMAN!
YEAH, ROLL IT JUST LIKE THAT.
IT'S GOTTA BE NICE AND ROUND.
ROLL
ROLL
THAT'S IT! NOW...
PUT THAT ONE ON TOP.
You got it?
BALANCE IS KEY HERE.

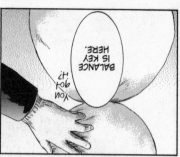

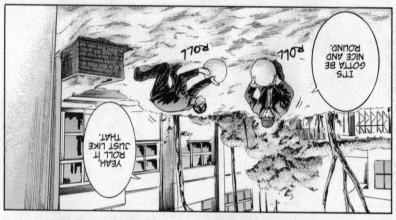

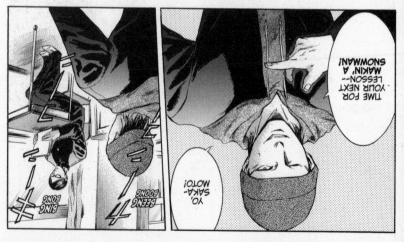

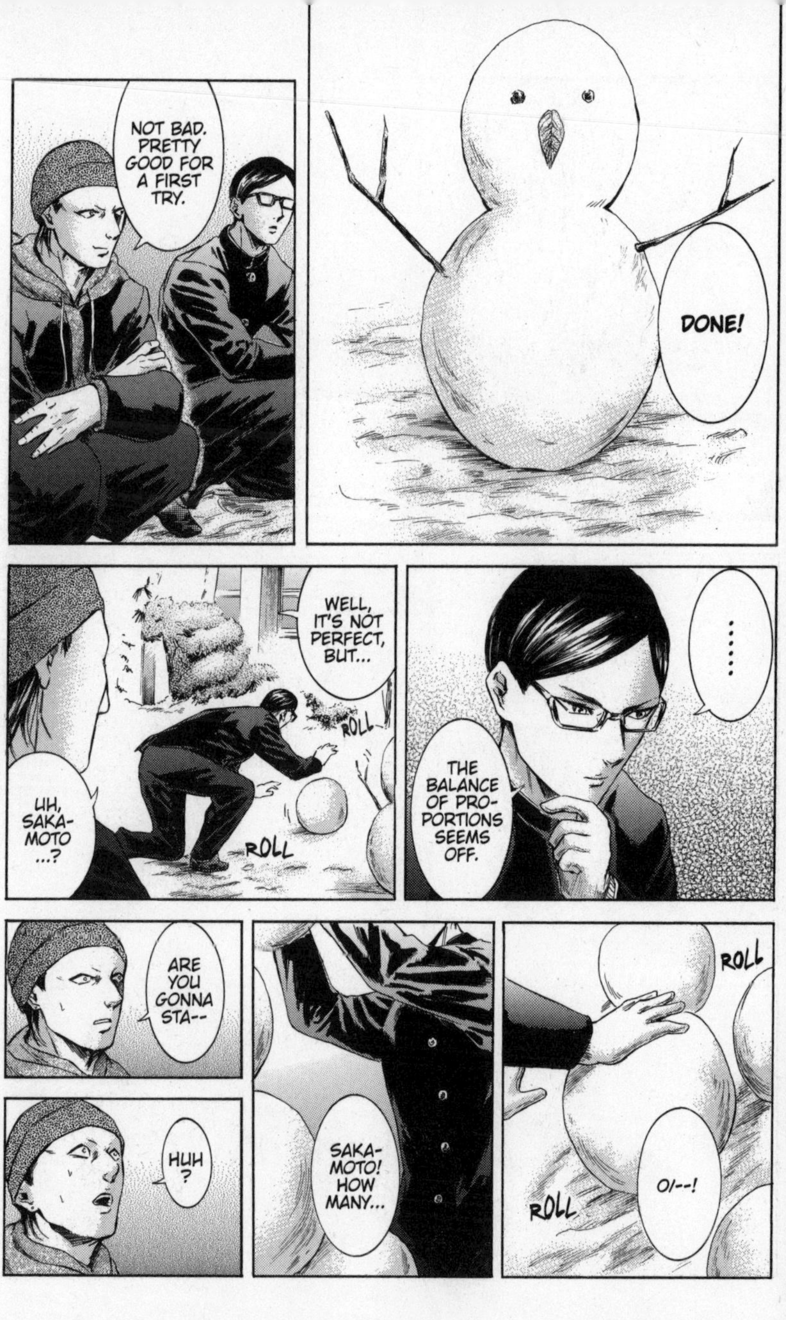
DONE!
NOT BAD. PRETTY GOOD FOR A FIRST TRY.
......
THE BALANCE OF PRO-PORTIONS SEEMS OFF.
WELL, IT'S NOT PERFECT, BUT...
ROLL
ROLL
UH, SAKA-MOTO ...?
ROLL
OI--!
ROLL
SAKA-MOTO! HOW MANY...
ARE YOU GONNA STA--
HUH ?

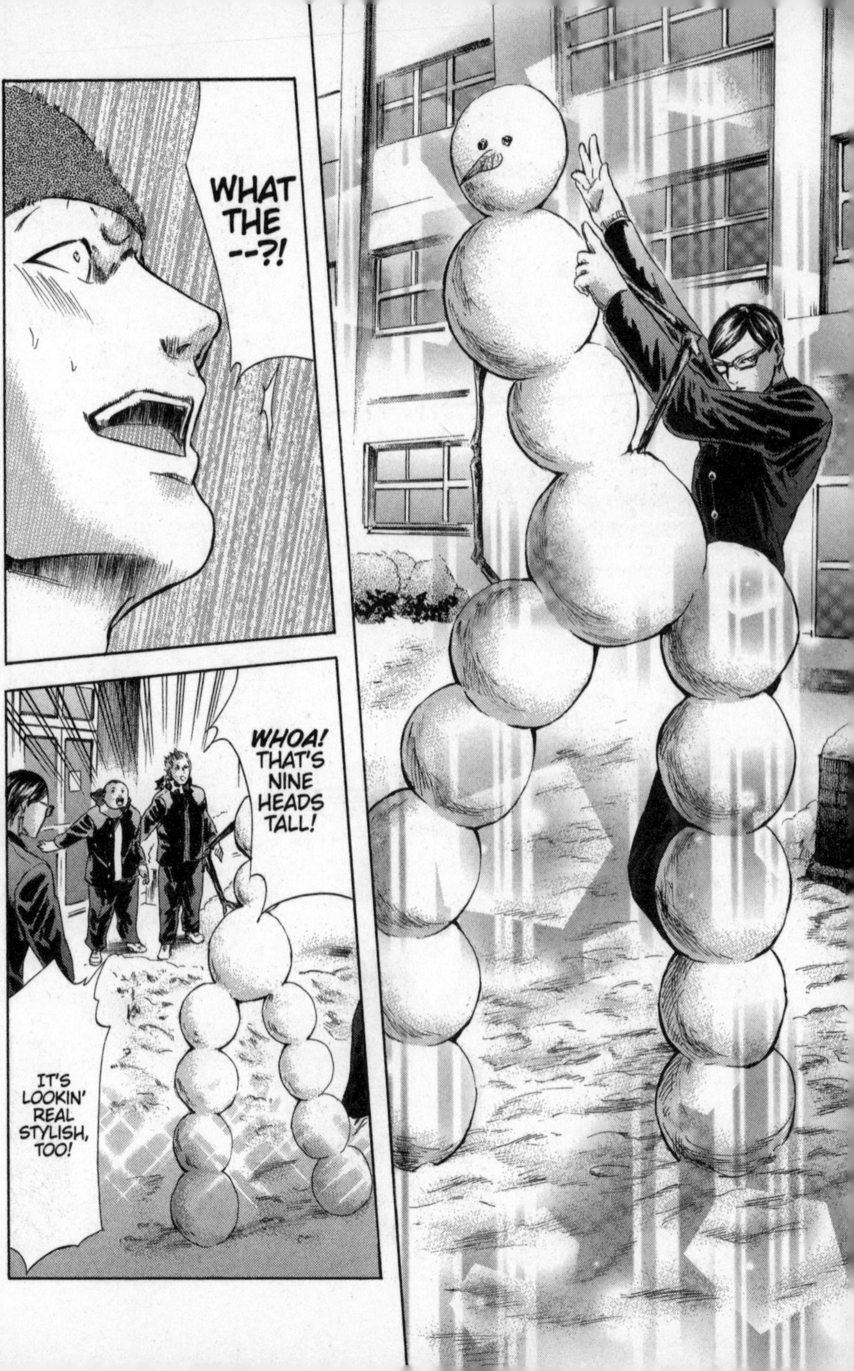

WHAT THE --?!
WHOA! THAT'S NINE HEADS TALL!
IT'S LOOKIN' REAL STYLISH, TOO!

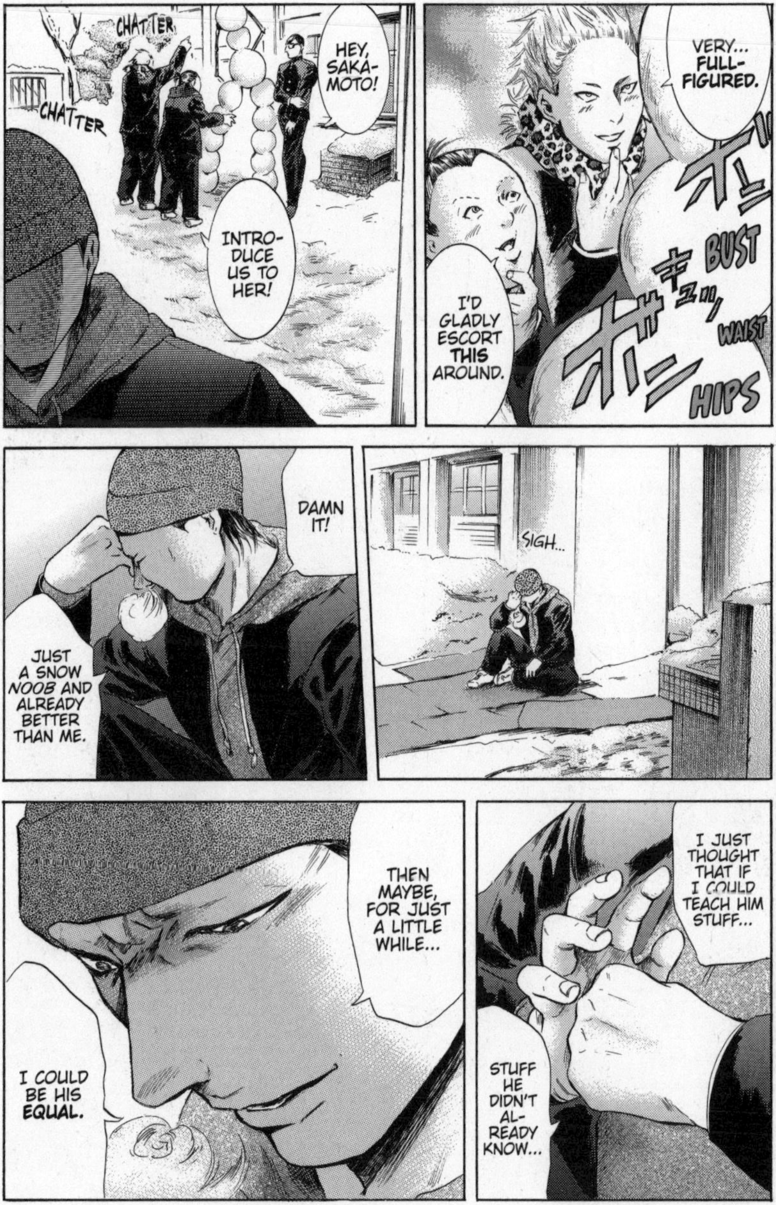
VERY... FULL-FIGURED.
BUST
WAIST
HIPS
I'D GLADLY ESCORT THIS AROUND.
CHATTER
CHATTER
HEY, SAKA-MOTO!
INTRO-DUCE US TO HER!
SIGH...
DAMN IT!
JUST A SNOW NOOB AND ALREADY BETTER THAN ME.
I JUST THOUGHT THAT IF I COULD TEACH HIM STUFF...
STUFF HE DIDN'T AL-READY KNOW...
THEN MAYBE, FOR JUST A LITTLE WHILE...
I COULD BE HIS EQUAL.

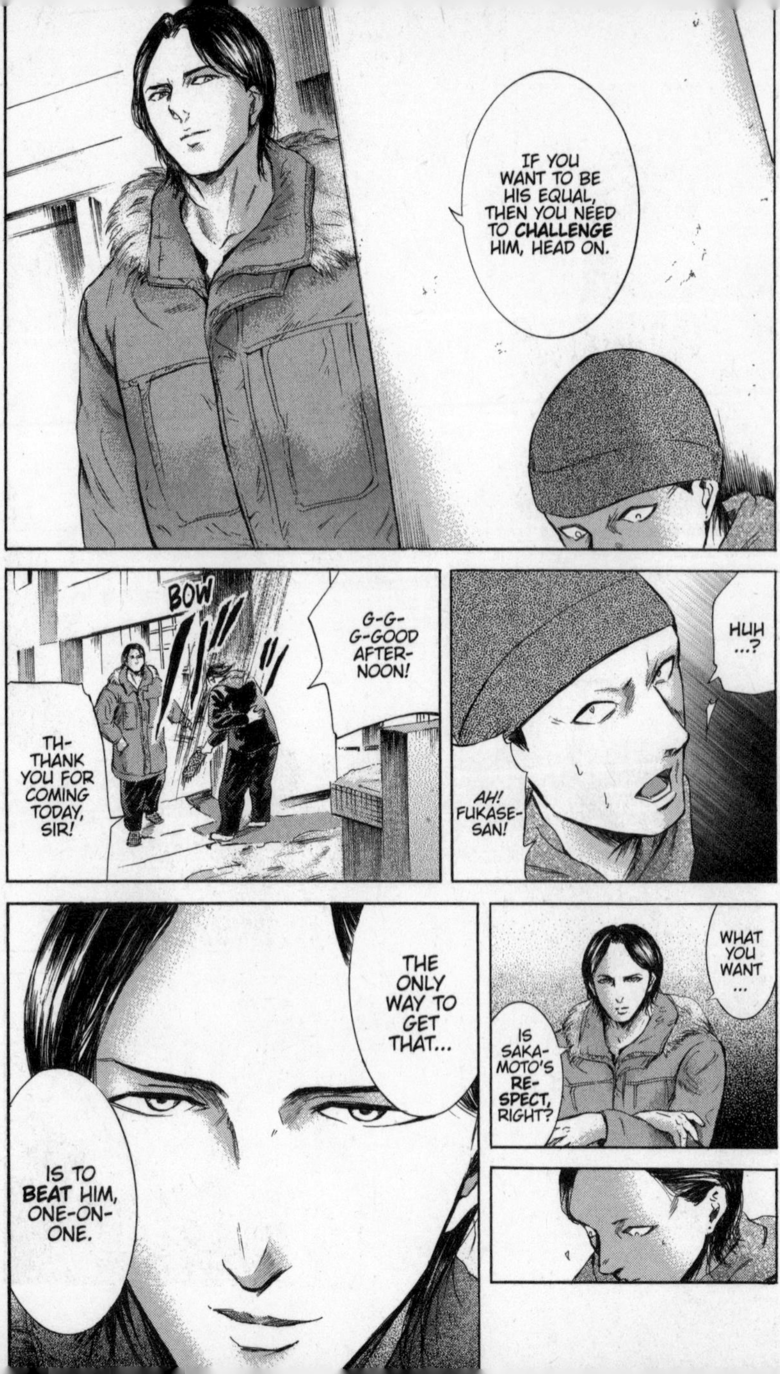
IF YOU WANT TO BE HIS EQUAL, THEN YOU NEED TO **CHALLENGE** HIM, HEAD ON.
HUH ...?
AH! FUKASE-SAN!
G-G-G-GOOD AFTER-NOON!
BOW
TH-THANK YOU FOR COMING TODAY, SIR!
WHAT YOU WANT ...
IS SAKA-MOTO'S RE-SPECT, RIGHT?
THE ONLY WAY TO GET THAT...
IS TO **BEAT** HIM, ONE-ON-ONE.

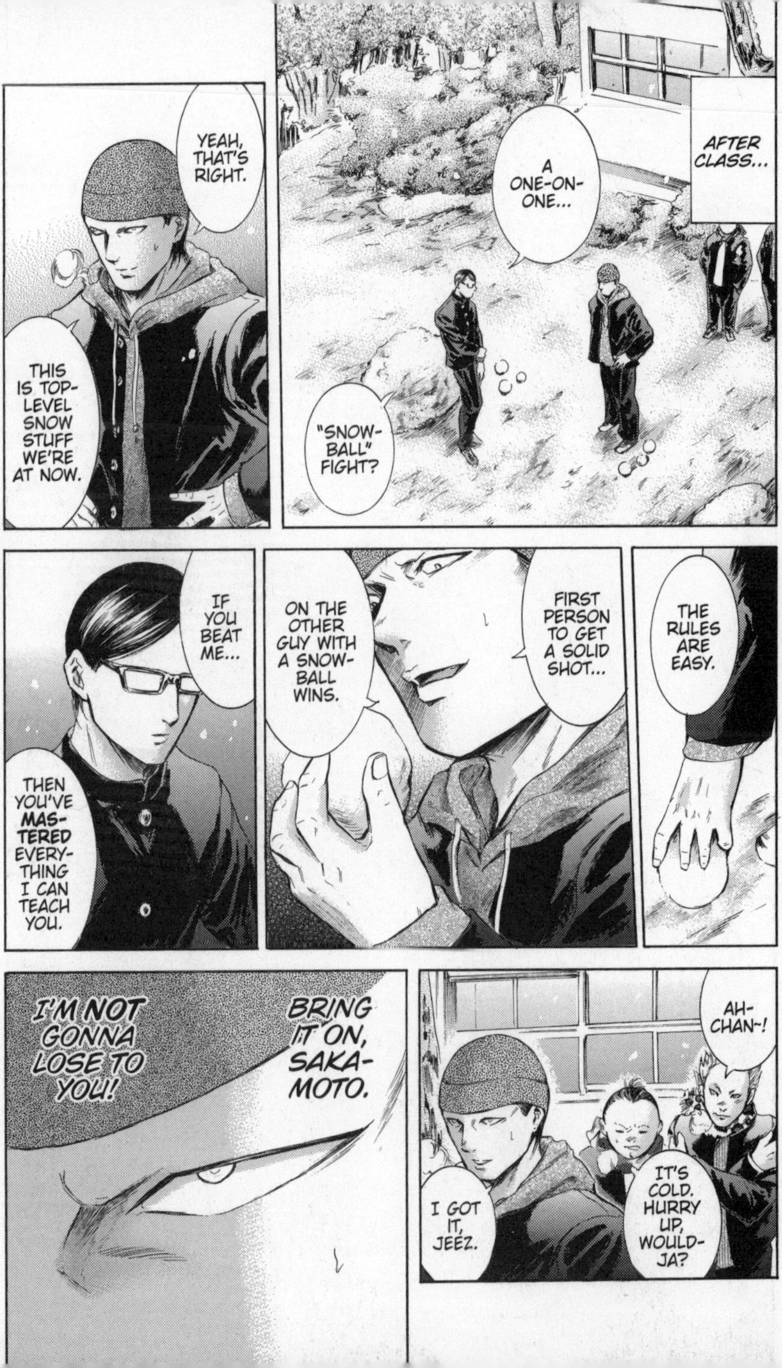
AFTER CLASS...
A ONE-ON-ONE...
"SNOW-BALL" FIGHT?
YEAH, THAT'S RIGHT.
THIS IS TOP-LEVEL SNOW STUFF WE'RE AT NOW.
THE RULES ARE EASY.
FIRST PERSON TO GET A SOLID SHOT...
ON THE OTHER GUY WITH A SNOW-BALL WINS.
IF YOU BEAT ME...
THEN YOU'VE MASTERED EVERY-THING I CAN TEACH YOU.
AH-CHAN~!
IT'S COLD. HURRY UP, WOULD-JA?
I GOT IT, JEEZ.
BRING IT ON, SAKA-MOTO.
I'M NOT GONNA LOSE TO YOU!

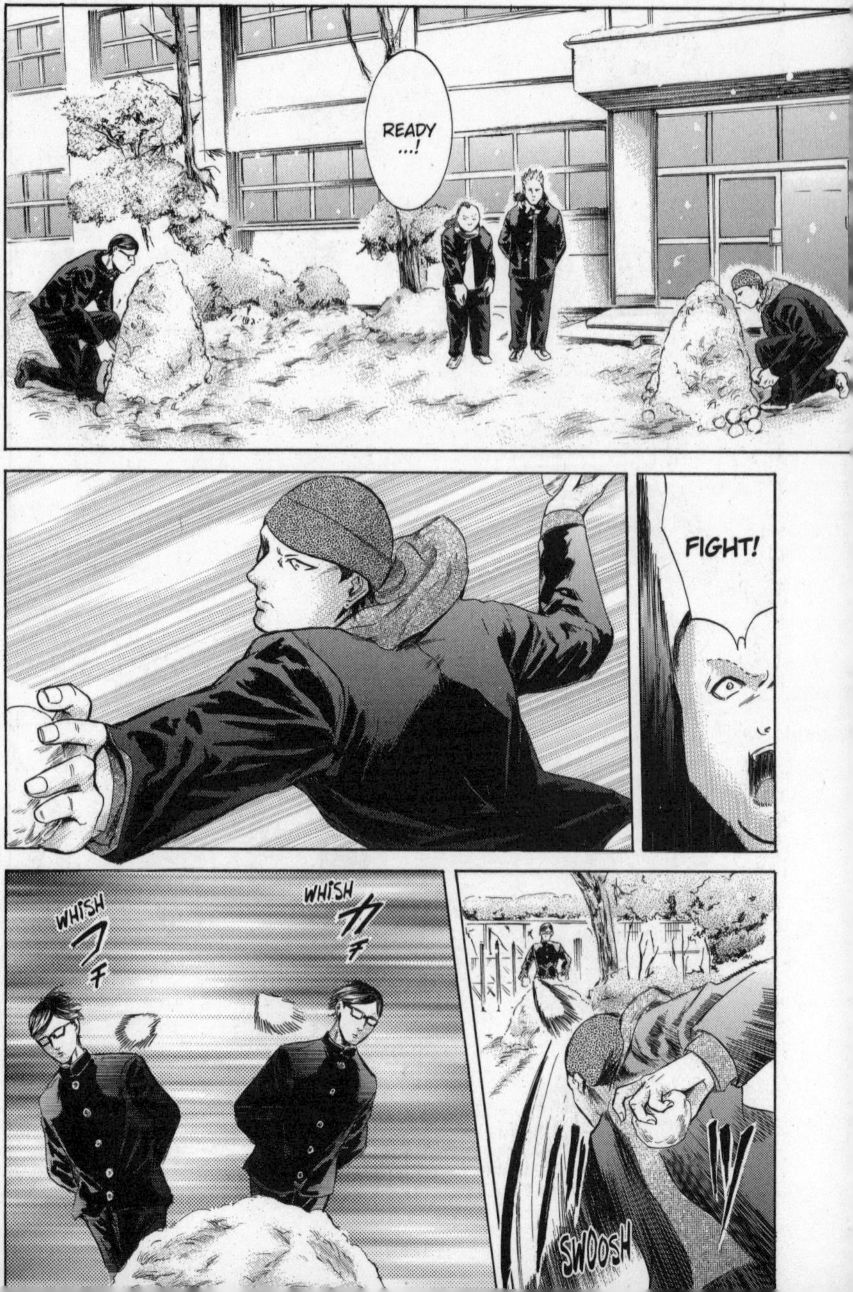
READY ...!
FIGHT!
SWOOSH
WHISH
WHISH

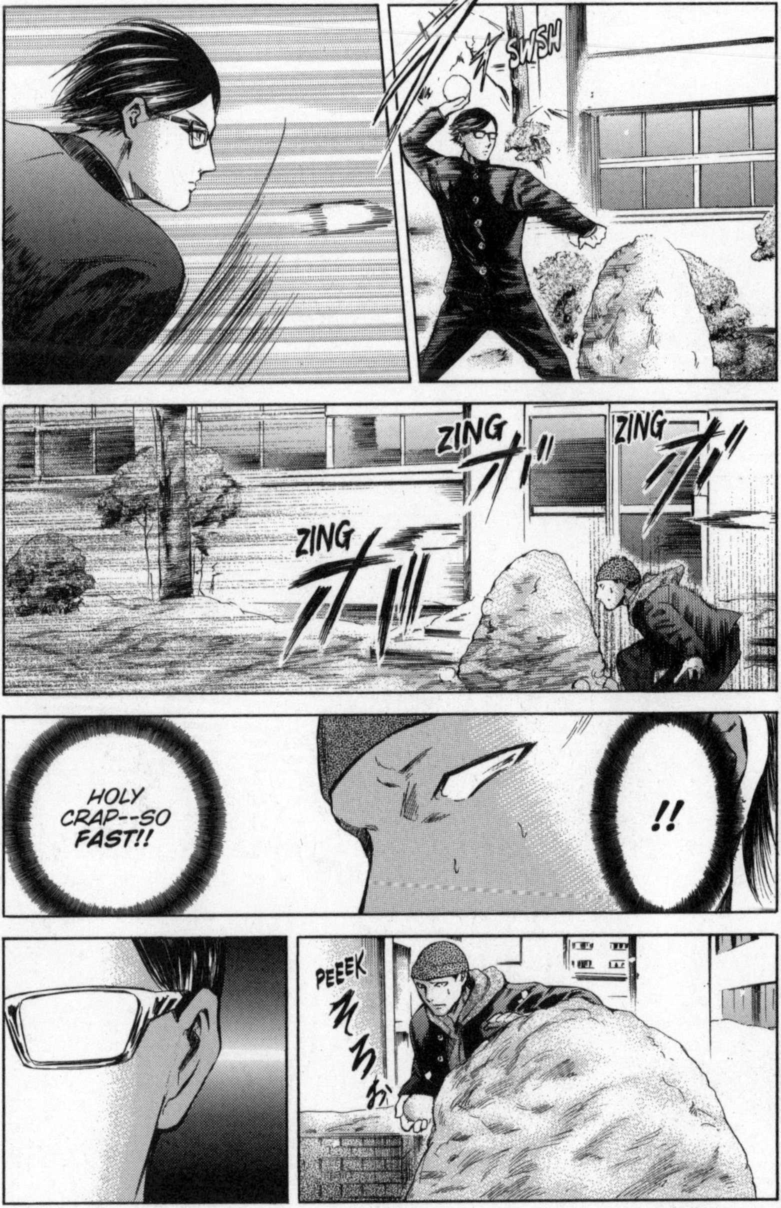
SWSH
ZING
ZING
ZING
!!
HOLY CRAP--SO FAST!!
PEEEK

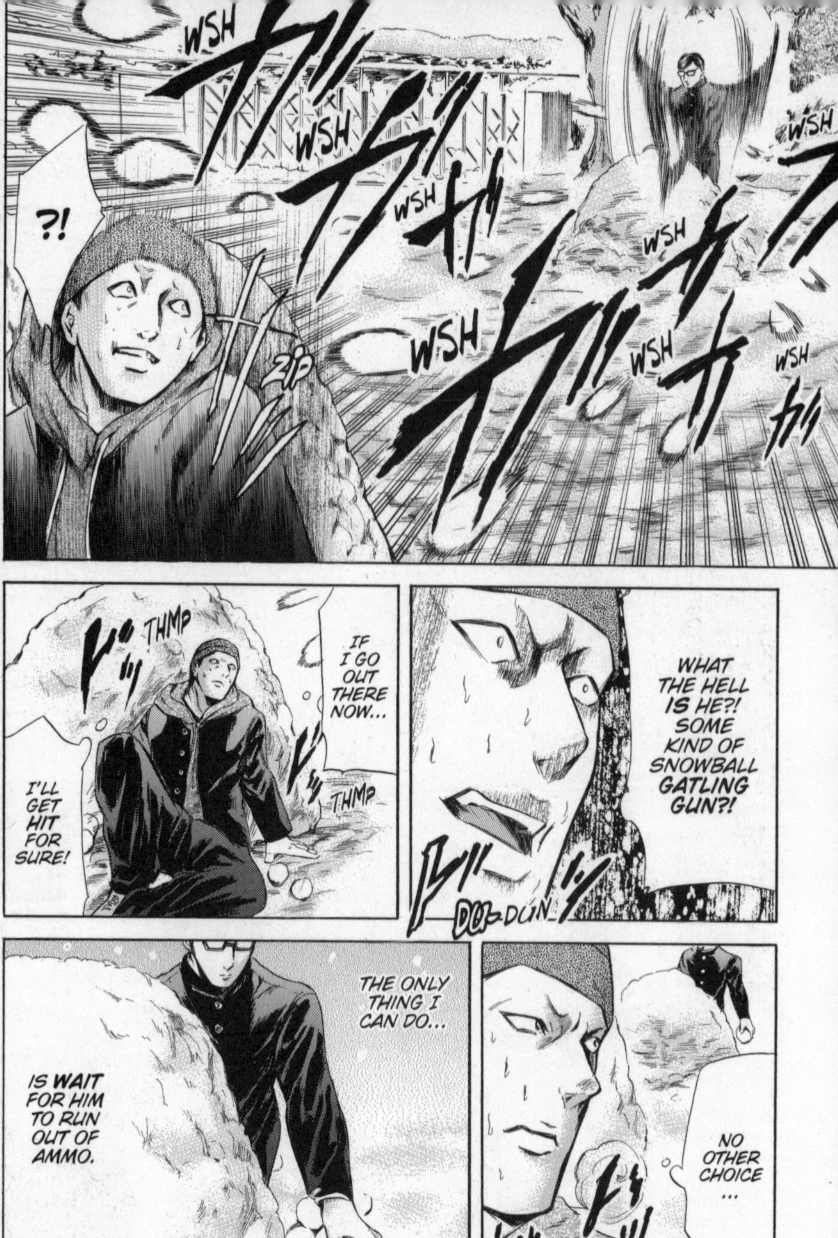
WSH
WSH
WSH
WSH
WSH
WSH
WSH
?!
ZIP
WHAT THE HELL IS HE?! SOME KIND OF SNOWBALL GATLING GUN?!
DO-DUN
IF I GO OUT THERE NOW...
THMP
THMP
I'LL GET HIT FOR SURE!
NO OTHER CHOICE ...
THMP
THMP
THE ONLY THING I CAN DO...
IS WAIT FOR HIM TO RUN OUT OF AMMO.

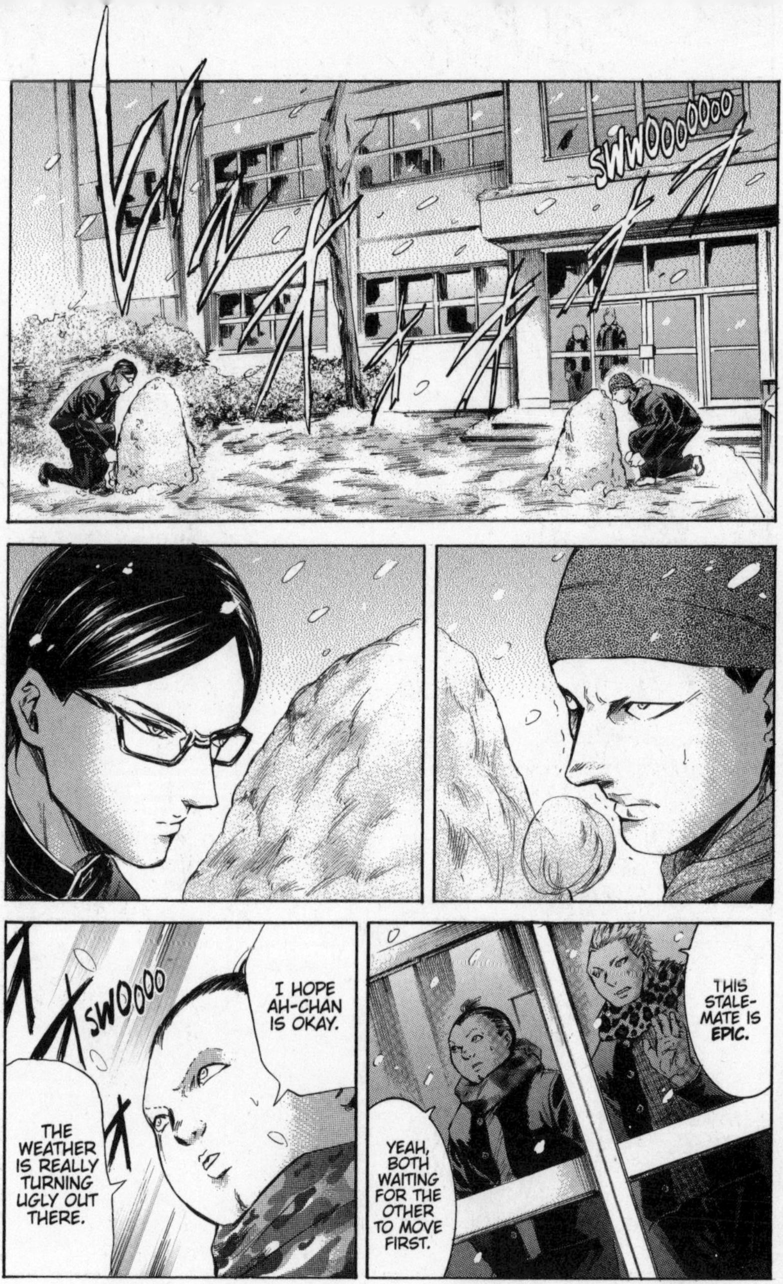
SWWOOOOOOO
THIS STALE-MATE IS EPIC.
YEAH, BOTH WAITING FOR THE OTHER TO MOVE FIRST.
I HOPE AH-CHAN IS OKAY.
SWOOOO
THE WEATHER IS REALLY TURNING UGLY OUT THERE.

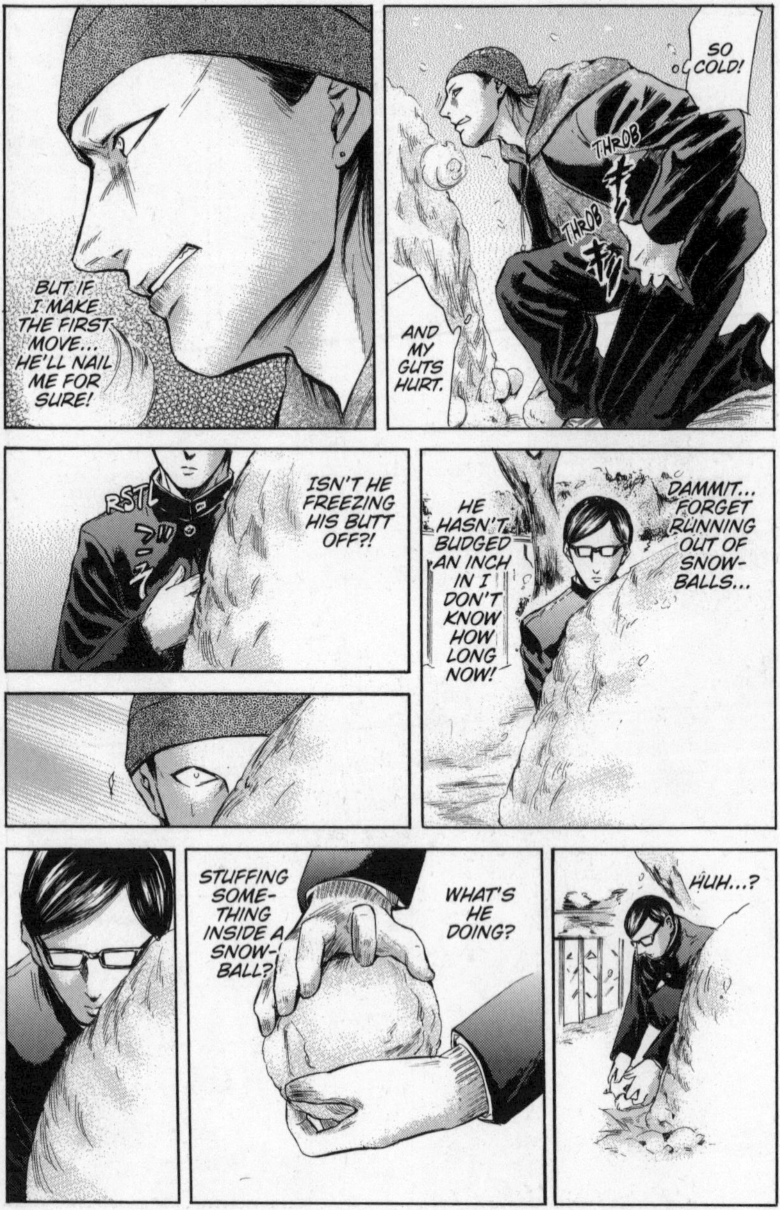
SO COLD!
THROB
THROB
AND MY GUTS HURT.
BUT IF I MAKE THE FIRST MOVE... HE'LL NAIL ME FOR SURE!
DAMMIT... FORGET RUNNING OUT OF SNOW-BALLS...
HE HASN'T BUDGED AN INCH IN I DON'T KNOW HOW LONG NOW!
ISN'T HE FREEZING HIS BUTT OFF?!
RSTL
HUH...?
WHAT'S HE DOING?
STUFFING SOME-THING INSIDE A SNOW-BALL?

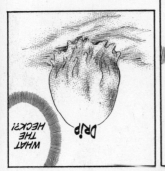

SWISH
ROLL
ROLL
ROLL
?!
ROLL
HUH ?!
DRIP
WHAT THE HECK?!
DRIP
WHAT'S IT DOING?
DRIP
WHAT DID HE PUT IN THERE?

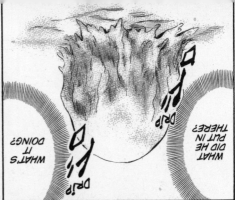

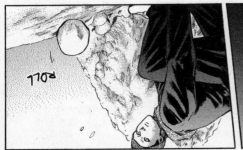

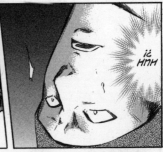

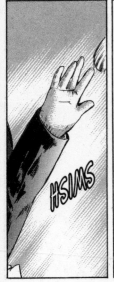

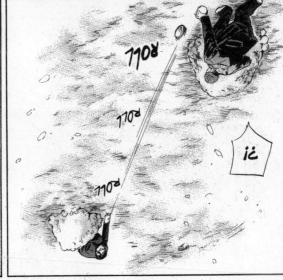

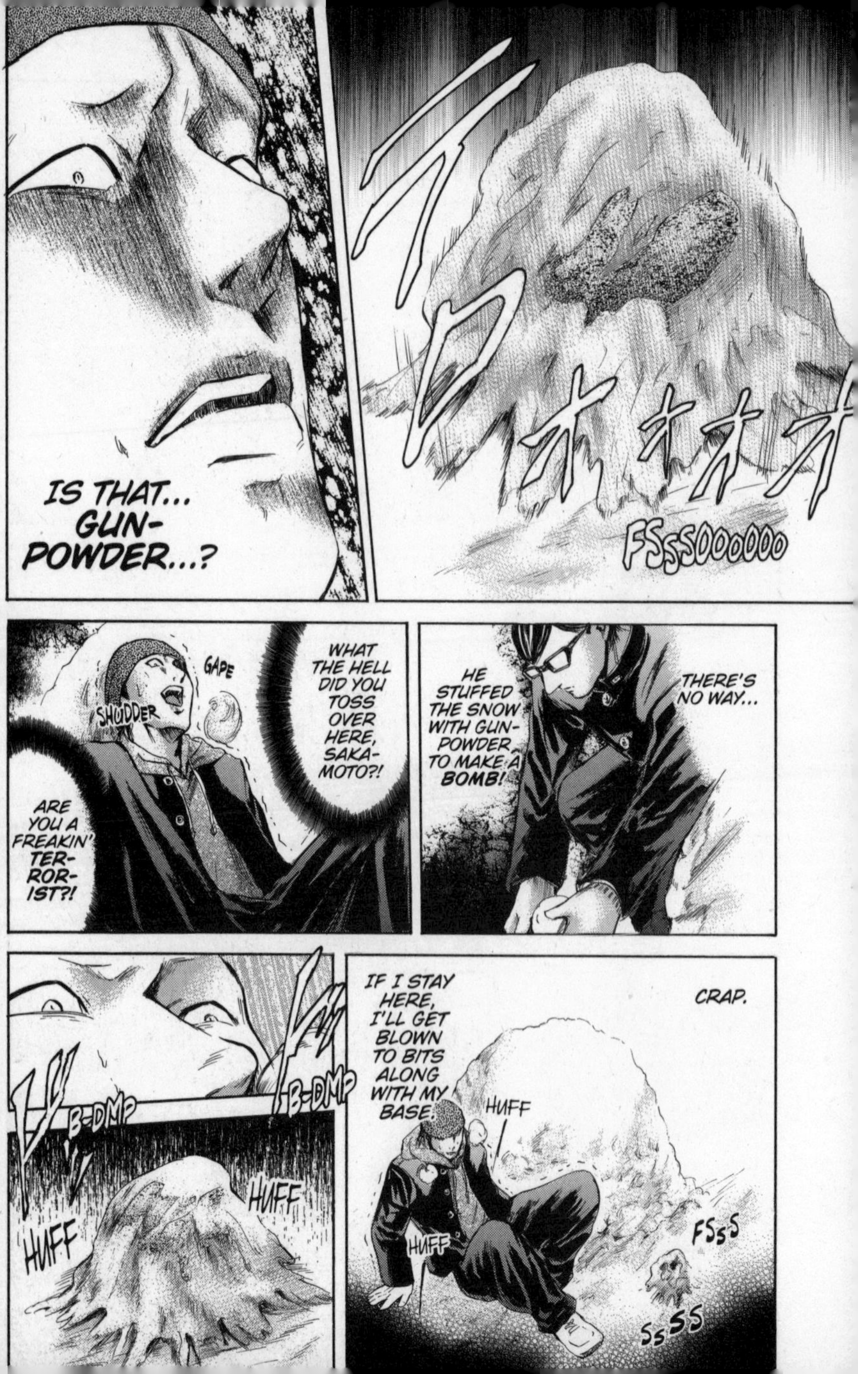
FSSSOOOOOO
IS THAT... GUN-POWDER...?
THERE'S NO WAY...
HE STUFFED THE SNOW WITH GUN-POWDER TO MAKE A BOMB!
WHAT THE HELL DID YOU TOSS OVER HERE, SAKA-MOTO?!
GAPE
SHUDDER
ARE YOU A FREAKIN' TER-ROR-IST?!
CRAP.
IF I STAY HERE, I'LL GET BLOWN TO BITS ALONG WITH MY BASE.
HUFF
HUFF
FSSS
SSSS
B-DMP
B-DMP
HUFF
HUFF

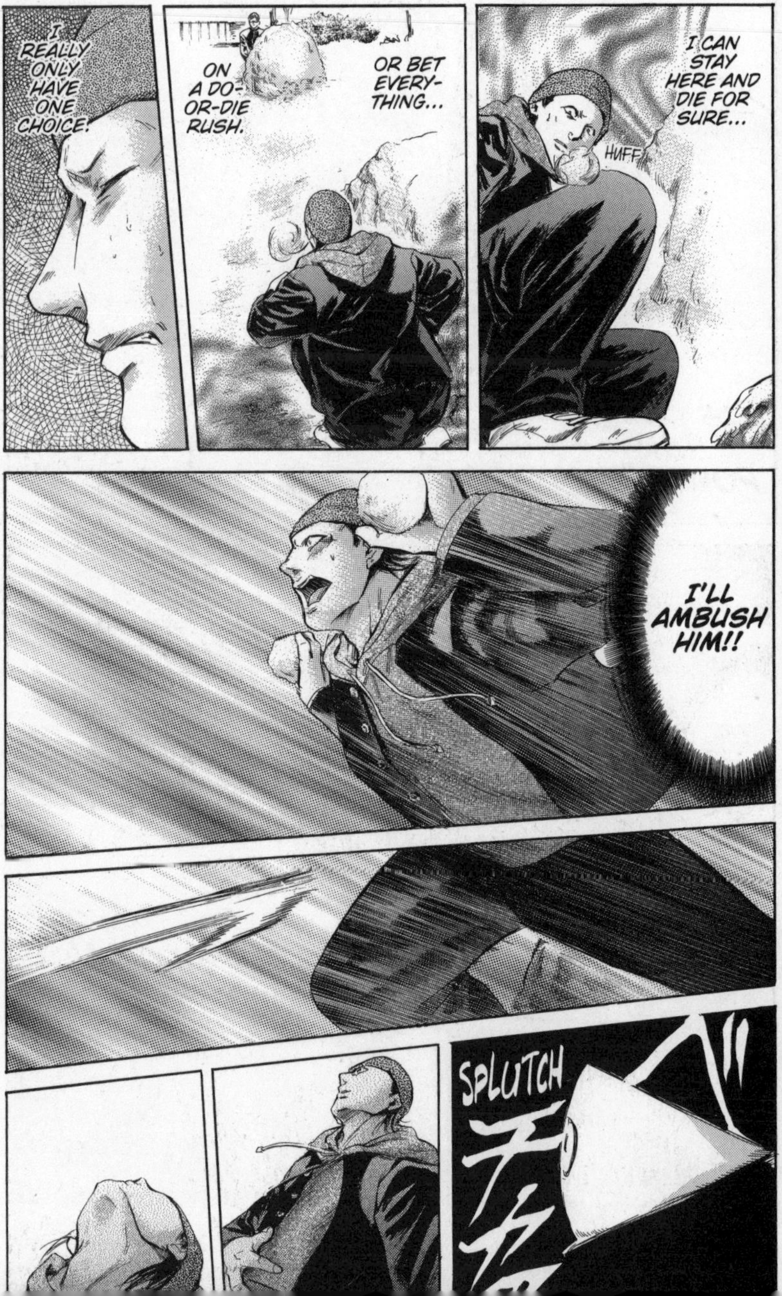
I CAN STAY HERE AND DIE FOR SURE...
HUFF
OR BET EVERYTHING...
ON A DO-OR-DIE RUSH.
I REALLY ONLY HAVE ONE CHOICE.
I'LL AMBUSH HIM!!
SPLUTCH

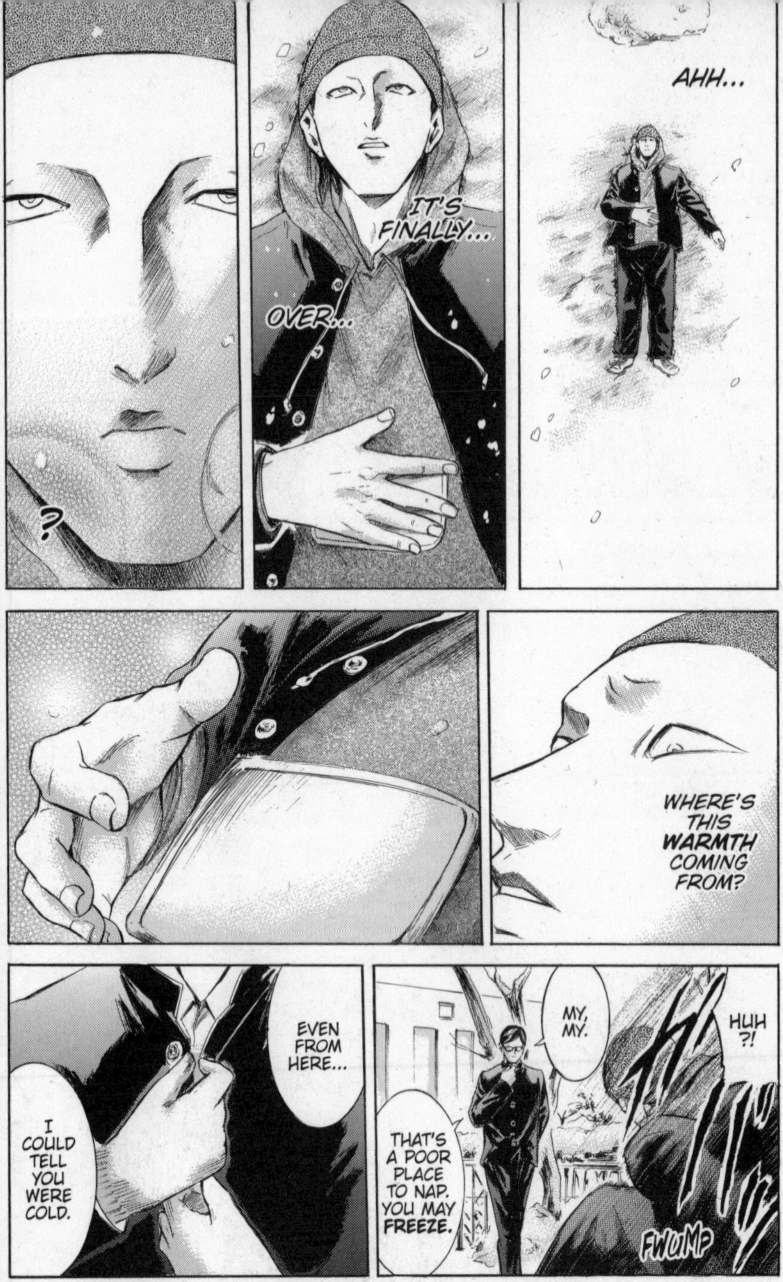
AHH...
IT'S FINALLY...
OVER...
?
WHERE'S THIS WARMTH COMING FROM?
HUH ?!
FWUMP
MY, MY.
THAT'S A POOR PLACE TO NAP. YOU MAY FREEZE.
EVEN FROM HERE...
I COULD TELL YOU WERE COLD.

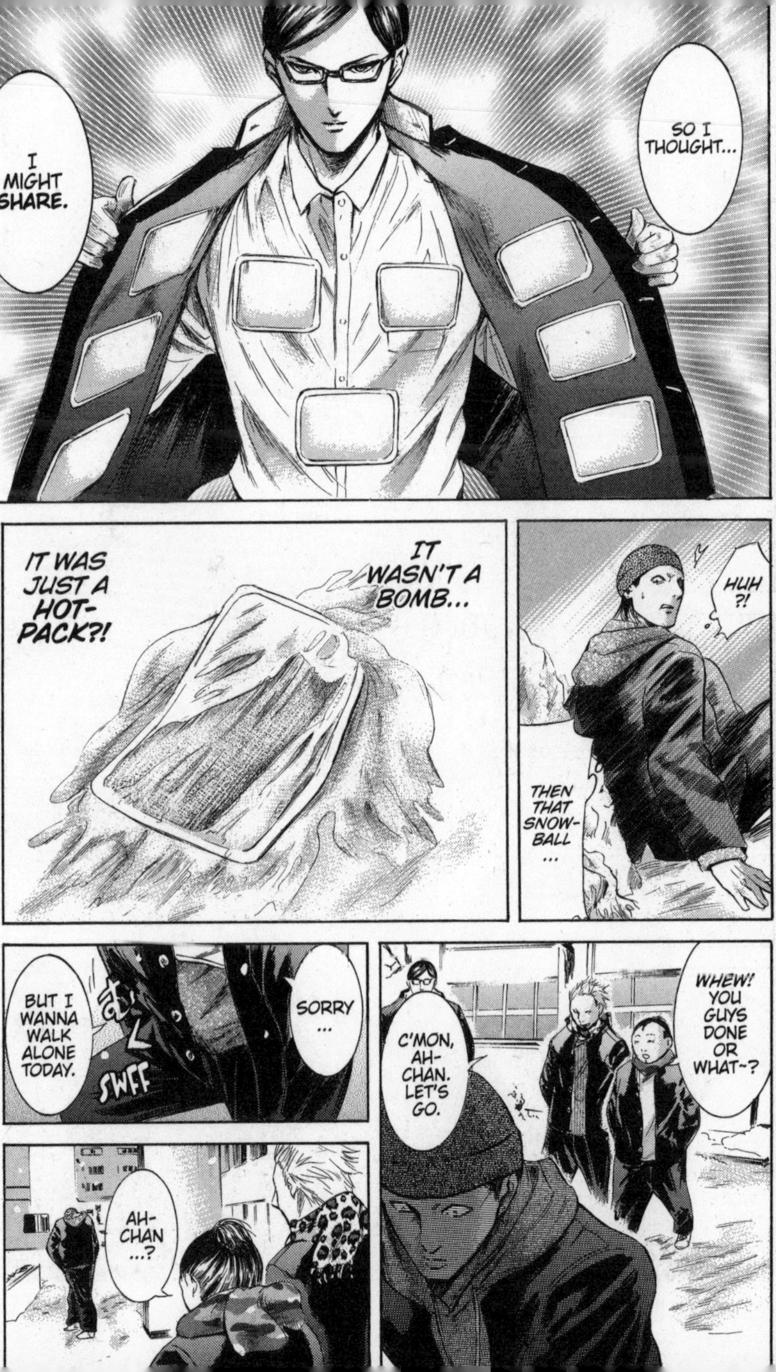
SO I THOUGHT...
I MIGHT SHARE.
HUH?!
THEN THAT SNOW-BALL...
IT WASN'T A BOMB...
IT WAS JUST A HOT-PACK?!
WHEW! YOU GUYS DONE OR WHAT~?
C'MON, AH-CHAN. LET'S GO.
SORRY...
BUT I WANNA WALK ALONE TODAY.
SWFF
AH-CHAN...?

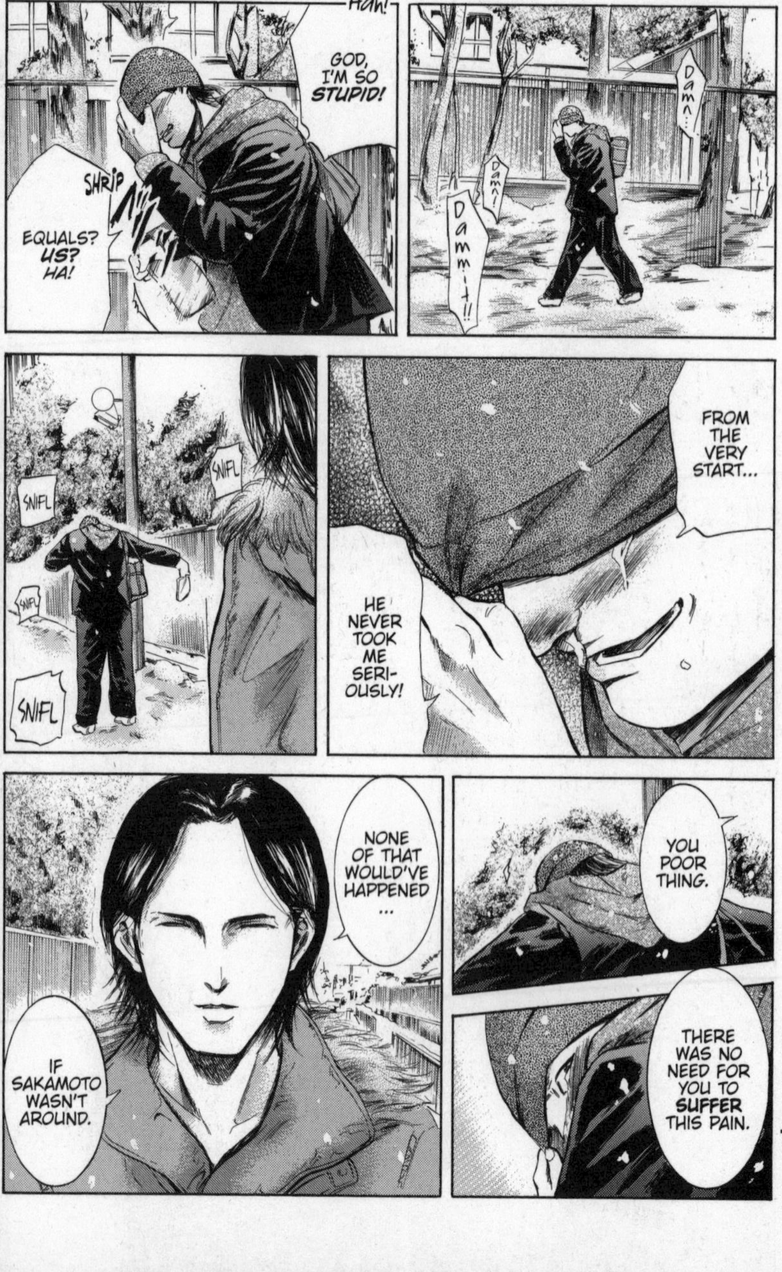
Damn...
Damn!
Dammit!!
Hah!
GOD, I'M SO STUPID!
SHRIP
EQUALS? US? HA!
FROM THE VERY START...
HE NEVER TOOK ME SERIOUSLY!
SNIFL
SNIFL
SNIFL
SNIFL
YOU POOR THING.
THERE WAS NO NEED FOR YOU TO SUFFER THIS PAIN.
NONE OF THAT WOULD'VE HAPPENED...
IF SAKAMOTO WASN'T AROUND.

End of Chapter 22

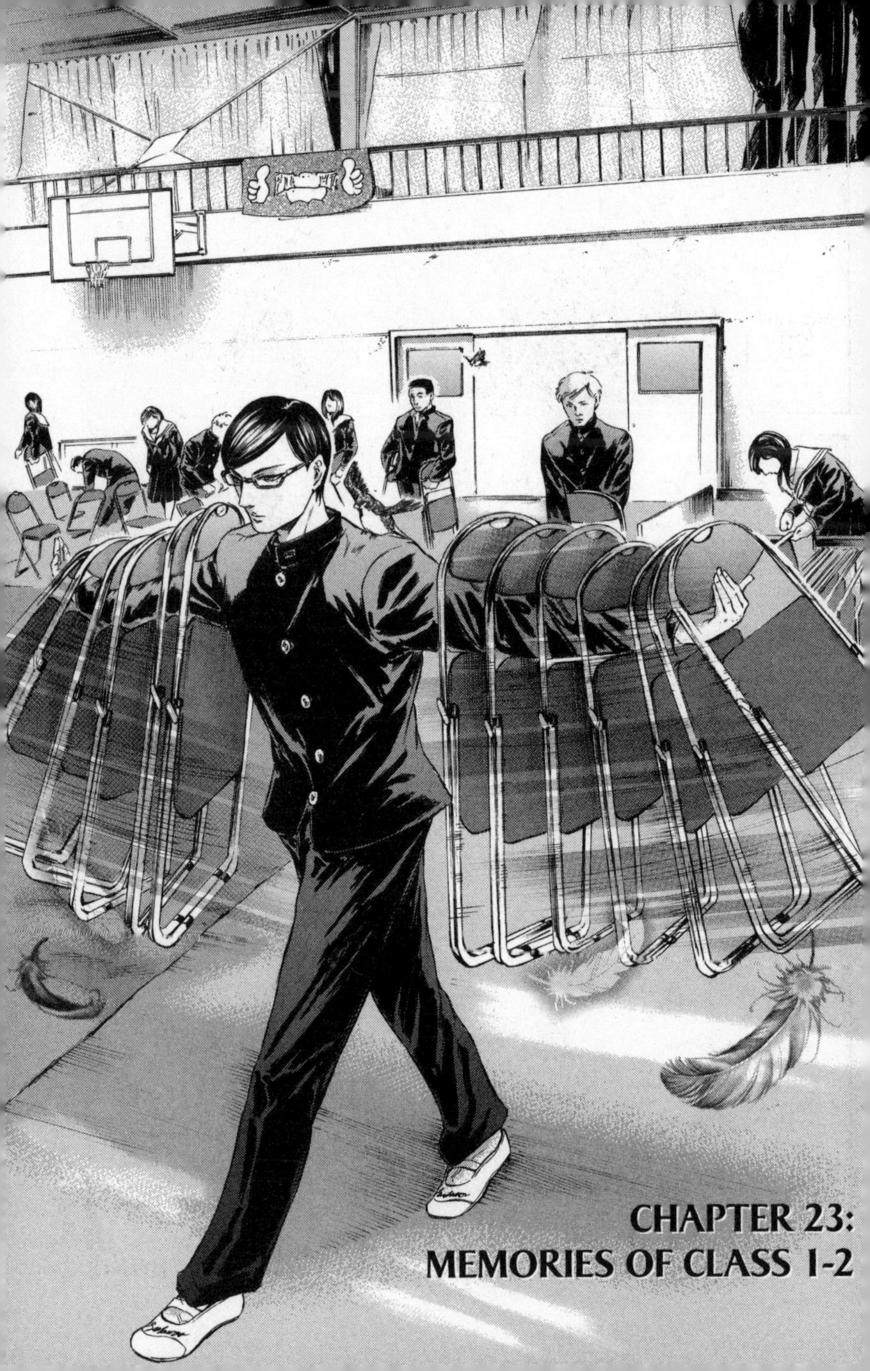

CHAPTER 23: MEMORIES OF CLASS 1-2

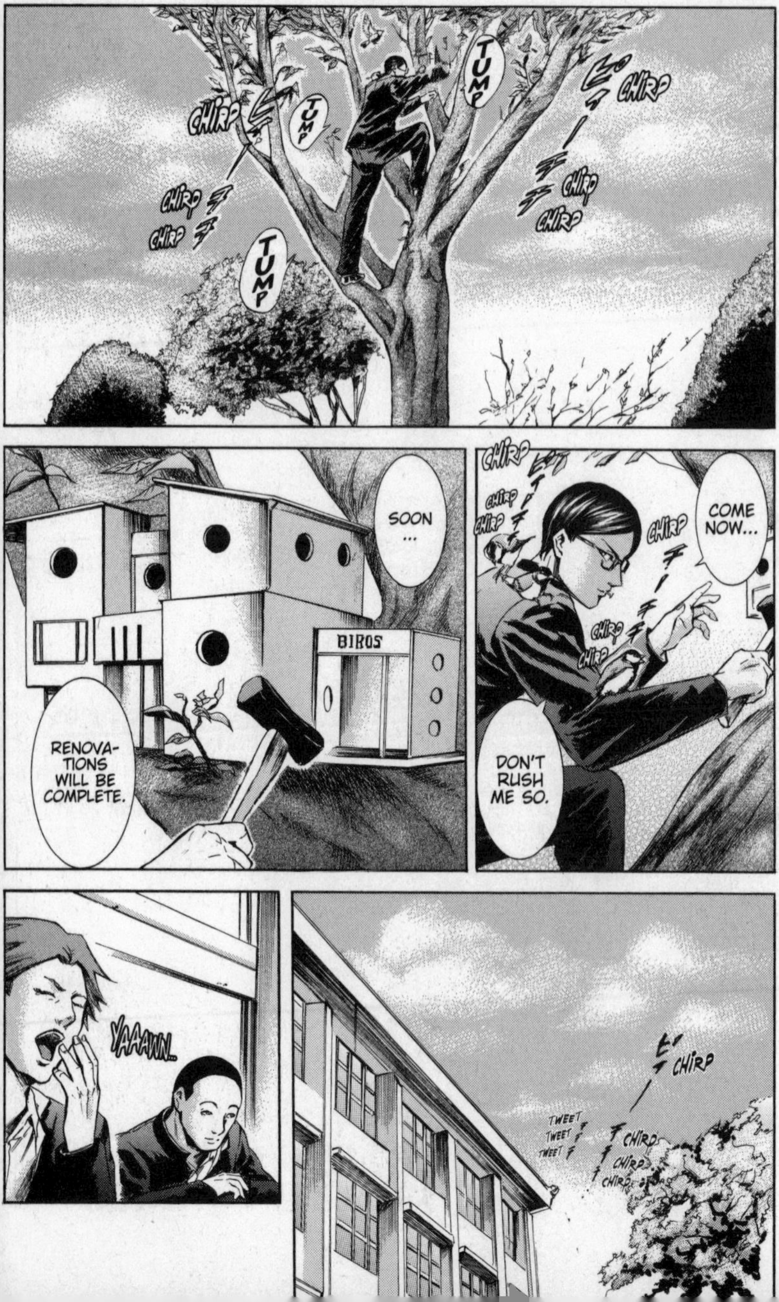
CHIRP
CHIRP
CHIRP
TUMP
TUMP
CHIRP
CHIRP
CHIRP
TUMP
COME NOW...
CHIRP
CHIRP
CHIRP
CHIRP
CHIRP
CHIRP
DON'T RUSH ME SO.
SOON ...
BIROS
RENOVATIONS WILL BE COMPLETE.
CHIRP
TWEET
TWEET
TWEET
CHIRP
CHIRP
CHIRP
YAAAWN...

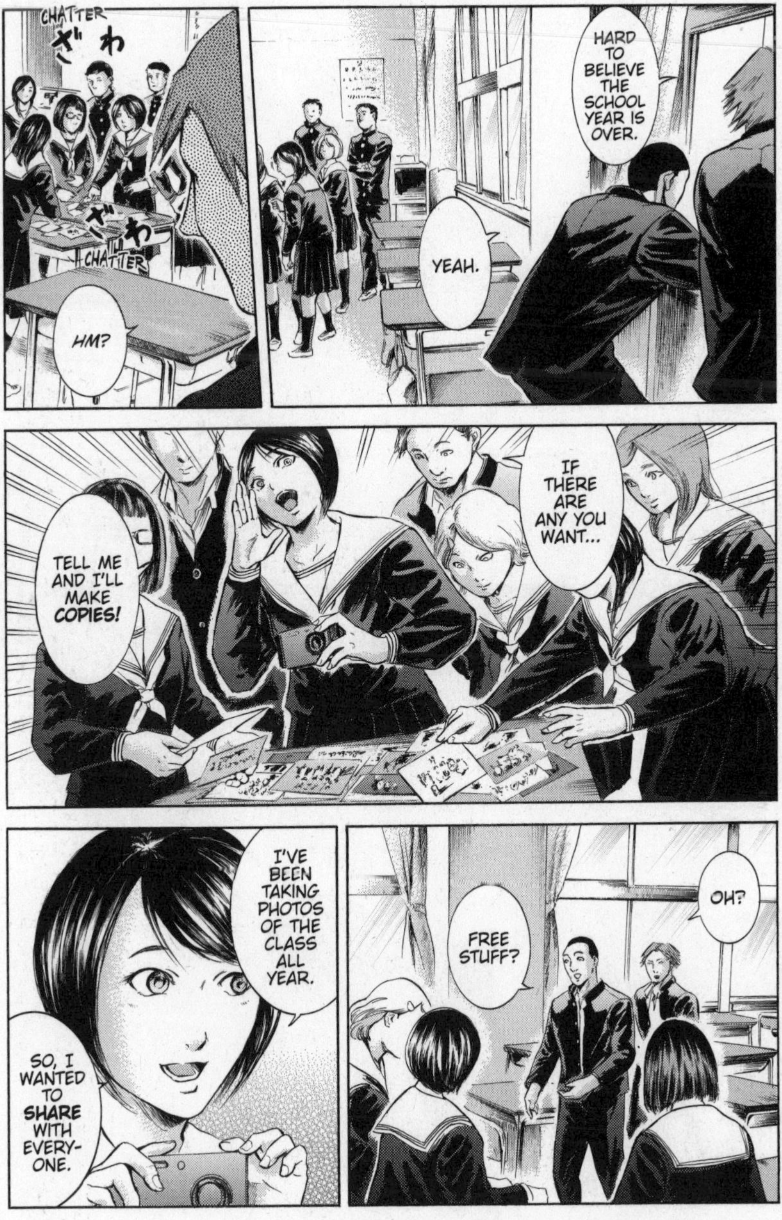
HARD TO BELIEVE THE SCHOOL YEAR IS OVER.
YEAH.
CHATTER
ざわ
ざわ
CHATTER
HM?
IF THERE ARE ANY YOU WANT...
TELL ME AND I'LL MAKE **COPIES!**
OH?
FREE STUFF?
I'VE BEEN TAKING PHOTOS OF THE CLASS ALL YEAR.
SO, I WANTED TO **SHARE** WITH EVERY-ONE.

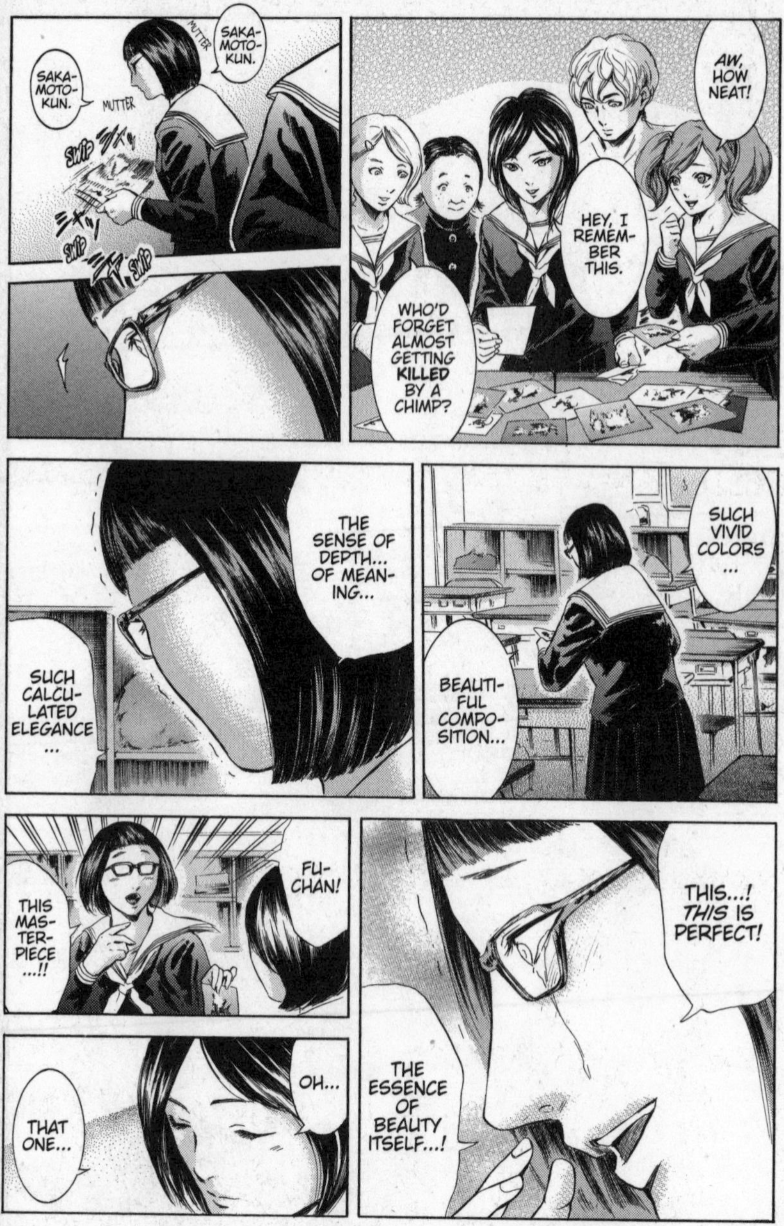
AW, HOW NEAT!
HEY, I REMEMBER THIS.
WHO'D FORGET ALMOST GETTING **KILLED** BY A CHIMP?
SAKAMOTO-KUN.
MUTTER
SAKAMOTO-KUN.
MUTTER
SWIP
SWIP
SWIP
SUCH VIVID COLORS...
BEAUTIFUL COMPOSITION...
THE SENSE OF DEPTH... OF MEANING...
SUCH CALCULATED ELEGANCE...
THIS...! *THIS* IS PERFECT!
THE ESSENCE OF BEAUTY ITSELF...!
FU-CHAN!
THIS MASTERPIECE...!!
OH...
THAT ONE...

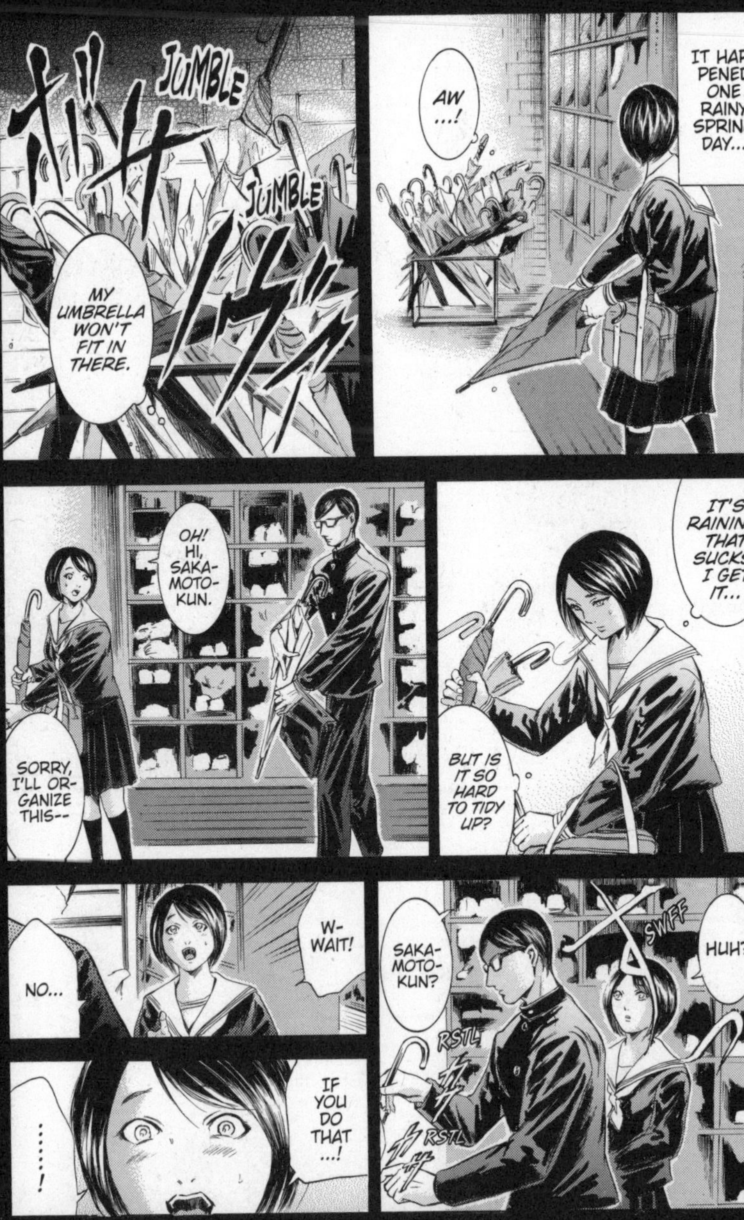
IT HAPPENED ONE RAINY SPRING DAY...
AW ...!
JUMBLE
JUMBLE
MY UMBRELLA WON'T FIT IN THERE.
IT'S RAINING. THAT SUCKS. I GET IT...
BUT IS IT SO HARD TO TIDY UP?
OH! HI, SAKAMOTO-KUN.
SORRY, I'LL ORGANIZE THIS--
HUH?
SWFF
SAKAMOTO-KUN?
RSTL
RSTL
W-WAIT!
NO...
IF YOU DO THAT ...!
......!

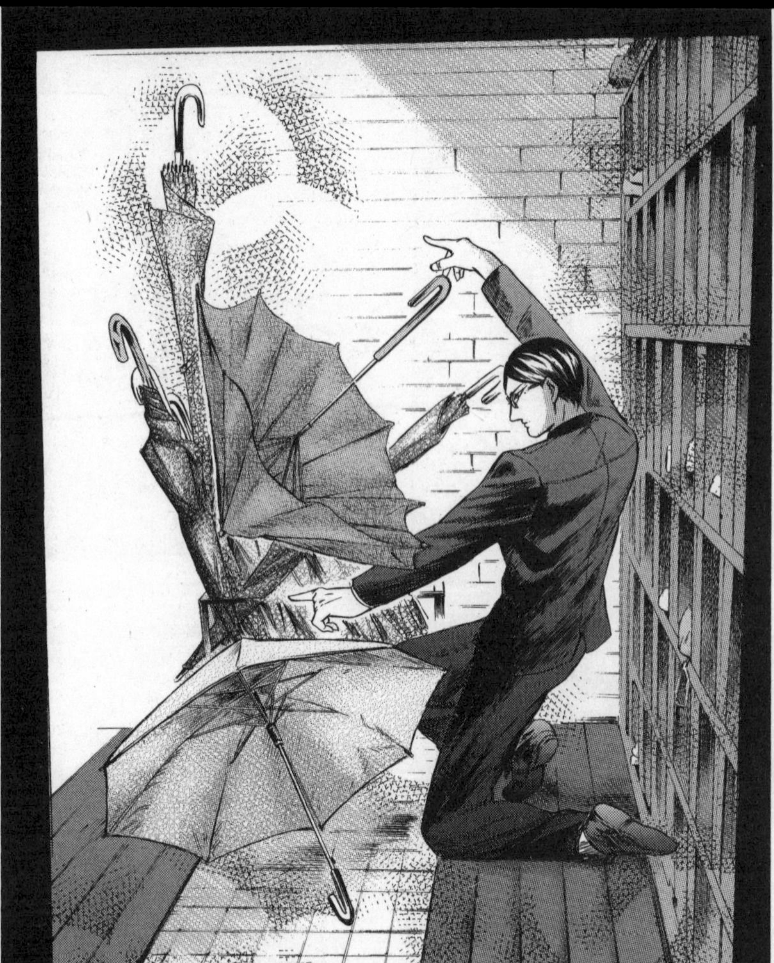

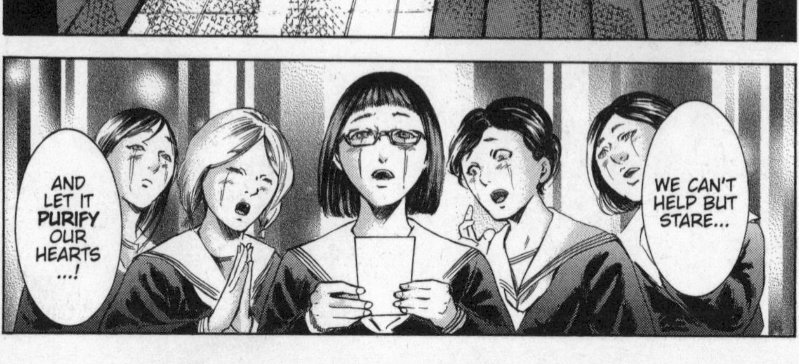
WE CAN'T HELP BUT STARE...
AND LET IT PURIFY OUR HEARTS ...!

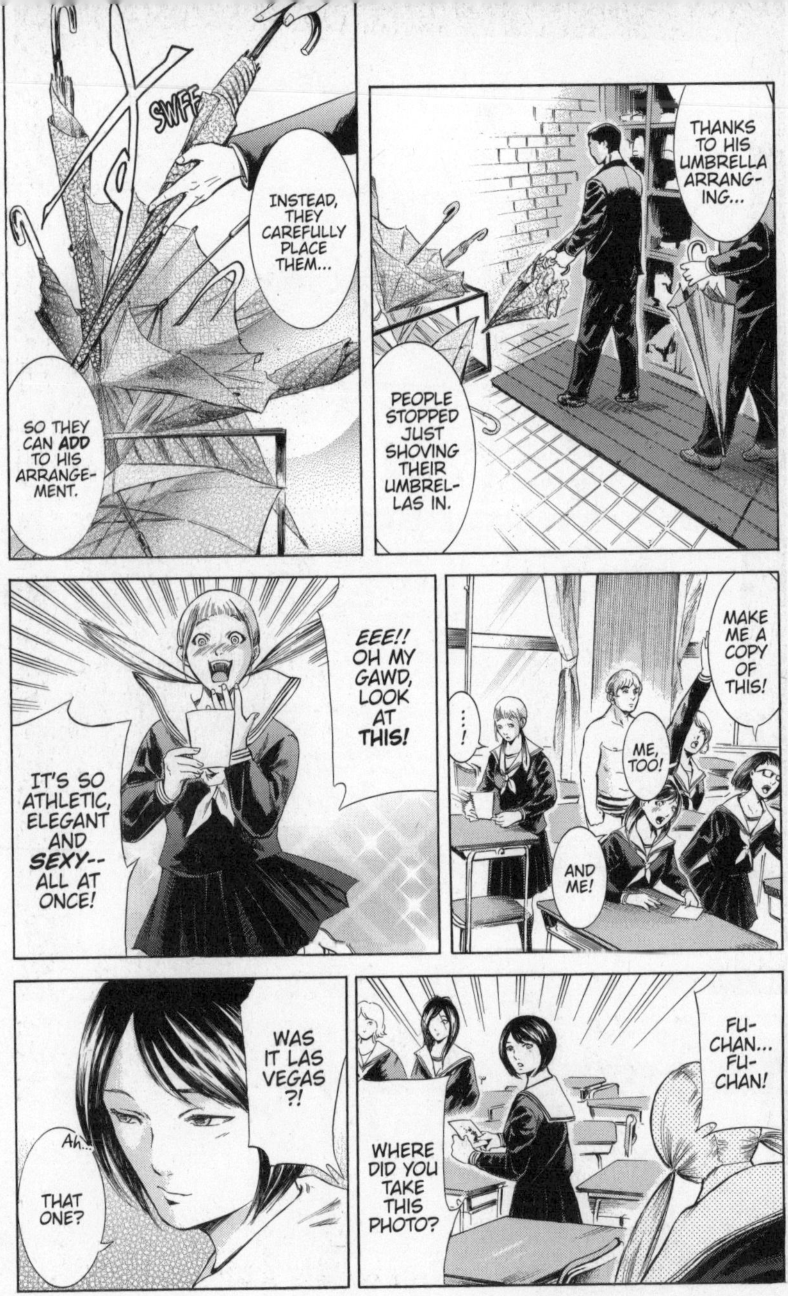
THANKS TO HIS UMBRELLA ARRANGING...
PEOPLE STOPPED JUST SHOVING THEIR UMBRELLAS IN.
INSTEAD, THEY CAREFULLY PLACE THEM...
SWFF
SO THEY CAN **ADD** TO HIS ARRANGEMENT.
MAKE ME A COPY OF THIS!
...!
ME, TOO!
AND ME!
EEE!! OH MY GAWD, LOOK AT **THIS!**
IT'S SO ATHLETIC, ELEGANT AND ***SEXY***-- ALL AT ONCE!
FU-CHAN... FU-CHAN!
WHERE DID YOU TAKE THIS PHOTO?
WAS IT LAS VEGAS ?!
Ah...
THAT ONE?

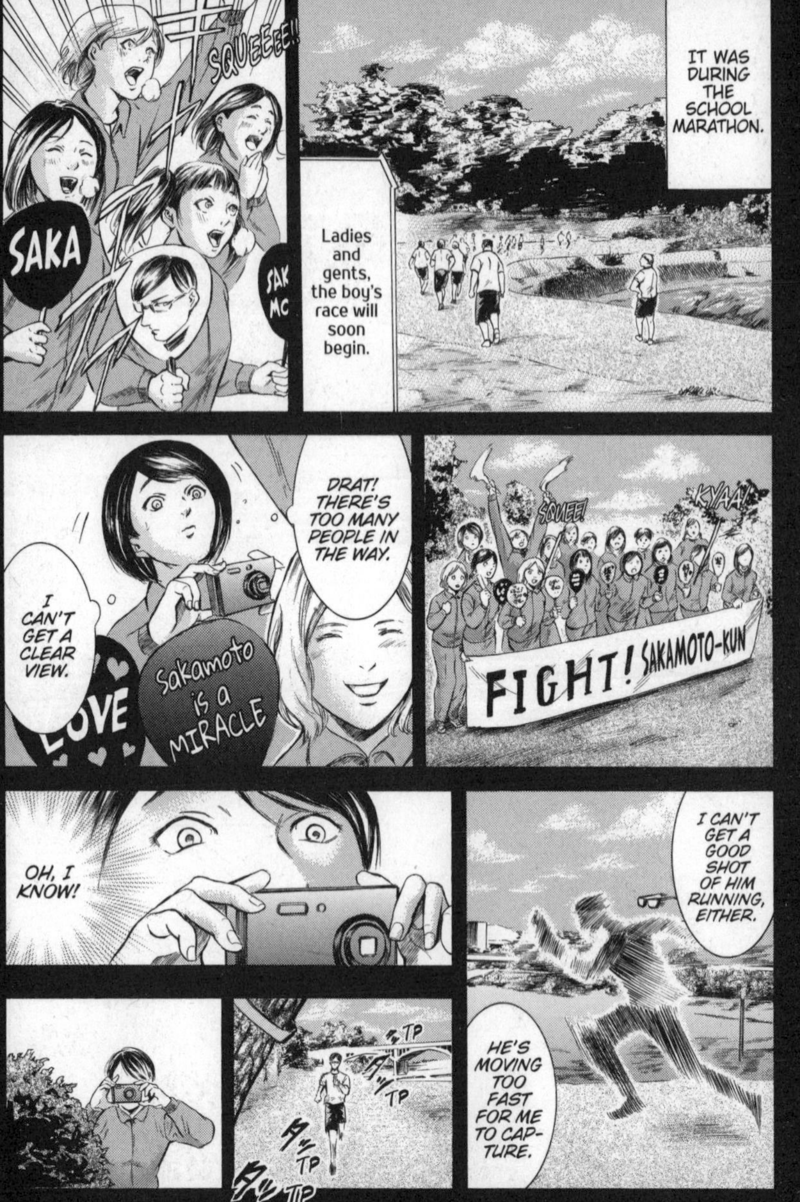
IT WAS DURING THE SCHOOL MARATHON.
Ladies and gents, the boy's race will soon begin.
SQUEEEE!!
SAKA
SAK MO
FIGHT! SAKAMOTO-KUN
SQUEE!
KYAA!
DRAT! THERE'S TOO MANY PEOPLE IN THE WAY.
I CAN'T GET A CLEAR VIEW.
LOVE
Sakamoto is a MIRACLE
I CAN'T GET A GOOD SHOT OF HIM RUNNING, EITHER.
HE'S MOVING TOO FAST FOR ME TO CAPTURE.
OH, I KNOW!
TP
TP
TP
TP

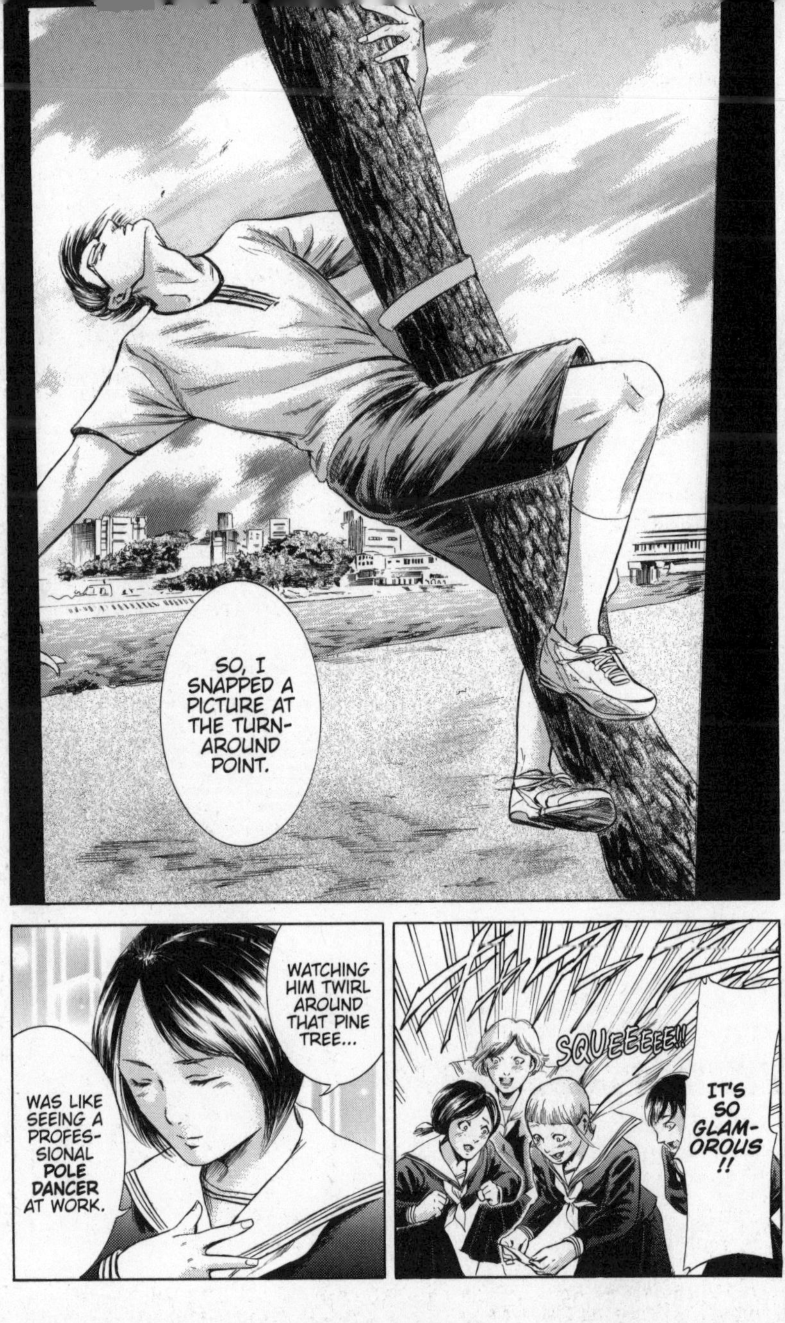
SO, I SNAPPED A PICTURE AT THE TURN-AROUND POINT.
SQUEEEEEE!!
IT'S SO GLAMOROUS!!
WATCHING HIM TWIRL AROUND THAT PINE TREE...
WAS LIKE SEEING A PROFESSIONAL POLE DANCER AT WORK.

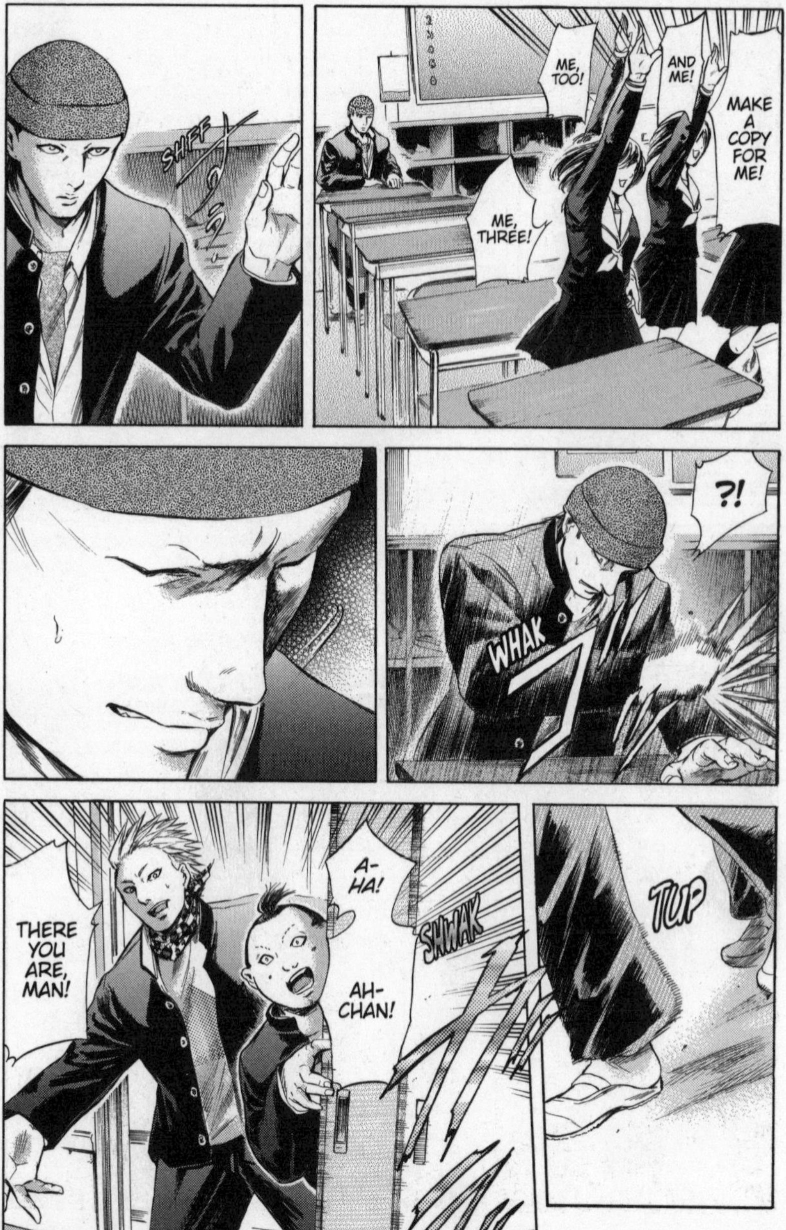
MAKE A COPY FOR ME!
AND ME!
ME, TOO!
ME, THREE!
SHIFF
?!
WHAK
TUP
SHWAK
A-HA!
AH-CHAN!
THERE YOU ARE, MAN!

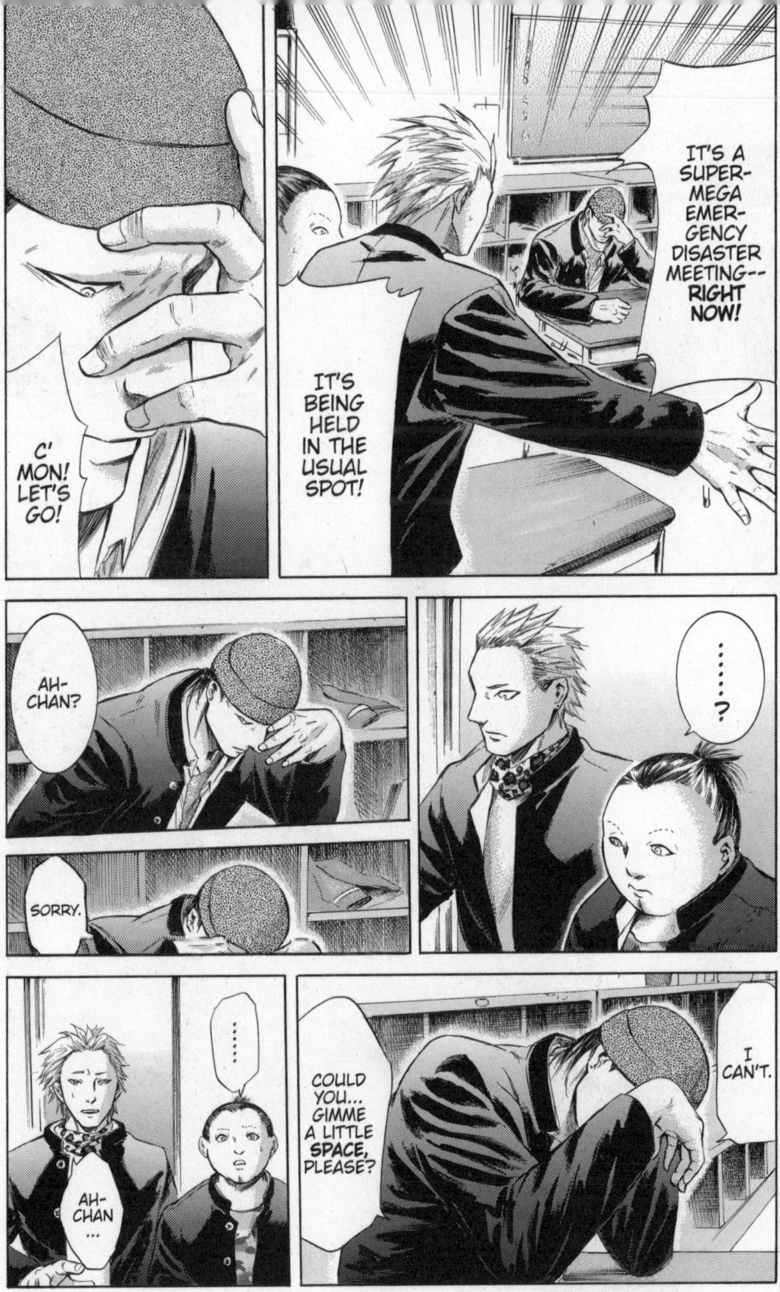
IT'S A SUPER-MEGA EMERGENCY DISASTER MEETING-- RIGHT NOW!
IT'S BEING HELD IN THE USUAL SPOT!
C' MON! LET'S GO!
......?
AH-CHAN?
SORRY.
I CAN'T.
COULD YOU... GIMME A LITTLE SPACE, PLEASE?
......
AH-CHAN ...

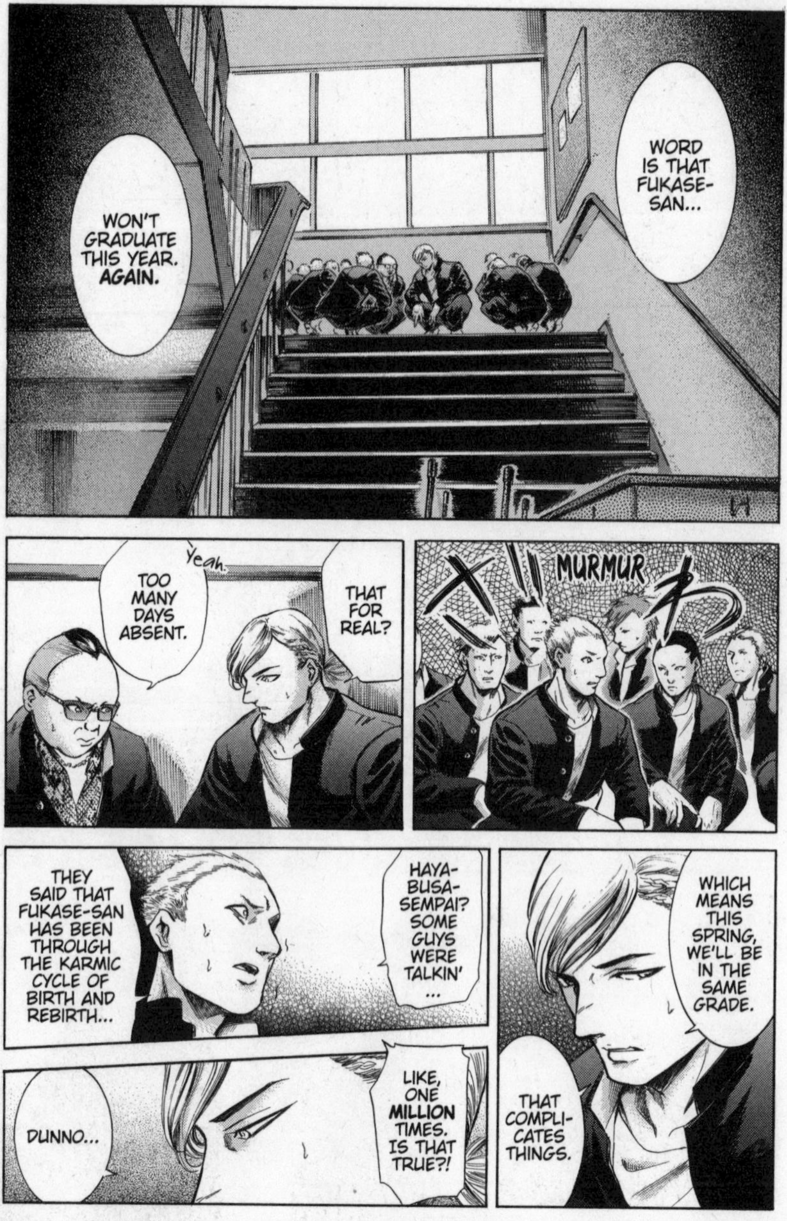
WORD IS THAT FUKASE-SAN...
WON'T GRADUATE THIS YEAR. AGAIN.
MURMUR
THAT FOR REAL?
Yeah.
TOO MANY DAYS ABSENT.
WHICH MEANS THIS SPRING, WE'LL BE IN THE SAME GRADE.
THAT COMPLI-CATES THINGS.
HAYA-BUSA-SEMPAI? SOME GUYS WERE TALKIN' ...
THEY SAID THAT FUKASE-SAN HAS BEEN THROUGH THE KARMIC CYCLE OF BIRTH AND REBIRTH...
LIKE, ONE MILLION TIMES. IS THAT TRUE?!
DUNNO...

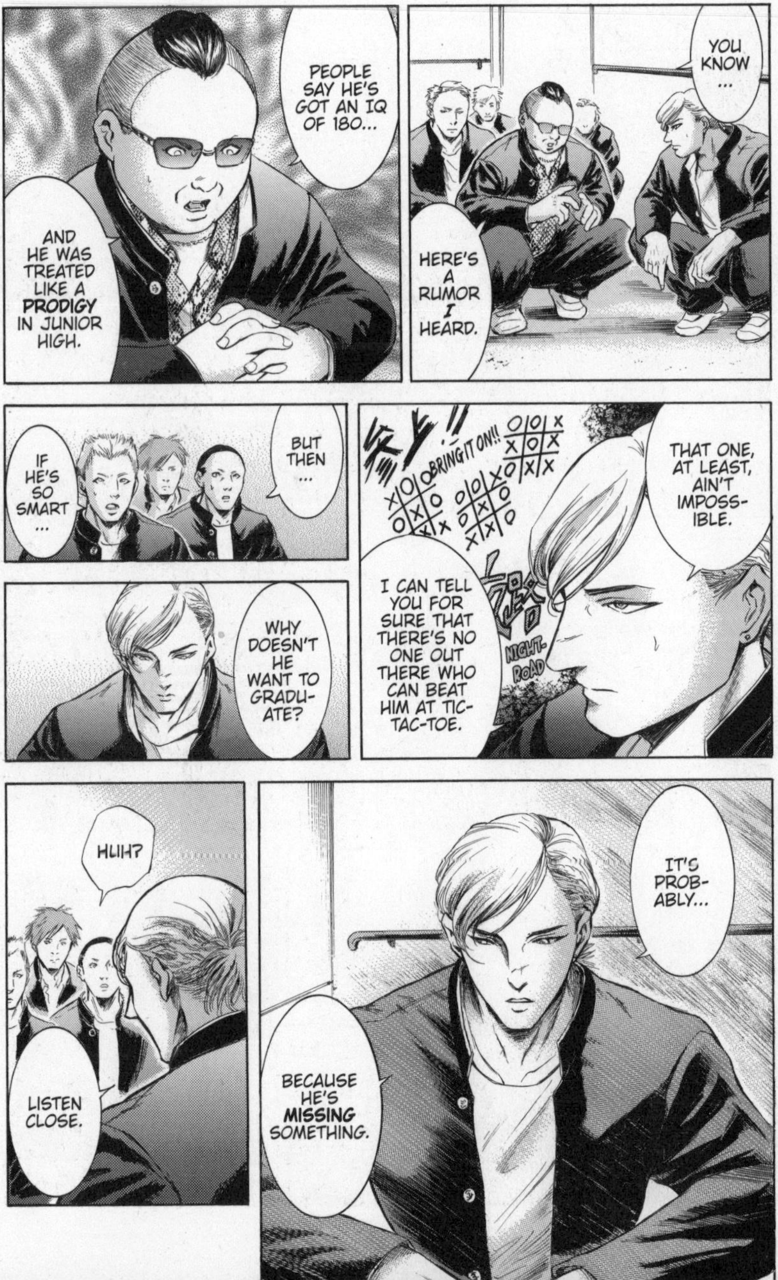
YOU KNOW ...
HERE'S A RUMOR I HEARD.
PEOPLE SAY HE'S GOT AN IQ OF 180...
AND HE WAS TREATED LIKE A PRODIGY IN JUNIOR HIGH.
BRING IT ON!!
THAT ONE, AT LEAST, AIN'T IMPOSSIBLE.
I CAN TELL YOU FOR SURE THAT THERE'S NO ONE OUT THERE WHO CAN BEAT HIM AT TIC-TAC-TOE.
NIGHT-ROAD
BUT THEN ...
IF HE'S SO SMART ...
WHY DOESN'T HE WANT TO GRADUATE?
IT'S PROBABLY...
BECAUSE HE'S MISSING SOMETHING.
HUH?
LISTEN CLOSE.

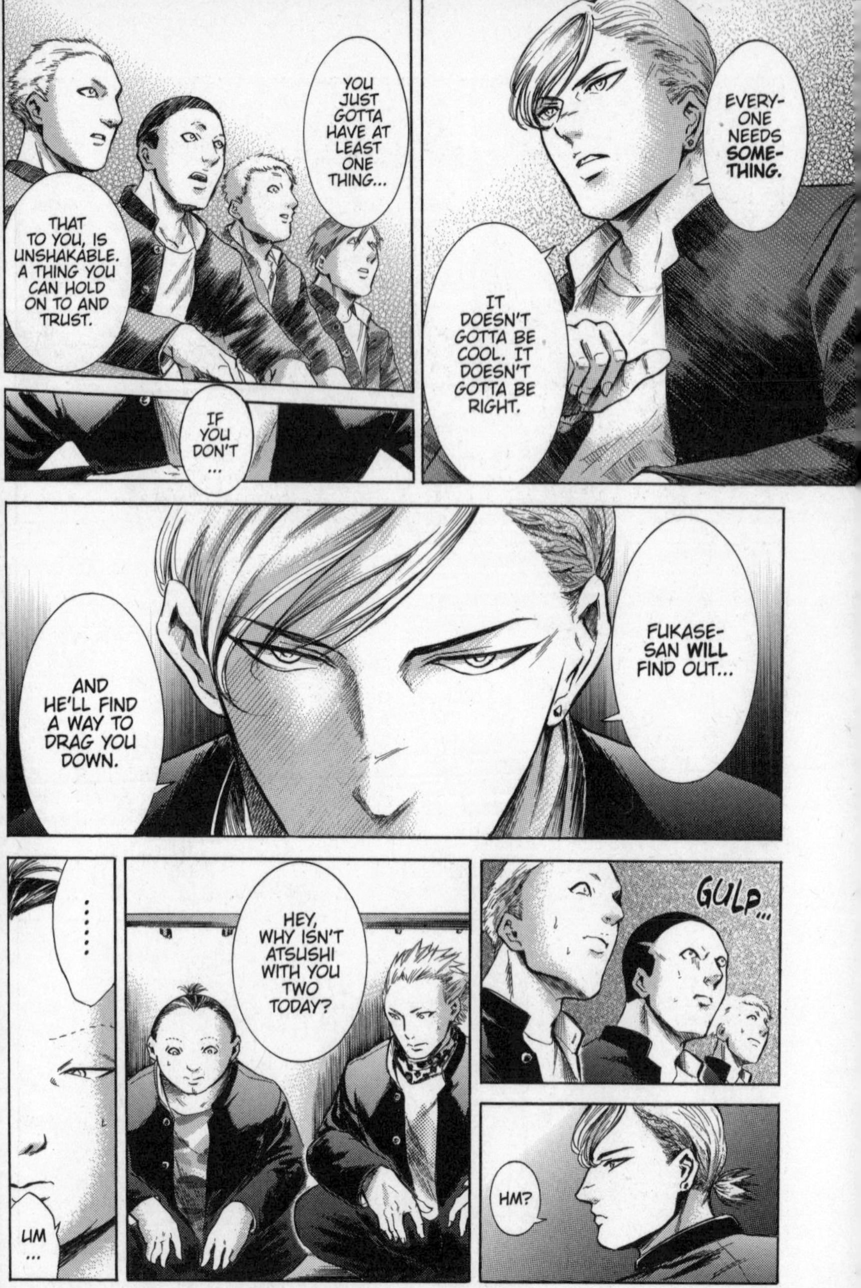
EVERY-ONE NEEDS SOME-THING.
IT DOESN'T GOTTA BE COOL. IT DOESN'T GOTTA BE RIGHT.
YOU JUST GOTTA HAVE AT LEAST ONE THING...
THAT TO YOU, IS UNSHAKABLE. A THING YOU CAN HOLD ON TO AND TRUST.
IF YOU DON'T ...
FUKASE-SAN WILL FIND OUT...
AND HE'LL FIND A WAY TO DRAG YOU DOWN.
GULP...
HM?
HEY, WHY ISN'T ATSUSHI WITH YOU TWO TODAY?
......
UM ...

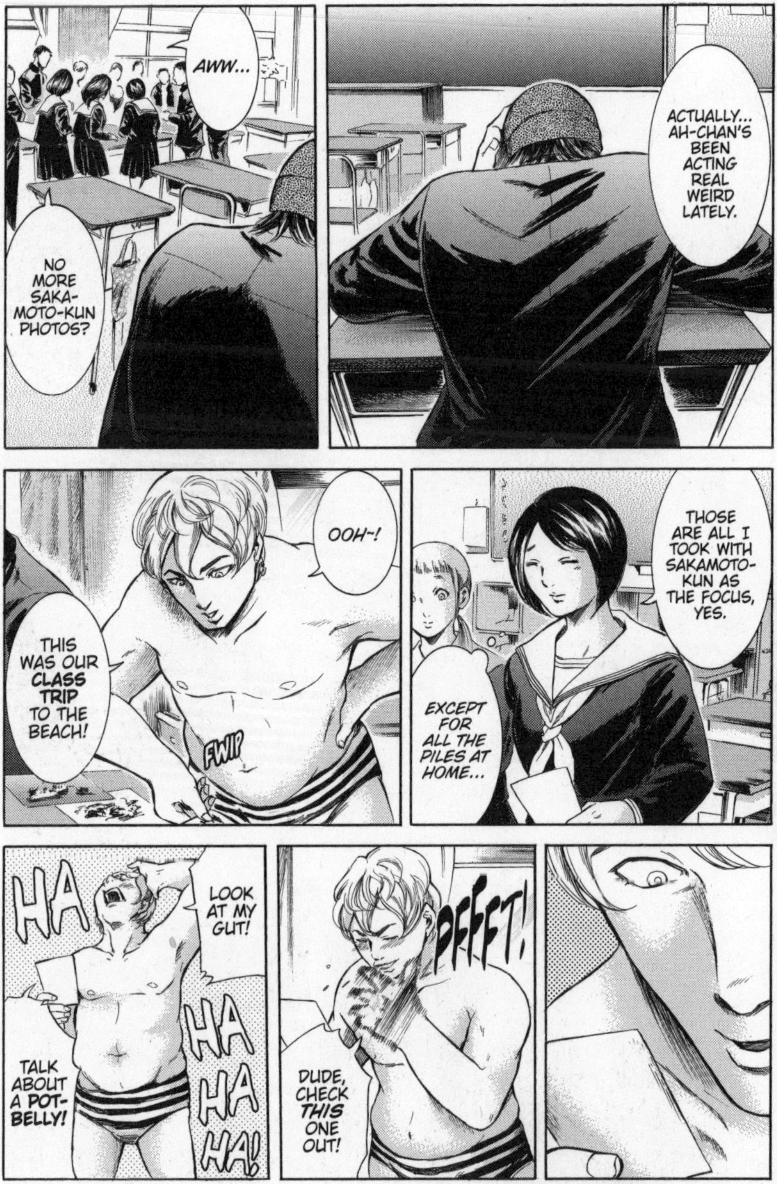
ACTUALLY... AH-CHAN'S BEEN ACTING REAL WEIRD LATELY.
AWW...
NO MORE SAKA-MOTO-KUN PHOTOS?
THOSE ARE ALL I TOOK WITH SAKAMOTO-KUN AS THE FOCUS, YES.
EXCEPT FOR ALL THE PILES AT HOME...
OOH~!
THIS WAS OUR CLASS TRIP TO THE BEACH!
FWIP
PFFFT!
DUDE, CHECK THIS ONE OUT!
LOOK AT MY GUT!
HA HA HA HA!
TALK ABOUT A POT-BELLY!

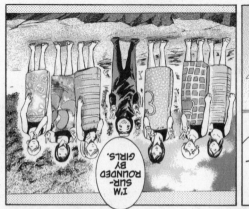

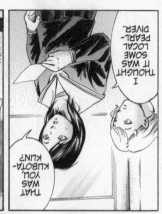

HUH ...?
YOU LOOK THE SAME TO ME.
HMM, LET'S SEE... DO YOU STILL...
HAVE THAT ONE PICTURE OF ME?
A-HA! HERE IT IS ...!
FOR THE FIRST TIME...
I'M SUR-ROUNDED BY GIRLS.
THAT WAS YOU, KUBOTA-KUN?
I THOUGHT IT WAS SOME LOCAL PEARL-DIVER.

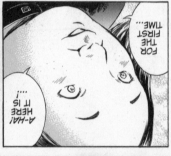

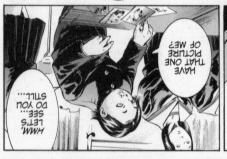

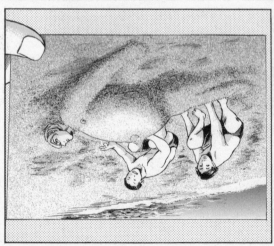

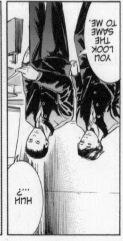

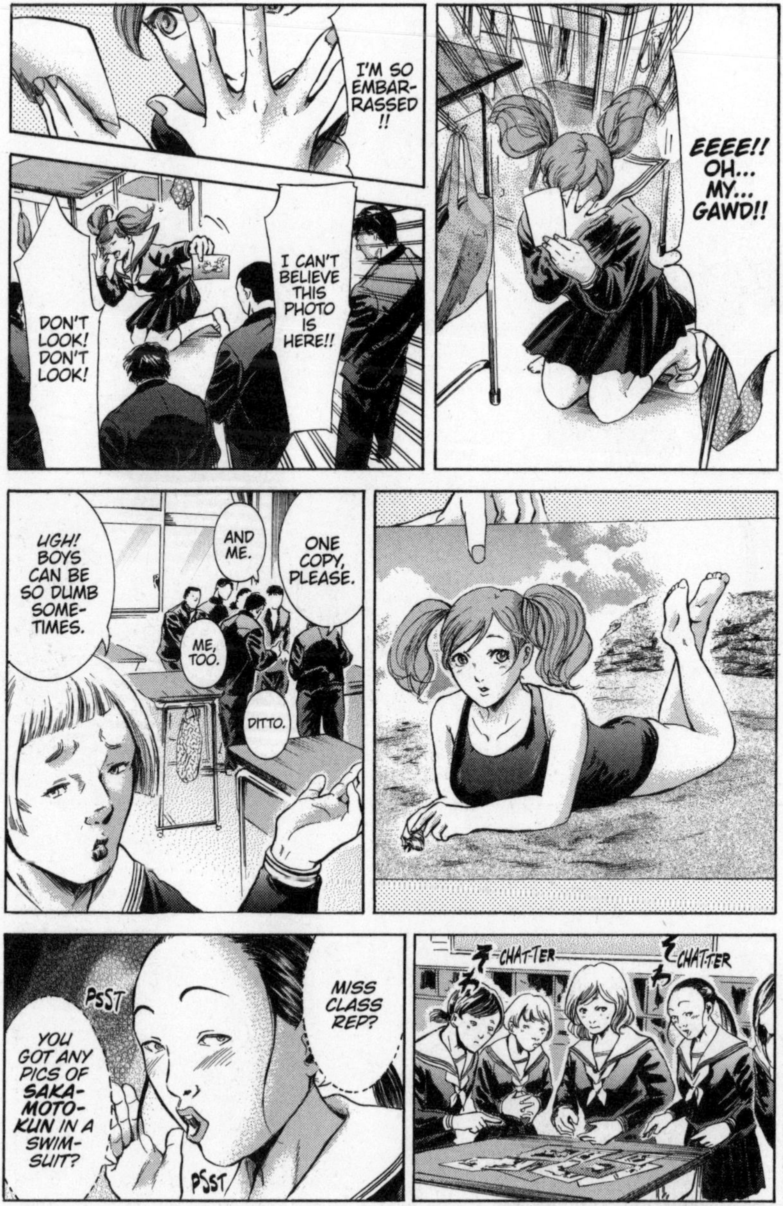
EEEE!! OH... MY... GAWD!!
I'M SO EMBARRASSED!!
I CAN'T BELIEVE THIS PHOTO IS HERE!!
DON'T LOOK! DON'T LOOK!
ONE COPY, PLEASE.
AND ME.
ME, TOO.
DITTO.
UGH! BOYS CAN BE SO DUMB SOMETIMES.
CHAT-TER
CHAT-TER
MISS CLASS REP?
PSST
YOU GOT ANY PICS OF SAKAMOTO-KUN IN A SWIMSUIT?
PSST

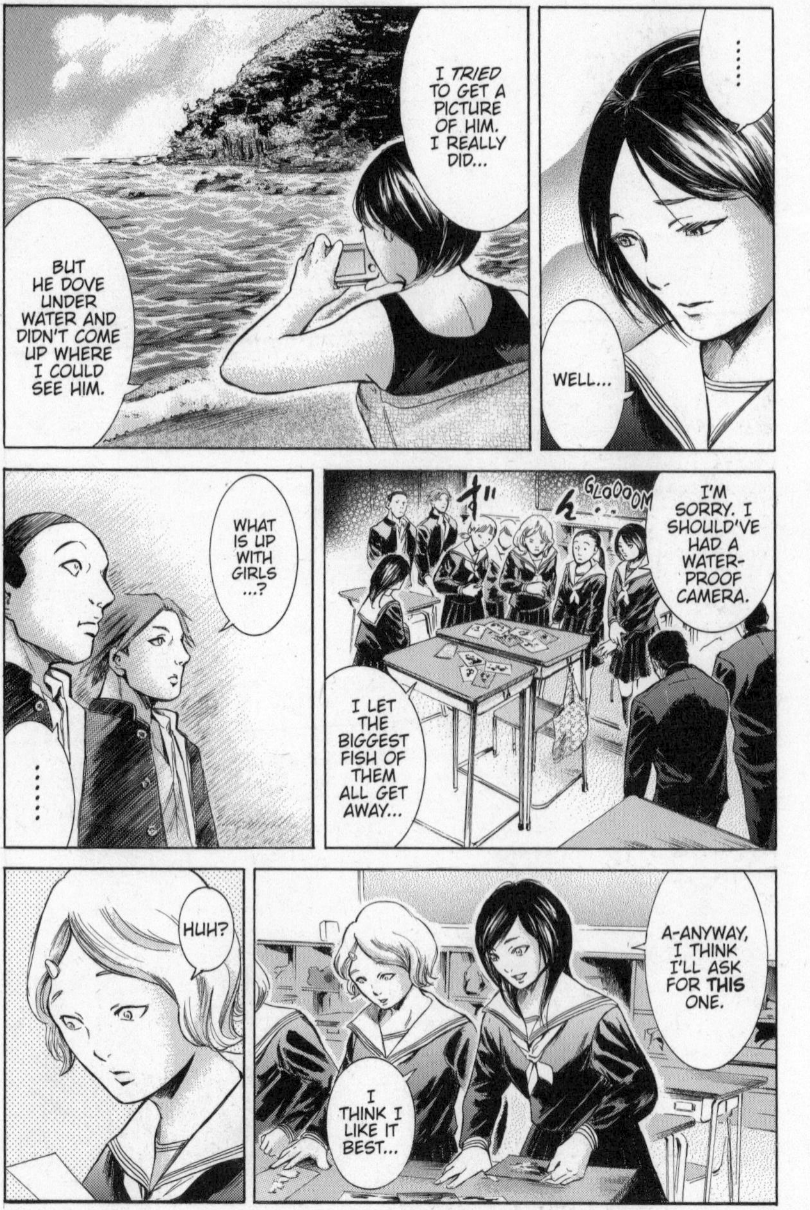
......
WELL...
I TRIED TO GET A PICTURE OF HIM. I REALLY DID...
BUT HE DOVE UNDER WATER AND DIDN'T COME UP WHERE I COULD SEE HIM.
GLOOOOM
I'M SORRY. I SHOULD'VE HAD A WATER-PROOF CAMERA.
I LET THE BIGGEST FISH OF THEM ALL GET AWAY...
WHAT IS UP WITH GIRLS ...?
......
A-ANYWAY, I THINK I'LL ASK FOR THIS ONE.
I THINK I LIKE IT BEST...
HUH?

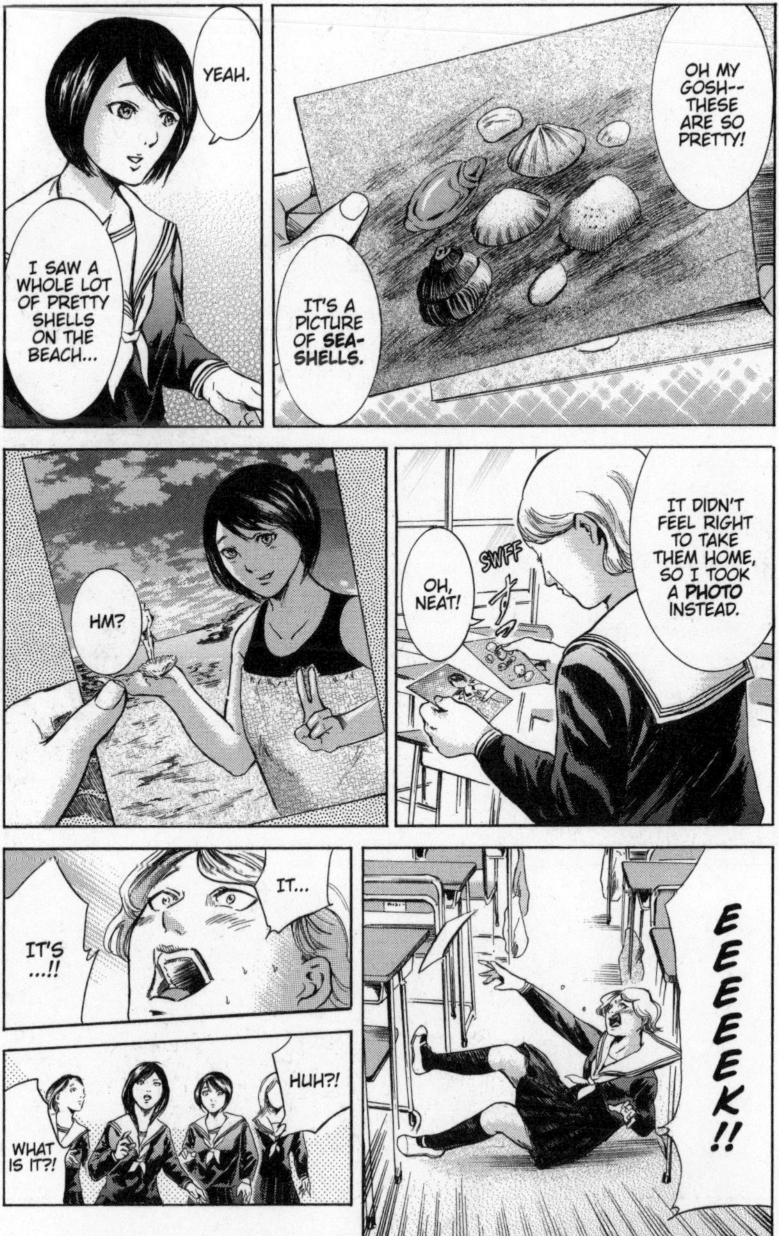
OH MY GOSH-- THESE ARE SO PRETTY!
IT'S A PICTURE OF SEA-SHELLS.
YEAH.
I SAW A WHOLE LOT OF PRETTY SHELLS ON THE BEACH...
IT DIDN'T FEEL RIGHT TO TAKE THEM HOME, SO I TOOK A PHOTO INSTEAD.
SWFF
OH, NEAT!
HM?
EEEEEEK!!
IT...
IT'S ...!!
HUH?!
WHAT IS IT?!

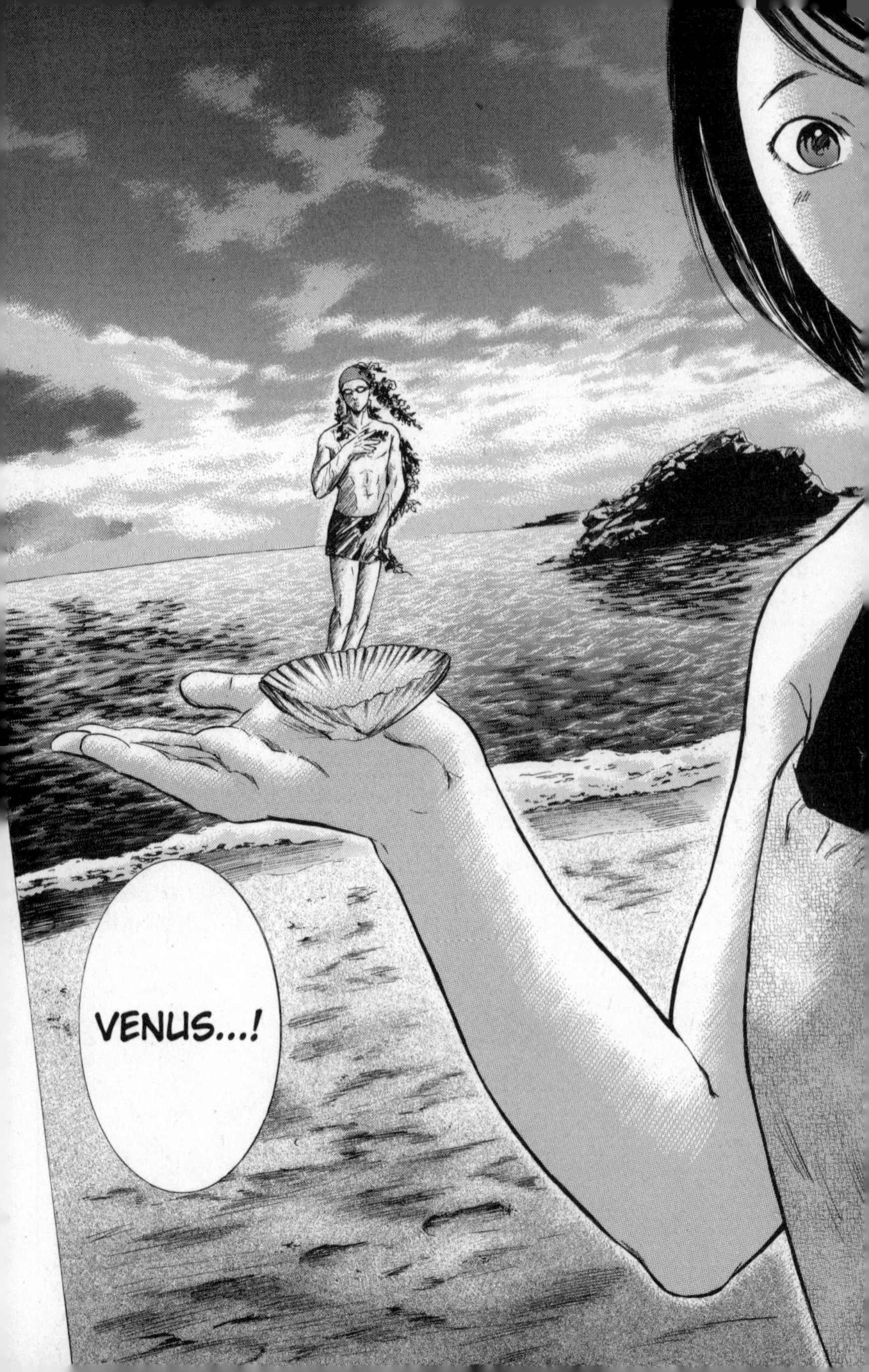
VENUS...!

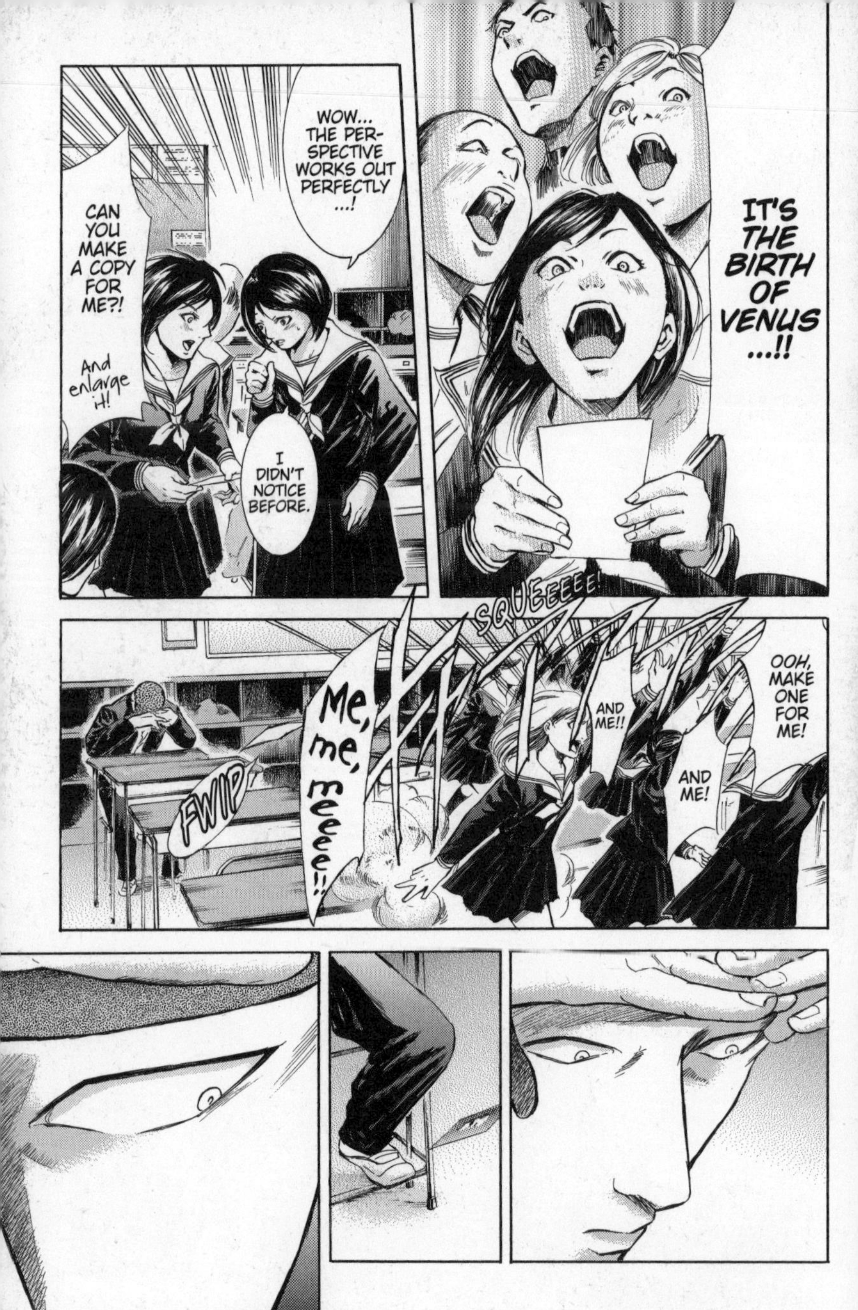
IT'S THE BIRTH OF VENUS ...!!
SQUEEEEE!
WOW... THE PER-SPECTIVE WORKS OUT PERFECTLY ...!
I DIDN'T NOTICE BEFORE.
CAN YOU MAKE A COPY FOR ME?!
And enlarge it!
OOH, MAKE ONE FOR ME!
AND ME!
AND ME!!
Me, me, meeee!!
FWIP

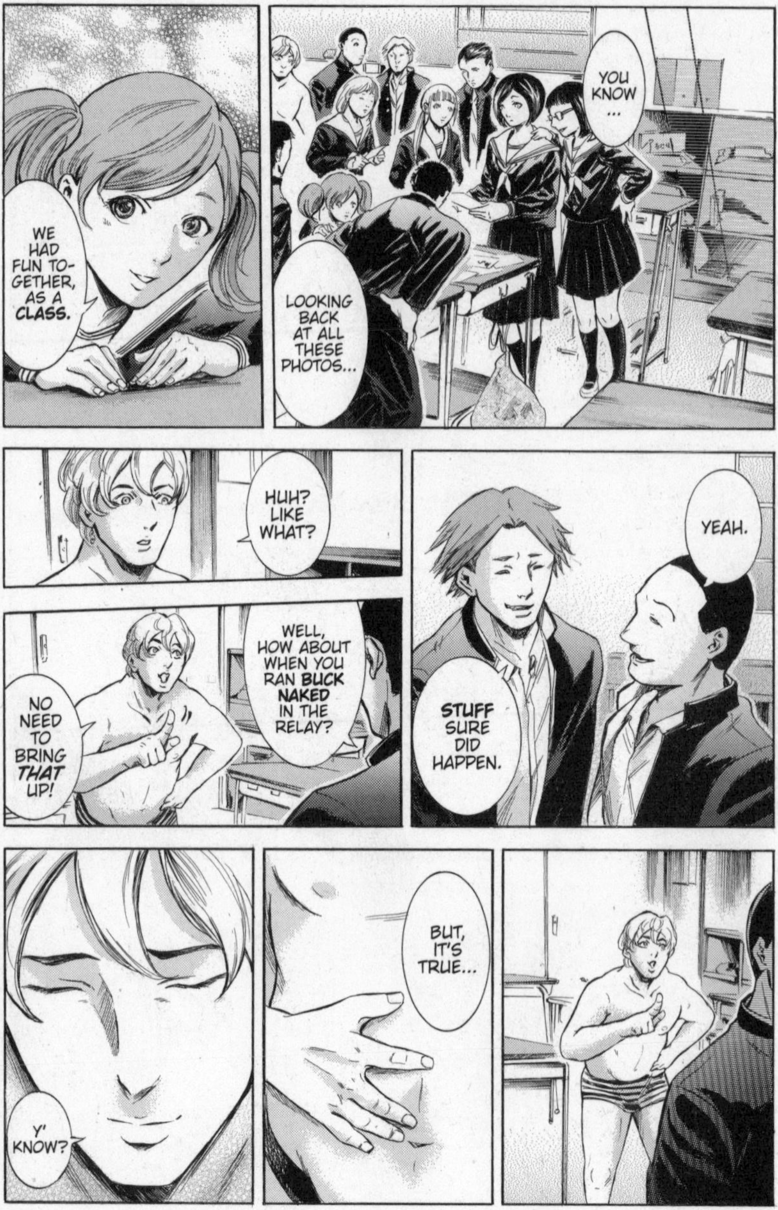
YOU KNOW ...
LOOKING BACK AT ALL THESE PHOTOS...
WE HAD FUN TO-GETHER, AS A **CLASS.**
YEAH.
STUFF SURE DID HAPPEN.
HUH? LIKE WHAT?
WELL, HOW ABOUT WHEN YOU RAN **BUCK NAKED** IN THE RELAY?
NO NEED TO BRING ***THAT*** UP!
BUT, IT'S TRUE...
Y' KNOW?

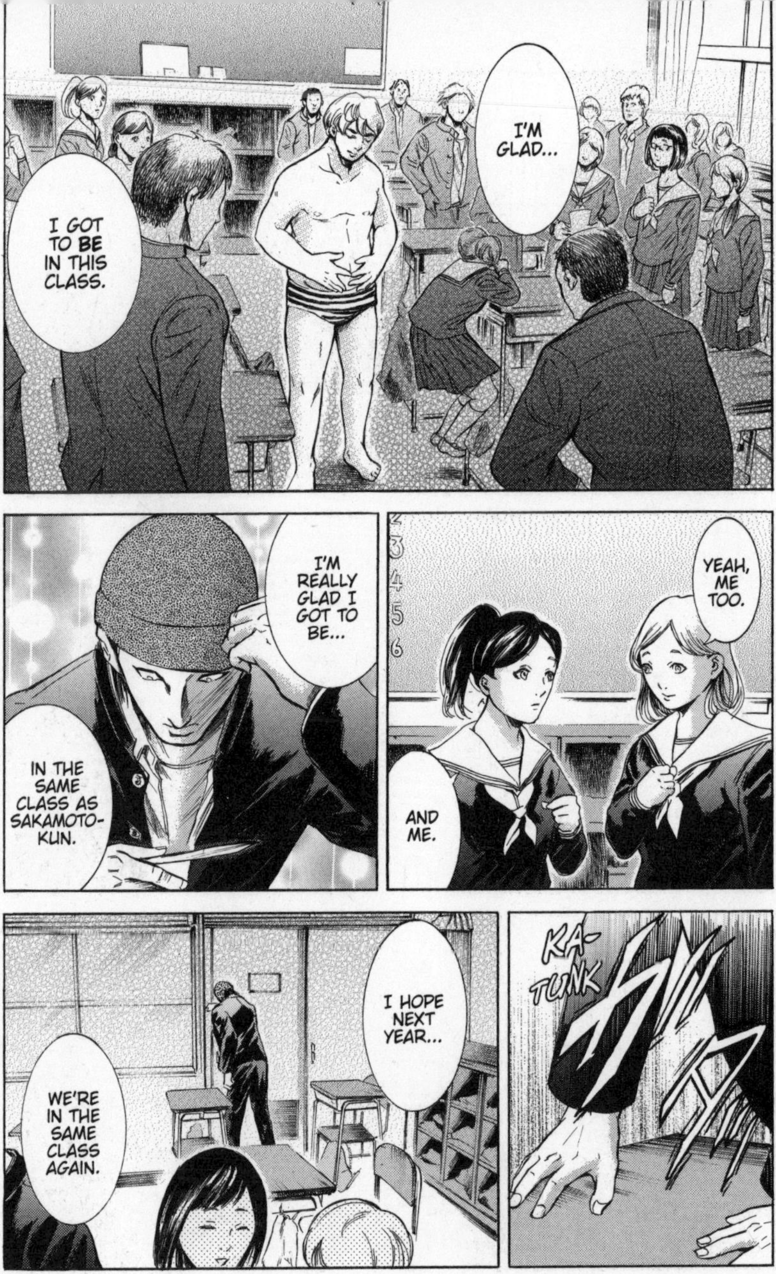
I'M GLAD...
I GOT TO BE IN THIS CLASS.
YEAH, ME TOO.
AND ME.
I'M REALLY GLAD I GOT TO BE...
IN THE SAME CLASS AS SAKAMOTO-KUN.
KA-TUNK
I HOPE NEXT YEAR...
WE'RE IN THE SAME CLASS AGAIN.

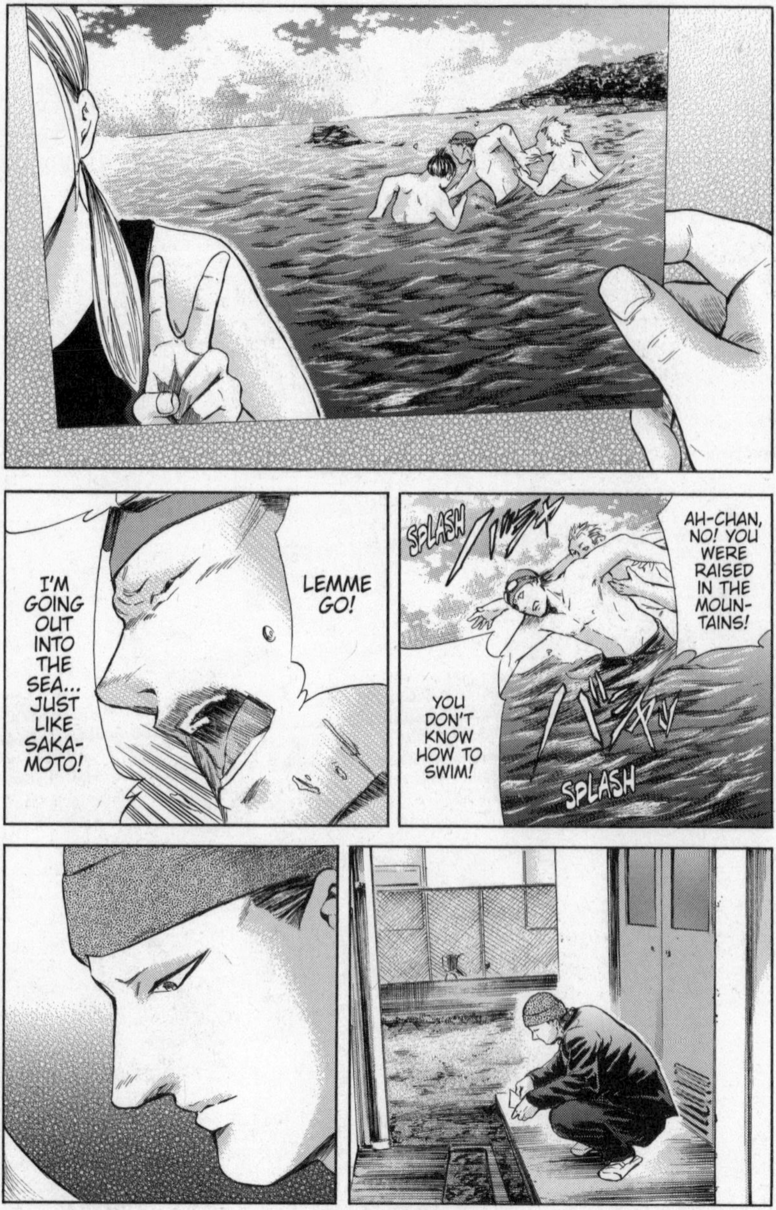
AH-CHAN, NO! YOU WERE RAISED IN THE MOUN-TAINS!
SPLASH
YOU DON'T KNOW HOW TO SWIM!
SPLASH
LEMME GO!
I'M GOING OUT INTO THE SEA... JUST LIKE SAKA-MOTO!

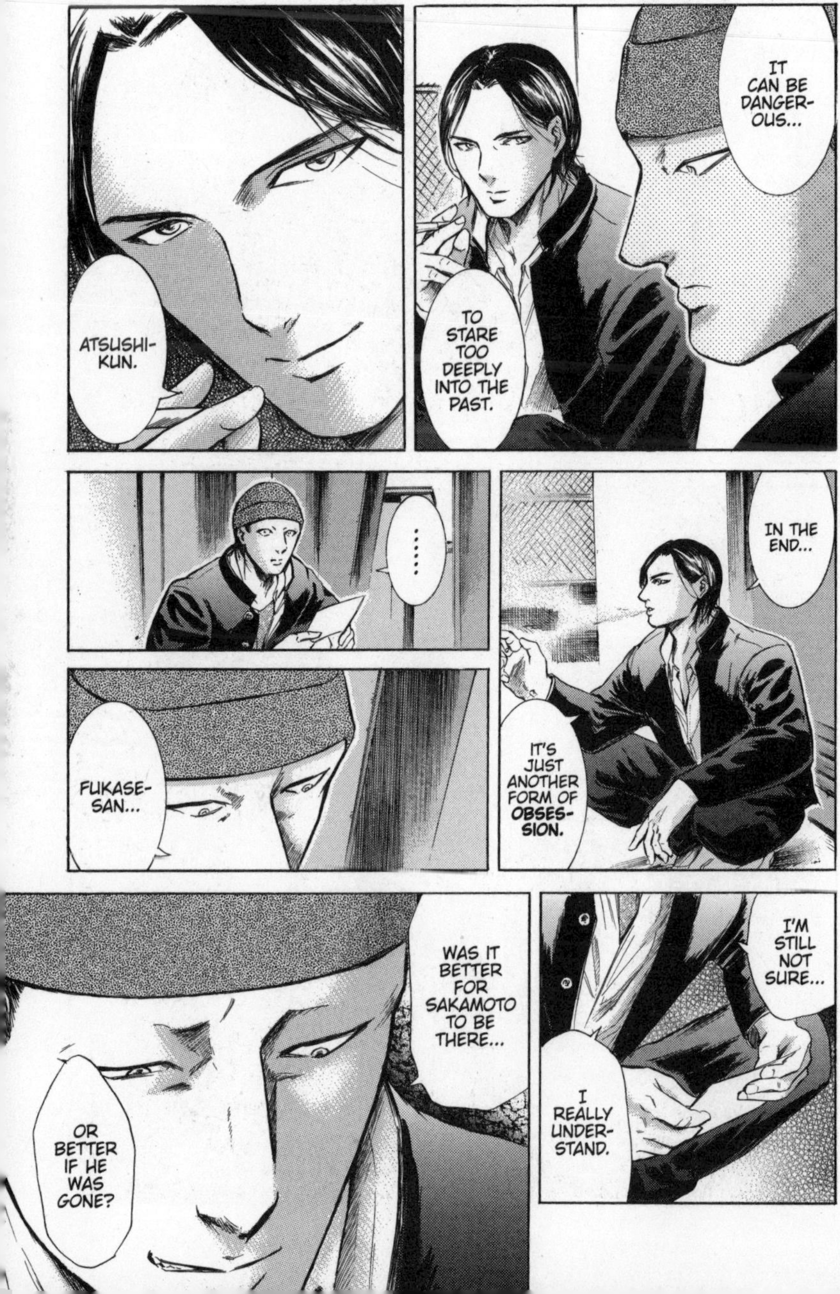
IT CAN BE DANGER-OUS...
TO STARE TOO DEEPLY INTO THE PAST.
ATSUSHI-KUN.
IN THE END...
IT'S JUST ANOTHER FORM OF OBSES-SION.
......
FUKASE-SAN...
I'M STILL NOT SURE...
I REALLY UNDER-STAND.
WAS IT BETTER FOR SAKAMOTO TO BE THERE...
OR BETTER IF HE WAS GONE?

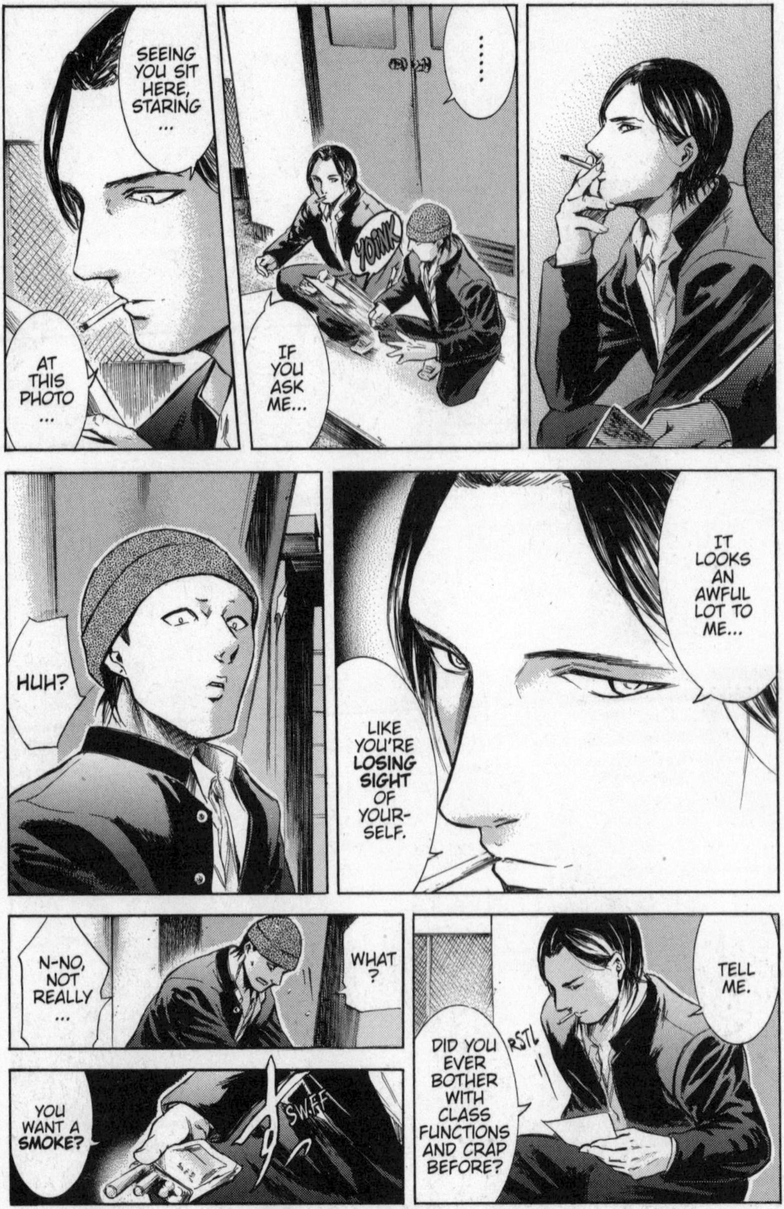
......
YOINK
IF YOU ASK ME...
SEEING YOU SIT HERE, STARING ...
AT THIS PHOTO ...
IT LOOKS AN AWFUL LOT TO ME...
LIKE YOU'RE LOSING SIGHT OF YOUR-SELF.
HUH?
TELL ME.
RSTL
DID YOU EVER BOTHER WITH CLASS FUNCTIONS AND CRAP BEFORE?
WHAT ?
N-NO, NOT REALLY ...
SWFF
YOU WANT A SMOKE?

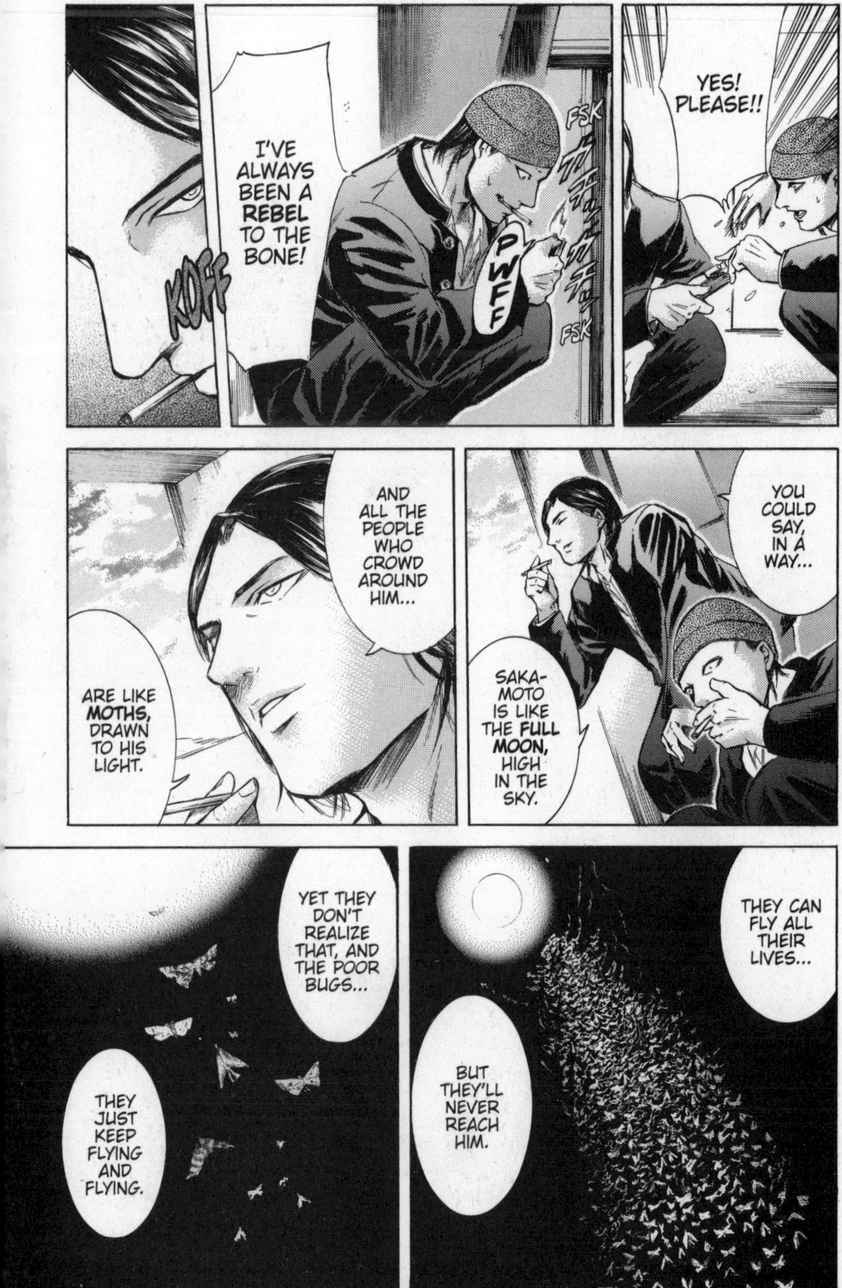
YES! PLEASE!!
I'VE ALWAYS BEEN A REBEL TO THE BONE!
PWFF
FSK
FSK
KOFF
YOU COULD SAY, IN A WAY...
SAKA-MOTO IS LIKE THE FULL MOON, HIGH IN THE SKY.
AND ALL THE PEOPLE WHO CROWD AROUND HIM...
ARE LIKE MOTHS, DRAWN TO HIS LIGHT.
THEY CAN FLY ALL THEIR LIVES...
BUT THEY'LL NEVER REACH HIM.
YET THEY DON'T REALIZE THAT, AND THE POOR BUGS...
THEY JUST KEEP FLYING AND FLYING.

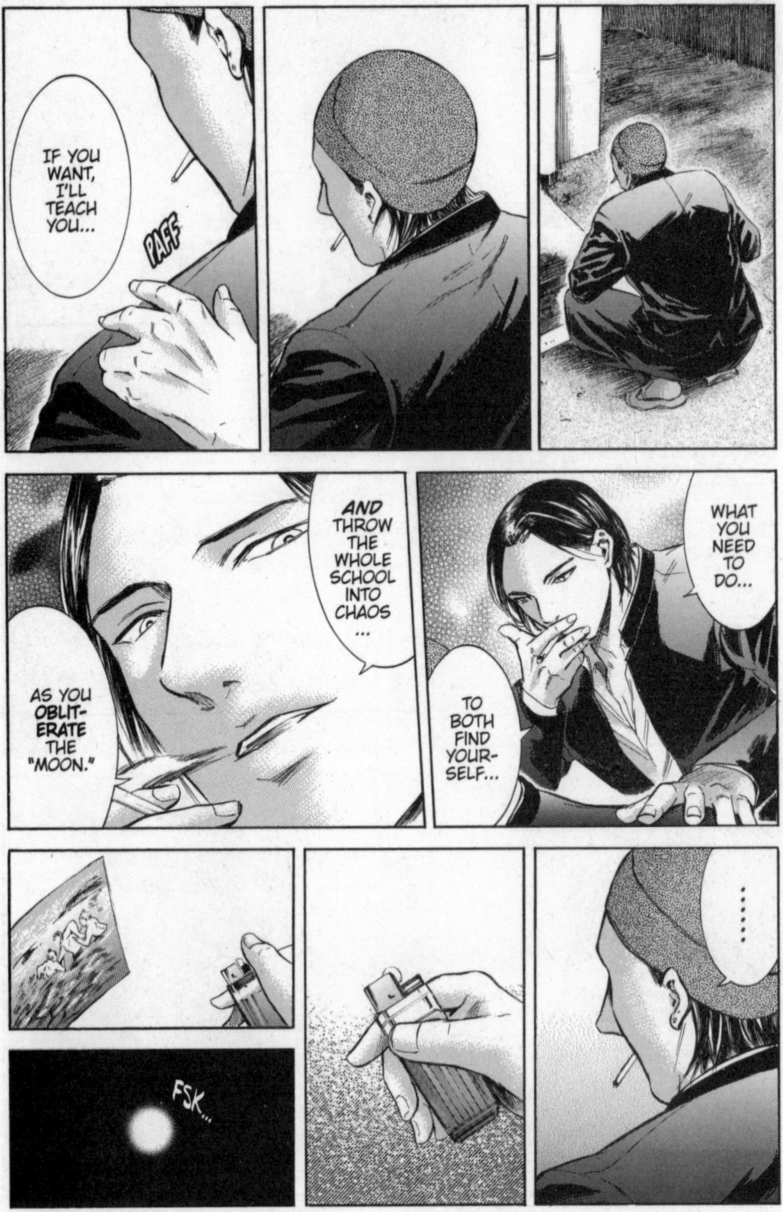
IF YOU WANT, I'LL TEACH YOU...
PAFF
WHAT YOU NEED TO DO...
TO BOTH FIND YOUR-SELF...
AND THROW THE WHOLE SCHOOL INTO CHAOS ...
AS YOU OBLIT-ERATE THE "MOON."
......
FSK...

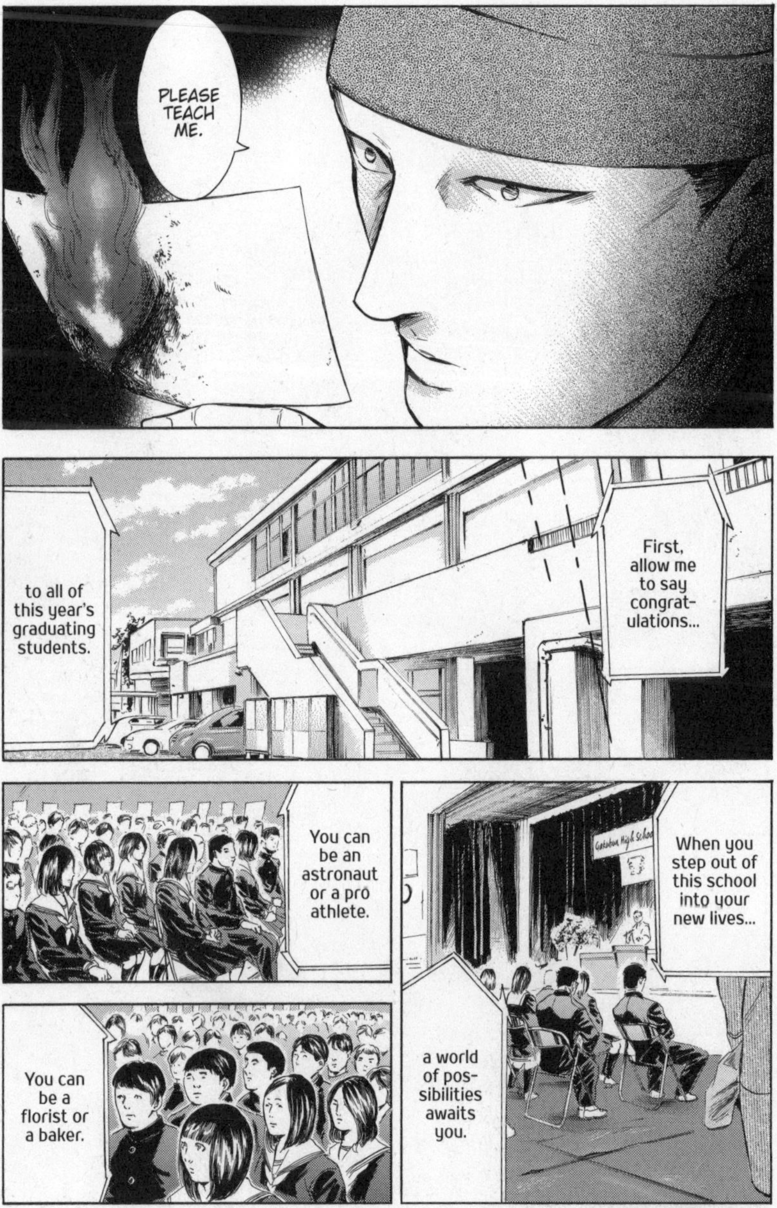
PLEASE TEACH ME.
First, allow me to say congratulations...
to all of this year's graduating students.
When you step out of this school into your new lives...
a world of possibilities awaits you.
You can be an astronaut or a pro athlete.
You can be a florist or a baker.

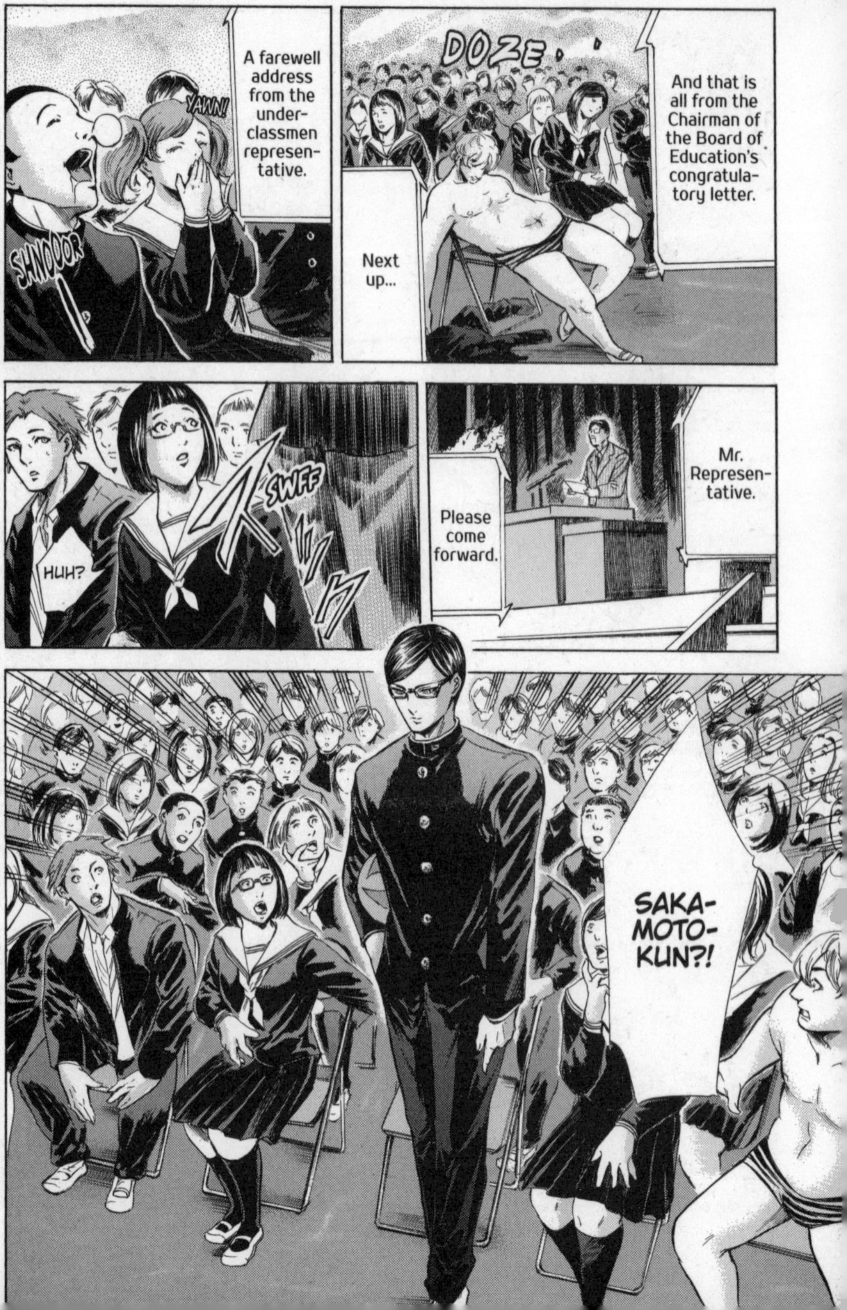
And that is all from the Chairman of the Board of Education's congratulatory letter.
DOZE
Next up...
A farewell address from the underclassmen representative.
YAWN!
SHNOOOR
Mr. Representative.
Please come forward.
SWFF
HUH?
SAKA-MOTO-KUN?!

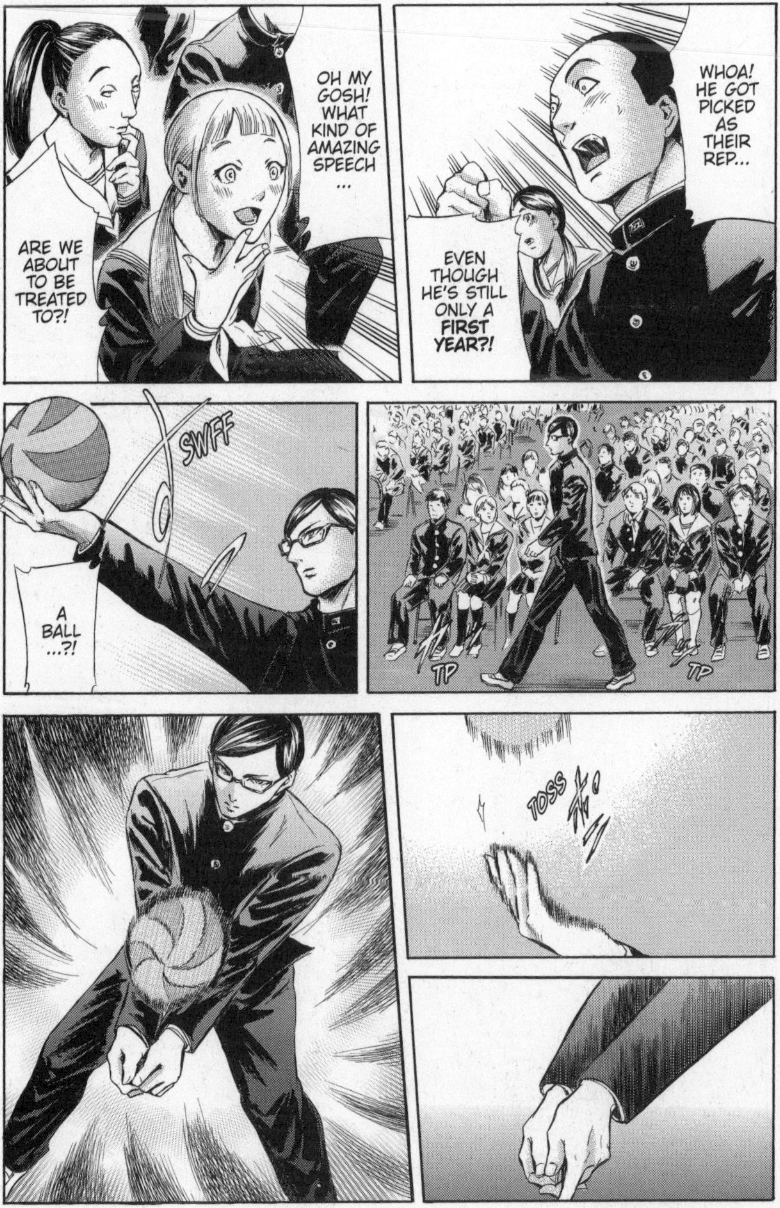
WHOA! HE GOT PICKED AS THEIR REP...
EVEN THOUGH HE'S STILL ONLY A FIRST YEAR?!
OH MY GOSH! WHAT KIND OF AMAZING SPEECH ...
ARE WE ABOUT TO BE TREATED TO?!
TP
TP
SWFF
A BALL ...?!
TOSS

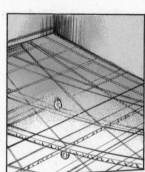

WHAT THE HECK IS HE DOING?!

HE HIT IT WAY UP TOWARDS THE CEILING...?!

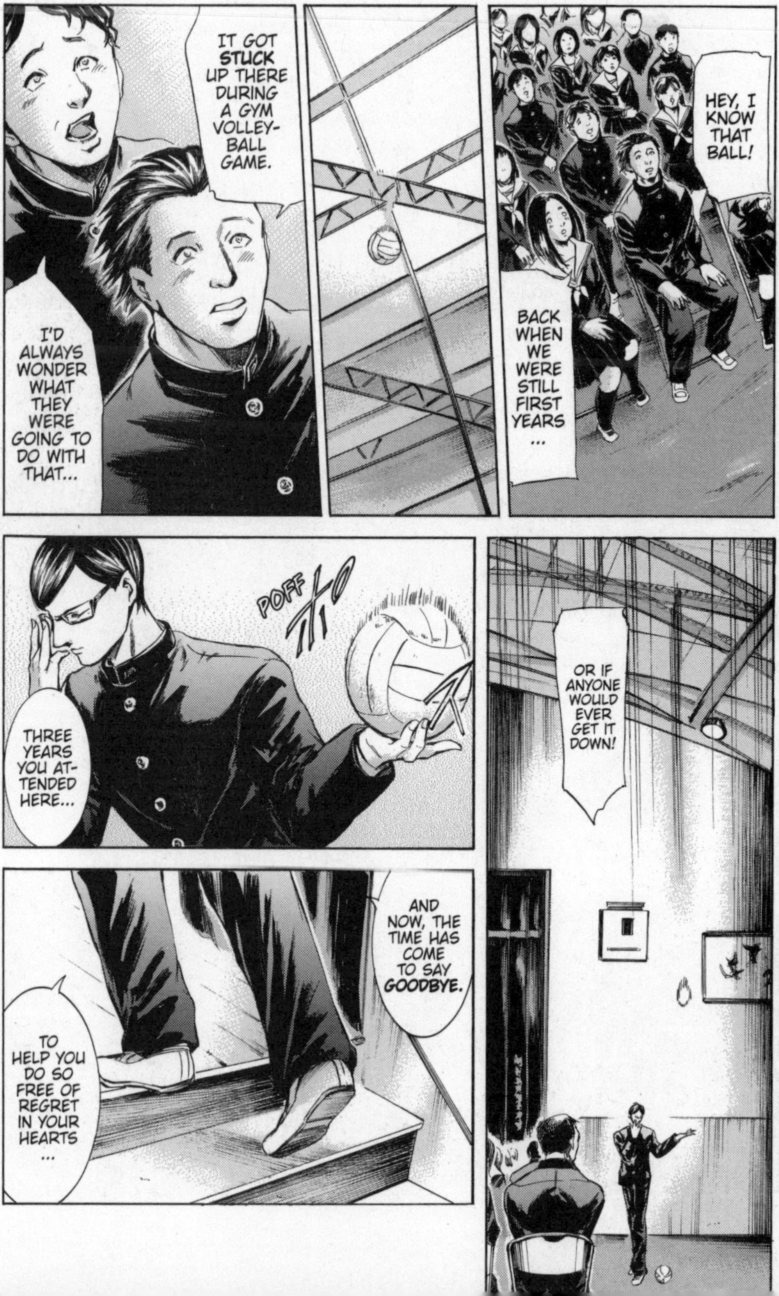
HEY, I KNOW THAT BALL!
BACK WHEN WE WERE STILL FIRST YEARS...
IT GOT STUCK UP THERE DURING A GYM VOLLEYBALL GAME.
I'D ALWAYS WONDER WHAT THEY WERE GOING TO DO WITH THAT...
OR IF ANYONE WOULD EVER GET IT DOWN!
POFF
THREE YEARS YOU ATTENDED HERE...
AND NOW, THE TIME HAS COME TO SAY GOODBYE.
TO HELP YOU DO SO FREE OF REGRET IN YOUR HEARTS...

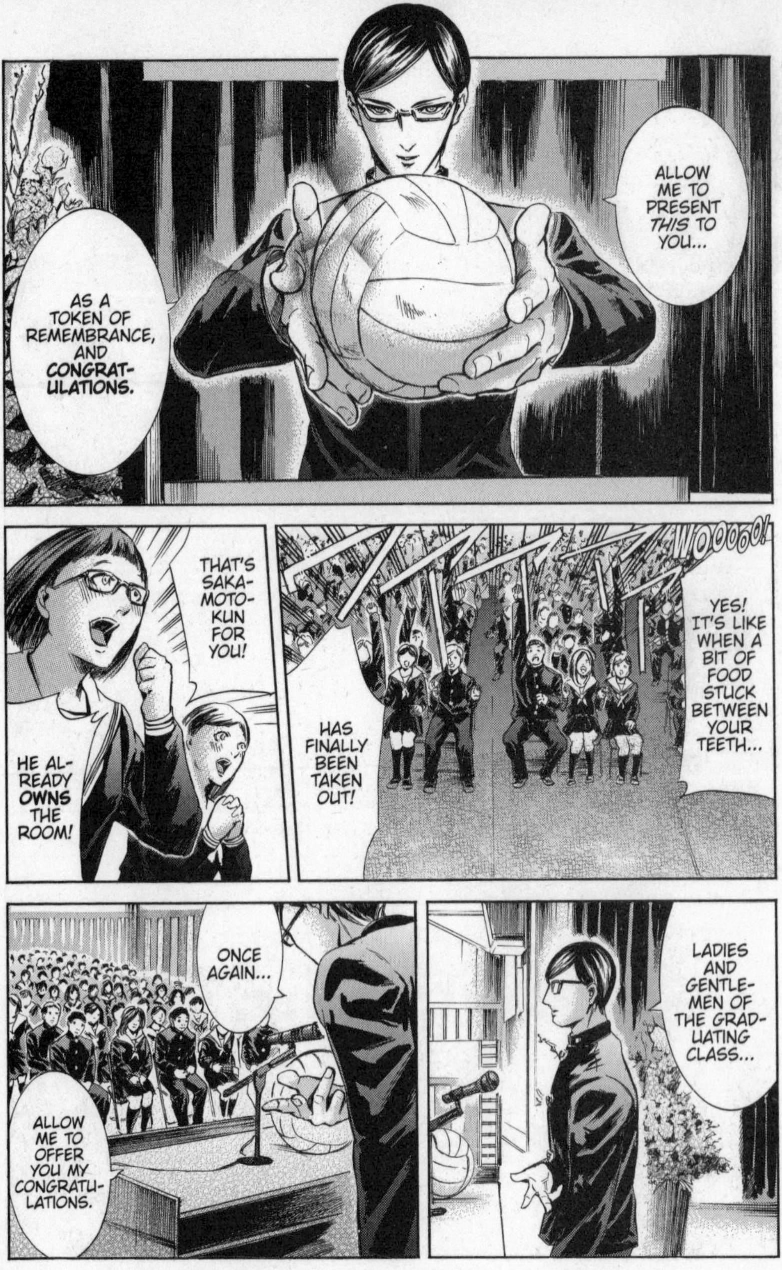
ALLOW ME TO PRESENT THIS TO YOU...
AS A TOKEN OF REMEMBRANCE, AND CONGRATULATIONS.
WOOOOO!
YES! IT'S LIKE WHEN A BIT OF FOOD STUCK BETWEEN YOUR TEETH...
HAS FINALLY BEEN TAKEN OUT!
THAT'S SAKAMOTO-KUN FOR YOU!
HE ALREADY OWNS THE ROOM!
LADIES AND GENTLEMEN OF THE GRADUATING CLASS...
ONCE AGAIN...
ALLOW ME TO OFFER YOU MY CONGRATULATIONS.

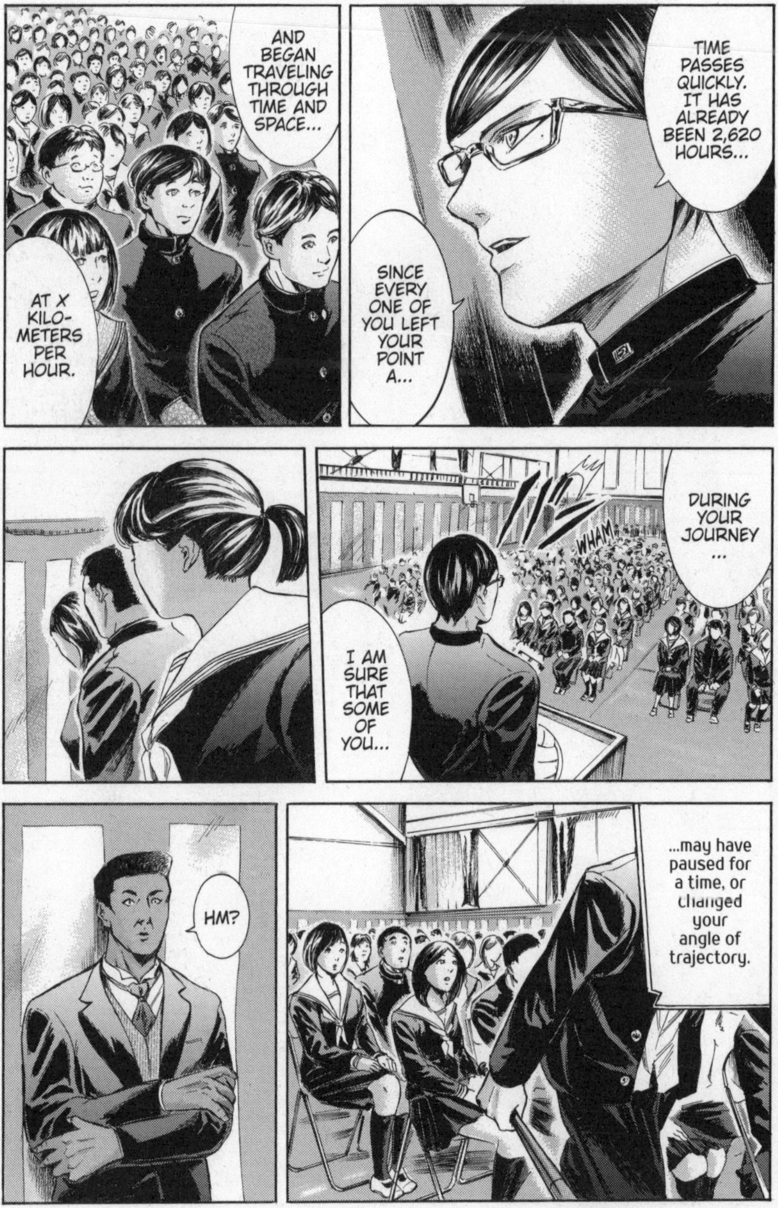
TIME PASSES QUICKLY. IT HAS ALREADY BEEN 2,620 HOURS...
SINCE EVERY ONE OF YOU LEFT YOUR POINT A...
AND BEGAN TRAVELING THROUGH TIME AND SPACE...
AT X KILO-METERS PER HOUR.
DURING YOUR JOURNEY ...
WHAM
I AM SURE THAT SOME OF YOU...
...may have paused for a time, or changed your angle of trajectory.
HM?

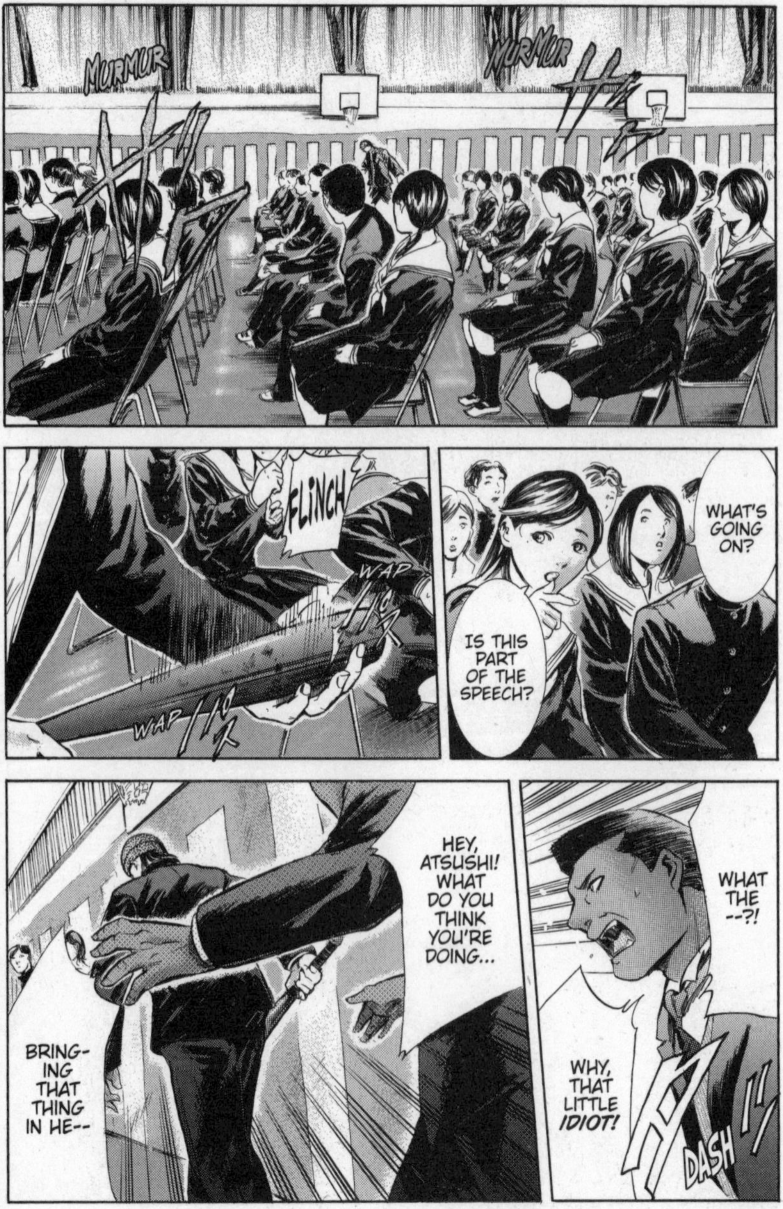
MURMUR
MURMUR
WHAT'S GOING ON?
IS THIS PART OF THE SPEECH?
FLINCH
WAP
WAP
WHAT THE --?!
WHY, THAT LITTLE IDIOT!
DASH
HEY, ATSUSHI! WHAT DO YOU THINK YOU'RE DOING...
BRING-ING THAT THING IN HE--

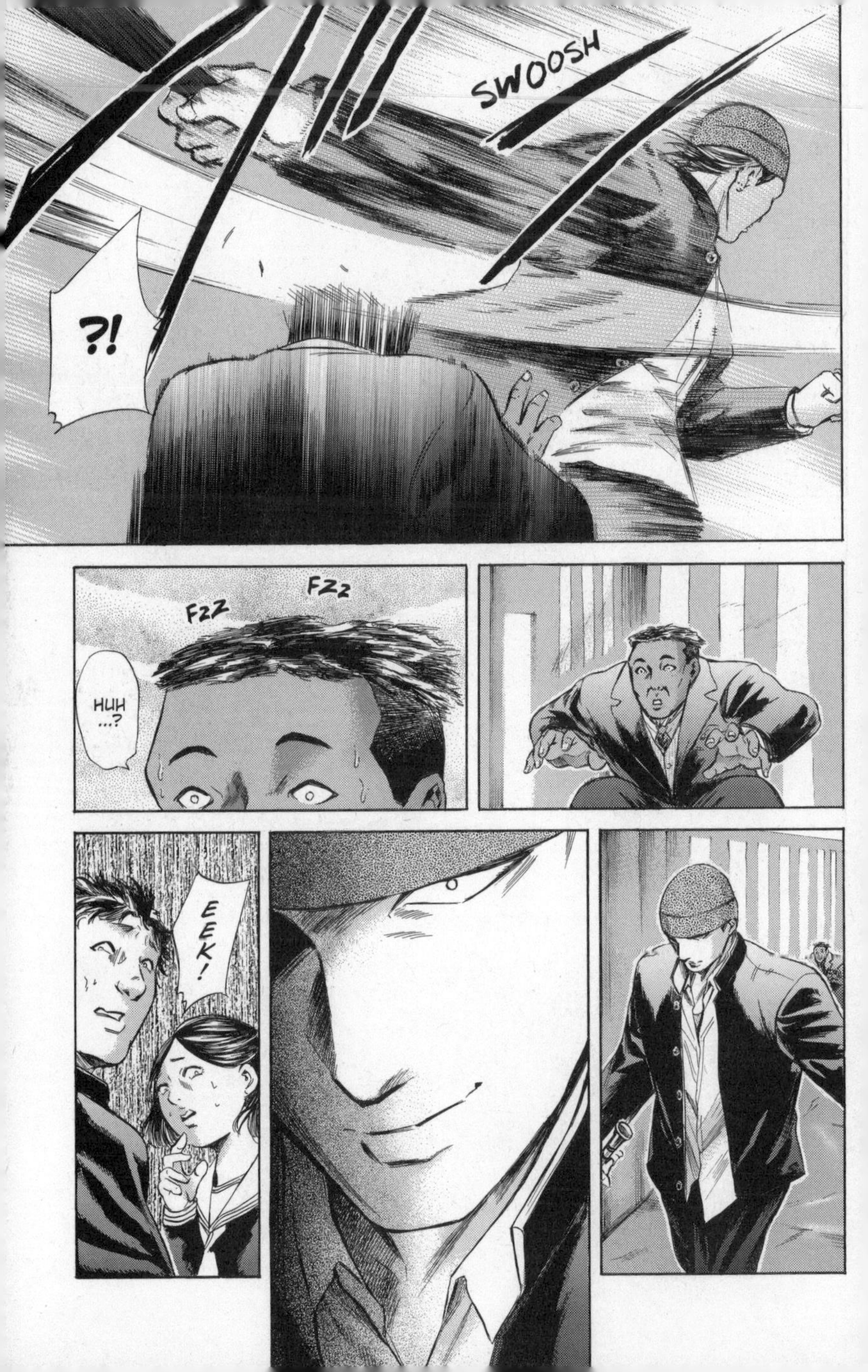
SWOOSH
?!
FZZ
FZZ
HUH ...?
EEK!

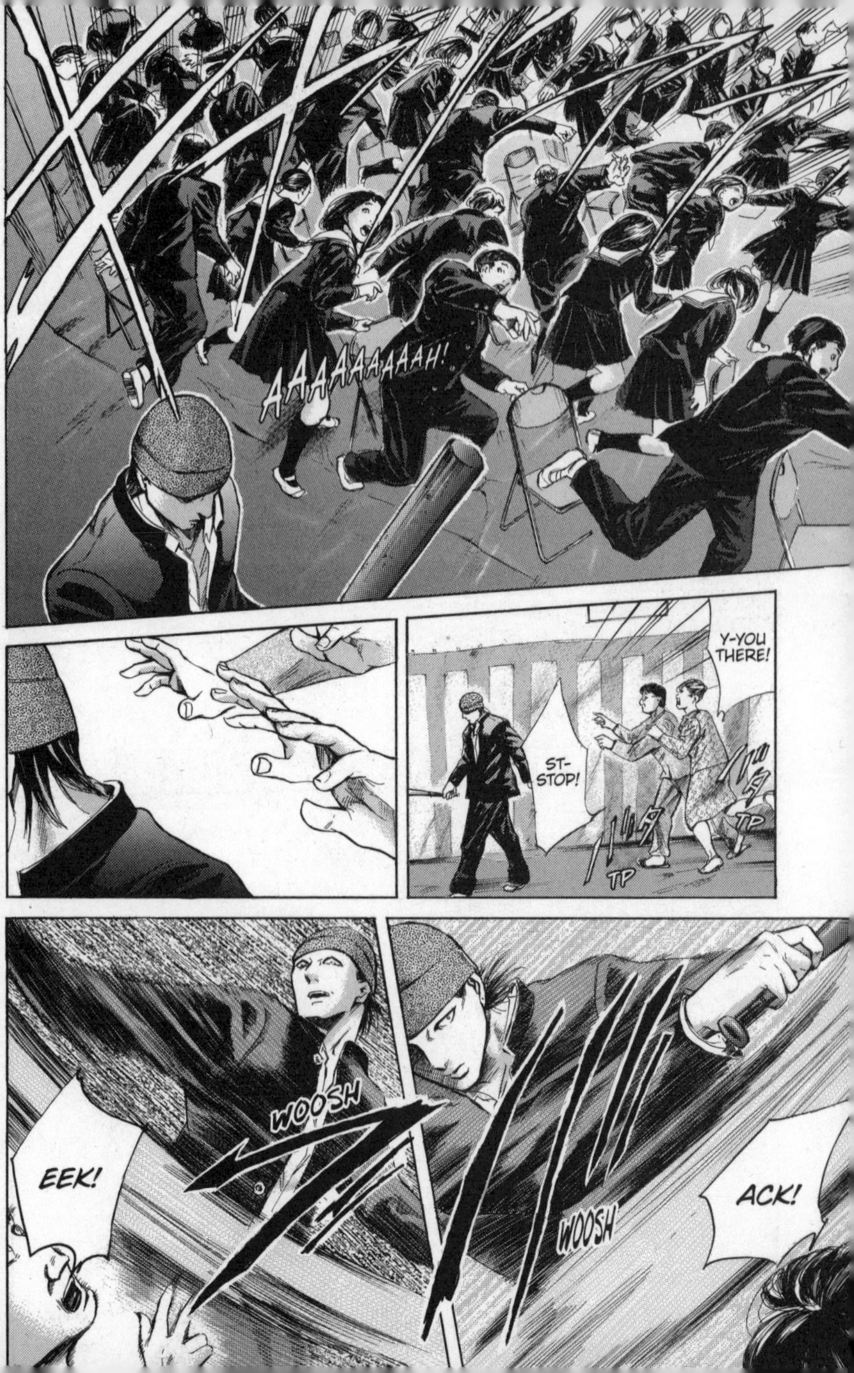
AAAAAAAAAH!
Y-YOU THERE!
TP
TP
ST-STOP!
ACK!
WOOSH
WOOSH
EEK!

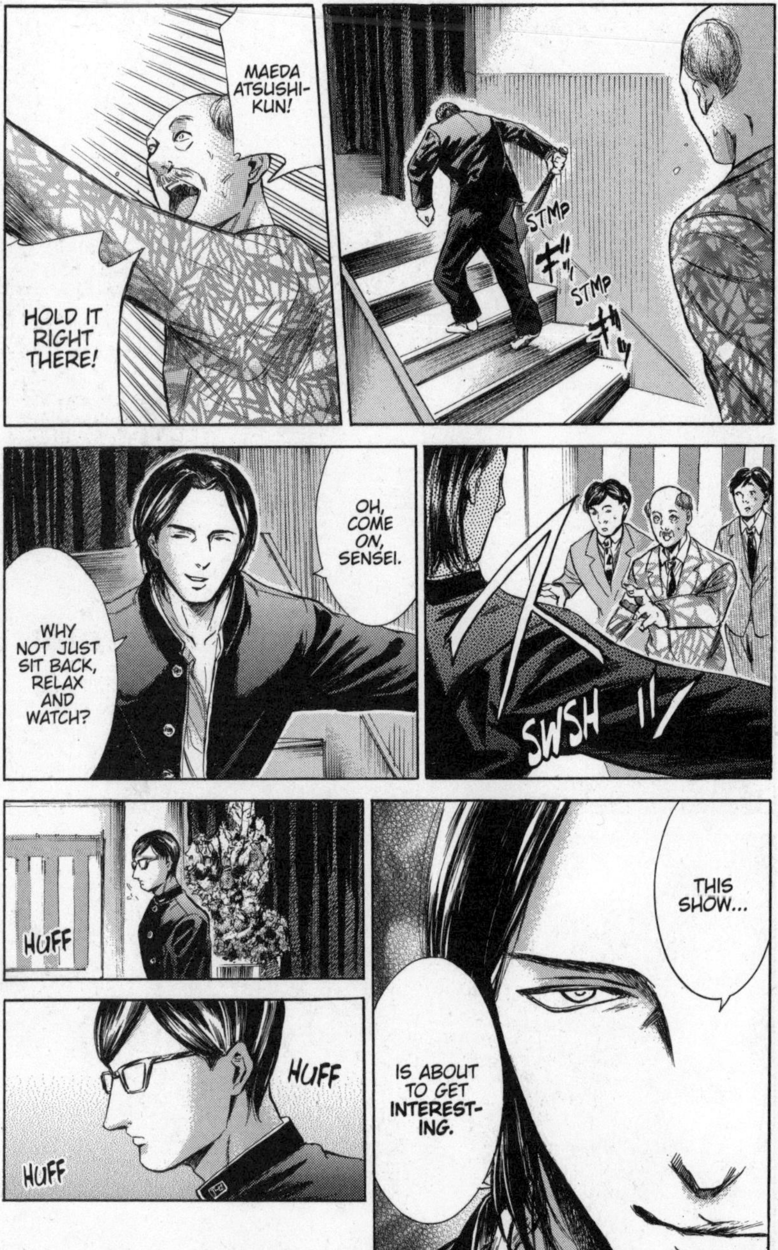
STMP
STMP
MAEDA ATSUSHI-KUN!
HOLD IT RIGHT THERE!
SWSH
OH, COME ON, SENSEI.
WHY NOT JUST SIT BACK, RELAX AND WATCH?
THIS SHOW...
IS ABOUT TO GET INTEREST-ING.
HUFF
HUFF
HUFF

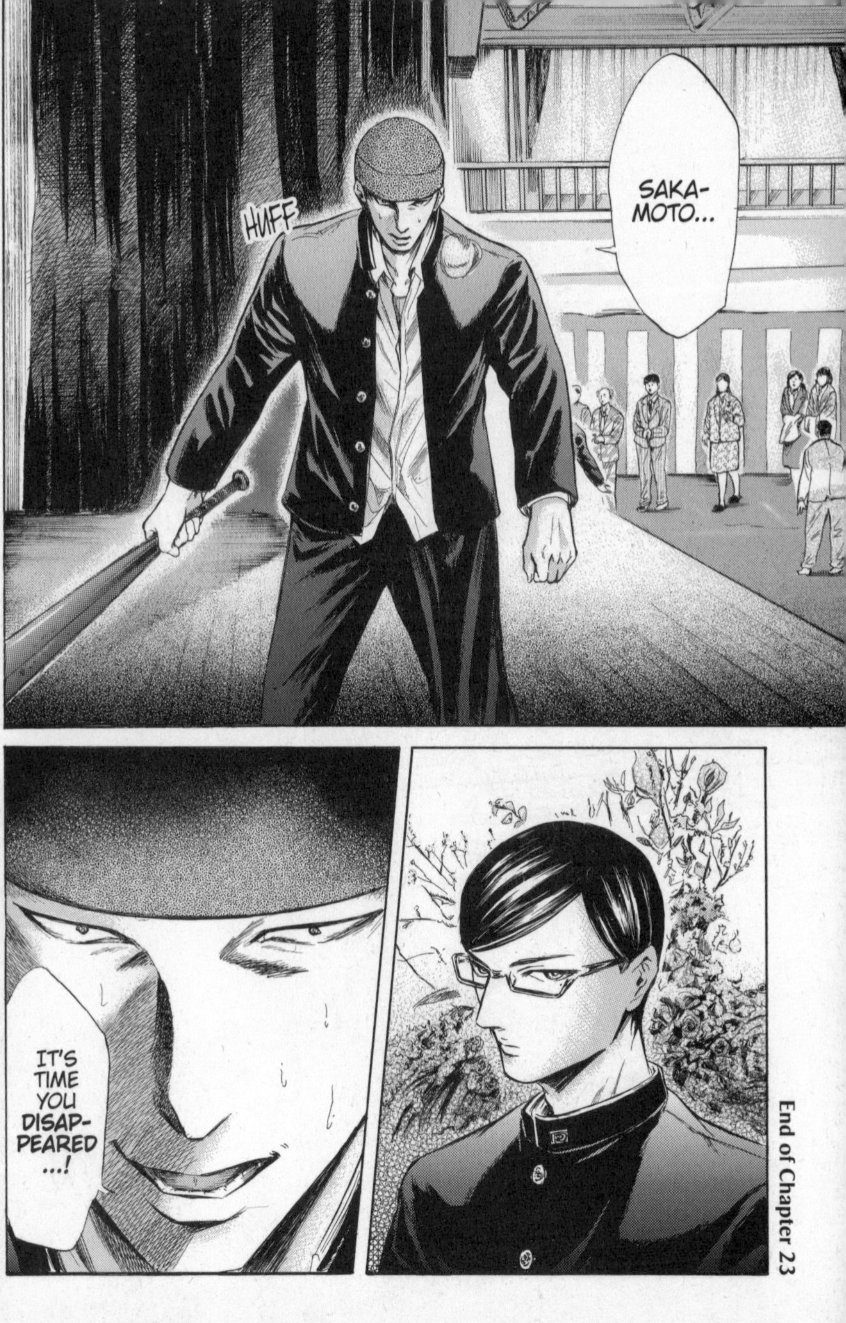
SAKA-MOTO...
HUFF
IT'S TIME YOU DISAP-PEARED ...!

End of Chapter 23

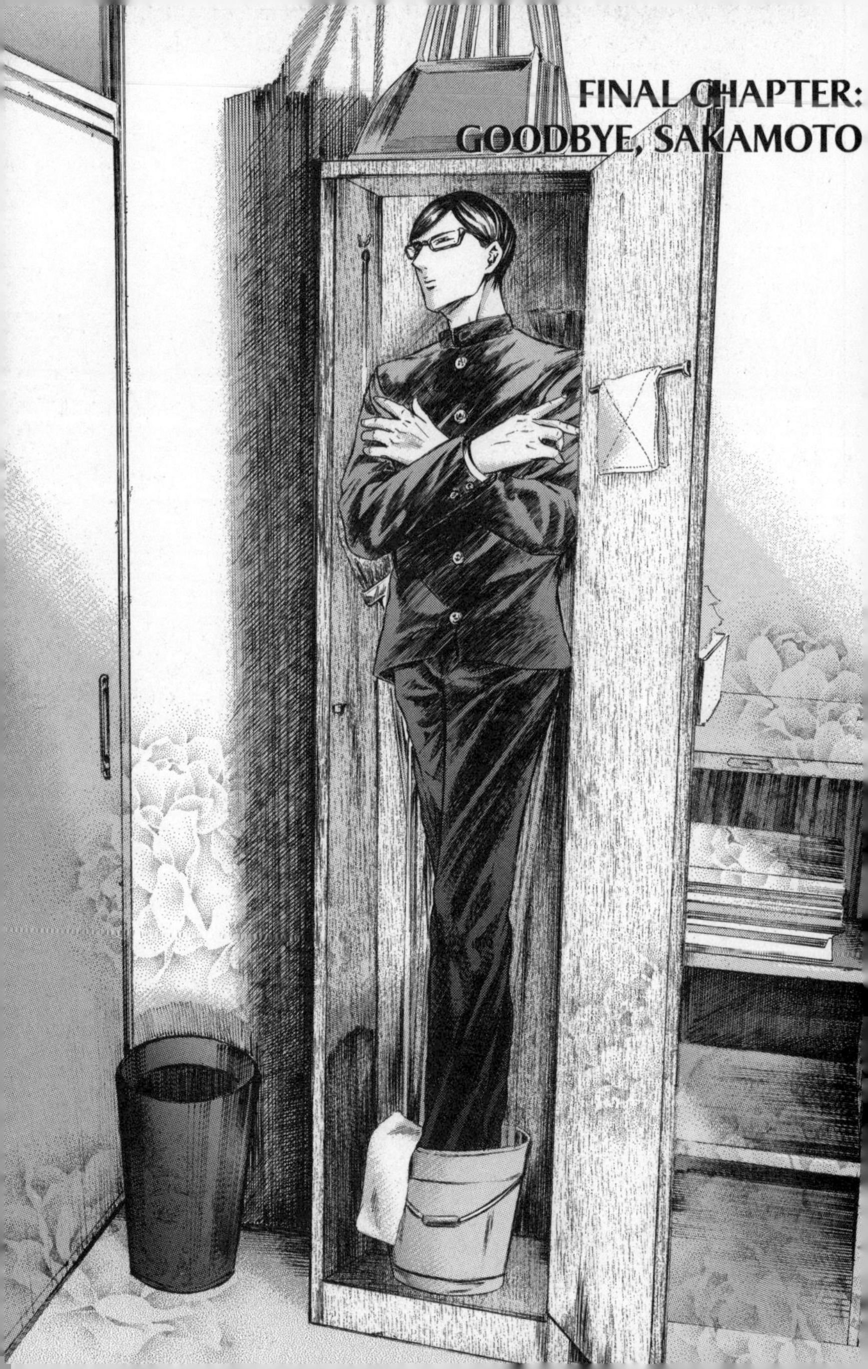
FINAL CHAPTER:
GOODBYE, SAKAMOTO

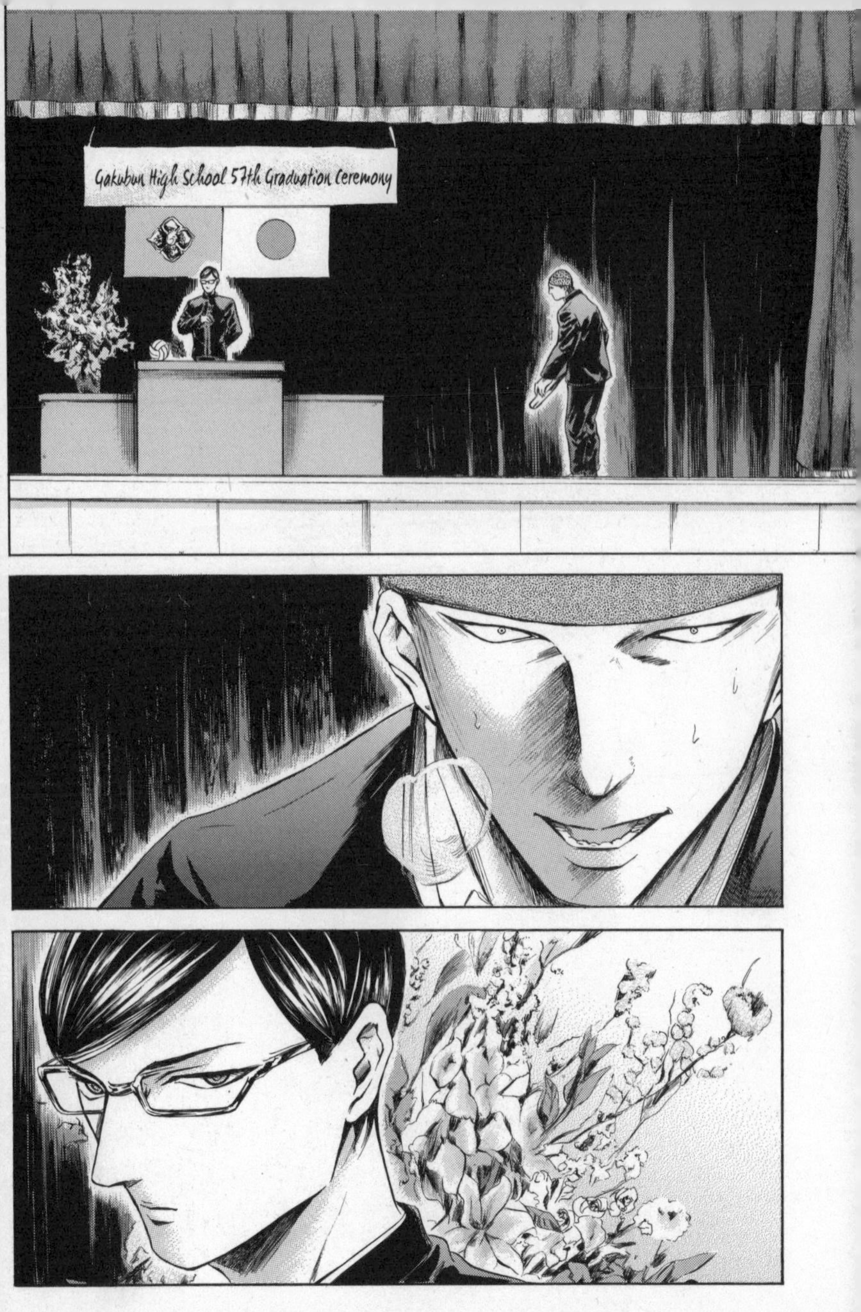
Gakubun High School 57th Graduation Ceremony

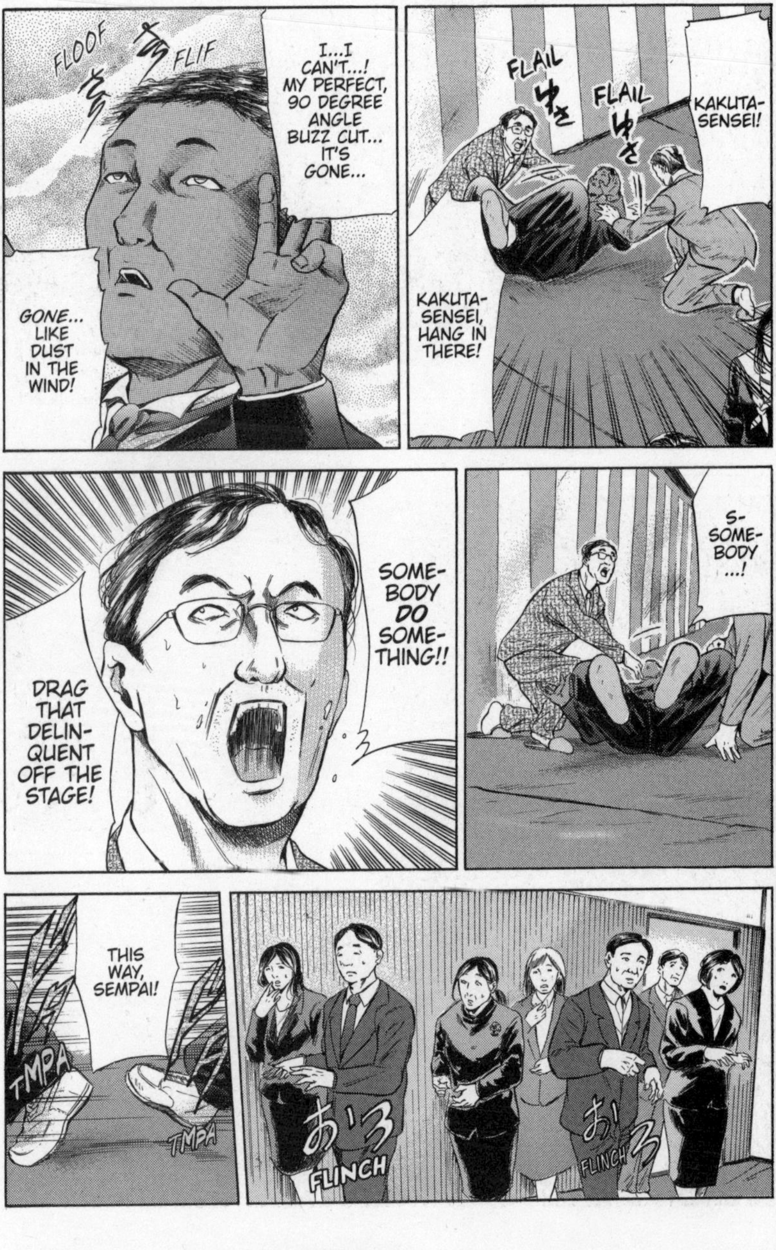
FLAIL
ゆさ
FLAIL
ゆさ
KAKUTA-SENSEI!
KAKUTA-SENSEI, HANG IN THERE!
I...I CAN'T...! MY PERFECT, 90 DEGREE ANGLE BUZZ CUT... IT'S GONE...
FLOOF
FLIF
GONE... LIKE DUST IN THE WIND!
S-SOME-BODY ...!
SOME-BODY DO SOME-THING!!
DRAG THAT DELIN-QUENT OFF THE STAGE!
おろ
FLINCH
おろ
FLINCH
THIS WAY, SEMPAI!
TMPA
TMPA

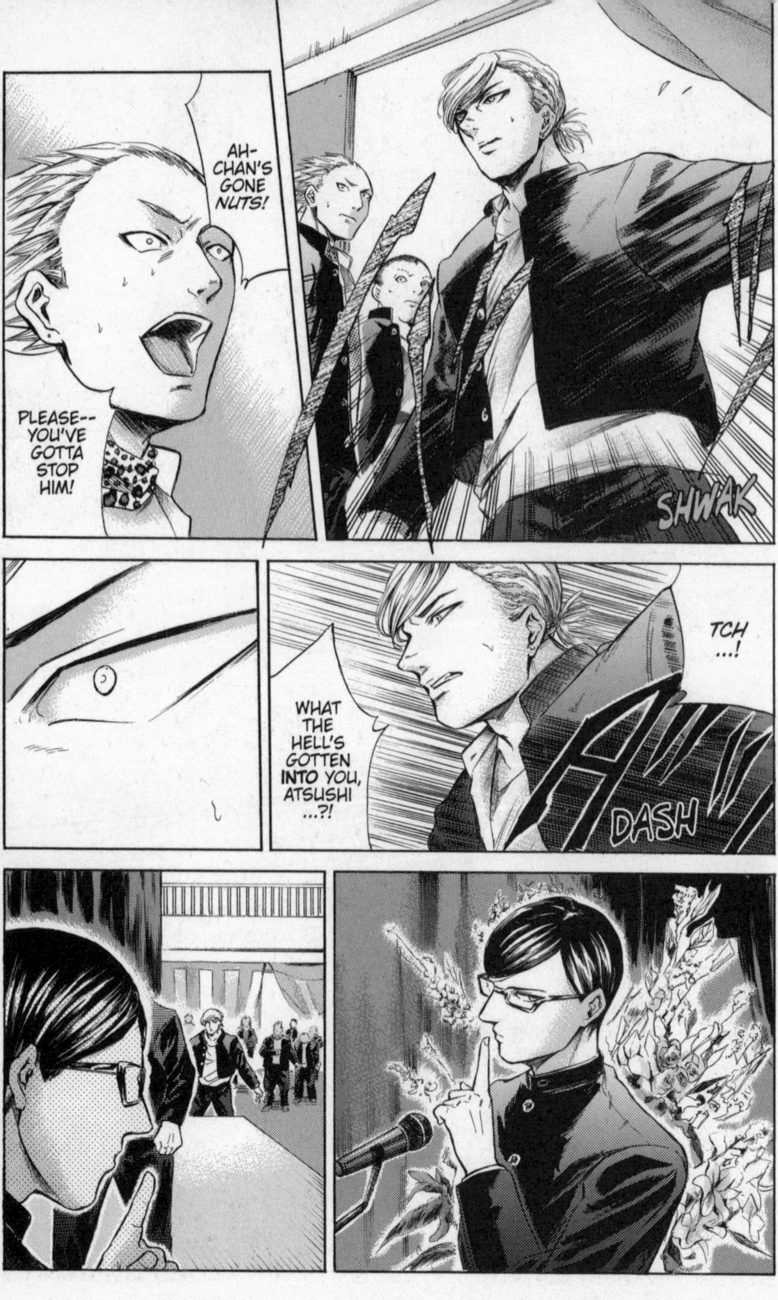
SHWAK
AH-CHAN'S GONE NUTS!
PLEASE--YOU'VE GOTTA STOP HIM!
TCH ...!
DASH
WHAT THE HELL'S GOTTEN INTO YOU, ATSUSHI ...?!

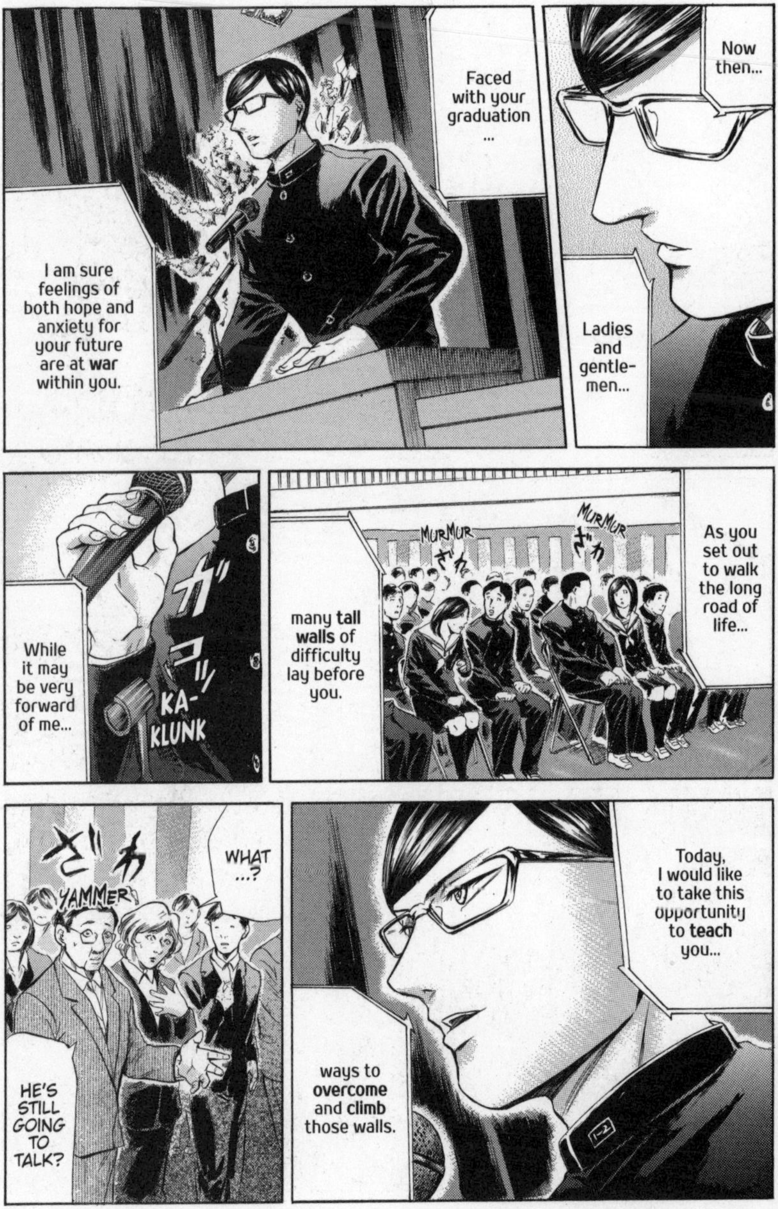
Now then...
Ladies and gentle-men...
Faced with your graduation ...
I am sure feelings of both hope and anxiety for your future are at war within you.
As you set out to walk the long road of life...
MURMUR
MURMUR
many tall walls of difficulty lay before you.
While it may be very forward of me...
KA-KLUNK
Today, I would like to take this opportunity to teach you...
ways to overcome and climb those walls.
WHAT ...?
YAMMER
HE'S STILL GOING TO TALK?

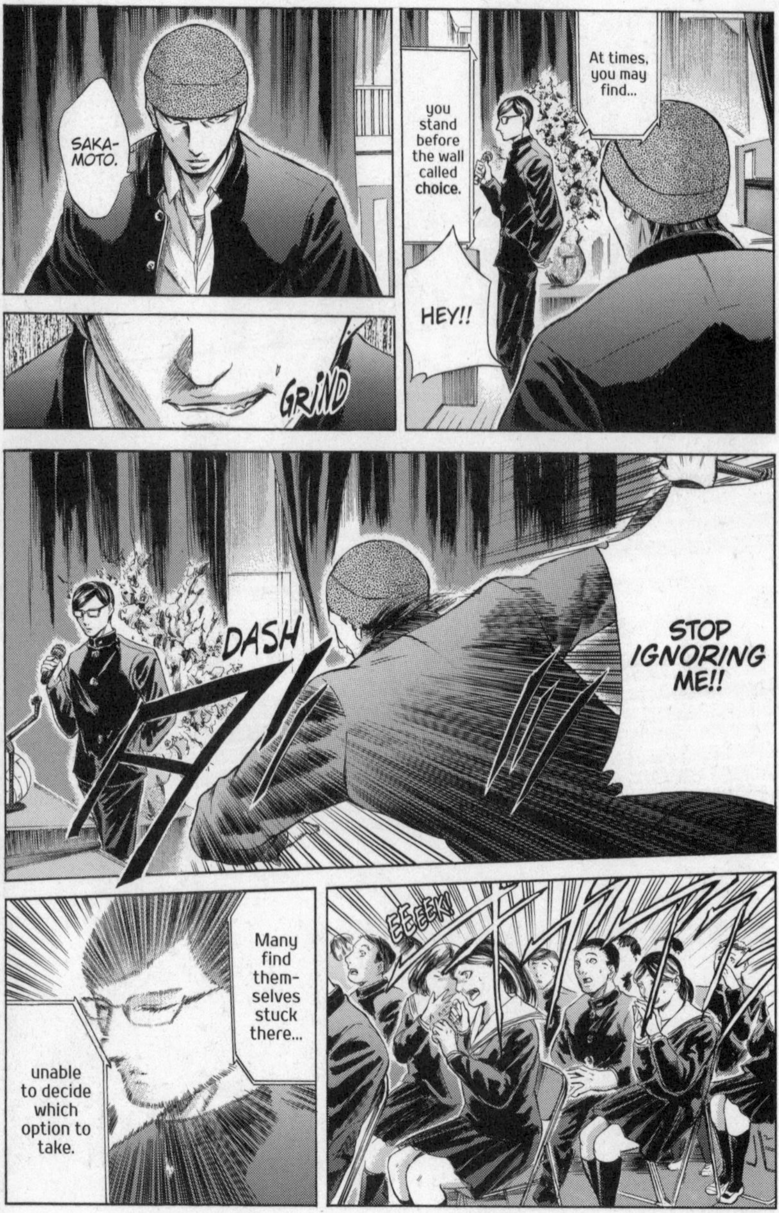
At times, you may find...
you stand before the wall called choice.
HEY!!
SAKA-MOTO.
GRIND
STOP IGNORING ME!!
DASH
EEEEK!
Many find them-selves stuck there...
unable to decide which option to take.

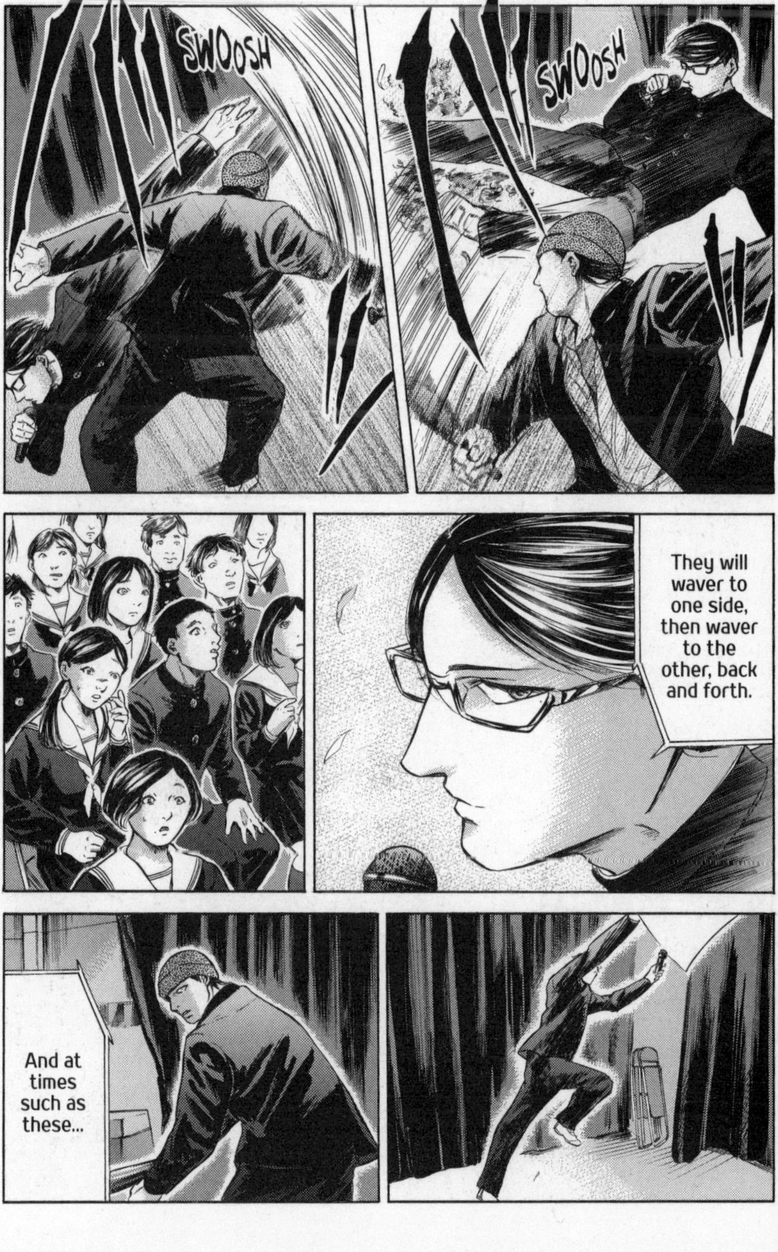
SWOOSH
SWOOSH
They will waver to one side, then waver to the other, back and forth.
And at times such as these...

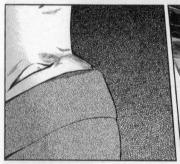

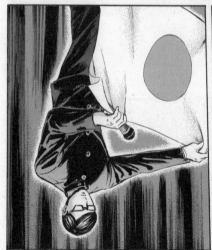

Remember, sometimes simplicity is best.

And perhaps a straight-forward charge...
is the answer you seek.
WOW! SO, THIS IS ALL AN ACT?!
EVEN THAT DELIN-QUENT IS IN ON IT!
YEEEAH!

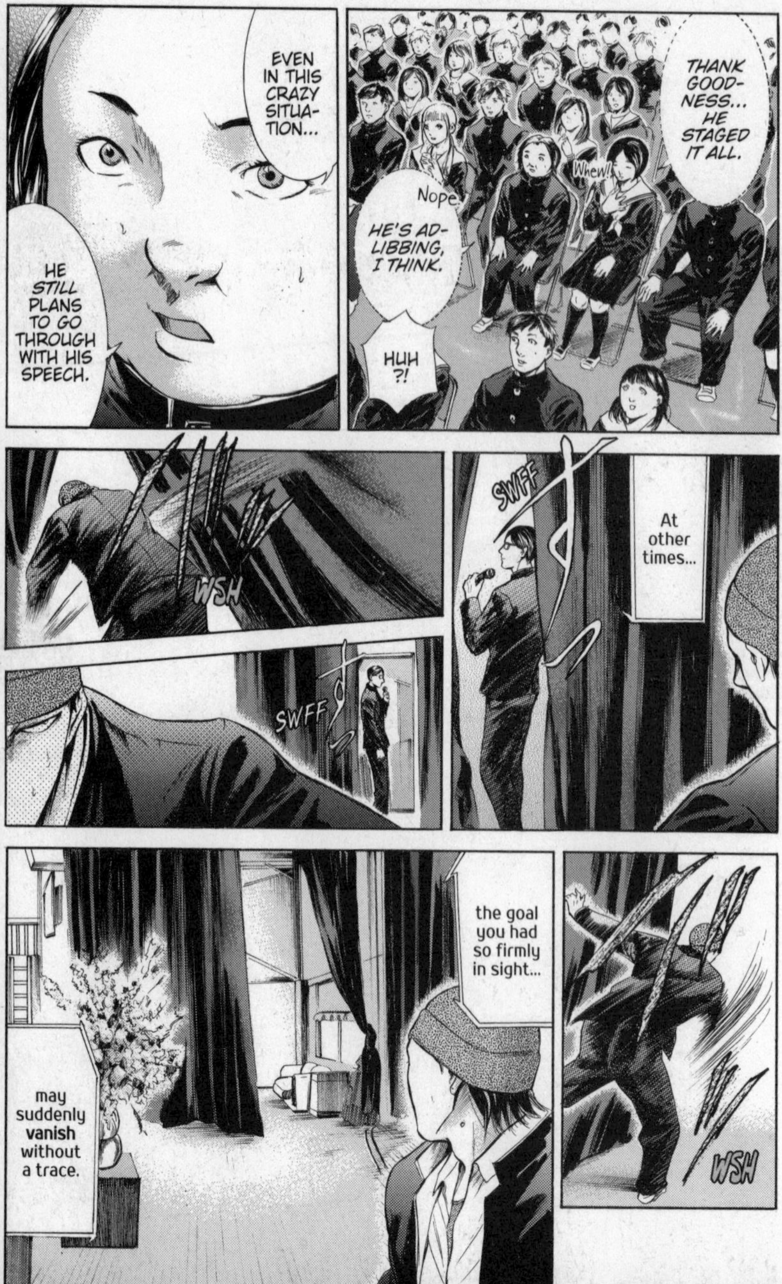
THANK GOODNESS... HE STAGED IT ALL.
Whew!
Nope.
HE'S AD-LIBBING, I THINK.
HUH ?!
EVEN IN THIS CRAZY SITUATION...
HE STILL PLANS TO GO THROUGH WITH HIS SPEECH.
At other times...
SWFF
WSH
SWFF
WSH
the goal you had so firmly in sight...
may suddenly **vanish** without a trace.

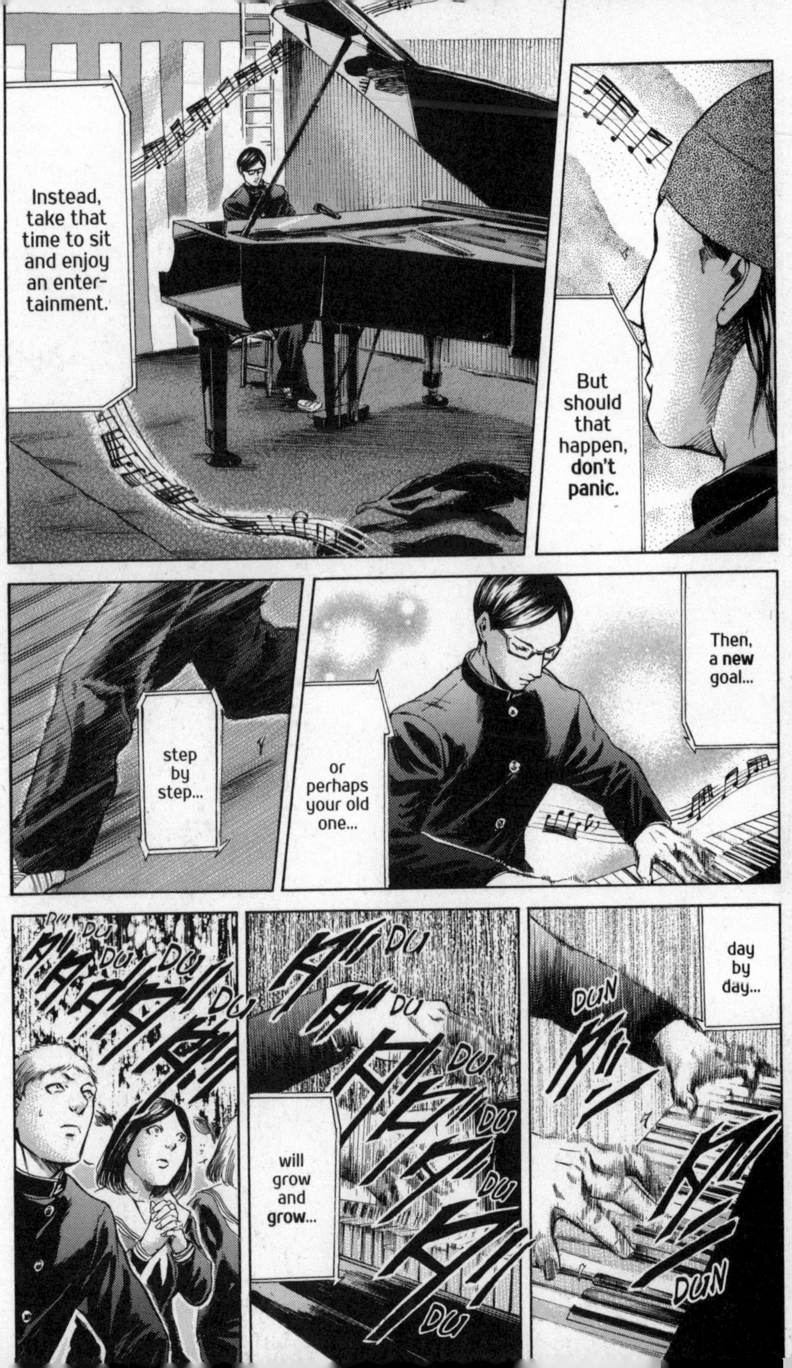
But should that happen, don't panic.
Instead, take that time to sit and enjoy an entertainment.
Then, a new goal...
or perhaps your old one...
step by step...
day by day...
DUN
DUN
will grow and grow...
DU
DU
DU
DU
DU
DU
DU
DU
DU
DU

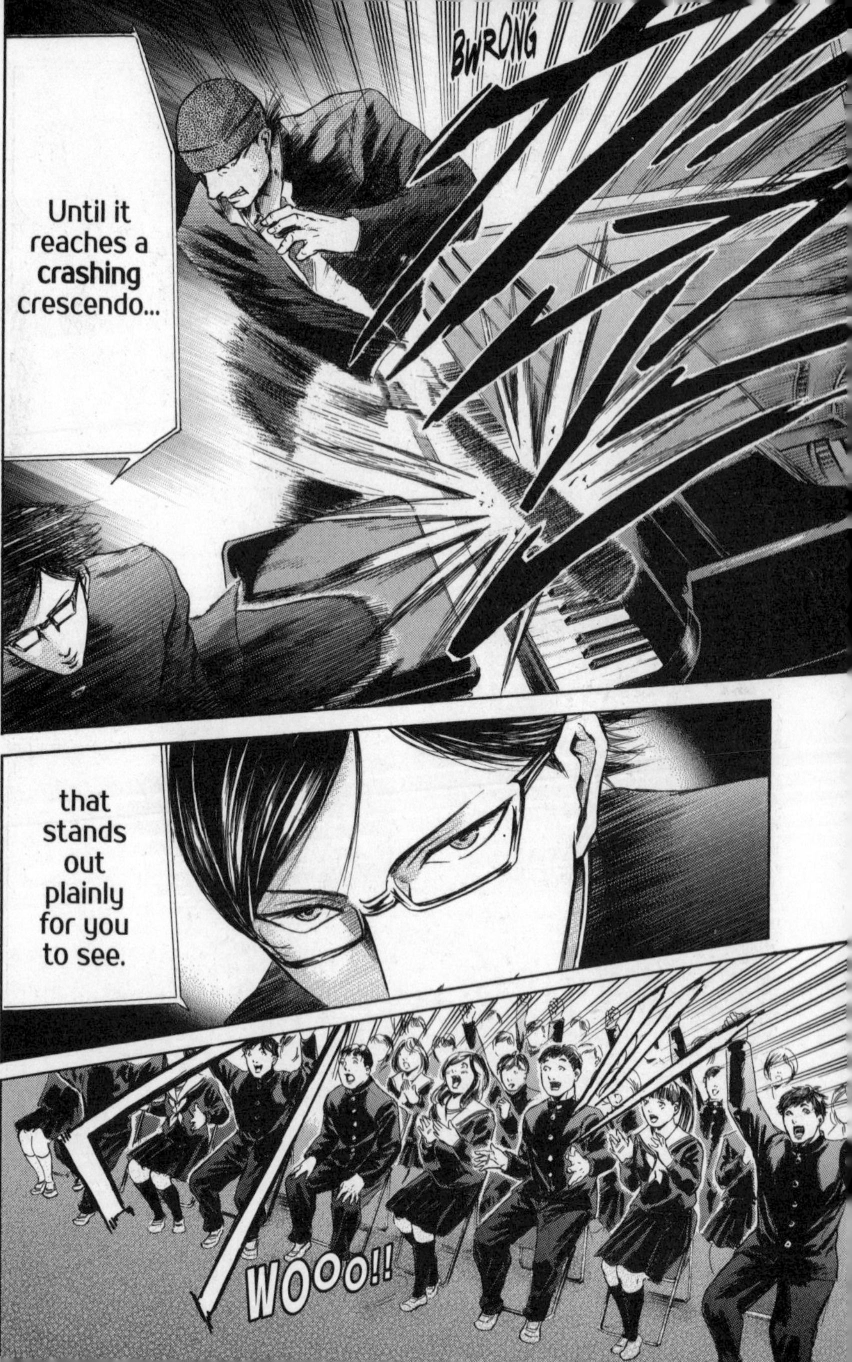
BWRONG
Until it reaches a crashing crescendo...
that stands out plainly for you to see.
WOOO!!

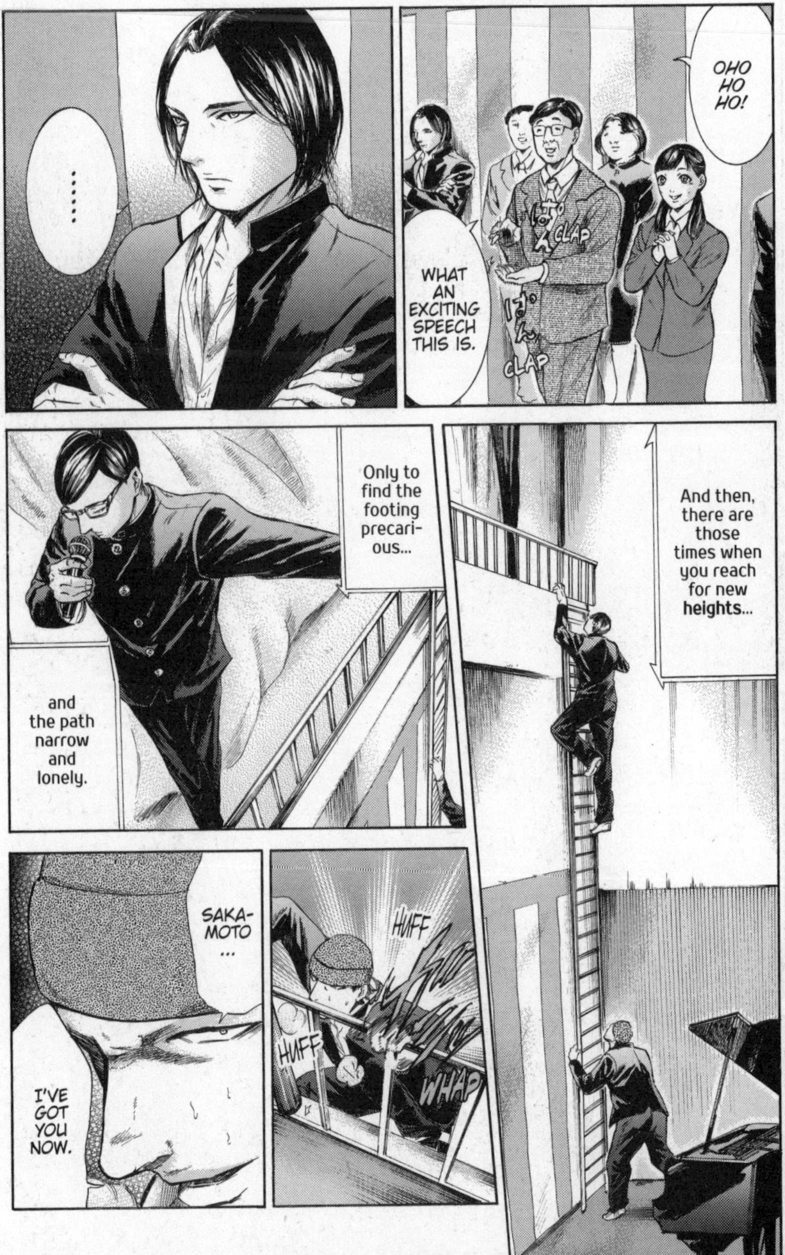
OHO HO HO!
WHAT AN EXCITING SPEECH THIS IS.
CLAP
CLAP
......
And then, there are those times when you reach for new **heights**...
Only to find the footing precari-ous...
and the path narrow and lonely.
HUFF
HUFF
WHAP
SAKA-MOTO ...
I'VE GOT YOU NOW.

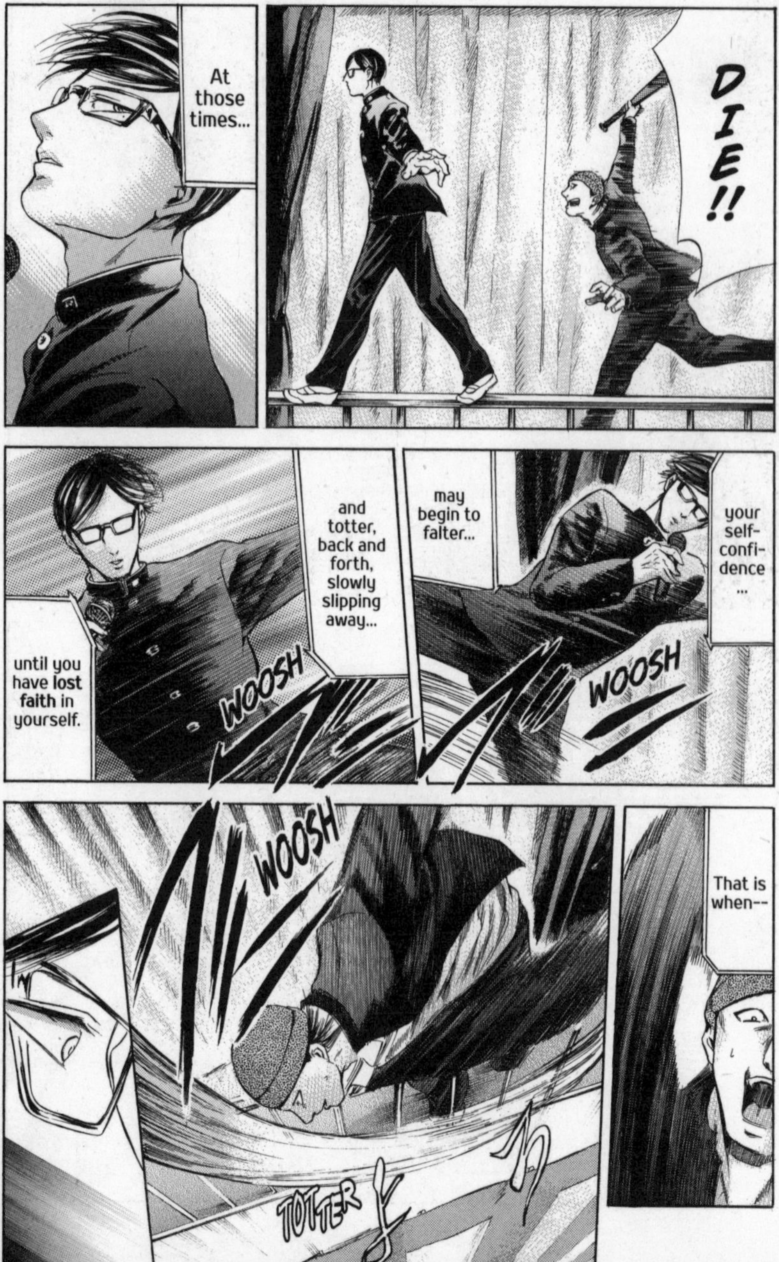
DIE!!
At those times...
your self-confidence ...
WOOSH
may begin to falter...
and totter, back and forth, slowly slipping away...
WOOSH
until you have lost faith in yourself.
That is when--
WOOSH
TOTTER

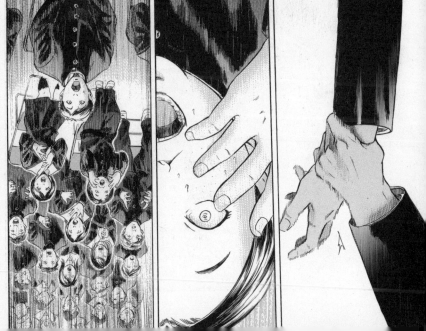

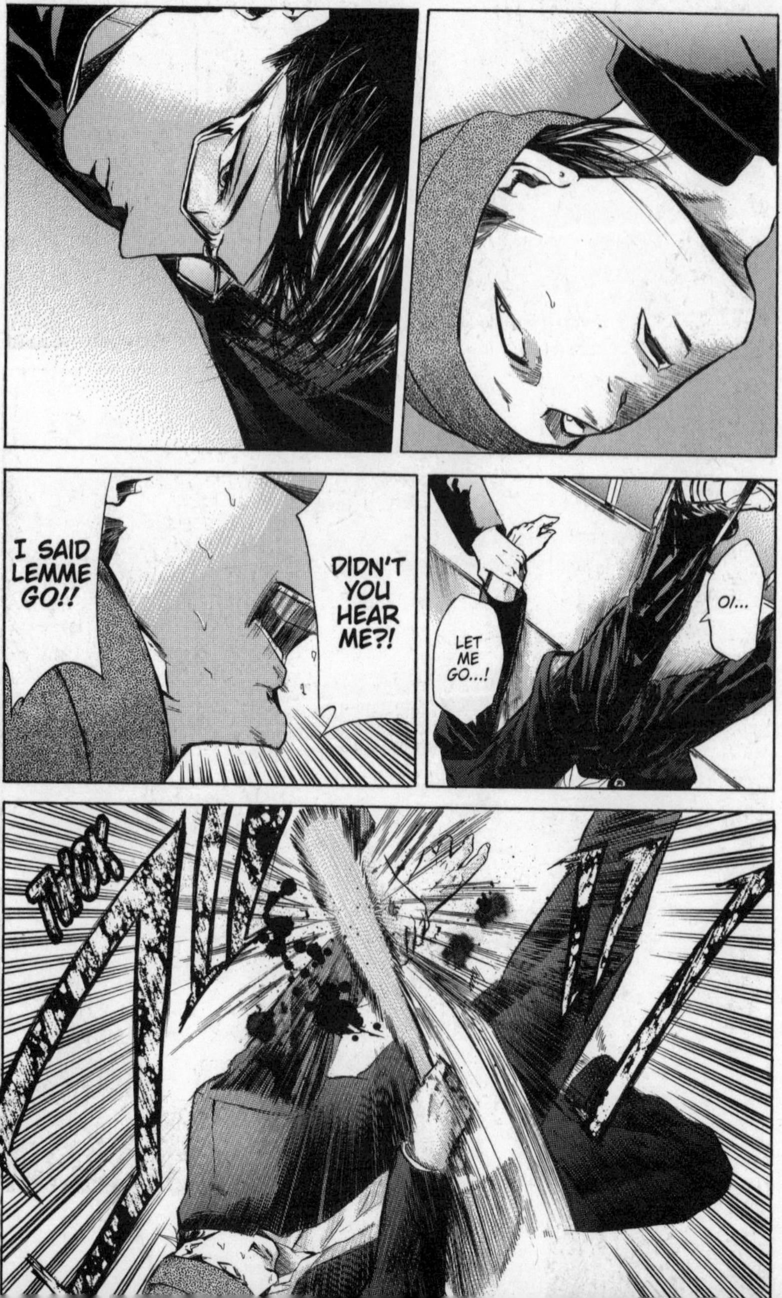
OI...
LET ME GO...!
DIDN'T YOU HEAR ME?!
I SAID LEMME GO!!
THOK

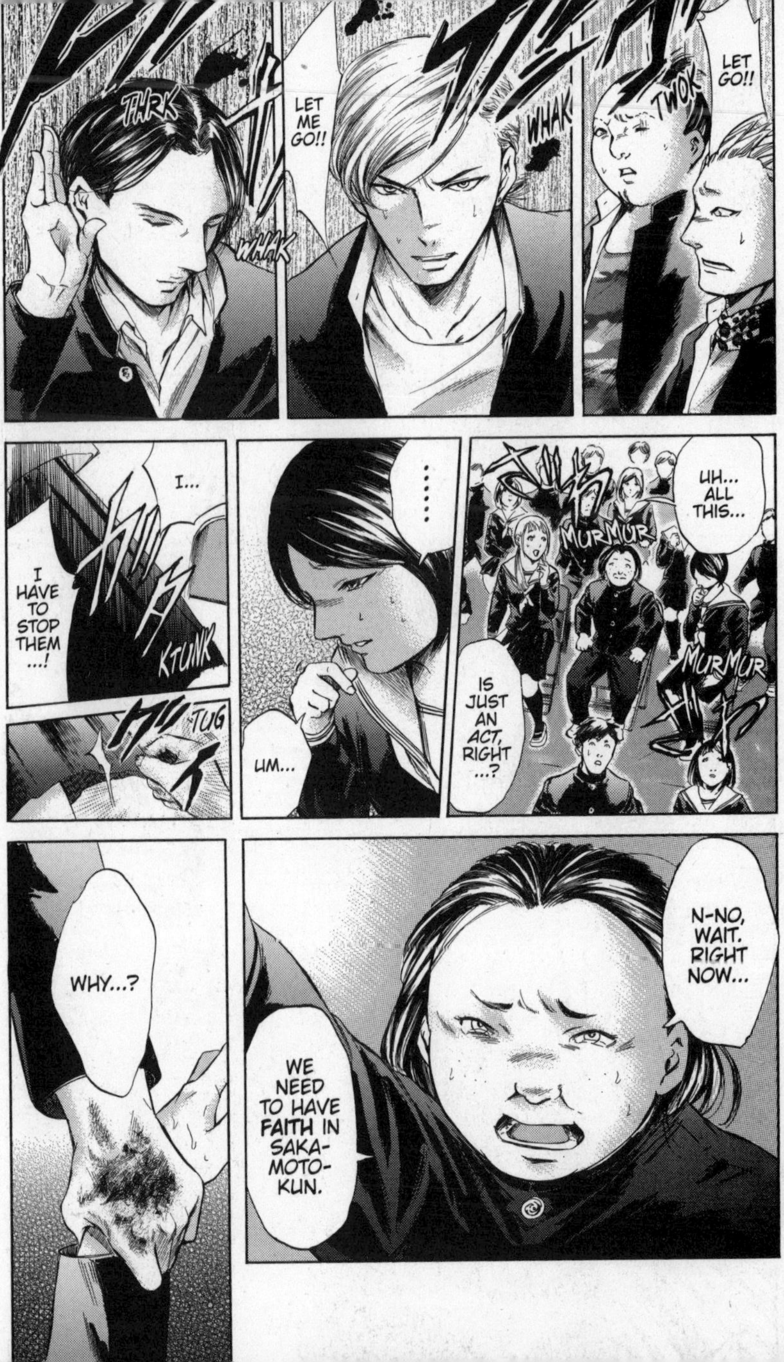
LET GO!!
TWOK
WHAK
LET ME GO!!
WHAK
THRK
UH... ALL THIS...
MURMUR
MURMUR
IS JUST AN ACT, RIGHT ...?
......
UM...
I...
I HAVE TO STOP THEM ...!
KTUNK
TUG
N-NO, WAIT. RIGHT NOW...
WE NEED TO HAVE FAITH IN SAKA-MOTO-KUN.
WHY...?

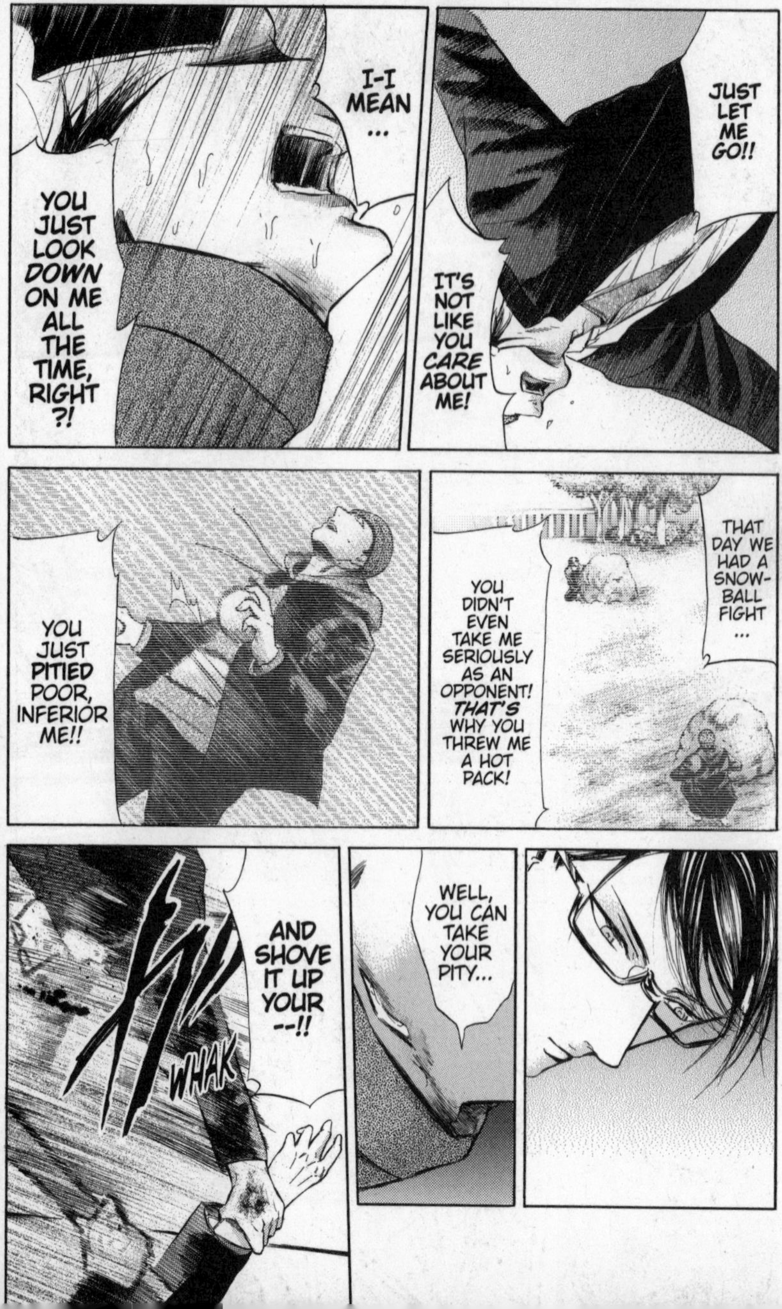
JUST LET ME GO!!
IT'S NOT LIKE YOU CARE ABOUT ME!
I-I MEAN ...
YOU JUST LOOK DOWN ON ME ALL THE TIME, RIGHT ?!
THAT DAY WE HAD A SNOW-BALL FIGHT ...
YOU DIDN'T EVEN TAKE ME SERIOUSLY AS AN OPPONENT! THAT'S WHY YOU THREW ME A HOT PACK!
YOU JUST PITIED POOR, INFERIOR ME!!
WELL, YOU CAN TAKE YOUR PITY...
AND SHOVE IT UP YOUR --!!
WHAK

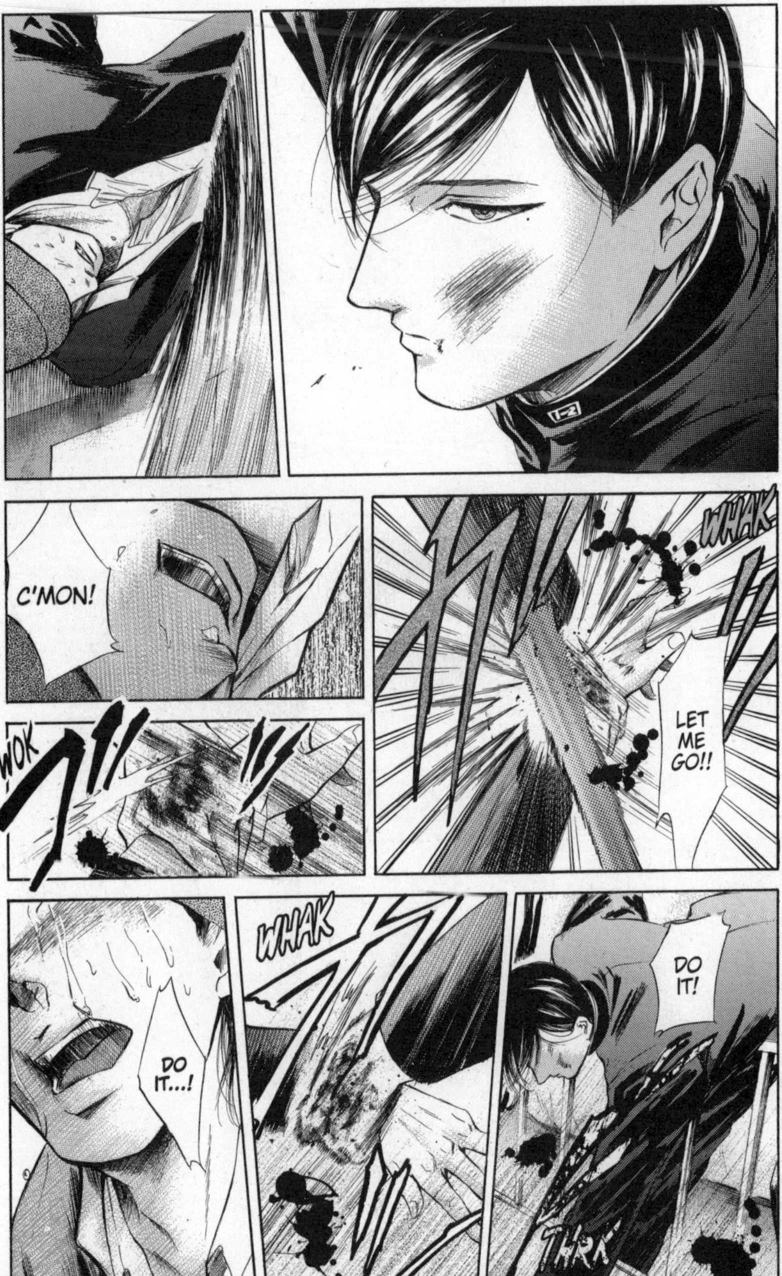
WHAK
LET ME GO!!
C'MON!
TWOK
DO IT!
THRK
WHAK
DO IT...!

C'MON, MAN... YOU'VE GOTTA BE...

SICK OF ME AND MY STUPID CRAP BY NOW.

I FIND YOUR ABILITY TO EXPOSE ALL THAT YOU ARE...

FOR THE WORLD TO SEE QUITE ADMIRABLE.

PERSONALLY...

Hah!

I-I'M NOT THAT GULLIBLE...

I DON'T BUY IT.

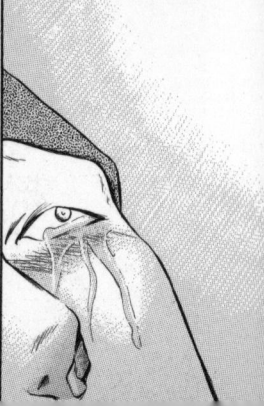

Should the time ever come...

when you no longer believe in your-self...

you must have faith.

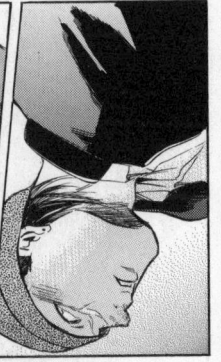

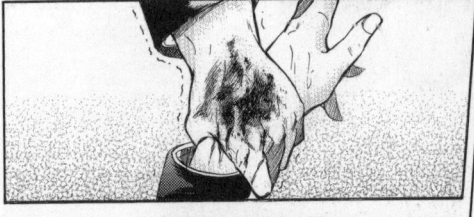

FAITH IN *WHAT*, HUH?

HAH!

QUIVER

QUIVER

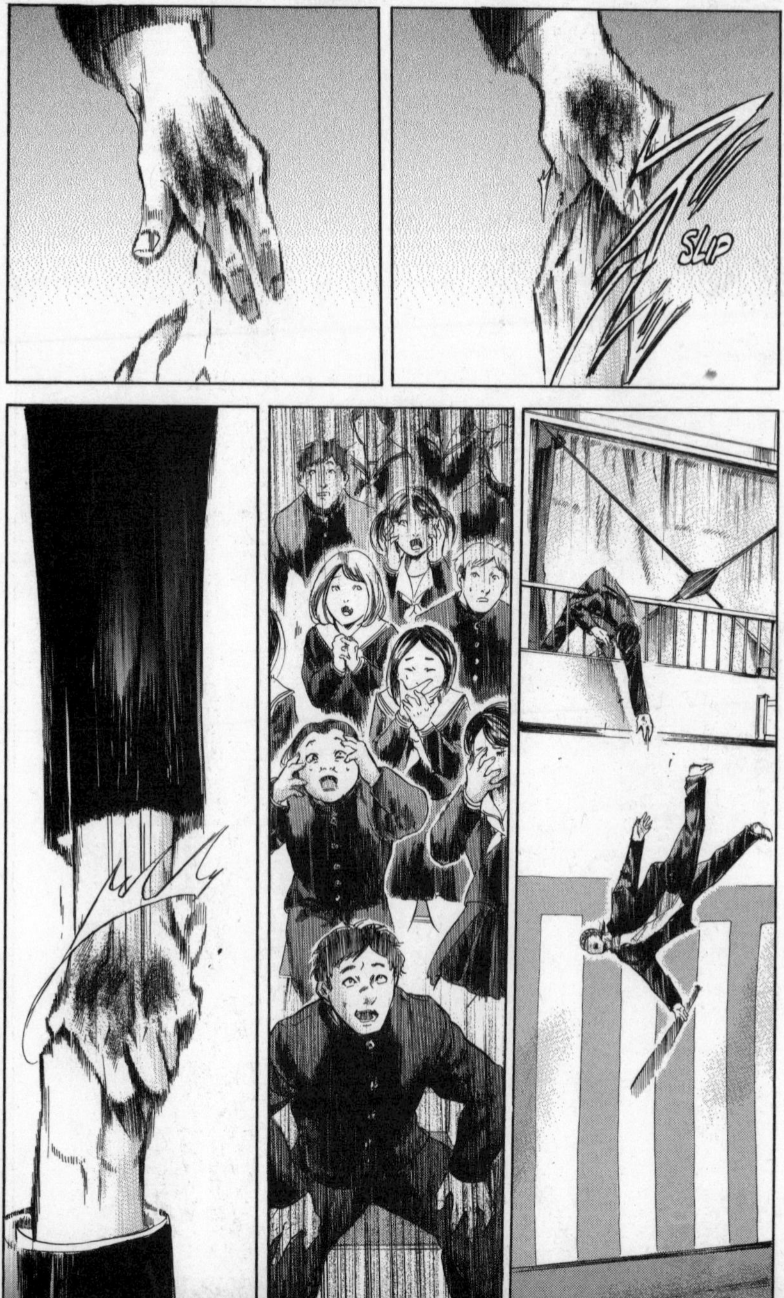
SLIP

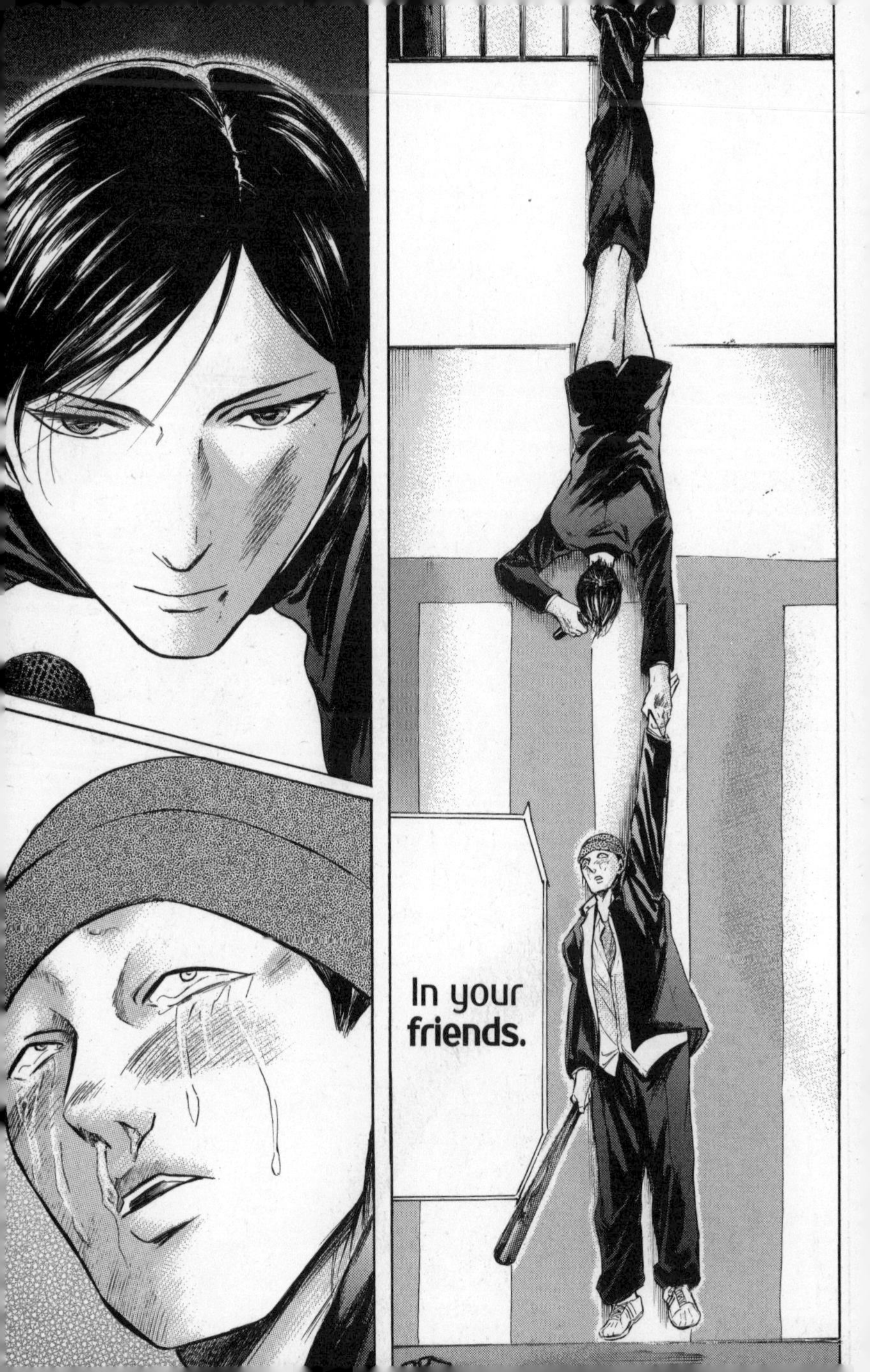
In your friends.

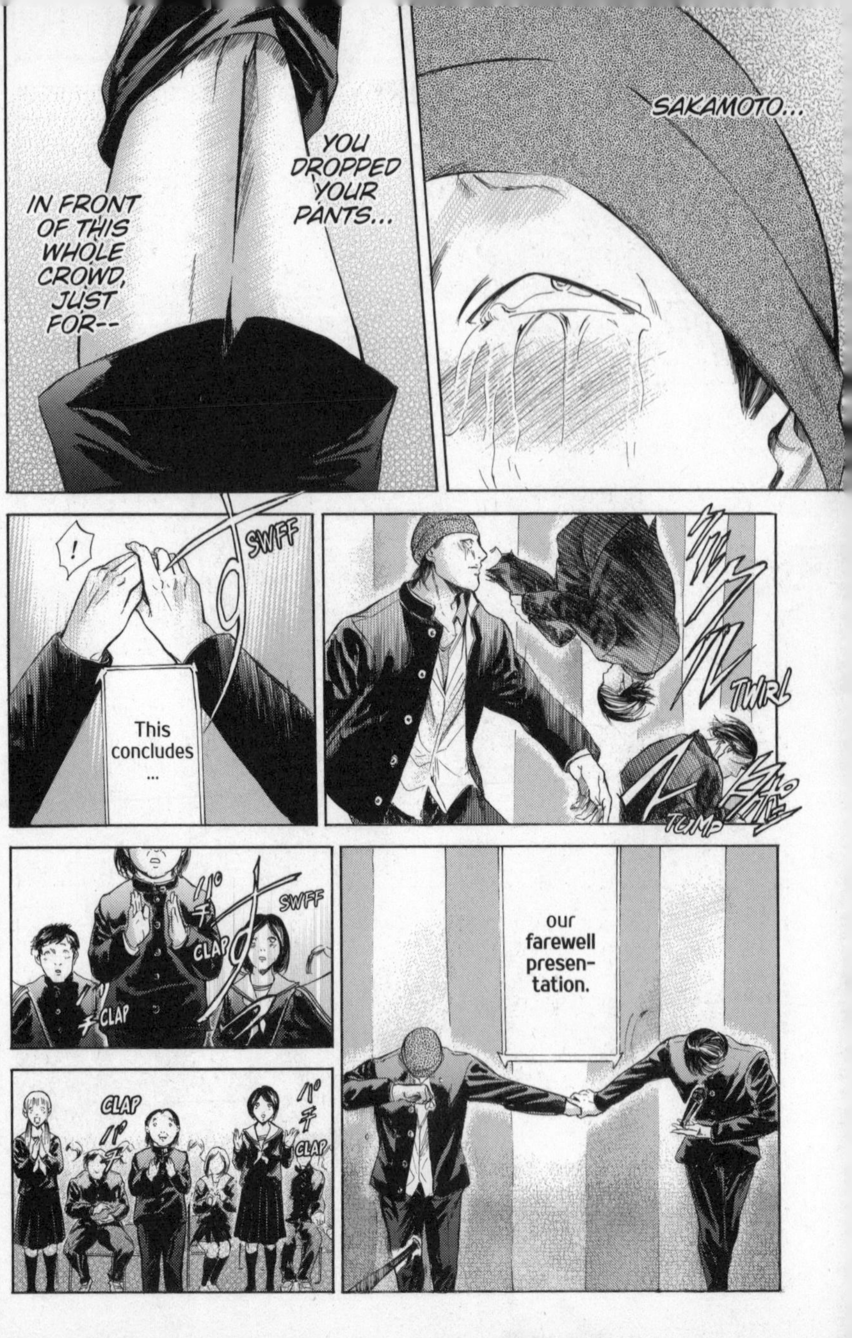
SAKAMOTO...
YOU DROPPED YOUR PANTS...
IN FRONT OF THIS WHOLE CROWD, JUST FOR--
TWIRL
TUMP
!
SWFF
This concludes ...
our farewell presen-tation.
パチ
CLAP
SWFF
パチ
CLAP
CLAP
パチ
パチ
CLAP

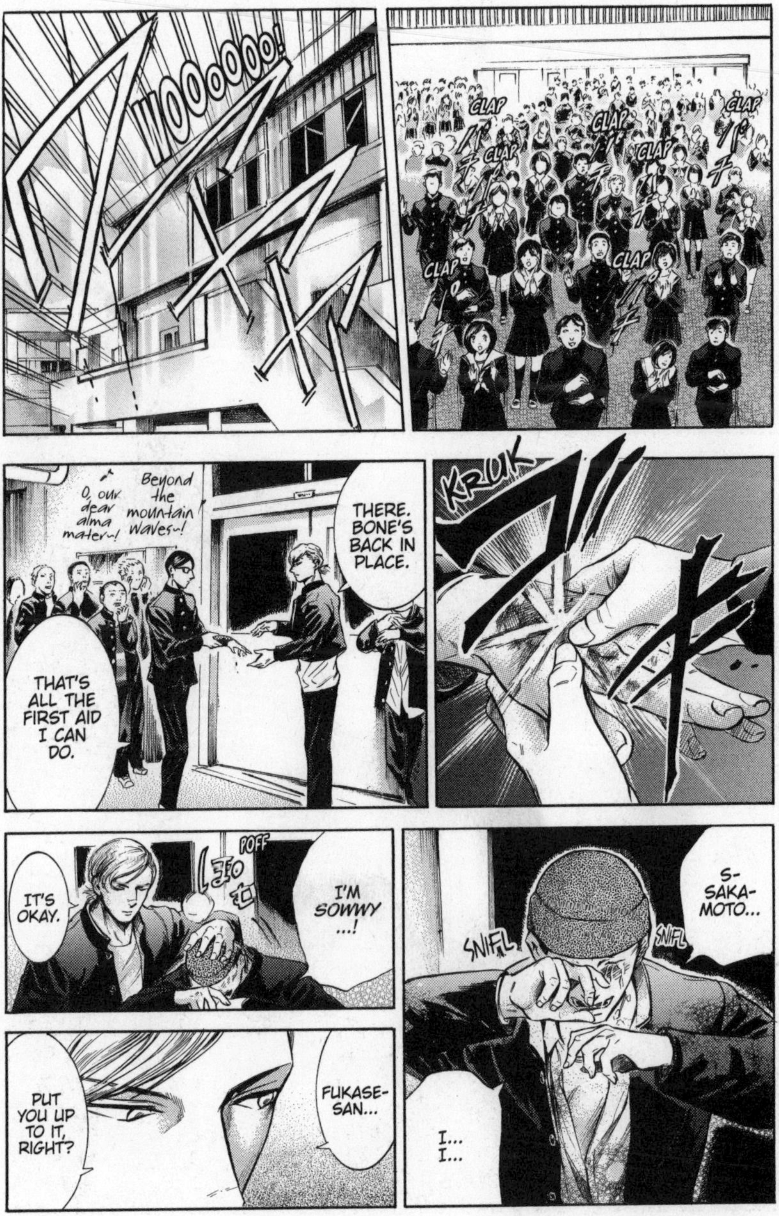

CLAP
CLAP
CLAP
CLAP
CLAP
CLAP
CLAP
WOOooooo!
KRUK
THERE. BONE'S BACK IN PLACE.
Beyond the mountain waves~!
O, our dear alma mater~!
THAT'S ALL THE FIRST AID I CAN DO.
S-SAKAMOTO...
SNIFL
SNIFL
I... I...
POFF
I'M SOWWY ...!
IT'S OKAY.
FUKASE-SAN...
PUT YOU UP TO IT, RIGHT?

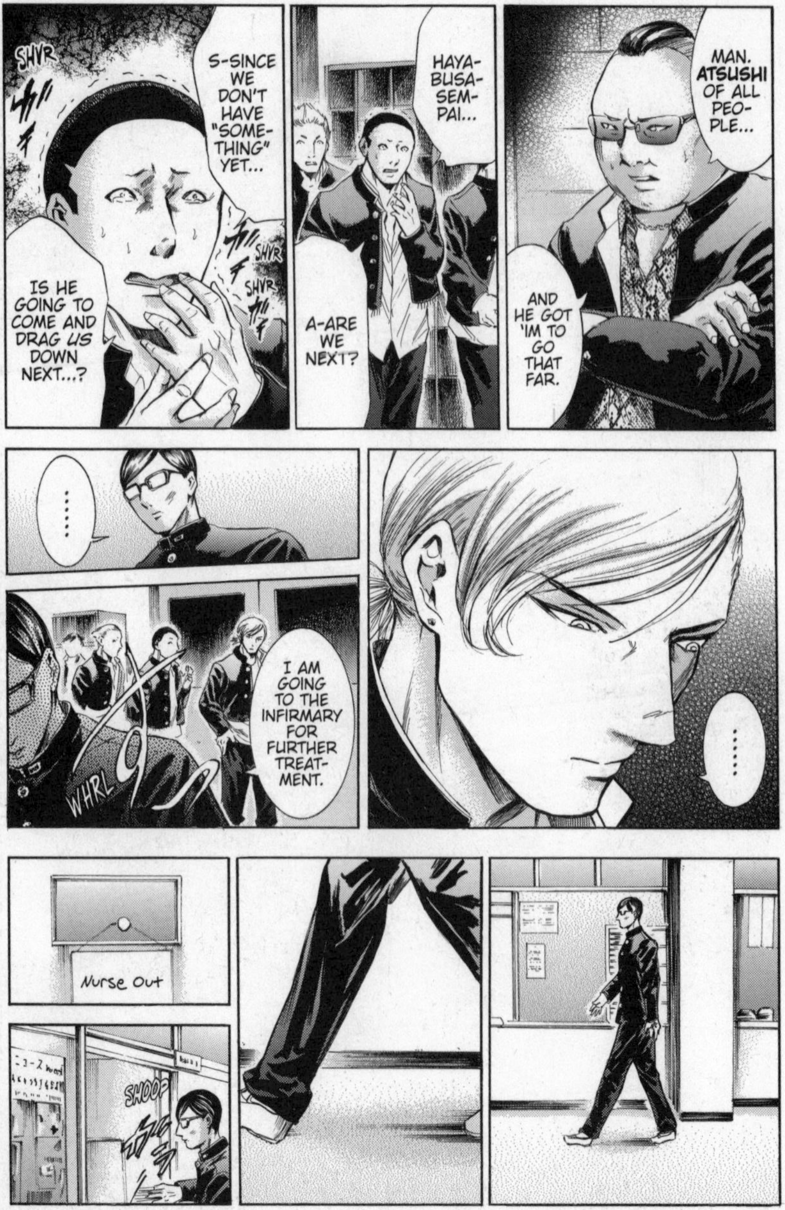
MAN. ATSUSHI OF ALL PEO-PLE...
AND HE GOT 'IM TO GO THAT FAR.
HAYA-BUSA-SEM-PAI...
A-ARE WE NEXT?
S-SINCE WE DON'T HAVE "SOME-THING" YET...
SHVR
SHVR
SHVR
IS HE GOING TO COME AND DRAG US DOWN NEXT...?
......
......
I AM GOING TO THE INFIRMARY FOR FURTHER TREAT-MENT.
WHRL
SHOOP
Nurse Out

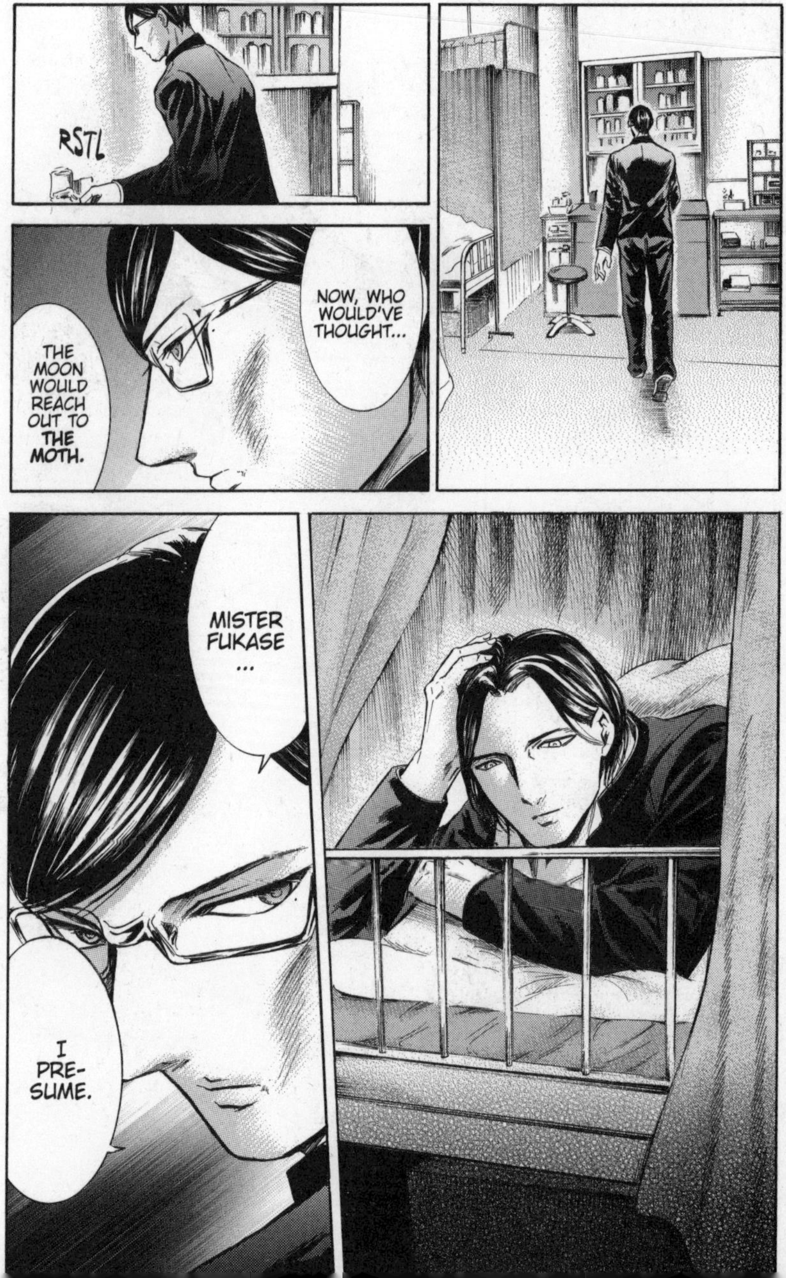
RSTL
NOW, WHO WOULD'VE THOUGHT...
THE MOON WOULD REACH OUT TO THE MOTH.
MISTER FUKASE ...
I PRE-SUME.

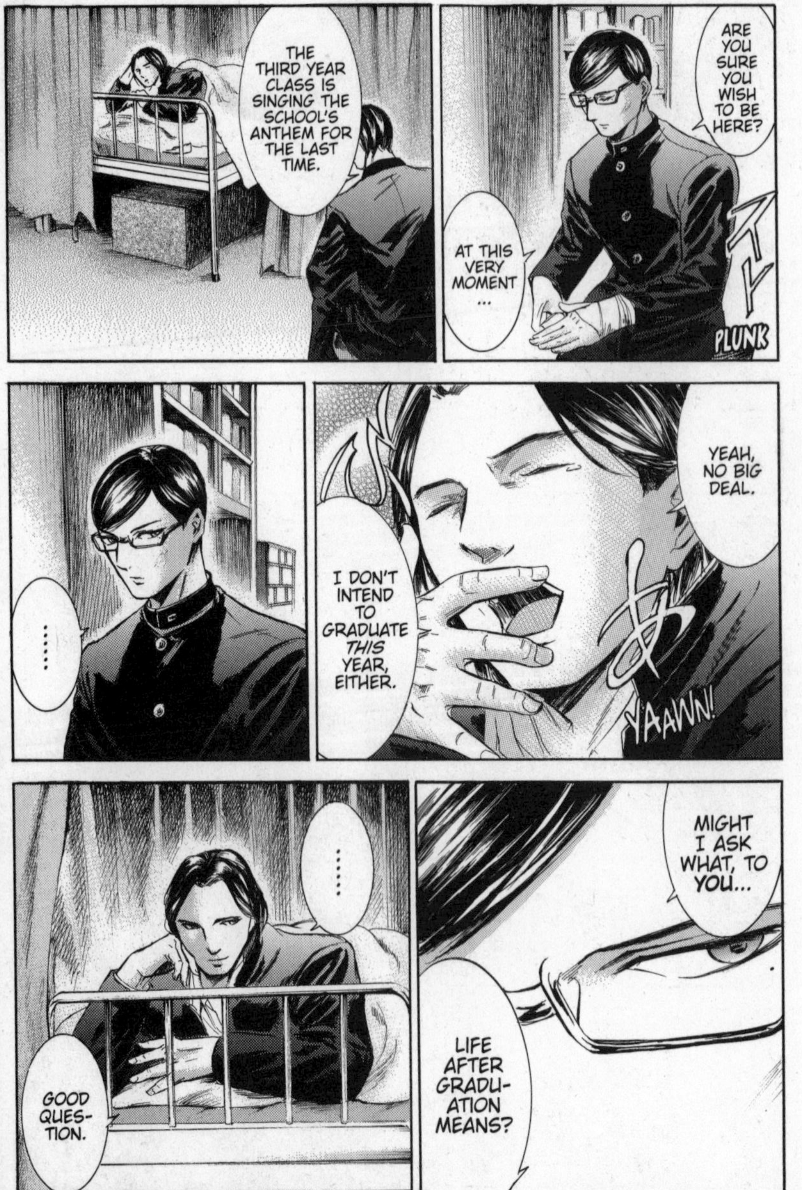
ARE YOU SURE YOU WISH TO BE HERE?
AT THIS VERY MOMENT ...
PLUNK
THE THIRD YEAR CLASS IS SINGING THE SCHOOL'S ANTHEM FOR THE LAST TIME.
YEAH, NO BIG DEAL.
I DON'T INTEND TO GRADUATE *THIS* YEAR, EITHER.
YAAWN!
......
MIGHT I ASK WHAT, TO YOU...
LIFE AFTER GRADU-ATION MEANS?
......
GOOD QUES-TION.

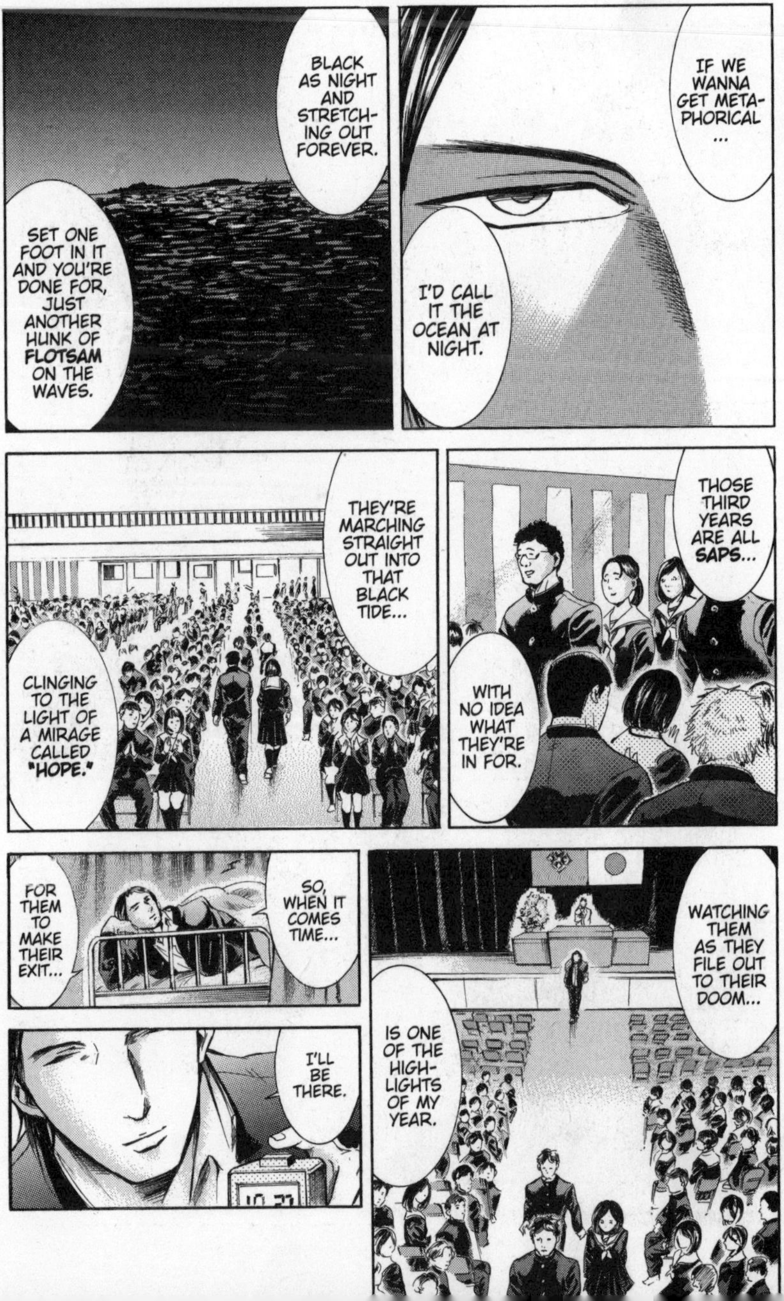
IF WE WANNA GET META-PHORICAL...
I'D CALL IT THE OCEAN AT NIGHT.
BLACK AS NIGHT AND STRETCH-ING OUT FOREVER.
SET ONE FOOT IN IT AND YOU'RE DONE FOR, JUST ANOTHER HUNK OF **FLOTSAM** ON THE WAVES.
THOSE THIRD YEARS ARE ALL **SAPS**...
WITH NO IDEA WHAT THEY'RE IN FOR.
THEY'RE MARCHING STRAIGHT OUT INTO THAT BLACK TIDE...
CLINGING TO THE LIGHT OF A MIRAGE CALLED **"HOPE."**
WATCHING THEM AS THEY FILE OUT TO THEIR DOOM...
IS ONE OF THE HIGH-LIGHTS OF MY YEAR.
SO, WHEN IT COMES TIME...
FOR THEM TO MAKE THEIR EXIT...
I'LL BE THERE.

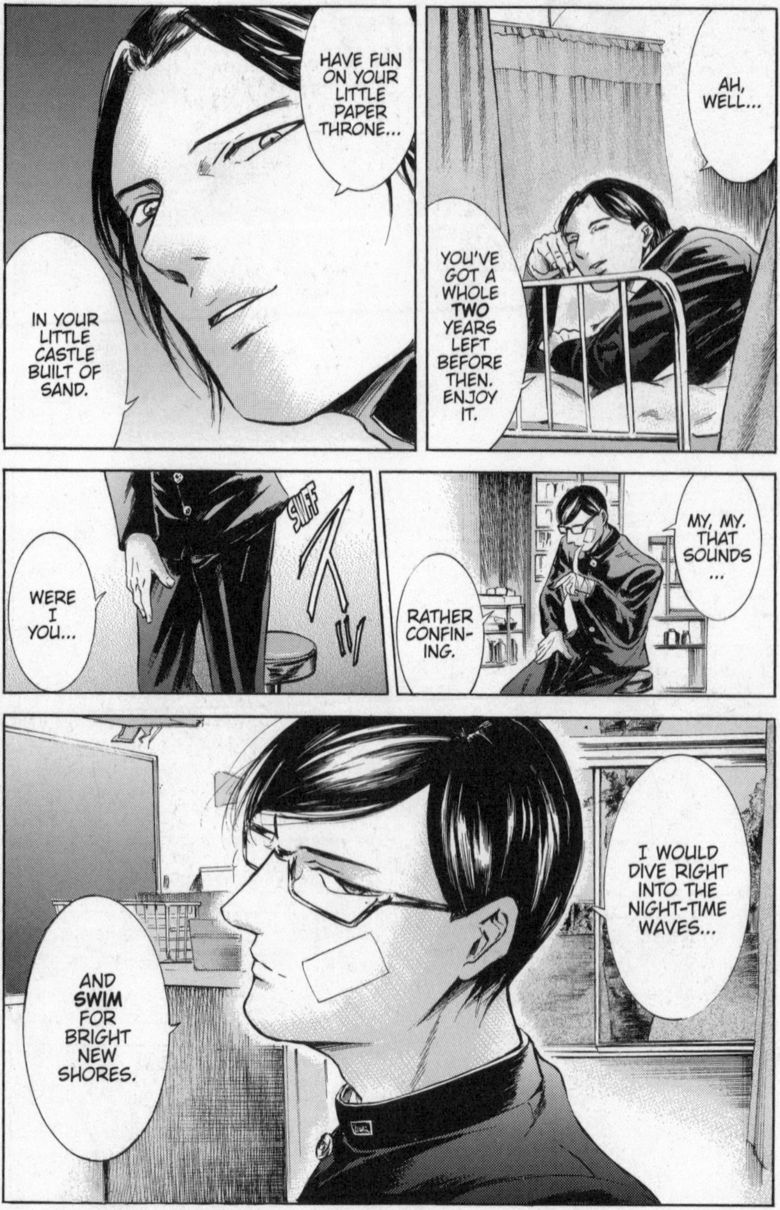
AH, WELL...
YOU'VE GOT A WHOLE **TWO** YEARS LEFT BEFORE THEN. ENJOY IT.
HAVE FUN ON YOUR LITTLE PAPER THRONE...
IN YOUR LITTLE CASTLE BUILT OF SAND.
MY, MY. THAT SOUNDS ...
RATHER CONFIN-ING.
SWFF
WERE I YOU...
I WOULD DIVE RIGHT INTO THE NIGHT-TIME WAVES...
AND **SWIM** FOR BRIGHT NEW SHORES.

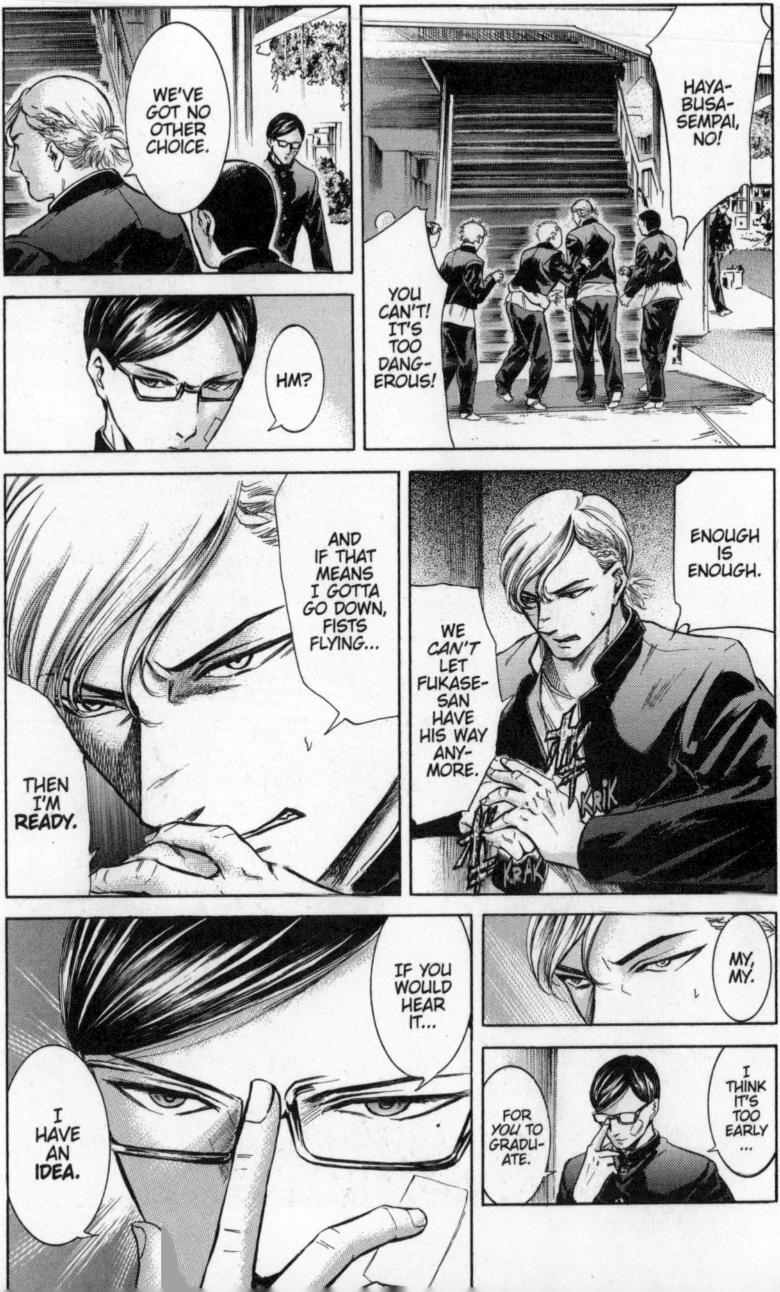
HAYA-BUSA-SEMPAI, NO!
YOU CAN'T! IT'S TOO DANG-EROUS!
WE'VE GOT NO OTHER CHOICE.
HM?
ENOUGH IS ENOUGH.
WE CAN'T LET FUKASE-SAN HAVE HIS WAY ANY-MORE.
KRIK
KRAK
AND IF THAT MEANS I GOTTA GO DOWN, FISTS FLYING...
THEN I'M READY.
MY, MY.
I THINK IT'S TOO EARLY ...
FOR YOU TO GRADU-ATE.
IF YOU WOULD HEAR IT...
I HAVE AN IDEA.

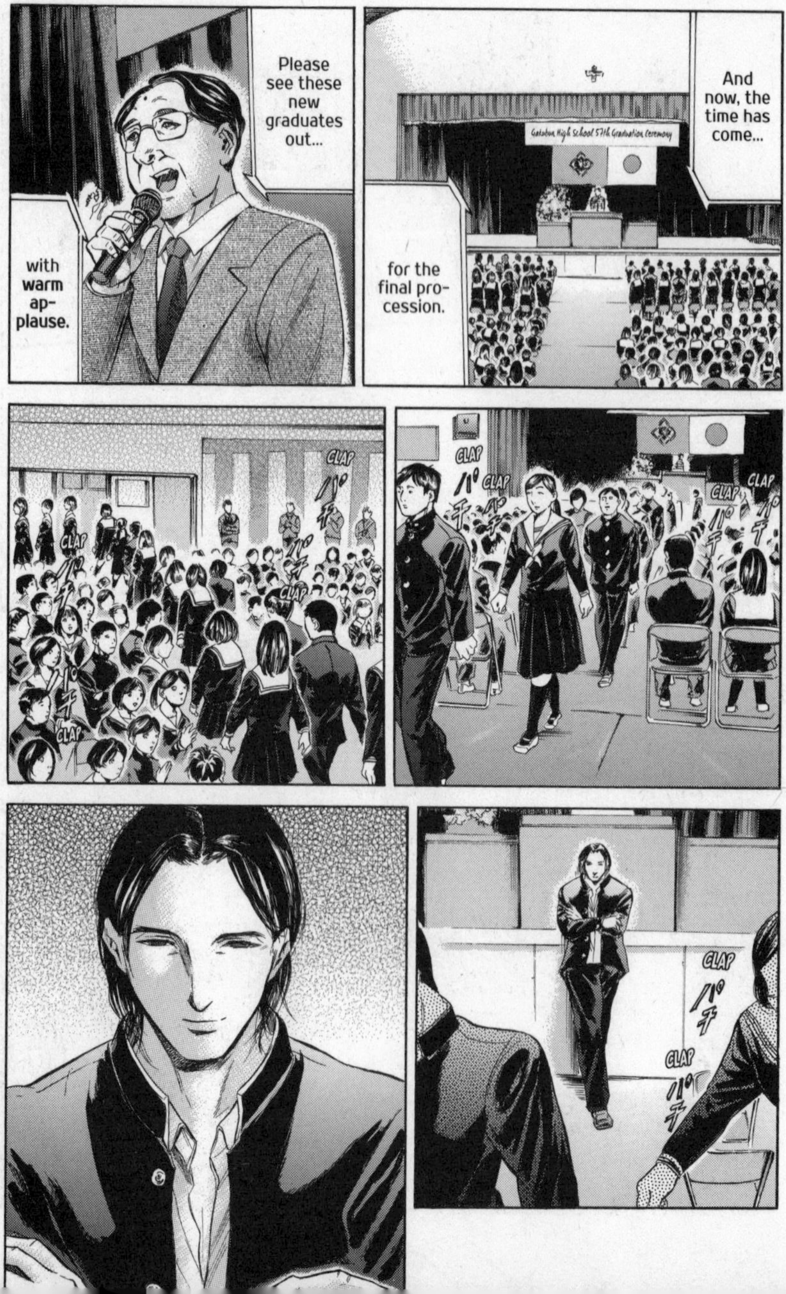
And now, the time has come...
for the final procession.
Gatoban High School 57th Graduation Ceremony
Please see these new graduates out...
with warm applause.
CLAP
CLAP
CLAP
CLAP
CLAP
CLAP
CLAP
CLAP
CLAP
CLAP

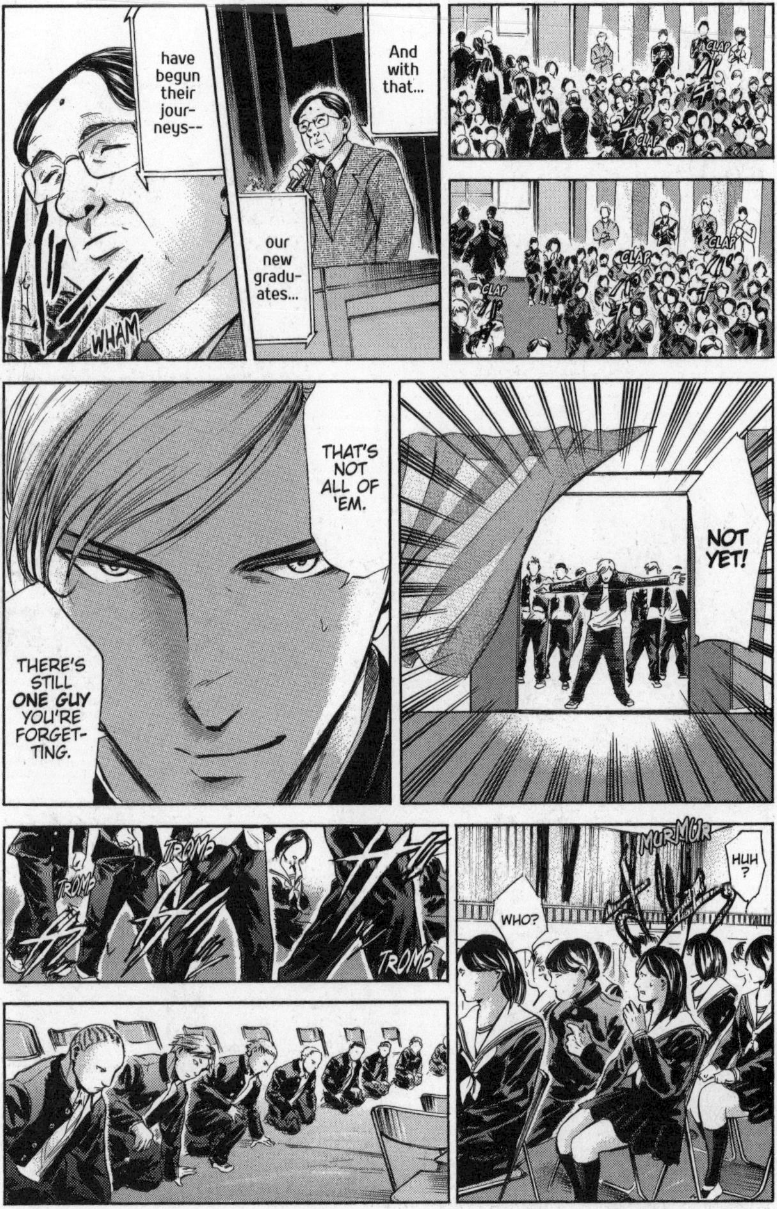
CLAP
CLAP
CLAP
CLAP
CLAP
And with that...
our new gradu-ates...
have begun their jour-neys--
WHAM
NOT YET!
THAT'S NOT ALL OF 'EM.
THERE'S STILL ONE GUY YOU'RE FORGET-TING.
MURMUR
HUH ?
WHO?
TROMP
TROMP
TROMP

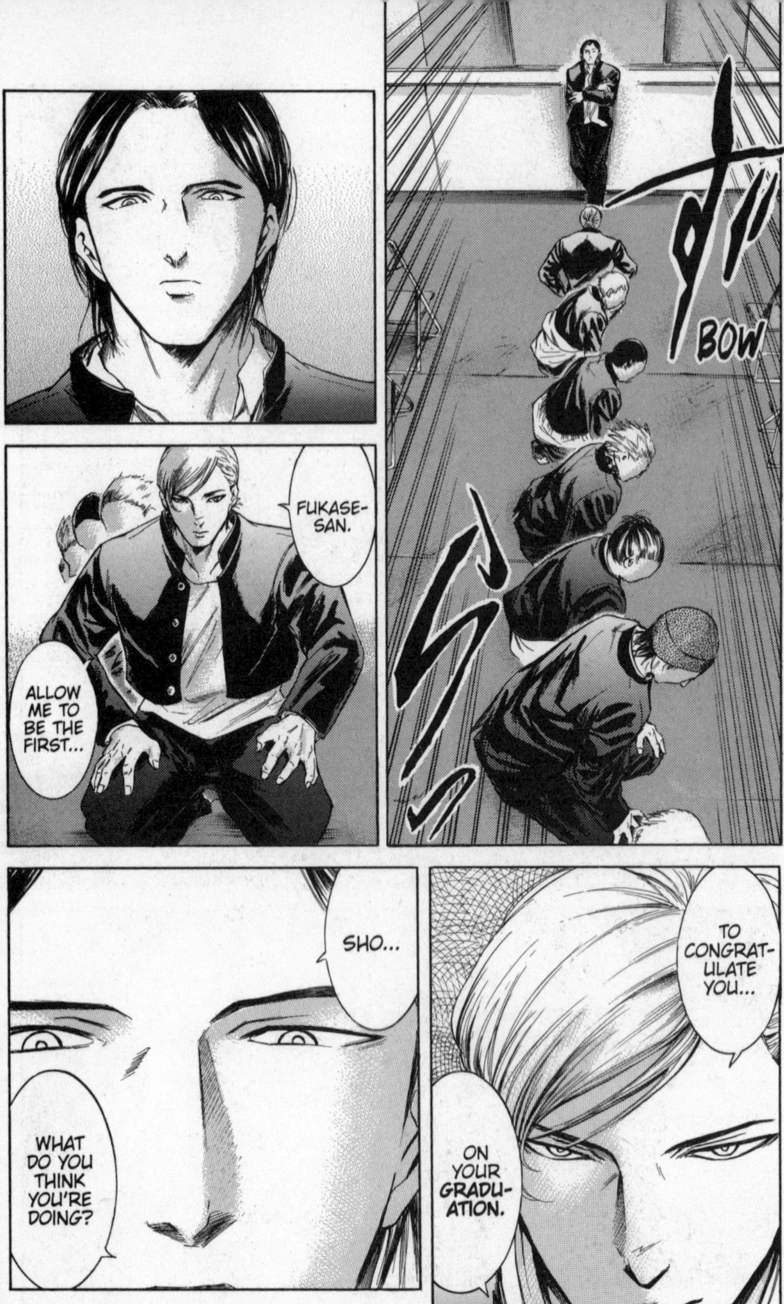
BOW
FUKASE-SAN.
ALLOW ME TO BE THE FIRST...
TO CONGRATULATE YOU...
ON YOUR GRADUATION.
SHO...
WHAT DO YOU THINK YOU'RE DOING?

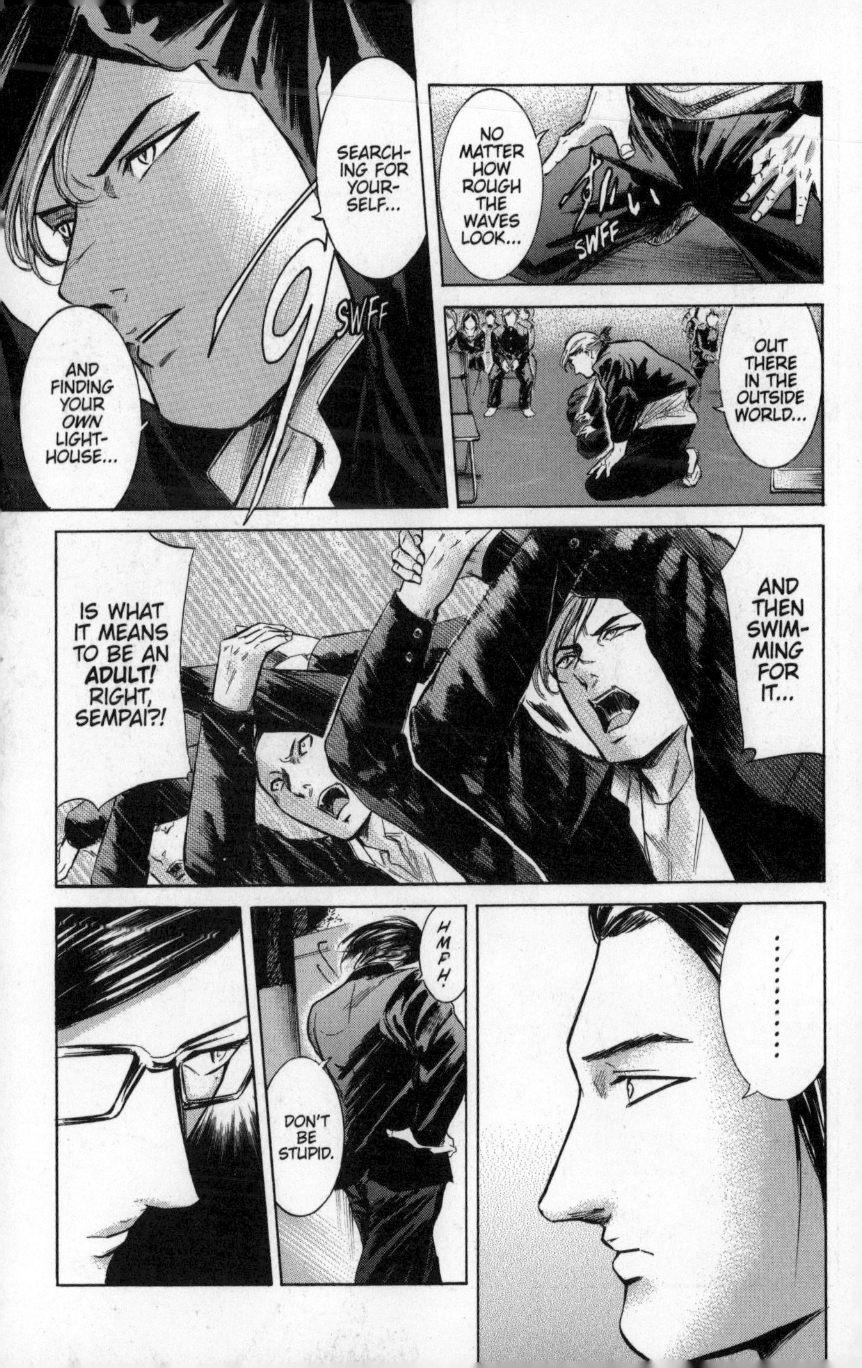
NO MATTER HOW ROUGH THE WAVES LOOK...
SWFF
OUT THERE IN THE OUTSIDE WORLD...
SEARCHING FOR YOURSELF...
SWFF
AND FINDING YOUR OWN LIGHTHOUSE...
AND THEN SWIMMING FOR IT...
IS WHAT IT MEANS TO BE AN ADULT! RIGHT, SEMPAI?!
....
HMPH!
DON'T BE STUPID.

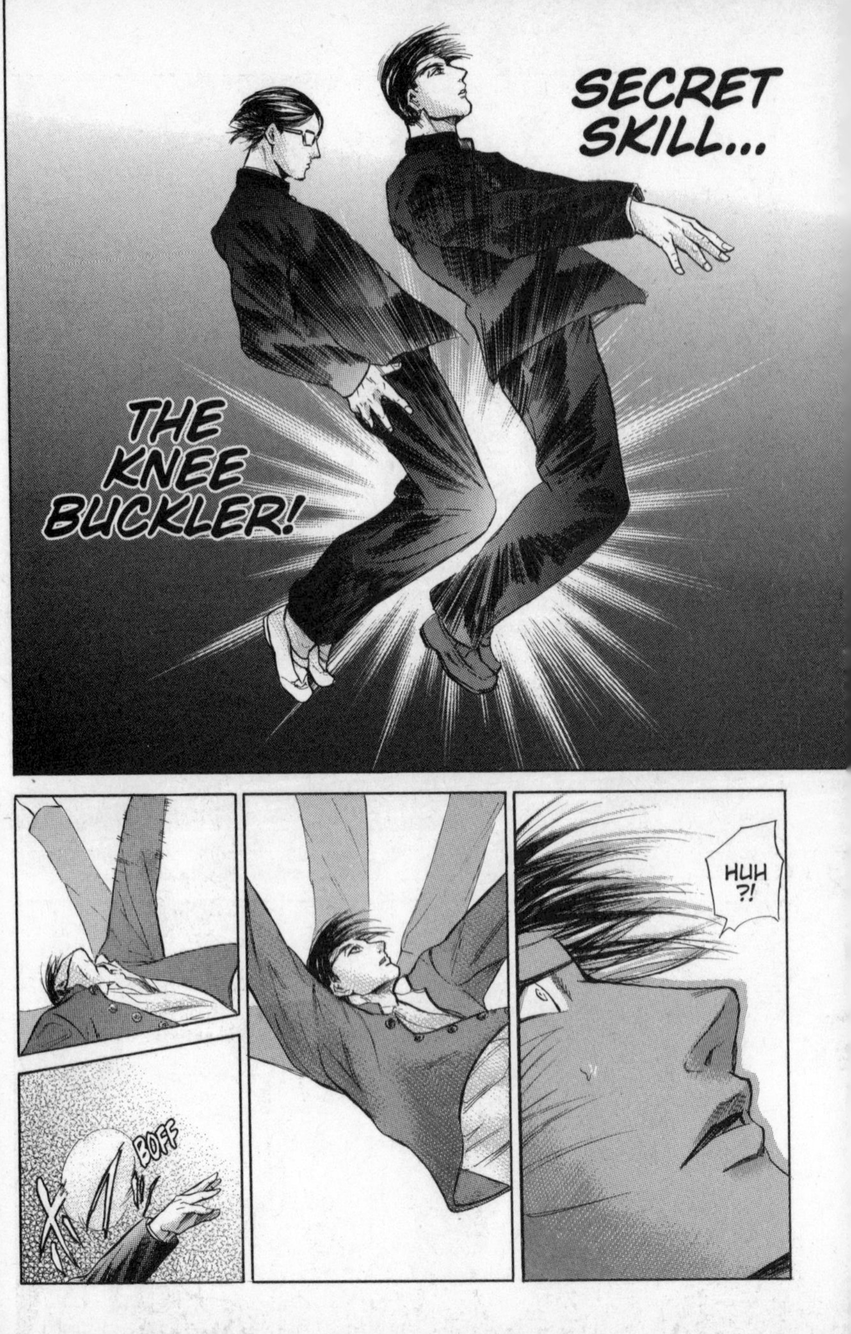
SECRET SKILL...
THE KNEE BUCKLER!
HUH ?!
BOFF

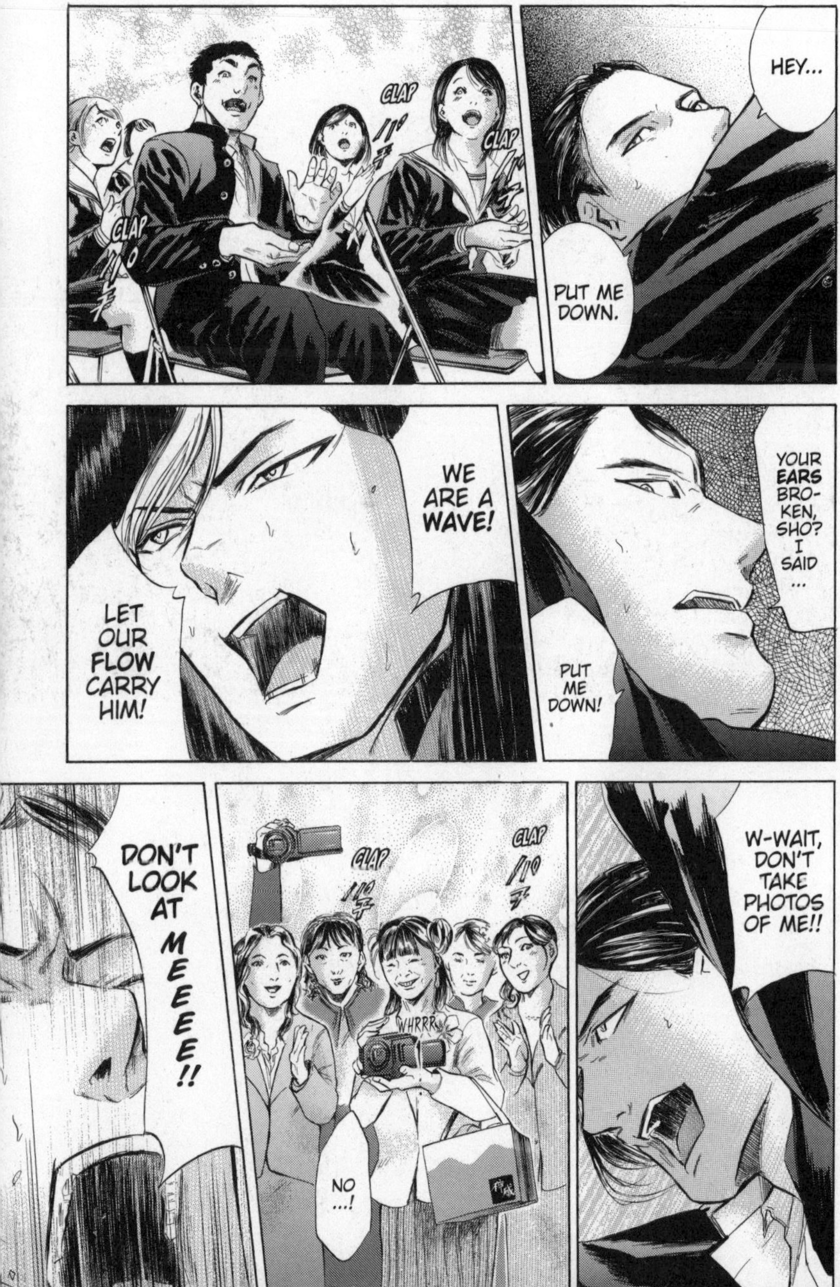
HEY...
PUT ME DOWN.
CLAP
CLAP
CLAP
YOUR EARS BRO-KEN, SHO? I SAID ...
PUT ME DOWN!
WE ARE A WAVE!
LET OUR FLOW CARRY HIM!
W-WAIT, DON'T TAKE PHOTOS OF ME!!
CLAP
CLAP
WHRRR
NO ...!
DON'T LOOK AT MEEEE!!

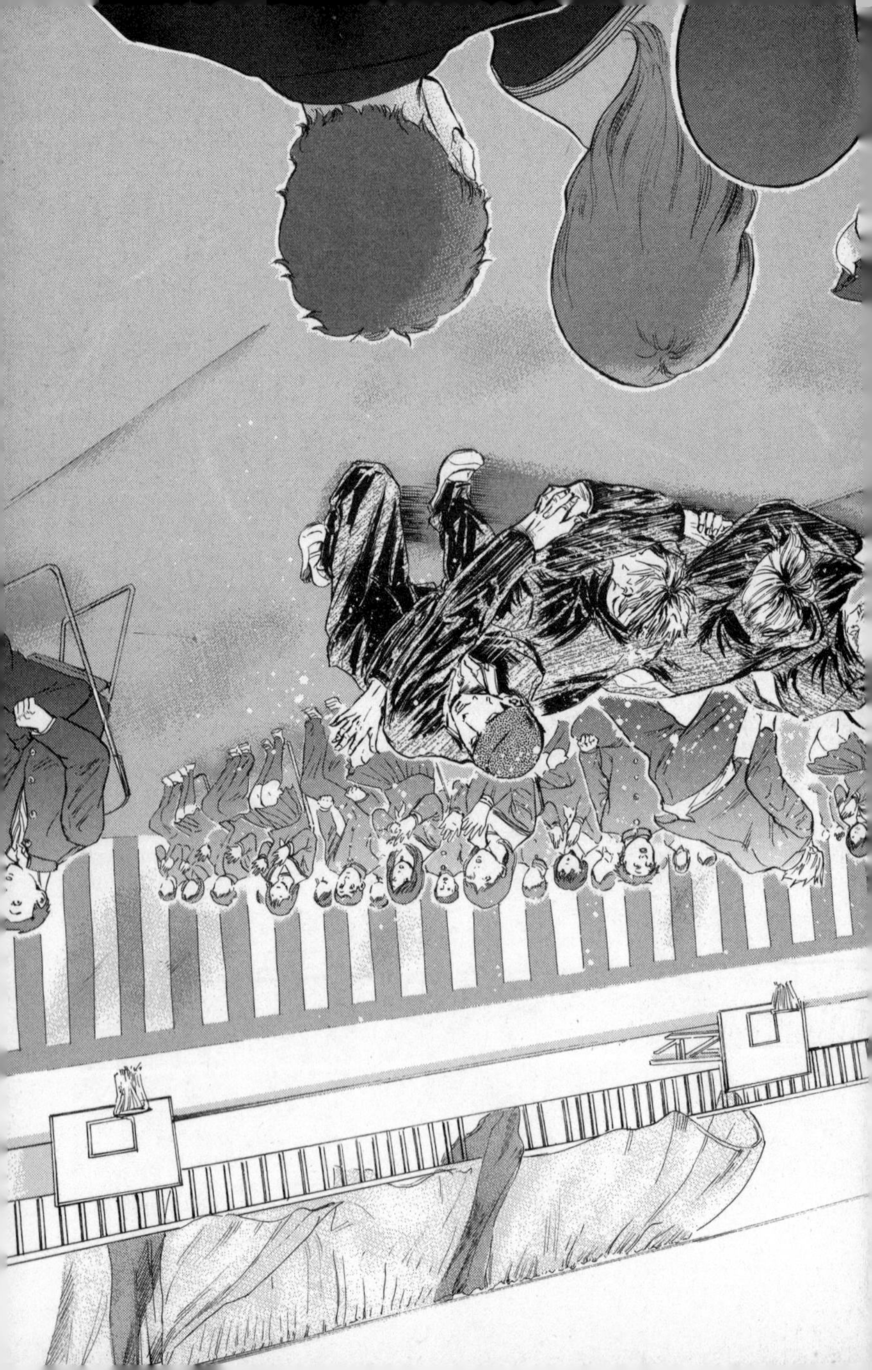

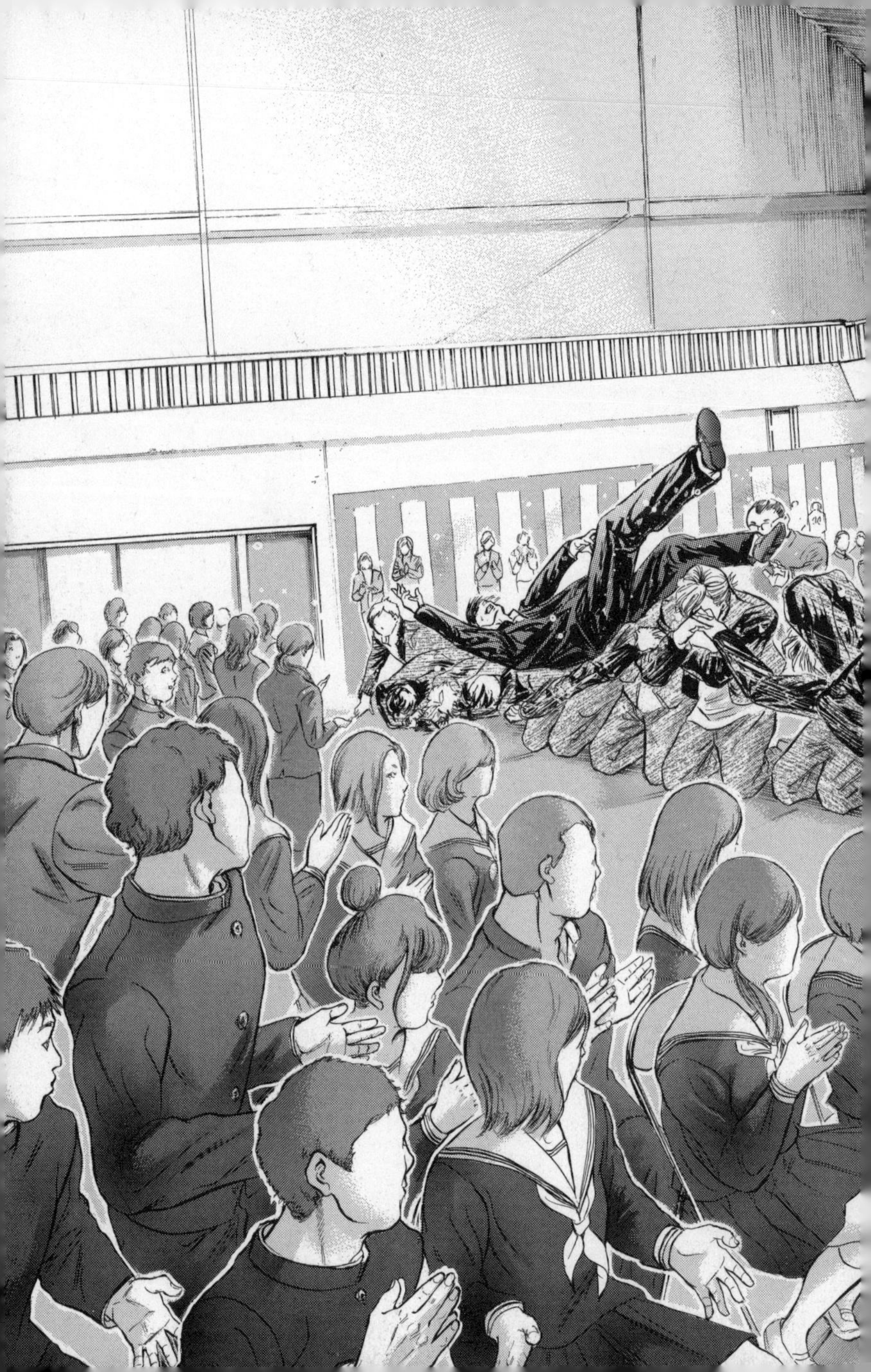

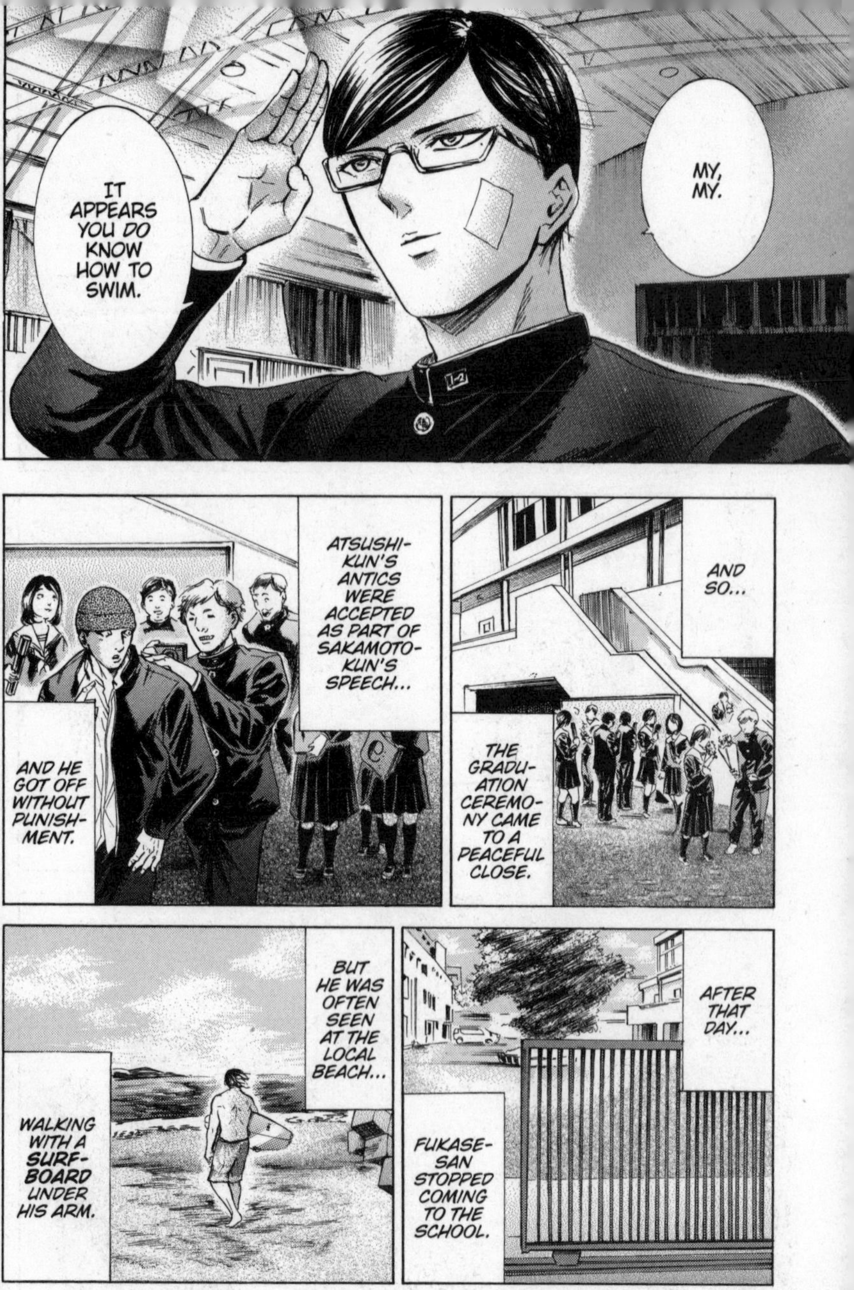
MY, MY.
IT APPEARS YOU DO KNOW HOW TO SWIM.
AND SO...
THE GRADUATION CEREMONY CAME TO A PEACEFUL CLOSE.
ATSUSHI-KUN'S ANTICS WERE ACCEPTED AS PART OF SAKAMOTO-KUN'S SPEECH...
AND HE GOT OFF WITHOUT PUNISHMENT.
AFTER THAT DAY...
FUKASE-SAN STOPPED COMING TO THE SCHOOL.
BUT HE WAS OFTEN SEEN AT THE LOCAL BEACH...
WALKING WITH A SURFBOARD UNDER HIS ARM.

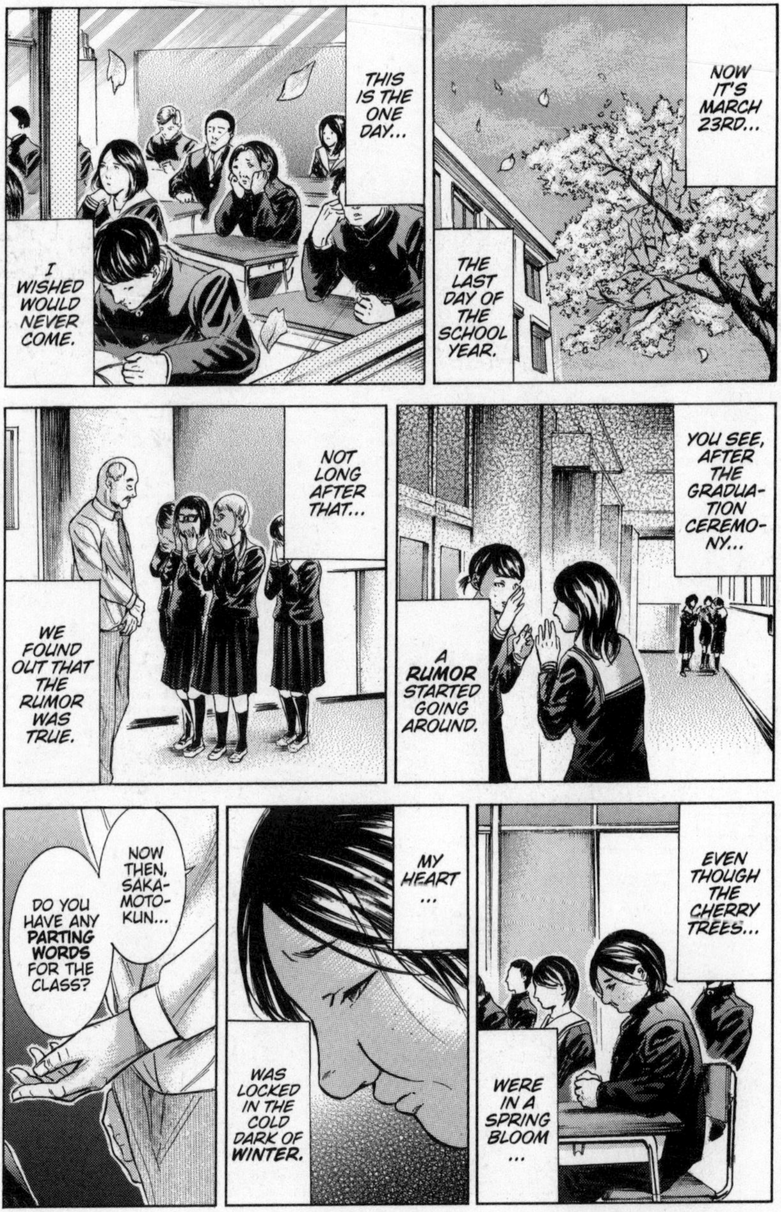
NOW IT'S MARCH 23RD...
THE LAST DAY OF THE SCHOOL YEAR.
THIS IS THE ONE DAY...
I WISHED WOULD NEVER COME.
YOU SEE, AFTER THE GRADUATION CEREMONY...
A RUMOR STARTED GOING AROUND.
NOT LONG AFTER THAT...
WE FOUND OUT THAT THE RUMOR WAS TRUE.
EVEN THOUGH THE CHERRY TREES...
WERE IN A SPRING BLOOM...
MY HEART...
WAS LOCKED IN THE COLD DARK OF WINTER.
NOW THEN, SAKAMOTO-KUN...
DO YOU HAVE ANY PARTING WORDS FOR THE CLASS?

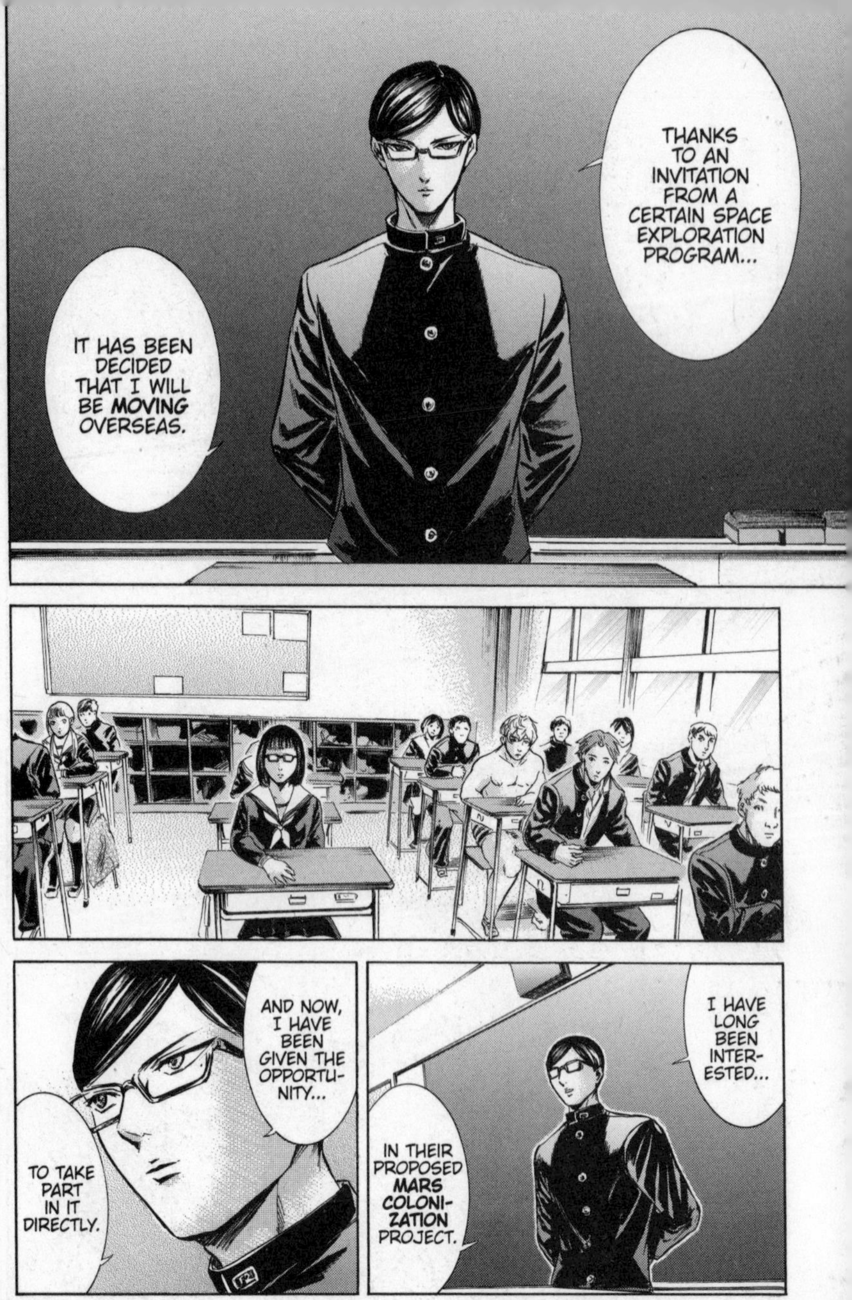
THANKS TO AN INVITATION FROM A CERTAIN SPACE EXPLORATION PROGRAM...
IT HAS BEEN DECIDED THAT I WILL BE **MOVING** OVERSEAS.
I HAVE LONG BEEN INTER-ESTED...
IN THEIR PROPOSED **MARS** **COLONI-ZATION** PROJECT.
AND NOW, I HAVE BEEN GIVEN THE OPPORTU-NITY...
TO TAKE PART IN IT DIRECTLY.

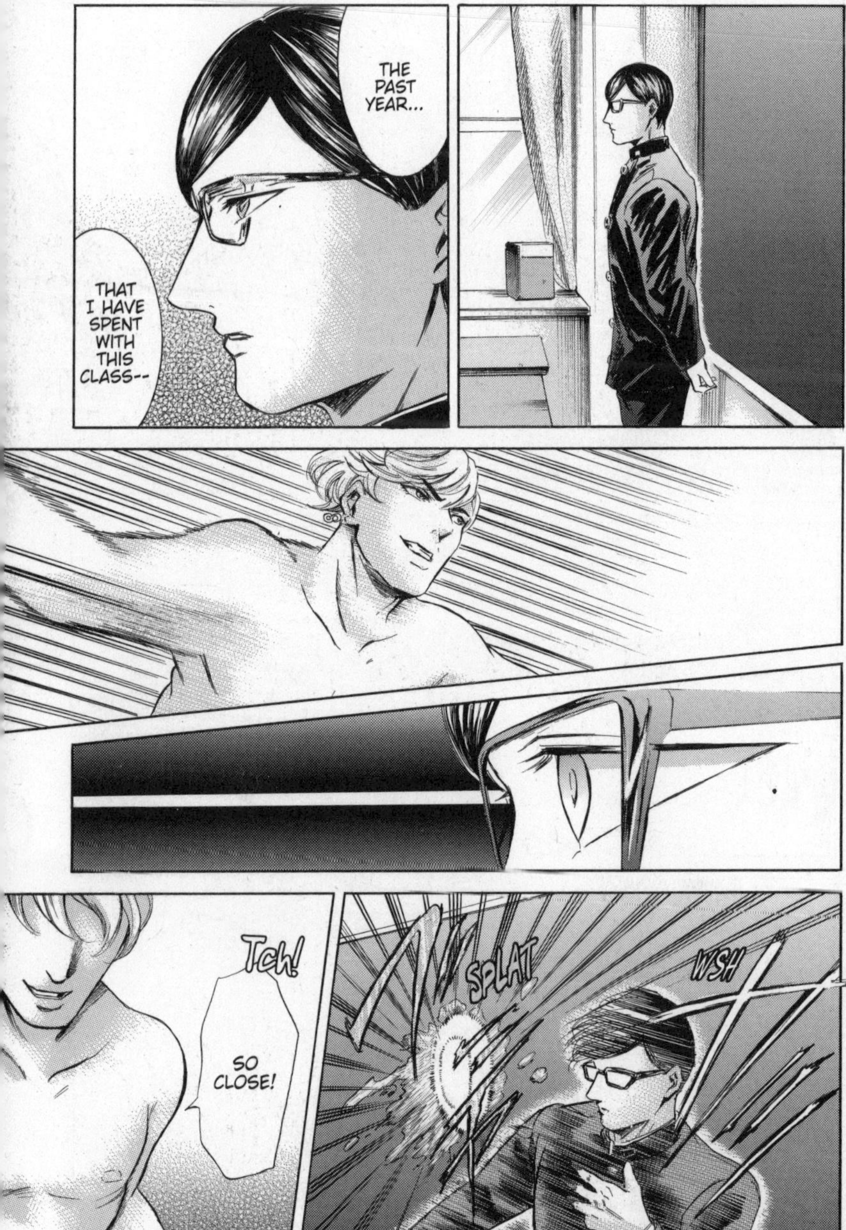
THE PAST YEAR...
THAT I HAVE SPENT WITH THIS CLASS--
WSH
SPLAT
Tch!
SO CLOSE!

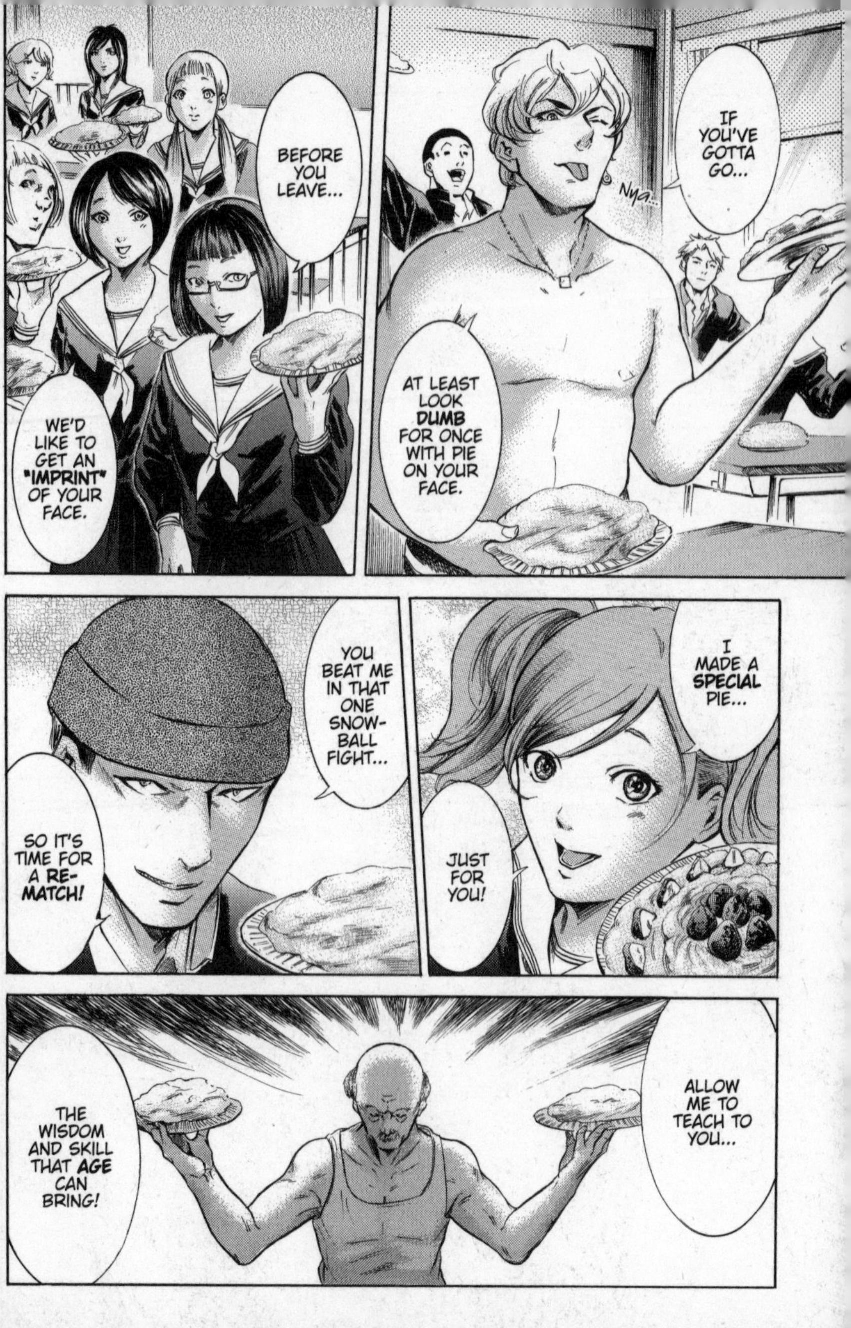
IF YOU'VE GOTTA GO...
Nya...
AT LEAST LOOK **DUMB** FOR ONCE WITH PIE ON YOUR FACE.
BEFORE YOU LEAVE...
WE'D LIKE TO GET AN **"IMPRINT"** OF YOUR FACE.
I MADE A **SPECIAL** PIE...
JUST FOR YOU!
YOU BEAT ME IN THAT ONE SNOW-BALL FIGHT...
SO IT'S TIME FOR A **RE-MATCH!**
ALLOW ME TO TEACH TO YOU...
THE WISDOM AND SKILL THAT **AGE** CAN BRING!

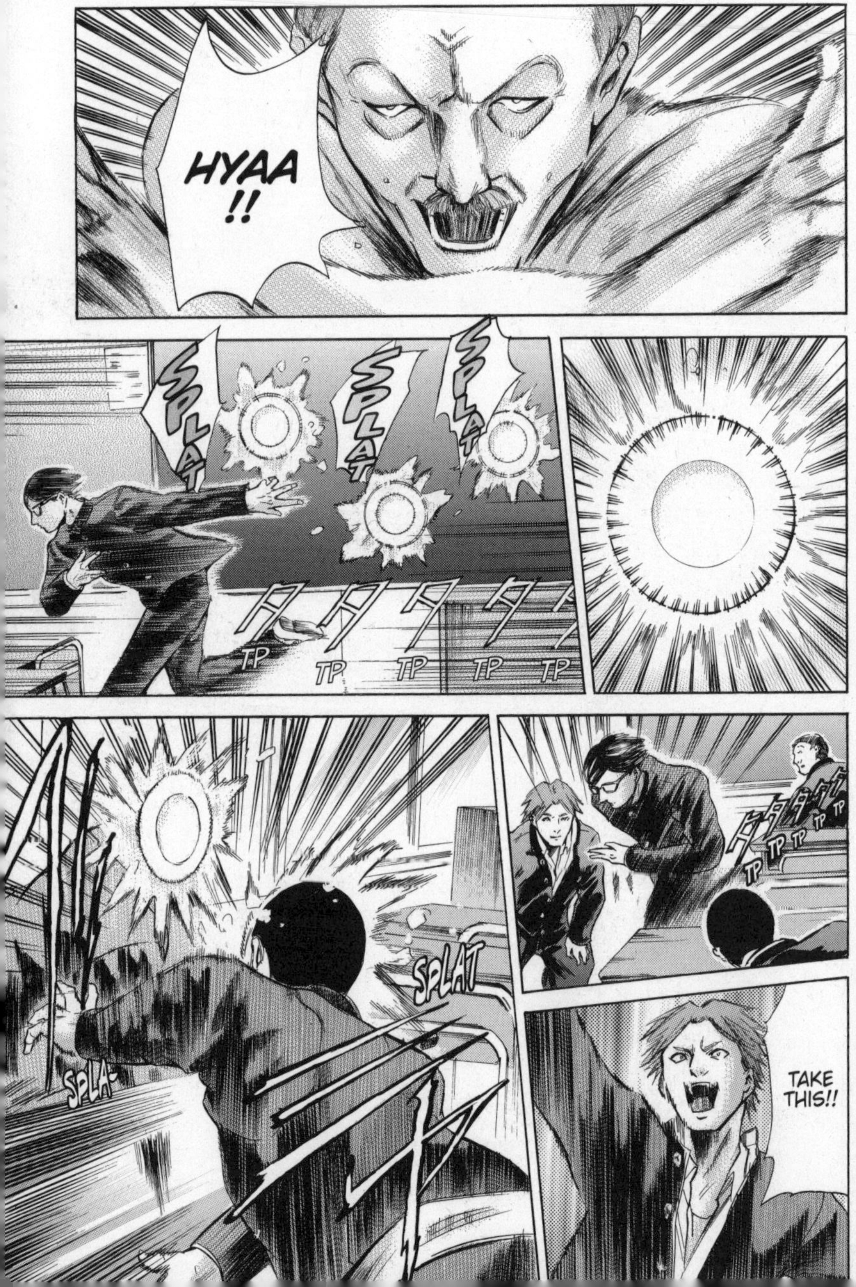
HYAA !!
SPLAT
SPLAT
SPLAT
TP TP TP TP TP
TP TP TP TP TP
TAKE THIS!!
SPLAT
SPLA-

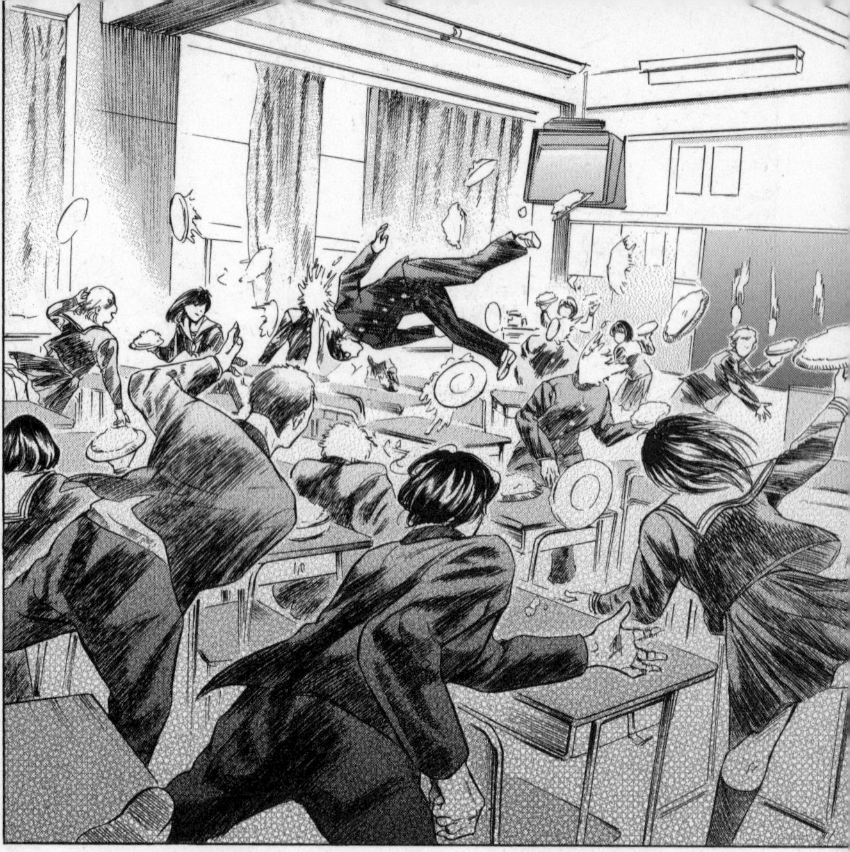

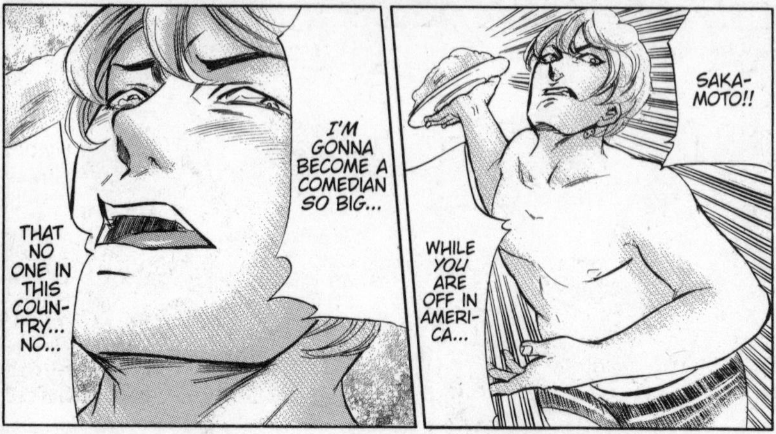
SAKA-
MOTO!!
WHILE
YOU
ARE
OFF IN
AMERI-
CA...
I'M
GONNA
BECOME A
COMEDIAN
SO BIG...
THAT
NO
ONE IN
THIS
COUN-
TRY...
NO...

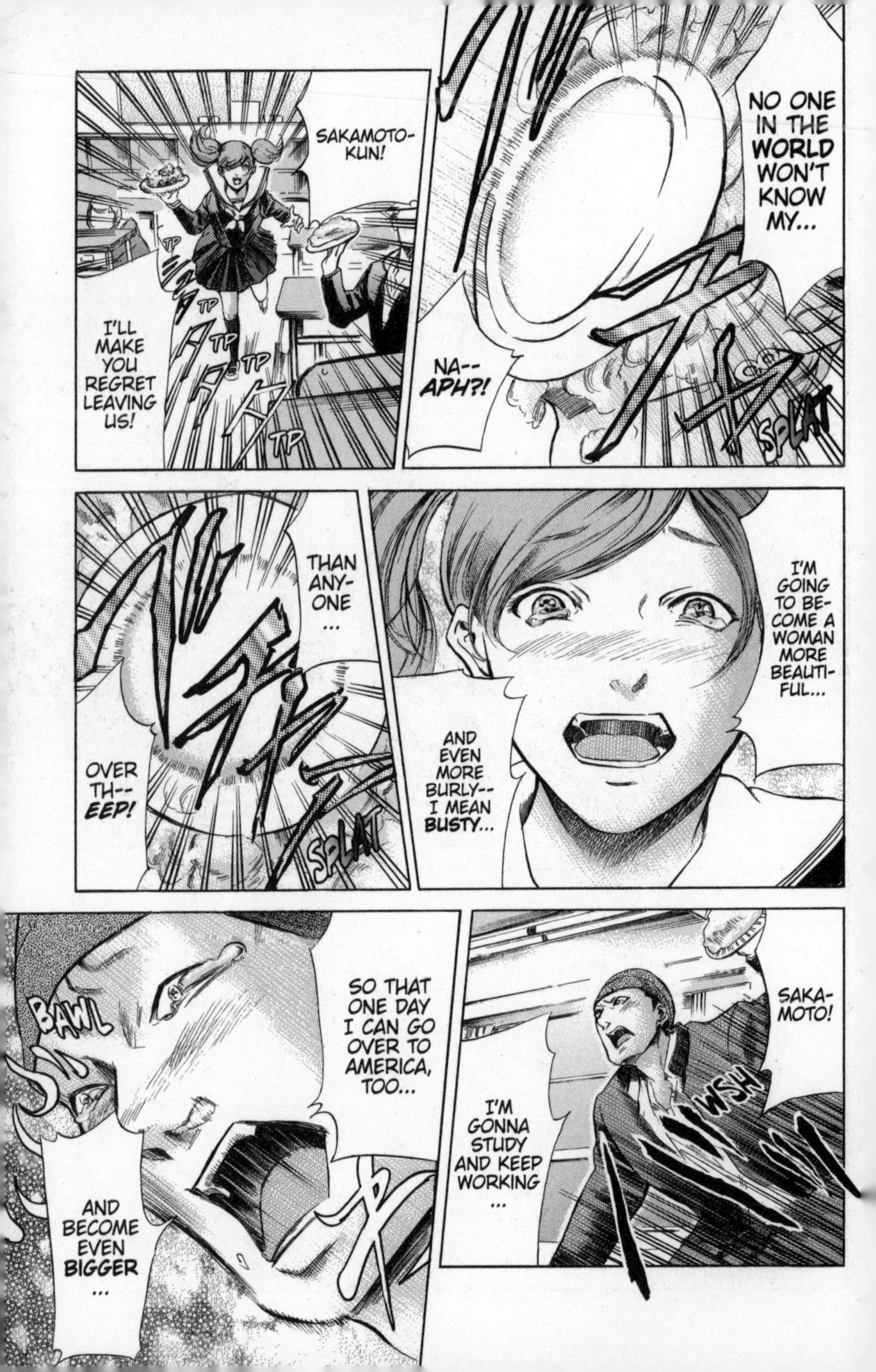
NO ONE IN THE WORLD WON'T KNOW MY...
NA-- APH?!
SPLAT
SAKAMOTO-KUN!
I'LL MAKE YOU REGRET LEAVING US!
TP TP TP TP TP
I'M GOING TO BECOME A WOMAN MORE BEAUTIFUL...
AND EVEN MORE BURLY-- I MEAN BUSTY...
THAN ANYONE...
OVER TH-- EEP!
SPLAT
SAKAMOTO!
I'M GONNA STUDY AND KEEP WORKING...
WSH
SO THAT ONE DAY I CAN GO OVER TO AMERICA, TOO...
BAWL
AND BECOME EVEN BIGGER...

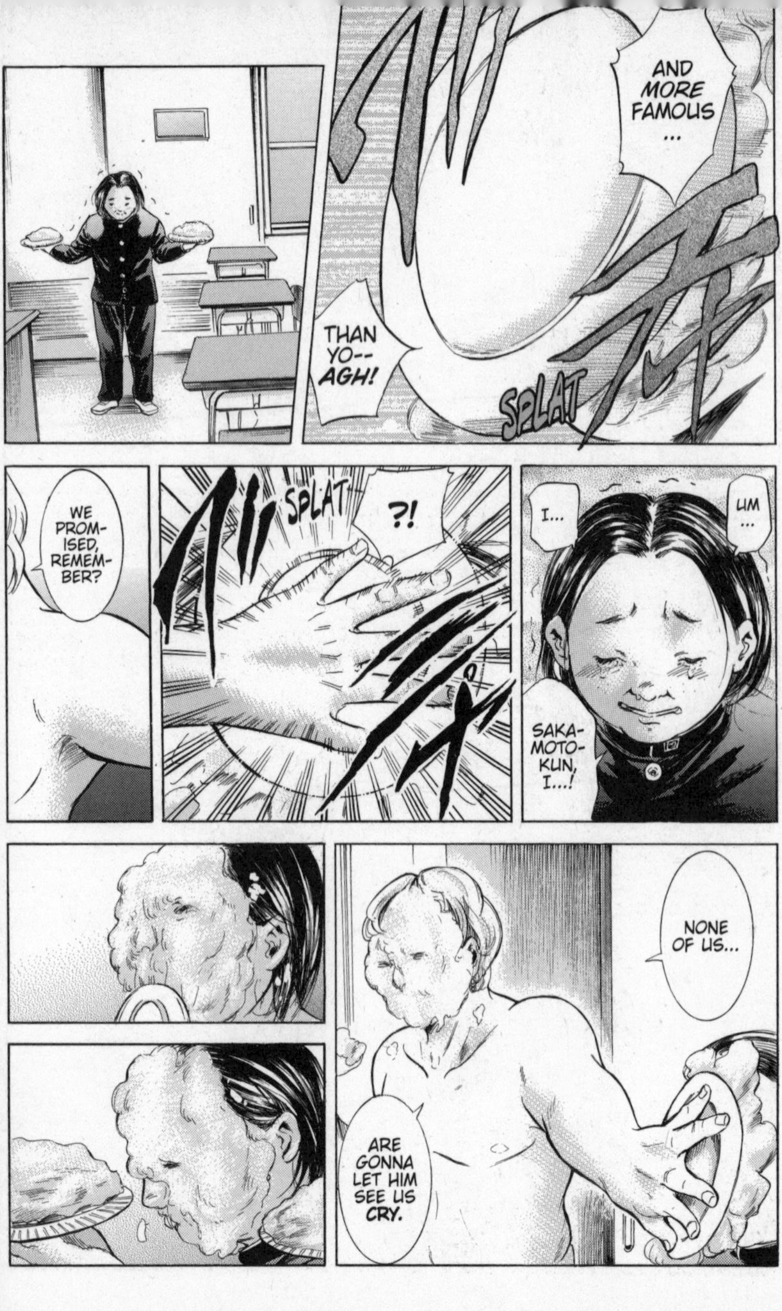
AND MORE FAMOUS ...
THAN YO-- AGH!
SPLAT
UM ...
I...
SAKAMOTO-KUN, I...!
?!
SPLAT
WE PROMISED, REMEMBER?
NONE OF US...
ARE GONNA LET HIM SEE US CRY.

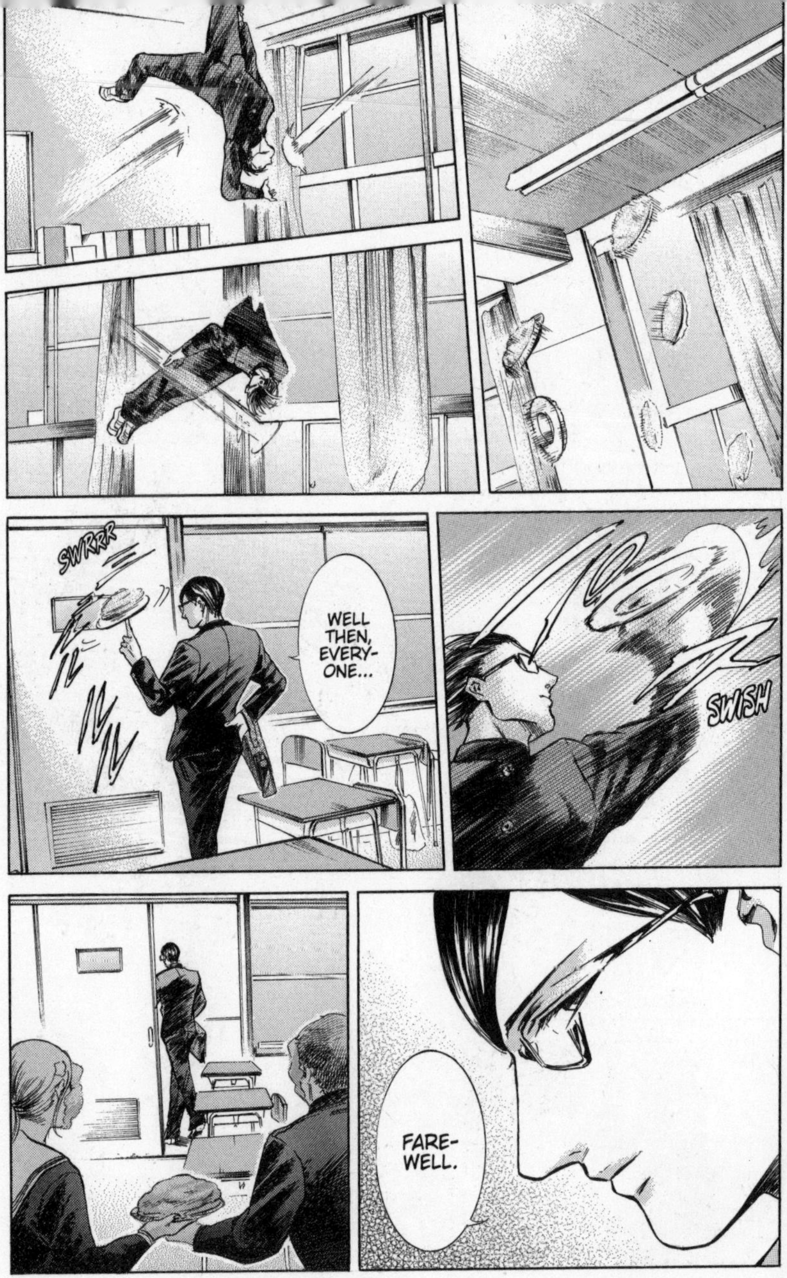
SWISH
WELL THEN, EVERY-ONE...
SWRRR
FARE-WELL.

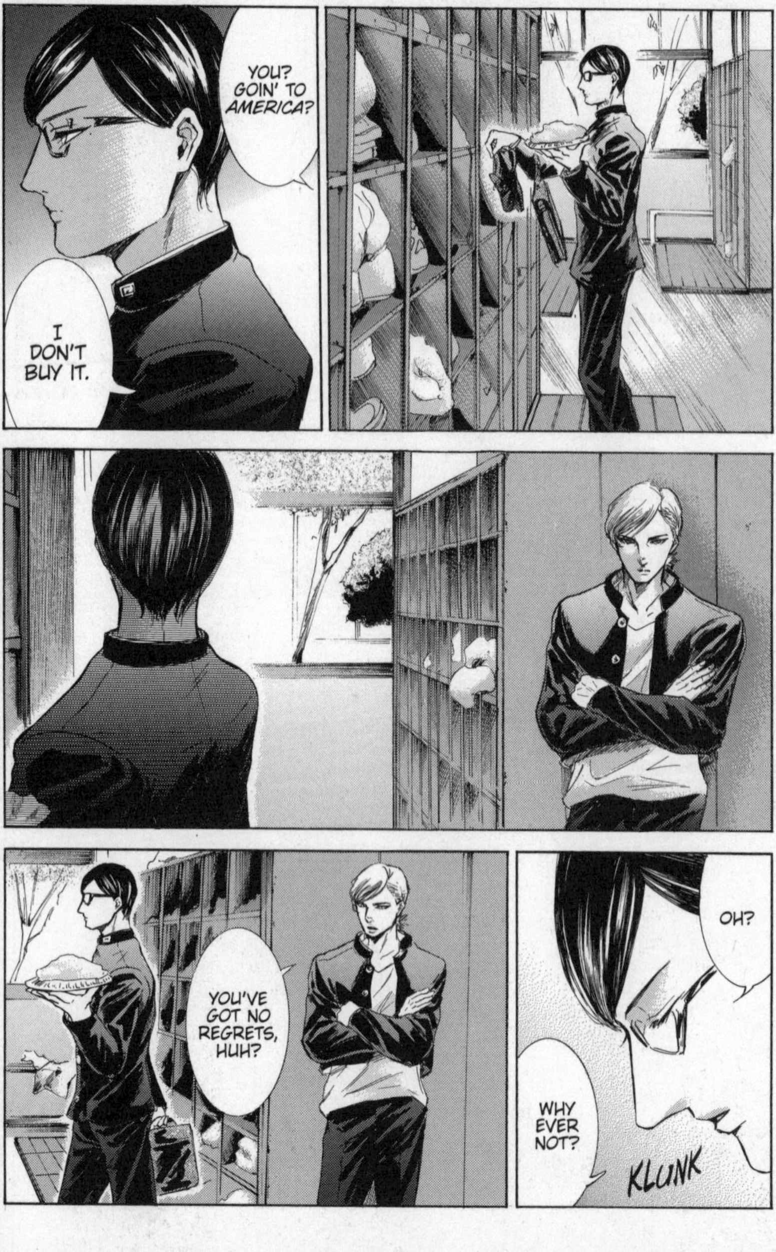
YOU? GOIN' TO AMERICA?
I DON'T BUY IT.
OH?
WHY EVER NOT?
KLUNK
YOU'VE GOT NO REGRETS, HUH?

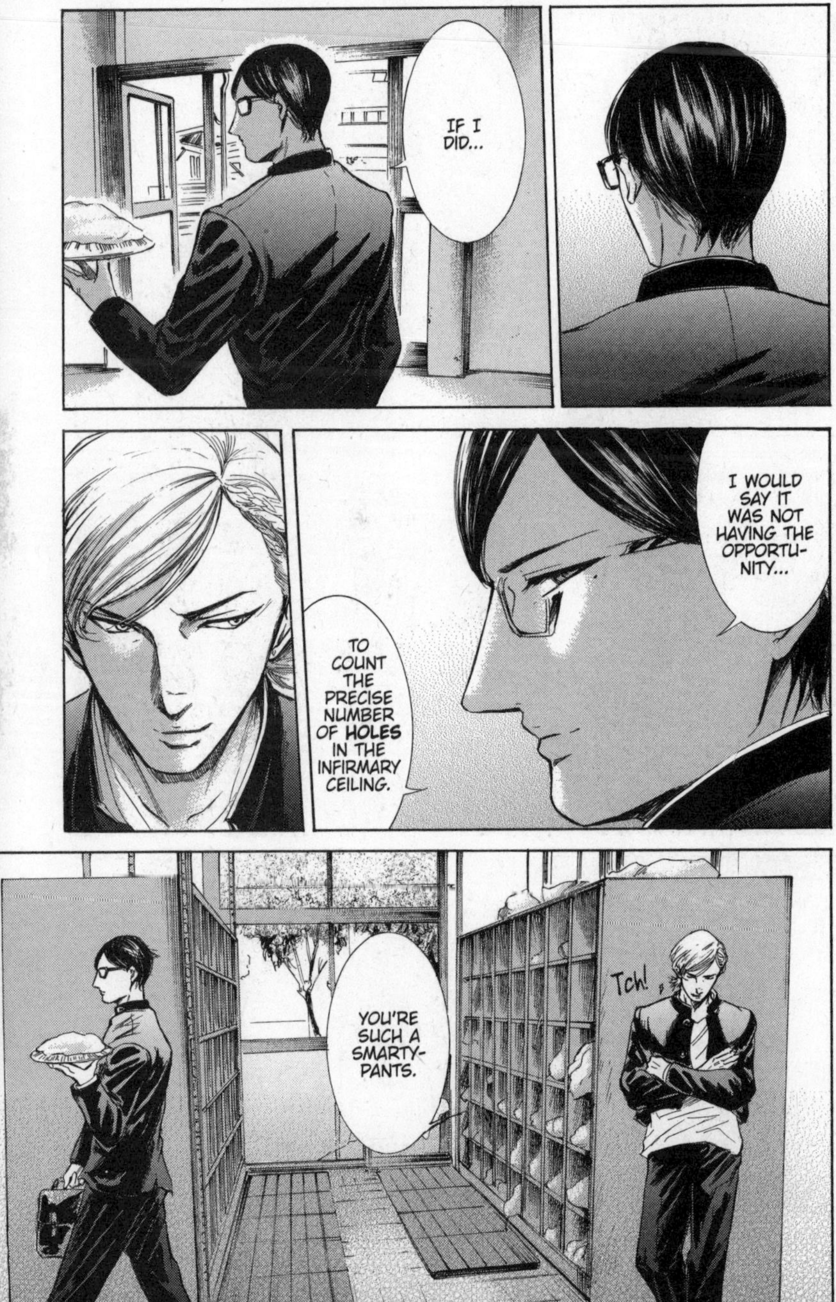
IF I DID...
I WOULD SAY IT WAS NOT HAVING THE OPPORTU- NITY...
TO COUNT THE PRECISE NUMBER OF **HOLES** IN THE INFIRMARY CEILING.
Tch!
YOU'RE SUCH A SMARTY- PANTS.

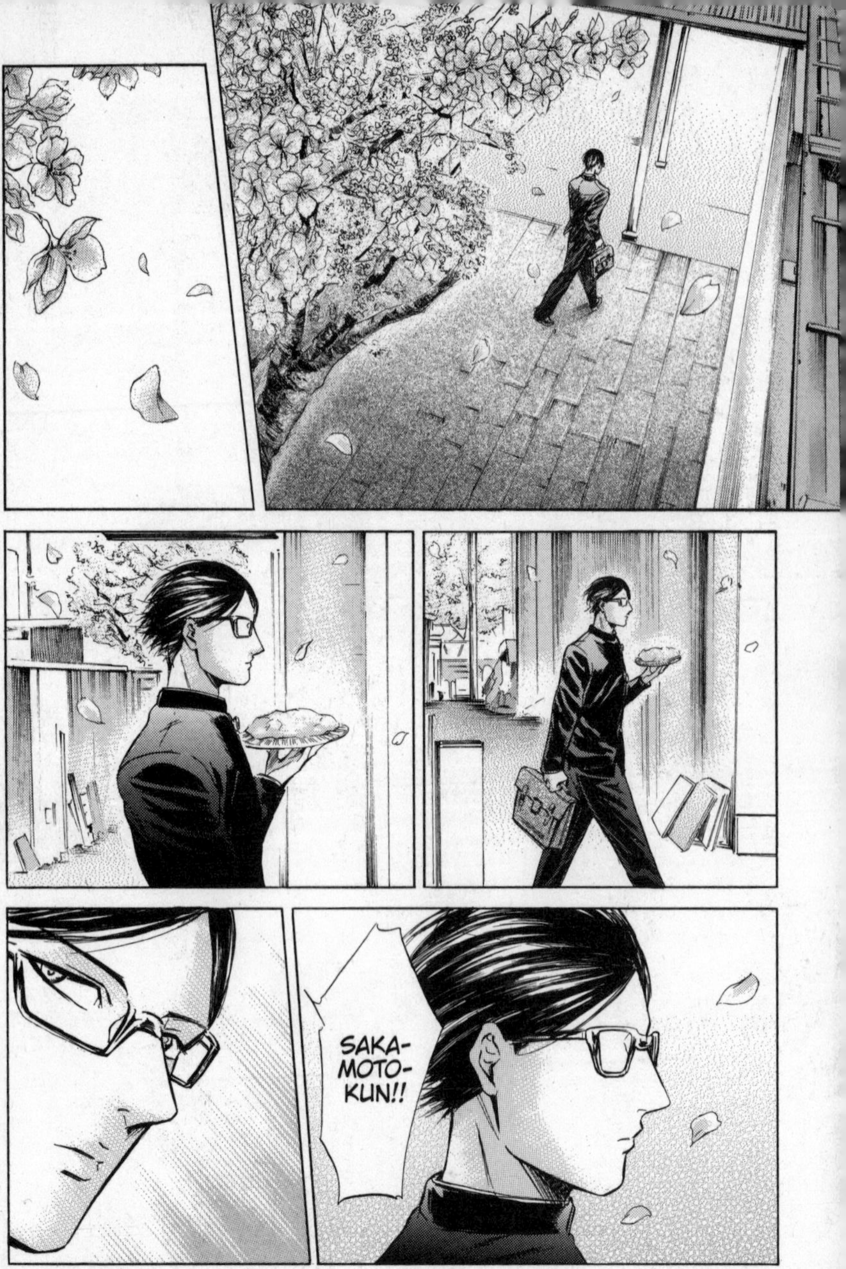
SAKA-
MOTO-
KUN!!

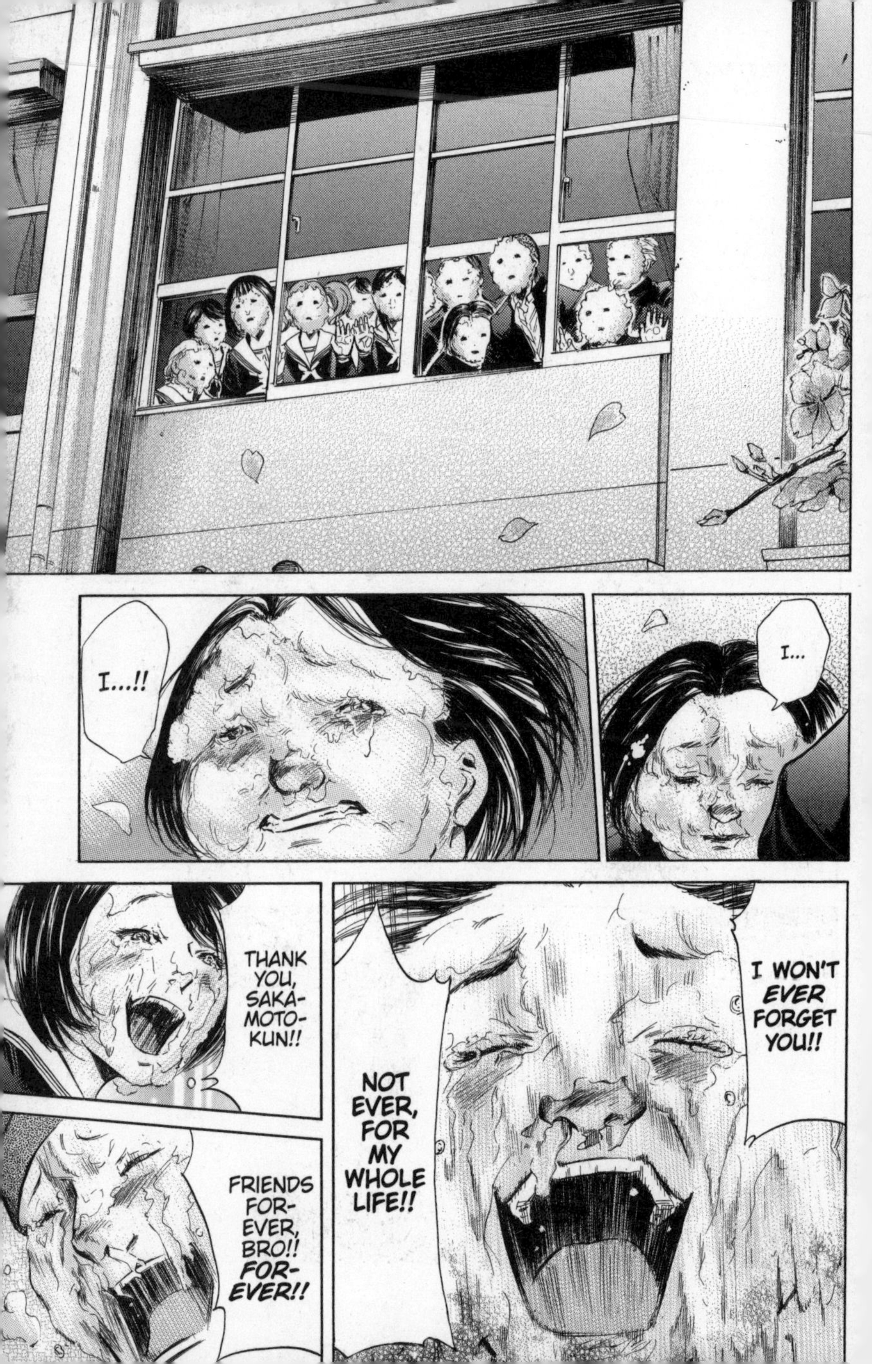
I...
I...!!
I WON'T *EVER* FORGET YOU!!
NOT EVER, FOR MY WHOLE LIFE!!
THANK YOU, SAKAMOTO-KUN!!
FRIENDS FOREVER, BRO!! *FOREVER!!*

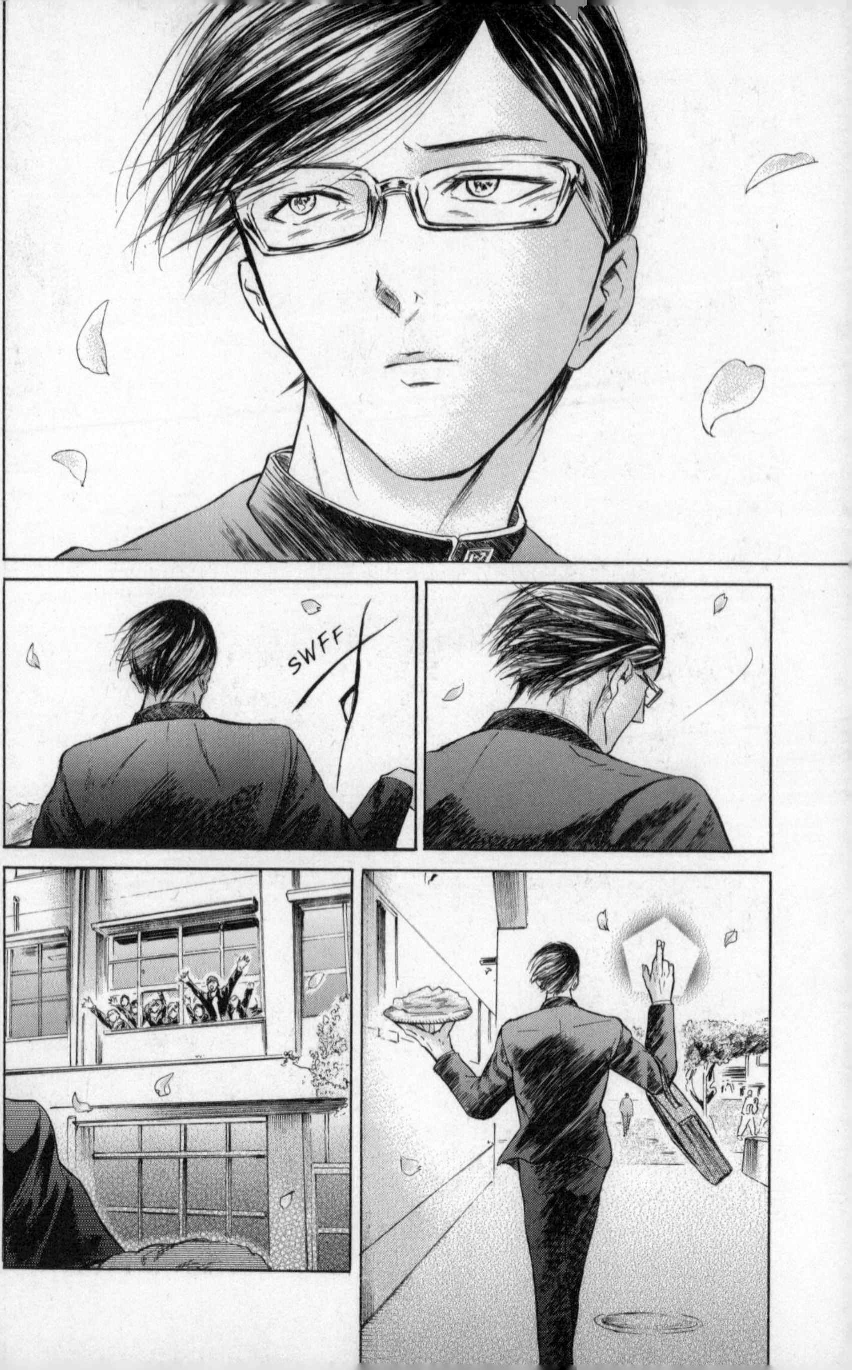
SWFF

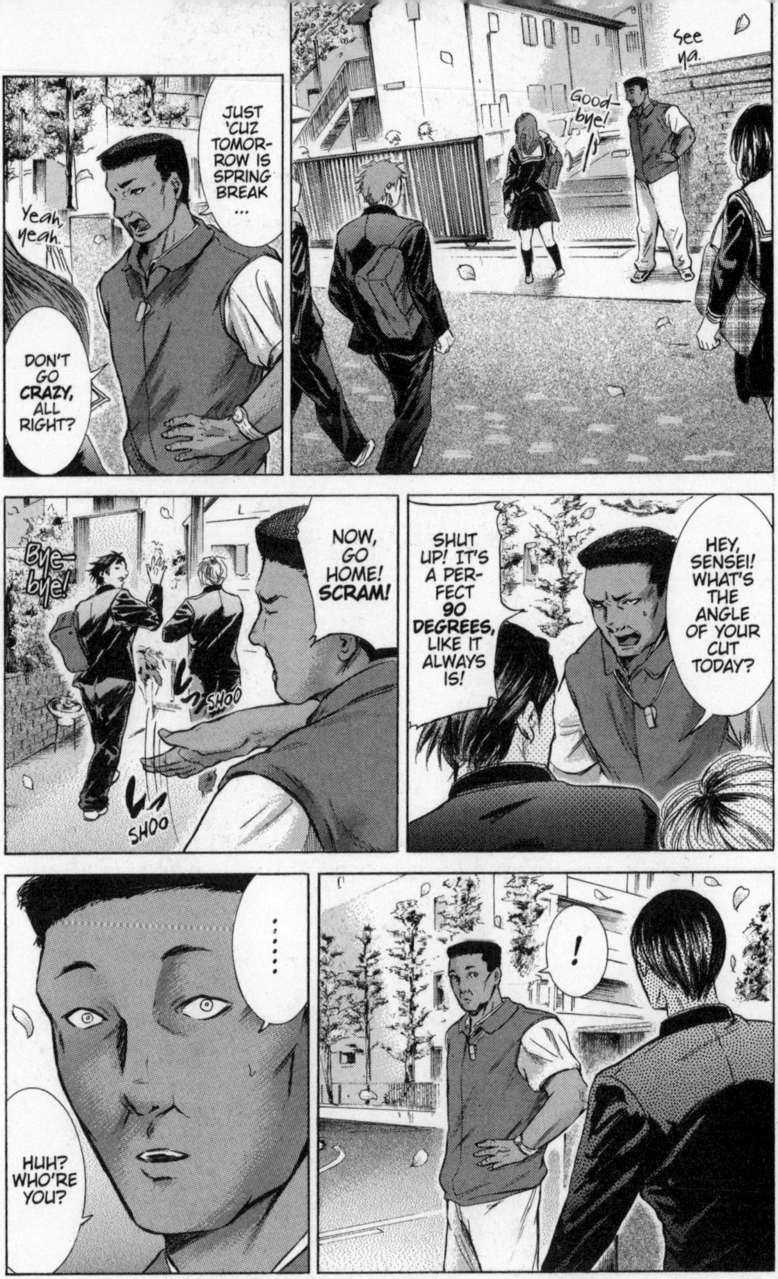
See ya.
Good-bye!
JUST 'CUZ TOMORROW IS SPRING BREAK ...
Yeah, yeah.
DON'T GO CRAZY, ALL RIGHT?
HEY, SENSEI! WHAT'S THE ANGLE OF YOUR CUT TODAY?
SHUT UP! IT'S A PERFECT 90 DEGREES, LIKE IT ALWAYS IS!
NOW, GO HOME! SCRAM!
Bye-bye!
SHOO
SHOO
!
......
HUH? WHO'RE YOU?

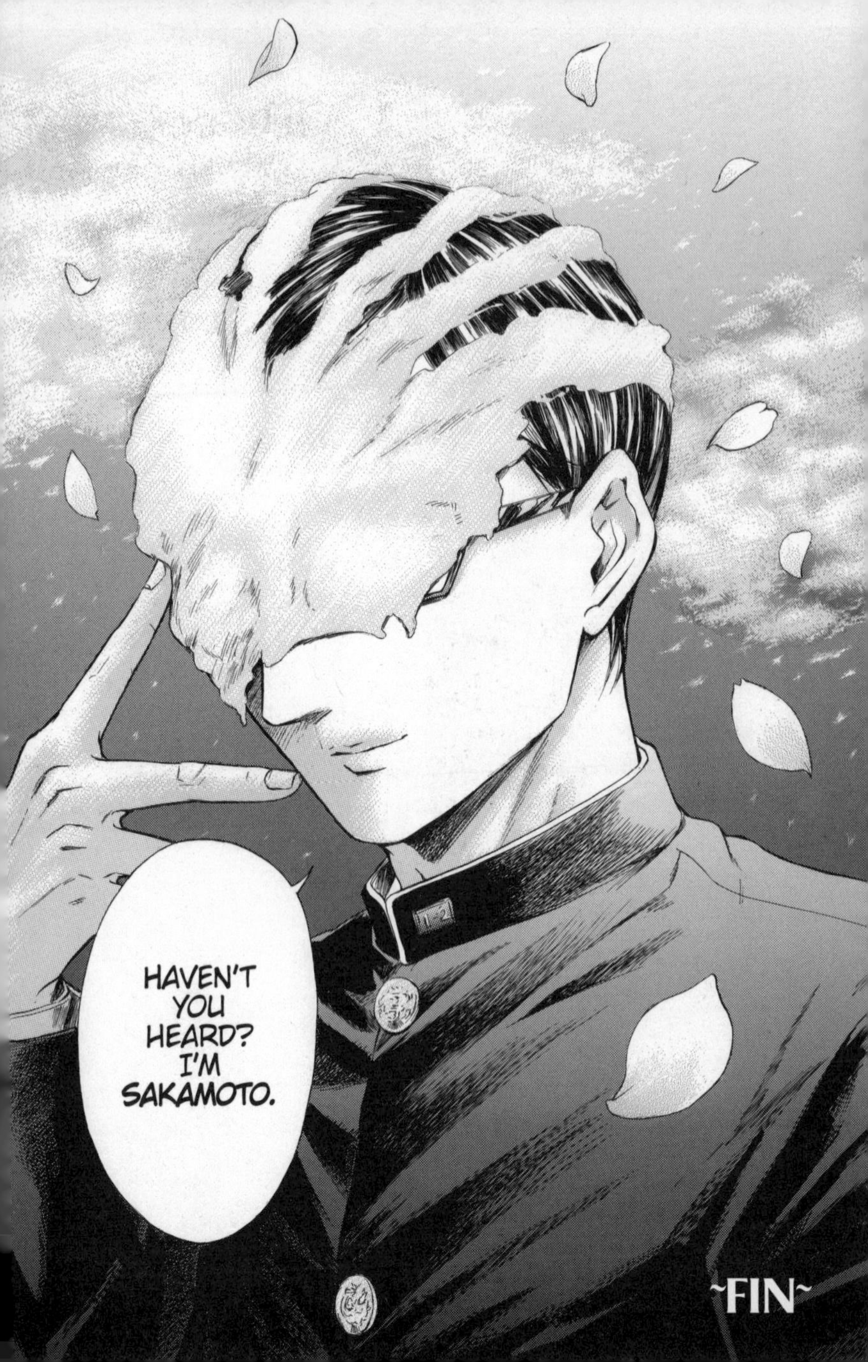
HAVEN'T YOU HEARD? I'M SAKAMOTO.
~FIN~

‹STAFF›

HARUNA ONOKI

KAORI SAKAGAMI

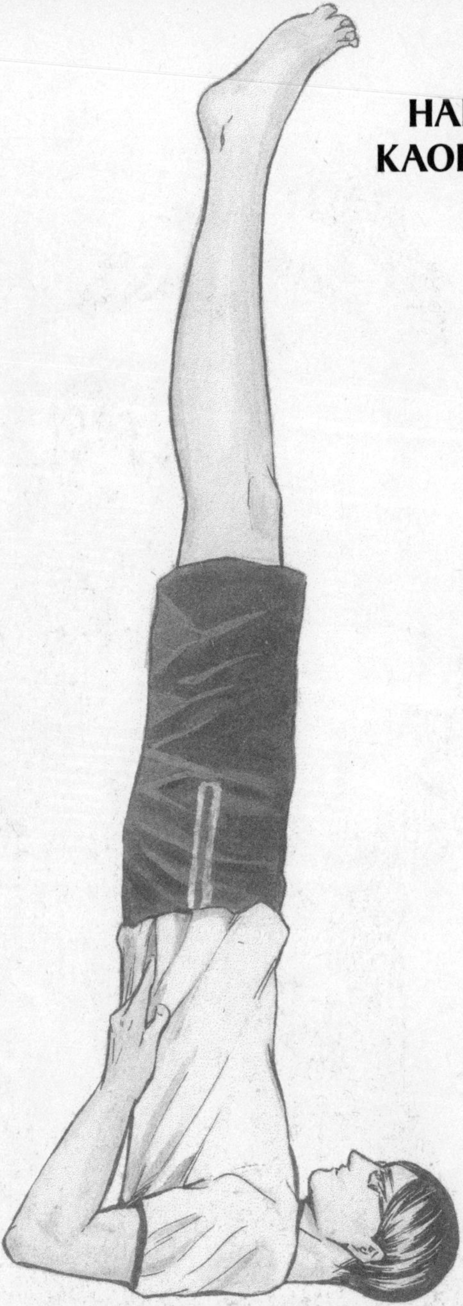

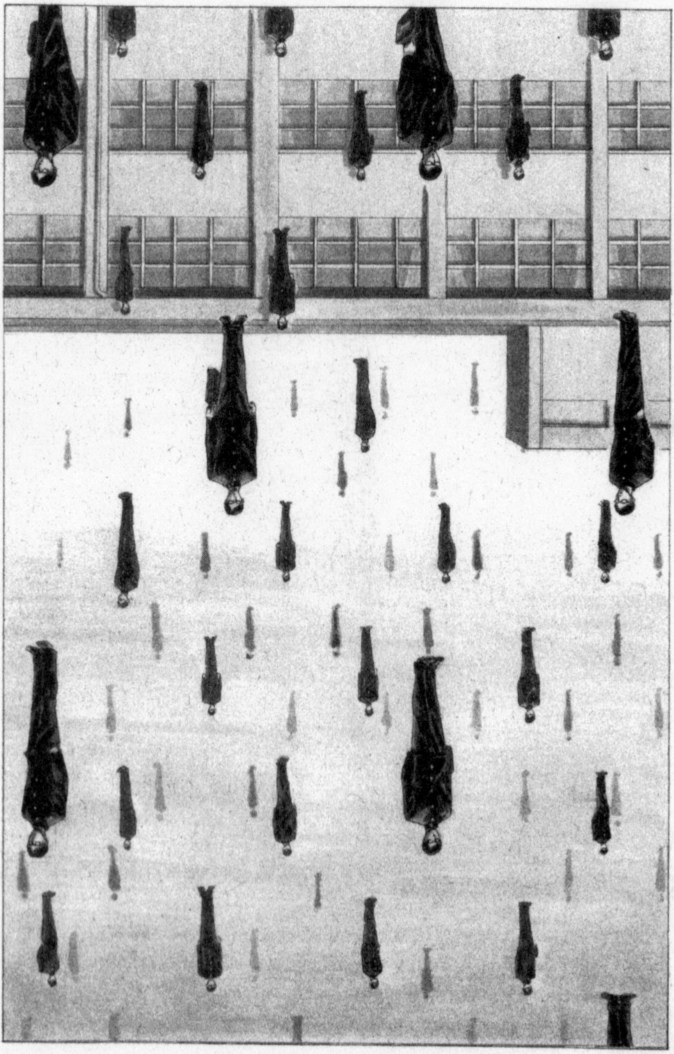